2021

Seeking to be Loved

To the reader, I apologize for any grammatical errors. The corrected version is available from Amazon Books.

by
Jeremiah Gagnon

Cover Art by
Gemarie K. Gagnon and Christie Valihura

ACKNOWLEDGEMENTS

I am thankful and very grateful for the commitment our parents, brothers and sisters had and have for each other. They, along with others, played the major role in the development of our character throughout our lives. Many experiences, challenges and personal contacts influence and shape us. It is through them we hope to inherit the greatest of gifts.

It is beyond expression the gratitude I have for my wife, Mary. If not for her assistance, patience, endurance, and tolerance in seeing me through the completion of this endeavor, I am not sure it would have been completed. Thanks to my dearest daughters Maureen and Gemarie and my son Emerson, for it is our dear ones that taught me how to love unconditionally.

Introduction:

Only one thing is prized so highly that its value ranks above all things. It is in a category of its own, yet the human race squanders it. We have been given examples of it throughout our history. Heroic paragons of ordinary people, drama from the great classics, martyrdom of prophets, and God sacrificing his only begotten son, to give us an exemplar of it.

The seeking of love awakens the spirit in each one of us. We can only find it within the soul of our being. When we look beyond that, it will become elusive.

Not only does it exist within us, it is all around us. The ruler of this world distracts us with temptations.

If we seek love for the wrong reasons, we will confuse it with other desires.

If we seek it through others, it cannot and will not be found.

We can only experience it in purity when we acknowledge its origin and where it is planted in the recesses of our being.

This book is about one man who does not know what he has lost, only that there is something he must find.

Who set him on this path?

"The bond of perfection," Colossians Chapter 3, Verse 14 is the definition of what love truly is. We live in an imperfect world. Can anything in this world be flawless?

This awareness does not prevent the desire to find perfection. Nor should it curb the will to strive for it in all we do in life.

If being perfect is the goal, we may have already lost the battle. I believe we should always strive and work towards being the best self we can, every moment of our existence.

Perfection may be the gold standard. We will likely never achieve it in our humanness. Only in our spiritualness can we ever come close, if we are willing.

The only way we can come close to flawlessness in this world is through the gift of love.

As one learns to love more excellently, that is, if one chooses to; only then can we take the necessary steps to become more flawless of mind, body, and spirit. Only through the most absolute faultless love can one find the most perfect peace!

Colossians Chapter 3 Verse 12 - 15,
"Put on then, as God's chosen ones, holy and beloved, heartfelt compassion, kindness, humility, gentleness and patience, bearing with one another and forgiving one another, if one has a grievance against another; as the Lord has forgiven you, so must you also do."

"And over all these put on love, that is, the bond of perfection."

Do you see what I mean?

"And let the peace of Christ control your hearts, the peace into which you were also called in one body."

Can perfect love survive in an imperfect world?

Can it exist in a world full of trials, tribulations and temptations that challenge the minds, bodies, and souls of each one's being?

Can love endure?

Can true love exist, survive, and flourish in our world?

The answer is a triumphant, factual, resounding yes, yes, Thank God, **Yes**!

True love can exist only if we commit with total resolve to love one another, to respect and accept each other's uniqueness and differences without imposing our own ideals.

This story is about two individuals who found each other and faced personal and worldly challenges. Two individuals who, diligently and defiantly, met each struggle with love and a promise of a better tomorrow.

The family characters, places, events, and circumstances are real. They are part of our family history and heritage.

I credit our mother, Natalie Pauline (Emerson) Gagnon, for the foundation of the history and the lineage of the main characters. She served in the Genealogic Department of the Public Library in Haverhill, Massachusetts, once she retired. She extensively researched and reviewed immigration records and archives in city and town halls. In search of our father's history, she traveled throughout New England and Canada, spending weeks, months and years reviewing records and documents.

Many questions have been left unanswered, partially due to the mass migration of French citizens to Québec, Canada prior and during World War One, and records that were destroyed, lost or incomplete. The mass death toll of the influenza epidemic of 1918-20, took the lives of the direct source of information.

Piecing together the oral history from our father, brothers, and sisters, plus the documented findings from our mother and author's research, and experience is what inspired this writing.

Seeking to be Loved

Chapter 1 <u>The Vow</u>

It was January 14, 1900, noon on a clear, brisk winter day in the village of Berg-Sur-Moselle in the Lorraine region of France. This small community is set along the banks of the river Moselle. Friends, relatives, and most of the inhabitants in the little town gathered at the chapel of St Michel's Église (Church). They were attending the wedding of William Gilbert Guyon to Marilda Natalie Berube. All was quiet inside the chapel. The Blessed Sacramental rite of the matrimonial vows were being performed between this man and woman. They were being joined together as one Holy and Blessed Spirit. This ceremony always calls for a great celebration when two young souls find each other; when two individuals can without a doubt acknowledge their absolute love for each other.

It is truly a blessed moment when the vow is taken with complete resolve on the part of both, and each agree to love and cherish one another. This is the reason for the excitement and gathering of many, to share and witness this special sacred moment. To see, hear and feel the fullness of love as William "Gilbert" Guyon and Marilda Natalie Berube exchange sacred vows. Vows that seal the commitment of a lifetime of dedication to love and honor each other. This commitment is a sign of maturity and fullness of one's human growth of body, mind, and spirit. The mature oneness of this young man and woman's spirit will, in the next few moments, begin to blend and gel together as one. This miracle is completed by a force greater than the sum of both these individuals and the families combined.

That force, that power is a Divine gift!

There is a pause in the ceremony as the priest introduced one of the parishioners, a friend of the bride and groom, to read Corinthians Chapter 13.

He began, "Our Savior inspired these words: 'I shall show you still a more excellent way. If I speak in human and angelic tongues, but do not have love, I am a resounding gong or clashing cymbal. And

Seeking to be Loved

if I have the gift of prophecy and comprehend all mysteries and have all knowledge; if I have all faith so as to move mountains, but do not have love, I am nothing.

'Love is patient, love is kind. It is not jealous, love is not pompous, it is not inflated, it is not rude, it does not seek its own interest, it is not quick-tempered, it does no injury, it does not rejoice over wrongdoing, but rejoices in and with the truth.

'Love never fails. If there is prophecy, they will be brought to nothing; if tongues, they will cease; if knowledge, it will be brought to nothing. For we know partially, and we prophesy partially, but when the perfect comes, partial will pass away. When I was a child, I use to talk and act as a child, think as a child, reason as a child. When I became a man, I set aside childish things.

'At present we see indistinctly, as in a mirror, but then face to face. At present I know partially; then I shall know fully, as I am fully known. So, _Faith, Hope_ and _Love_ remain, these three; but the greatest of these is _LOVE_.' "

As the lector takes his seat, all the congregation returns its attention to the altar and the two standing there.

They await the words of the devotional promise.

The priest stated, "William Gilbert Guyon, will you take this woman, Marilda Natalie Berube, to be your lawfully wedded wife?"

"I DO!"

"Marilda Natalie Berube, will you take William Gilbert Guyon, to be your lawfully wedded husband?"

"I DO!"

"At this time if anyone present knows of any reason William and Marilda should not be wed, speak now, or forever hold your peace."

There is a hush within the chapel, a blessed moment of silence. Then the minister of this Blessed Sacrament surveyed the congregation. He observed the two standing together before him, then he gazed above. In a strong voluminous voice, he announces, "By the power invested in me by our Lord and Savior, I now

Seeking to be Loved

pronounce you Husband and Wife! What God has bound together this day, let no man put asunder!"

The priest turned his attention to William.

"William, you may now kiss your bride!"

An eruption of cheers and applause, mixed with laughter and tears, fill the parish. The two embrace and seal their pact with a kiss, followed by a blessing from the priest.

They both secretly want to go straight to the carriage and make their way to the bungalow. However, there was still the grand reception that many anticipated. Much preparation on the part of both families awaited them. Their special moment together that Gilbert had planned many years before he even met Marilda must wait.

The guests were already making their way to the banquet hall. The reception line was long. They endured, welcoming and thanking everyone for their attendance and support which they had experienced throughout their entire lives from family, friends, relatives, and the whole community.

After cutting the cake, Gilbert and Marilda were given a toast by his brother Philippe. It started with the first verse of Chapter 14 in First Corinthians.

"Pursue love, but strive eagerly for the spiritual gifts, above all that you may prophecy. We all wish for both of you a long, healthy and fruitful marriage."

They gave one final thanks to all the guests and bid them farewell. They made their way to the carriage that awaited.

His brother George met him at the carriage, whispering in his ear that his new home would be quite cozy. "Also, it will be well stocked with provisions, good for a few days at least. A few bottles of father's best wine will be waiting for you. I wish you well, my brother and your beautiful bride. We will see you in a few days. Enjoy your honeymoon."

Gilbert shook hands with his brother and thanked him. He wrapped the blanket around himself and his wife, shook the reins

Seeking to be Loved

and the horse began to make its way through the cheers of the crowd.

They had just a few kilometers to travel, a few hundred meters along the cobblestone streets of their little town. Then, down a one lane dirt path, that could hardly be considered a road, to where they would begin their new life together. The sun was already setting on a clear brisk evening. As they reached the outskirts of town, their carriage slowly made its way up to the ridge. The sun was already setting on the horizon. Other than the time of year and the coolness of the night air, it was just as Gilbert had imagined for many years.

Reaching the bungalow, Gilbert helped Marilda from the carriage. Keeping her in his arms, he carried her to the front door. She opened it and he leaned, turned slightly, he stepped over the threshold. He put her down, they faced each other and embraced, kissing once again. Several moments passed before they surveyed the warm glow about them. He said to Marilda, "George told me our home would be ready, warm and provisioned." They were both thankful for that, as they were exhausted from the last few days of preparation. He suggested Marilda open a bottle of wine while he took care of the horse and carriage.

Exiting the door, he noticed the last glimmer of light from the setting sun, the fading colors of yellow, orange, purple and pale blue, to the darkening blue sky above his head. He thanked God for this day, his wife, and the life they are about to share together. It was a magnificent sight. He called Marilda to join him for a moment. She grasped his hand and whispered, "Isn't it beautiful?"

Gilbert, not turning his head from the scene, wrapped his arm around her shoulder, drawing her close to him. In a barely audible voice he exclaimed, "This is God's wedding gift to us."

"What a glorious gift it is," she replied as she squeezed herself closer against him.

He unharnessed the horse and with a pat on its rump released it to the field for the evening. His memory drifted back to

Seeking to be Loved

when he, his brothers and father had worked this section of land. He always imagined one day he would have a home on this very knoll. It would be overlooking the pastures and the Moselle River beyond, which marked their border. This was his favorite spot of all his father's family land that they had worked for generations.

His mind flashed back, he can see himself as a boy spending the night on this very knoll where he would one day construct his bungalow. He could feel the peacefulness inside that he experienced years ago as he tended the flock of goats and sheep. In the early days of his youth, he enjoyed the openness, along with the sense of freedom it gave him. He also reflected on the fact that it gave him a sense of pride that his father trusted him. He was a youthful boy ten years of age, guarding and protecting the flocks.

Surely, he thought as he reminisced, that same feeling would have been experienced by his brothers. He never remembered ever having to spend more than a single night alone with the flocks. He knew he would have if it were expected of him. Even on this cold January night, he sensed the warm gentle breeze blowing against his face, just as it had done on those warm summer nights on this ridge years ago.

He thought to himself, "For twenty-six years he had worked this land." His entire life, which seemed insignificant compared to his father's and the generations of his family before him. "What is twenty-six years?" He thought to himself, when this land had been worked by his family for over four hundred years. Now he would do his part, raise a family, work, and care for the land, as his ancestors had done.

This last thought brought him back to the brisk night and his beloved Marilda, now his wife, awaiting him inside the bungalow. He slapped the mare on her rump a little firmer this time and off she went to graze on the hay left in the field. He hurried to the front door. He turned for one last glance to survey the ten acres where he and Marilda would begin their life together. He opened the door and was immediately struck by what appeared to be a soothing, glowing

Seeking to be Loved

warmth, inviting him in. He closed the door behind him. All he acknowledged was the sight of his bride. She was sitting by the hearth where two chairs and a small table had been placed between them. There were two glasses of wine, bread, and cheese on the table. Her body seemed to be radiating its own light, reflecting the flickering flames of the fire. The blaze was casting lively shadows, dancing, and bouncing off the curves of her body. It seemed to make her stillness come alive with an intoxicating motion, inviting him to share in the dance.

He felt a welling of moisture in his eyes. His spirit and soul rejoiced at the site, the loveliness of her.

He took off his jacket, loosening his tie, he stepped toward the fireplace and seated himself next to his dearest.

She had never taken her eyes off him from the moment the door had opened and he entered. Without saying a word, as he stared at the fire, he reached his hand toward her. It was met halfway. Their fingers intertwined into one, he turned his head to the right, seeing the sparkling radiance of Marilda's beauty. Gazing into her eyes, he struggled to say the words that were in his heart. Solemnly and softly, he uttered through the tension in his chest and throat, "Je t'aime(I love you). I have always loved you, from the moment I first saw you, across the aisle two pews down in church, that Sunday nearly thirteen years ago."

She laughed and said, "How can you love such a young girl of ten years of age? A girl you have never seen, or should I say, noticed before, nor even talked to. As I recall, you never even spoke to me until I was 14 or 15 years old. I believe it was when you bumped into me with a basket of fruit, or was it vegetables, at the marketplace. If I remember correctly, there was no acknowledgement of your clumsy behavior. Non(no), 'Excusez-moi, mademoiselle!' Nor, non apology," she stated in a humorously questioning manner.

"Ah oui," said Gilbert, "Arrr mais(but), I noticed the sparkle and the excitement in your eyes during the moment of that first meeting."

Seeking to be Loved

Laughing, she said, "Non-non (No no) that was more of a surprised and startled look that you saw in my eyes," she emphasized. "I was thinking, 'Who is this person, plowing his way so clumsily through the market?"

They laugh at each other's recollection. They reach for their glasses and raise them to each other and sip, never taking their eyes off each other. She cuts a piece of cheese and lifts it to his mouth. She placed it on his tongue. He kissed her fingers as she looks into his eyes.

He saw nothing but her, she only him. Moments, maybe only seconds, it could have been hours, before they rise together hand-in-hand and step into the next room.

Gilbert surveyed the room. He was thankful as he recalled his brother George's comment. "The bungalow will be warm and cozy, also provisioned."

He noticed the warmth and the soothing light of coals, piled in a bed of ash radiating their heat from the fireplace in the bedroom. He was thankful for his brother's consideration.

Lying beside each other, Marilda gently blew out the candle on the stand next to their bed and they embraced.

Gilbert awoke during the night, still embracing his bride, as his eyes adjusted to the darkness. He noticed the moonlight shining through the window, casting its soft beams of light onto Marilda. He is amazed at the peaceful beauty lying beside him. He whispered, "Merci(Thank you) Dear Lord. I promise to always love and cherish this woman beside me." He dozed off into a deep peaceful sleep.

Seeking to be Loved

Chapter 2 <u>The family</u>

William Gilbert(Gil) and Marilda Natalie("Nattie"), quickly set out to make their bungalow a home. Gilbert began calling her "Nattie," as she was called by her close friends and family, her nickname based on her middle-given name. Just as he is called by his middle name after his father.

When he was a young boy, he never left his father's side. He enjoyed the opportunity to assist him with chores. He liked helping his father with all the necessary tasks required of farm and stock husbandry.

Gilbert and Marilda both wanted a home that would keep them, and hopefully, in the not too distant future, their children, safe and warm. A home full of life, sounds of joy, laughter, prayer, and teaching. A new generation full of promise and hope, to learn, to love, to fight, cry and to be part of this land. The land Gilbert prized, the land his ancestors fought and died on for centuries.

The two looked forward to the promise of a fruitful marriage and abundant crops. For they both were willing to put forth their best effort. They had learned their trades well from their parents and had the support and backing of a strong and willing family, if ever they were in need.

Despite the diligence and love for one another, children did not come to them that first year, nor the second. Families and friends encouraged and teased them. Nattie so wanted children to raise. Gilbert would need them to assist with chores and help with the farm as it prospered and grew. After two years there was no conception.

Attending mass each week they both secretly had prayed for a child. The service ended and upon making their way out of the parish, they were approached by a neighbor, Mrs. Raibeau. She placed her hand on Nattie's shoulder and said, "May I speak with you for a moment?"

Seeking to be Loved

Once out of the church, Mrs. Raibeau informed them that her nephew and his wife had recently died unexpectedly. Both died from injuries sustained when their carriage rolled over a steep ridge, while hauling their crops to town. She said, "They had a son not yet two years old. My nephew was an only child when my sister's family moved to Besancan, which is south of here, close to the Swiss border."

She explained she was not familiar and knew little of her nephew's wife or her family. "He had met her in the south of France many years ago. We had no contact with her family. My sister and her husband, the grandparents of the child, are several years our elder and are not in good health. Well, surely you can see, we are too old to be raising the child and they are older than us. We have been praying for a proper home to place the boy. I understand from speaking with your mother, you have been trying for a Bé bé(Baby)."

As she was speaking, Gilbert and Nattie looked at each other. He read from her expression in her eyes the embarrassment, or was it shame, maybe both, he thought. At the same time both their hearts soared. Nattie nearly bursting with joy in anticipation of Mrs. Raibeau's probable request. Gilbert was excited also and it reflected in his own eyes. He looked at Nattie again and he could see the change in her expression.

He now could see something more familiar to him. It was the love, hope and joy in her eyes. He immediately turned to Mrs. Raibeau and said, "We would like to see the child!" Nattie squeezed his hand.

Mrs. Raibeau declared, "Of course you would. I can arrange a meeting at your convenience, he is staying with my sister Eva and her husband, the child's grandparents. They live in Gavisse, a few kilometers from here, 30 minutes if the road is not muddy. I will send them a message and request a time for a meeting."

They bid each other farewell. Nattie graciously thanked her for considering them as possible adoptive parents of the child.

Seeking to be Loved

In the carriage on the way home, she squeezed Gilbert's arm tightly. She was so full of excitement and anticipation that she was nearly cutting off the circulation in his arm. He was struggling to keep control the reins.

He also was excited about the possibility. Gil did not want to discourage Nattie, although on the other hand he did not want her to get her hopes to high. He conveyed to her, "Do not get too anxious. We do not know anything about the child. Other relatives or people in their village may want the boy. Let us not get our hopes up just yet.

She whispered, "I know," she began to cry. For in her heart she wanted to bear children and dreamed of the day when she would. Neither the vision nor desire of bearing and raising children ever left her. She was thankful for this gift that they may potentially receive if it was to be God's will.

Gilbert placed his arm around her and held her close. He wants to comfort her. Her tears stopped as they approached their bungalow.

The days dragged on the following week. Both went about their daily chores and business. They did not say much to one another as the days passed. Each day they hoped to hear news from Mrs. Raibeau about meeting her nephew's young son. Nearly a week passed without receiving any word. Saturday evening they walked through the new grass, still warm from the spring sun. The day was ending and the sun lay low in the sky. They shared each other's thoughts and wondered why they had not heard anything about the child. They thought that maybe another family member had offered to take the child to raise in their home. It was a consoling thought. Even though neither would admit it, there was a sorrow in their hearts.

"All week long I thought about raising him as our son," she told Gilbert. Having a child in the home brought on a wantonness in them both. Since they married, both secretly desired, hoped and prayed for children.

Seeking to be Loved

They stopped and watched the sunset, overlooking the sheep grazing on the fresh green spring grass. As the sun passed over the horizon, they turned and looked at each other. He kissed her on the forehead. Holding hands, they strolled back to the house.

In the morning they woke, kissed, and went about their chores, without much being said. They ate breakfast, readied themselves for church and were off. The 3 1/2 km carriage ride seemed slow and solemn. The service and sermon were a blur for Marilda, as it was for Gilbert. They prayed in their own minds, hearts, and deepest recesses of their souls, only for God's will, for what is to be. They were afraid to ask the Creator for such a precious gift; that of a child.

Their faith and belief is God's will is divine, not to be questioned, just trusted!

When the service was over, they were in no hurry to leave. They sat in silence for several minutes as the rest of the congregation made their way out. The church was nearly empty. A few still lingered and were talking at the door. Gilbert squeezed Nattie's hand; they looked at each other and nodded. They bowed reverently toward the altar, then turned to leave the church. When they reached the rear of the church, they noticed Madame Raibeau with another elderly couple they did not know.

They stepped forward toward Madame Raibeau to ask about the child. Madame was wearing a gentle pleasing smile on her face.

The others had a stern appearance about them. One would say it was more of a cross demeanor, somewhere between a worried and concerned look on their face.

Madame Raibeau introduced them. "This is my sister Eva and her husband," They noticed something behind the elderly couple's legs. Nattie took a step forward to greet them, extending her hand toward the woman. The woman reached for Nattie's hand. She and her husband stepped ever so slightly to the side. There before her eyes was a child, barely able to stand. He stood between the couple as content and unassuming as a sheep being led to a barn.

Seeking to be Loved

Marilda's attention was instantly drawn to the child. His eyes opened wide. They were bright, full of joy and cheer. Marilda released the most pleasant sounding sigh. Smiles and laughter broke the silence, as she knelt before the child. She stretched out her arms toward the child, so he may step towards her.

An onlooker later described that there appeared to be beams of light coming from Marilda's eyes, that enveloped around the child. Some say there was an aura radiating from both. Still, others described a force that could be felt beckoning both Marilda and the child. It was that strange force that drew the child right into Marilda's arms.

"Non," another said, "The beam of light drew the child right into her heart."

The elderly gentleman standing beside Monsieur Raibeau looked at Gilbert. In a matter-of-fact manner spoke with a strong monotone voice, "I believe the deal has been sealed. It is done. His name is Ernest James Dionne," he expressed to Gilbert.

Marilda shed tears of joy. She asked Ernest James, "Would you like to come live with us?" He nodded his head up and down.

Gilbert shook hands with Monsieur Dionne and thanked him graciously. Then he shook hands and hugged all who were present.

Monsieur Dionne led Gilbert to his wagon. He pointed to a trunk. "There are clothes, blankets and things made for or given to him by his mother and relatives." It was full of items they wanted the boy to have. Monsieur Dionne thanked them and gave them his blessing, then bid them farewell.

Gilbert shouted as their carriage rolled away, "Merci. We promise to take care of him and raise him as our own. When the time comes, we will let him know who his mother and father were, as well as both of you. You will always be welcome in our home."

Even though the sky was cloudy and overcast it could not shed the slightest bit of gloom on this glorious spring day. Gilbert and Marilda were filled with joy and happiness; it seemed to emanate from the child as well.

Seeking to be Loved

The team reached the final stretch of road that led to their home. Their home looked quaint and inviting. However they both thought something was a bit odd. Neither said anything to the other, for they knew not what it was that struck them funny about the scene. It was not until Gilbert exited the house a second time to retrieve more items from the wagon, he realized what was different. He had been so distracted by the child, he had not even noticed that he needed to push sheep and a few of the goats, along with fowl, aside.

It was very unusual, he recalled thinking, how strange. Even when he would drive them very close to the house to corral them for shearing, the animals always seemed to avoid getting near the residence. When he entered the house, he mentioned it to Nattie. "They never come this close to the house."

She looked at him, smiled, and after a brief thought, laughed. "They wanted to see the new family member and welcome him to their home." The three of them embraced, laughing. Gilbert turned to Ernest, who was held between them in their arms. He spoke to him, "Those sheep will know who to follow one day," touching the little boy's nose.

Those first few days were filled with joy and heartache. The only words Ernest could say clearly were "Ma ma, Da dee." He would say them as tears filled his eye lids. When Nattie heard the words, she stopped whatever she was doing. Her attention turned to the child and she would then wrap him tightly in her arms. She would whisper in his ear, "Dieu bénisse votre enfant(God Bless you child), Je suis désolé'(I am so sorry)," and then say, "Je t'aime(I love you) so much. I will be your Ma mee."

Each time after a few moments the child would let out a soft, quiet giggle. Only then would Nattie loosen her embrace enough to look into his eyes. She would see a happy little boy with a pleasant smile looking at her. Then once again her spirit soared.

Seeking to be Loved

Time passed, the crops grew, the herds flourished, as did the Guyon family. Marilda conceived and bore a daughter the following spring, Mary Alice. A little more than a year later, Henry Augustine, followed in September 1904. In January 1906, Gilbert was born. February 1908, Ludger Joseph, was born, later that year in July at five months of age he died of cholera. April 1909, Blanche Marie, came into the world, and June, 1910 Joseph William, joined into the Guyon family.

Yes, things were going well for Gilbert and Marilda, other than the death of their infant son Ludger, and they felt very blessed. The rumor around town was that William Gilbert Guyon Jr., was going to surpass his father in his manly hood and marital duties. On September 30, 1913, Phillip Joseph, was born.

The life and the home Gilbert always dreamed of had become his reality. Their home was full of joy, laughter, tears, sorrow and in a constant state of ruckus. The family was growing, working, and reaping the fruit of their labors.

There was something a bit unsettling in the air. Nattie and Gilbert both had an uneasy feeling. It was similar to the sensation one gets when a terrible storm is approaching and you see it coming on the horizon.

Occasionally, once all the children were tucked into bed, they sat on the porch, overlooking the field and the river beyond. They enjoyed the peacefulness of the fading light at the end of another day.

From the beginning of the year, there had been rumors that Germany and France wanted to reclaim land lost during the Prussian War. It was part of the territory between the Moselle and Rhine river valleys. The land the Guyon family had worked for nearly five hundred years was within this region. It all seemed very unlikely, so they felt secure. Yet there was a nagging unrest within them. It was the consensus of many that war was on the horizon.

Other conflicts had come and gone from within and outside the French borders throughout history. They had always survived, although not without casualty and loss. Although, there had not been any serious threat to France from invading countries or great battles since the Napoleonic campaigns, over 100 years ago.

Seeking to be Loved

Chapter 3 <u>The Coming Storm</u>

Tension was mounting across Europe. The imminence of war was in the winds. Among the populace of France in the year 1914, especially along the northeastern boundaries, the threat would soon become a reality. It was in the air, and the French citizens along the eastern borders saw the signs and acknowledged the fact that war was a very real possibility. With the threat becoming ever more evident, the French government, military leaders and citizens in the region were faced with the dilemma of what to do with the populace.

History notes that, there were three categories or stages of displacement about to take place in France, before and during the Great War.

First, there were people concerned more for the safety of their loved ones than their property and worldly possessions. They departed in the first phase of displacement, packing belongings they felt were necessary and important to them. The rest was sold for whatever they could get, or it was left behind. Most headed south or west to Paris, others to the coastal regions. Many hoped to obtain passage to leave the country to join family across the Atlantic. Some felt they had no place to go, wanting just to create distance between themselves and danger.

Others were unwilling to leave their homes and property, their heritage. This was the way of life that their family had lived and worked for generations. They were stalwarts, determined to keep their way of life, alive and well, willing to risk what they must to weather the storm. The thinking was that with a neutral stance, they might be left alone. They knew their land and property would be ransacked and ruined. Despite the horror of war they vowed never to leave what they lived and worked for from cradle to grave. Nor, would they leave their beloved France. Some realized they would be putting their lives and everything they possessed at risk. Still others

Seeking to be Loved

felt that the tensions would blow over, or not happen for many years.

The second stage of the displacement of the French people came about in the summer of 1914 in the northern and Northeast strongholds of France. In the eastern sectors, it was determined by the government and the military leaders that evacuation should take place. It was decided that any residents living and working in these areas, if not directly involved in the war efforts for the defense of France, must leave. If war broke out, as it most assuredly would, these people would hinder the defense efforts. It was quoted these countrymen will, "Be useless mouths to feed." Thus came the decisions leading to the second stage of displacement. They were to move away from the border areas to the interior or southern areas of France. During this phase they had no choice; they were forced to move.

Many left France and crossed borders into the surrounding countries hoping to wait out the coming clouds and storm of destruction that war would bring. Their plan and hope were to return one day.

The war broke out with the German army invading sooner than anyone suspected with a force and destructiveness no one imagined.

The French can be a stubborn, determined populace; a fierce, indomitable people as the Romans found out centuries before. Many did not want to be dictated to by anyone, whether it be their own government or an invading force. It was this along with love and patriotism which led to the third stage of displacement. This is where love becomes greater than fear and life itself.

Many of the individuals who fled to these bordering countries rallied. They returned to the motherland to help defend her against a war machine which the world had never seen before. This was the Third Stage of displacement, the call that rang in the heart of every Frenchman. The call to return to stop the senseless slaughter of

Seeking to be Loved

humanity, a cry heard by many men and women around the world, "Vive la France," to stop the spread of evil.

"What greater love is there than to lay down one's life for another" (paraphrased from the book of John).

This is where our story begins. Gilbert, Marilda and their seven children lived and worked their farm. The land, which earned them a livelihood, had been in his family for generations. They grew up in the post Prussian War era and felt safe within the borders of their powerful and beloved France. The Guyons knew the destruction of war, for Gilbert's father and forefathers fought in many wars. His grandfather served in Napoleon's army.

Men of the community attended town meetings, where many of the town leaders and business owners shared the rumors brought on by dealing with their contacts across the border. They conveyed their stories and experiences dealing with business associates on the other side of the border.

They shared what they observed with neighbors when visited and transporting their goods to and from the country to the east. They noticed the buildup of its forces and the preparation of an army, although it was never spoken of or mentioned when questioned. It all seemed to be just talk and no immediate threat, although heightened their suspicion.

Gilbert shared the news with Marilda. They discussed many possibilities, if in fact things should happen, and what options would be available in such an emergency. The thought of having a plan in place seemed to be a good idea.

Marilda informed Gilbert, "We have seven young children to think about and to assure a future."

Many believed war was no immediate threat. Although it was more than mere talk and speculation about the possibilities of the coming war. Forces were being staged and encampments on the German side of the border were growing ever larger and closer.

Seeking to be Loved

Chapter 4 <u>Life on the farm</u>

It was a beautiful spring morning; the sky was brilliant blue. Gil stepped outside his back door. Marilda joined him.

He determined, "This will be a good day to plow the fields." He went about morning chores, while Marilda went back inside to prepare breakfast. The children were beginning to rise. She told Ernest, Henry, and Gilbert Jr., to go about their chores while Mary Alice and Blanche would help her inside.

Gil and the boys returned as breakfast was being set on the table. The children gathered and took their seats, a prayer was said, and the meal began. Gil announced that he and the older boys, Ernest 12, Henry 9, soon to be 10, and Gilbert Jr. who had recently turned 8 years old, would join him in the fields on this glorious day.

That announcement was met with grumbling and mixed emotion. Ernest and Henry knew what to expect, whereas young Gilbert in his excitement about being with his older brothers and father in the fields, could not wait to start. This was the first time he would be joining his father and brothers for such work. He was thinking, "I am growing up. I am a big boy now. I am taking on more man chores!"

He was glad to not be confined to the house or the area immediately surrounding it with the women folk. "I will now be out in the fields with the men and I will be working." He was quite proud to be considered ready for the test.

It was always exciting this time of year, with spring just around the corner. Preparation for a new season, it is time to get the fields ready to accept seed. "The seeds of promise," as Gilbert like to put it, explaining to his sons that each seed planted in well prepared soil meant a future crop. The growing of food that would help sustain them and hopefully many others. It was a privilege, as well as their duty, to care for and work the land so that it would yield abundantly. Gilbert took every opportunity to guide, teach and educate his sons on the virtues of working diligently. Teaching them to prepare well,

Seeking to be Loved

to cherish and care for all that they had. He taught them to properly use and maintain equipment, tools, beast, property, each other and neighbors. He would always state, for it was his favorite saying, no matter what the occasion, "Seek a good harvest, for you will reap what it is you sow."

The late April sun rose higher into the sky and warmed the land. Gilbert plowed the field with his team, two fine Percheron stallions. The two older boys' job was to work with their hoes and break up the large chunks of sod that the plow turned. Gilbert Jr.'s, job was pick out the stones and put them into a bucket. He did well until it had gotten too heavy to carry. At that point he then had to carry his bucket full of stones and stack them on the outside edge of the field.

The growing pile added height to the stone wall. This wall served as a fence to keep out the cattle and sheep. The goats always mysteriously found their way into the garden and field crops each year, despite the wall.

They were just finishing the section of field when they heard the yell from Nattie. That meant that dinner would be ready by the time they got back to the house. They finished the row and Gilbert steered the team back to the barn. He instructed the boys to finish breaking up the sod in the last row and remove the stones. Then they cleaned up and hauled water to their mother. Gilbert unharnessed the team, filled the trough with water, brushed down their coats, and gave each two scoops of grain and oat mix. He patted their heavily muscular necks, telling them they did well for the first day in the fields. They whinnied, snorted, and nodded their heads.

Gilbert washed and joined his family at the table. He led the family in grace and thanksgiving for the food that they had on the table and for each one sitting there. Nattie asked her young son Gilbert how his first day went in the fields with his big brothers and father.

Seeking to be Loved

He had to blink his eyes a few times, to wake himself up. Smiling, he said, "I enjoy being with father and my brothers. Man's work is hard work."

His sister Mary just rolled her eyes.

Marilda noticed Mary was about to comment about their household duties and caring for the little ones. She gently smiled at her, shaking her head no, signifying to let his comment be.

Gilbert Jr.'s father commented on his sons performance, "And he did a fine man's work today."

When the meal was finished, Marilda carried little Gilbert to his bed and laid him there, sound asleep. The two older boys went with their father to clean and sharpen the tools for tomorrow's work. They made repairs on the buildings, house, and barn. The final chore was checking the herd and flocks before calling it a day.

It had been a typical day inside the home and out in the barnyard. Marilda and the girls were busy doing the spring-cleaning. Many chores needed to be done, beating the rugs, feather mattresses and quilts, which had compiled a winter's worth of dust.

They thoroughly cleaned the house top to bottom. There was not an inch in the entire house that was not washed clean. Every nook and cranny had been swept, cleaned, and swept again. Plus, they had to milk the cows and goats, care for two very young children, a baby and prepare meals for nine hungry mouths.

All in all, the entire family was a well-oiled working unit. Each knew their role, fulfilling their duties with joy and gratitude, for what they had and each other. They had all they needed, although it came at a price. That price was labor, love and respect for one another. They all had a sense of duty to each other, the animals and the land which provided their livelihood. Except, of course, for the two youngest, although Joseph, who was almost four years old, had his work to do as well. His job was not an easy one, with three busy women constantly in motion, moving about the house. His duty was to stay out from under their feet and let mother know if his younger brother needed anything. This kept him busy as the ladies of the

Seeking to be Loved

house buzzed about them. This kept him and baby Phillip from being harmed, most of the time!

At the end of each day the family settled in for the evening after another day well spent. Their father would tell stories, many of which were told to him by his father and grandfather. The stories had been passed down by each generation. The tales always attempted to instill a strong sense of right and wrong. Prudence and morality were also themes, to develop a conscience in his children. It was their father's intent as well to instill a sense of duty and responsibility that extended to one's family, friends, community, and country.

Once weekly the children, five to fifteen years of age, were strongly encouraged (forced) to go into the town meeting hall. There was a circuit teacher who would present and assign lessons and give assignments for each child to complete by the next week's session. It was not much of a school, however expectations were high for each individual student. Families would be assigned textbooks, they were responsible for returning them in good condition. If not the student or family were required to replace them at their expense. Some were quite old, yet still in good condition. Many an evening, families would discuss the lessons with their children. With such a large family, the Guyons learned a lot from the lessons each had brought home to complete.

They were well into spring, the fields were cultivated and seeded. Sprouts were springing forth and spirits were high.

The sheep had lambed, and goats had given birth to their kids. It looked to be another promising, fruitful year on the Guyon's farm.

On this early May evening the children were playing in the yard near the patio, each had completed their assignments for school. Marilda and Gilbert were sitting on the porch holding hands, watching the children, as they unwound from the days toil. They watched the sun as it was getting closer to the horizon. The beautiful shades of yellow, orange, light purple and blue painted the sky on

Seeking to be Loved

the horizon to the west and the day was at its end. "Another gift from above, for all to see and acknowledge and enjoy," Gilbert stated aloud. They both knew how fortunate they are.

They turned to each other, looked into each other's eyes, and said the exact same words simultaneously. "We are blessed!"

They watched the sunlight as it faded from the sky. Gilbert whispered, "Marilda Natalie Guyon, Je t'aime so much!"

Nattie never turned her head from the horizon. Gilbert saw the smile as it appeared on the right side of her face. Then he, too, returned his gaze, watching the colors fade, knowing she heard and was pleased.

Seeking to be Loved

Chapter 5 <u>The Vision</u>

All the children slept well that night, even young Phillip. He was nearly seven months old and beginning to sleep through the night. The night was quiet and peaceful, though both Nattie and Gil had an uneasiness about them throughout the evening and it kept them awake. Sleep was light and restless for them both.

Gilbert was the first to rise, and he sat silently on the edge of the bed. Nattie, not falling asleep until wee hours of the morning, was still in bed. She laid in silence, listening for Phillip's first cry of hunger, to greet a new day. After a few moments, she noticed her husband had not moved from the edge of the bed. She asked if he felt well.

He replied, "Oui, I am fine."

She sensed he must have also felt the same uneasiness just as she had throughout the night.

Nothing else was said. He reached for his trousers, dressed, and quietly left the room. He stopped at the fireplace and stoked the remaining embers in the hearth. He added kindling and a few sizable pieces of wood for the fire so it would still be warm when Nattie arose. He grabbed his boots and went outside to put them on. He did not want to wake his family. He knew the heavy sound of him walking across the floor with his boots on was bound to stir them. It was too early to start their day. He closed the door behind him and turned to face the day. He enjoyed the brisk, fresh crispness of the early morning, noticing it first on his cheeks as he took a deep breath of the fresh morning air. It smelled sweet from the new blossoms starting to appear. He liked the mornings when he arose before the birds began their first chirps on a new day. He can distinguish the difference of their initial cries which eventually turned to calls. The birds progressed to their songs later in the morning. Gil believed it was probably due to the fact their chores were done, their nestlings fed, or seeking a mate. He had noticed over the years it was not until

Seeking to be Loved

the sun rose and warmed the land that the birds chirps and calls turned to songs, each unique to its species.

He sat on the step to pull on his boots. He stepped off the front porch, gazed at the western sky, and recognized the signs of another clear spring day. He took a deep breath and with a bit of relief went about his business, getting an early start on the morning chores. He hoped to turn the ground in the eastern field of his property today.

He was thinking his father and his brothers, Joseph, and Philippe, would be working the field alongside his. He was looking forward to seeing them. His three older brothers George, Frank, and Louis, had left France with their families almost three years ago, heading to the Eastern Canadian Province of Québec.

Turning the corner of the house, walking toward the barn, he noticed the eastern sky. He took note that it did not look as promising as he had thought a moment ago. He saw that it was not clear, and clouds were moving west. He thought to himself, "It does not look threatening," as he sniffed the air. He acknowledged, "I cannot smell a hint of rain, at least not yet. Maybe we will be able to get another good day in."

He was pleased how well the boys worked yesterday. He laughed when he thought of young Gilbert, lugging the less than half full bucket of stones to the edge of the field to dump. He thought, what a little trouper he was!

"Ahhh, there are my little birds, starting to awaken, adding chirps to the morning sounds as he is rustling here and there." He welcomed the company on this quiet morning. Soon all the animals will be awake, ready to be fed, watered, and led to the fields.

Gilbert enjoyed this life. He felt great purpose in the routine and the diligence required to care for the beasts. They were the animals that helped him make a living off the land and provide for his family and community. It was good, hard, and laborious work. It gave his life purpose. The fact that he was outside and in the open working appealed to him. Also, he was proud to be a part of what he

Seeking to be Loved

and his family had owned and had been their heritage for generations. He did not have to have anyone telling him what he needed to do. His father had taught him well. He often wondered how people could work in the factories for such long days. How could those that live in the confines of the cities, day in and day out, not feel claustrophobic? He often thought how his brothers, since leaving his beloved France, could enjoy their new life. They appeared to, at least from the letters they wrote to his parents, which he had also read. He recalled them describing the jobs they had in the factories along the great St. Lawrence River.

He thanked God that he and Nattie had the life they did.

First light started to brighten the sky. Nattie had not realized she had finally dozed off into such a deep sleep after Gilbert had left the house. Light shone in the room from the windows, and the thought occurred to her that she was getting a late start on the day. She paused a moment, listening for Phillip. She heard cooing sounds coming from his crib. She instantly felt a broad, proud mother's smile growing across her face, knowing her child was content.

She quickly went to him and whispered, "Good morning my dear sweet child. How are you this morning? Are you patiently waiting for Ma mee, to change and feed you, my little one?"

Phillip, smiled and started to make other resonance, the happy greeting sounds, and reactions at the sight of his mother. He begins to kick his feet in his great expectation. His anticipation is readily recognized. Nattie sees it in his actions and his eyes, the excitement he displayed when seeing and hearing the person he knows best, who cares for his needs.

The joy of recognition was in his whole little being, when their eyes meet, mother and child. Even the most casual observer could recognize the sparkle in both their eyes. They shared each other's expressions of joy radiating from both of them. Time stood still during those moments. Nothing else in the world mattered or was even acknowledged. Just the warm, trusting, comfortable feeling of the love that emanated all around them.

Seeking to be Loved

Marilda(Nattie, Nat) and William(Gil) loved all their children dearly and equally. Each are different, unique individuals. They had their own personality, likes, dislikes, talents, and gifts. All assumed their duties, the family was a unit where each played their own role. Each are of independent mind and pursued their own interests, with the things they showed favor.

As parents, they taught them diligently with patience, caring and love, for it was their duty to do so. They wanted to teach their children what they believed was important. Their mission was to instill in each the skills they needed to survive in this world and lead them to the next. They taught through their example to honor God, others, and themselves by their actions and also to be independent and of strong moral character. They wanted to teach them that life may not be easy. However it will definitely be, "What you, yourself make it."

Nattie felt a special connection with Phillip. It was not obvious, for she loved all and thanked God for each one of her children. Even though she was healthy and strong, she knew her childbearing years would be ending soon. It took more than three years to conceive her last child, causing her to realize Phillip may be her last. She wanted to savor her final gift of motherhood and mothering as long as she could, for she knew that one day this part of her life would be gone forever.

Even before she and Gilbert were married, they would speak of one day having children, maybe even as many as his father and grandfather. Marilda's prayer had been, "If that is to be the case, may I be up to the task."

The rain held off, and with the gloomy light of the gray sky, Gil and the boys were able to get the next field plowed. Now that the soil had been turned and broken, it was ready to accept seed. As he expected, his father and his brothers were working in the field adjacent to them. They planned their breaks to eat and rest their animals to coincide. They would meet where their fields bordered each other. Gilbert William Guyon shared the letters he had recently received from his three older sons with Gil and his grandsons. All three had steady work in the canning industry.

Gil's older brothers shared their concerns of news of an upcoming war in Europe. The boys feared for their homeland and family, particularly those on the eastern border of France. His brothers sent their warning of caution, as well as their love to all. Gilbert senior also mentioned that his sons in Québec can offer housing and shelter. He told Gil, their letters said work is nearly guaranteed. Jobs were plentiful for anyone that would wish to come to Canada.

Gil's father would share the news he heard from friends in the community who had trade across the border. The businessmen who bought and sold from each other, and have known each other well for many years. They did not have much to say when they inquired about the rumors. All he could tell his boys was the trade which once had been pleasant, now made them feel awkward. He was told the tension and hostility was noticeable when dealing with them. These were men, business associates and merchants whom they had agreements with across the border for years. Many were considered friends, rather than just business contacts. Some had suspected something sinister was manifesting itself. It was obvious they were trying to keep something from them. Some buildings were being reinforced behind the scenes in Germany. One could not help wondering when noticing many vacant and empty buildings in the towns close to the border.

During the last rest break of the day, the Guyons met with each other once again. Gilbert's father wanted to talk to Gil before they left the fields and returning to their home. He told Joseph to take the team and finish the row. "I want to talk awhile with Gil." He took Gil aside so the young ones would not hear them. Gil sensed his father had something important to say to him. He told his boys to keep breaking up the clods of soil and picking out the stones and he would take the team in a few minutes.

Seeking to be Loved

Gilbert Sr. put his arm over Gil's shoulder and walked away from the boys. He said, "You have a lifetime yet to live. You have been blessed with a large family, strong and healthy. You need to protect them. I know how much you love this land and this farm. I want you to listen, my son, you must not risk exposing them to harm from the dangers that may be coming our way. You must do whatever is necessary to protect your family, your young ones."

Gil looked at his father in bewilderment. He knew his father would stay and be buried on the land that his family had owned and defended for so long. The land which he himself loved, labored on, and dedicated his life to. The land that had been fruitful for him many years. He knew this land was a gift to his family from above, to care for and protect, to sow and reap in earnestness. Oui, a gift on earth.

Or, is it yet another trial presented to him? Is it a test that determines where he places his value?

The terra firma had always provided for those who respected it. His father knew how much his son loved the land. He knew especially this particular patch of pastureland on the hillside overlooking the Moselle river. It had been one of his son's dreams, ever since he was a child. His father reminded him, "I remember how you would say, 'This is where I want to build my own home. I want to be able to overlook these pastures, with the river beyond'."
He knew his son's dreams and his future ambitions had never been far from this parcel. He knew Gil would do anything within his power to nurture, nourish and protect the ground which he and his family inherited and had rights to for generations.

Monsieur Guyon knew his son's sense of duty, honor, moral and personal obligation was as strong as his own, if not more. He himself loved the land. Gil was his son and he knew what was in his heart. He knew nothing was more precious than his sons, daughters, and his family.

His words were intended to impress upon Gilbert that there is something greater. He told Gil, "The land, our heritage and all of the

Seeking to be Loved

worldly things that we possess are not worth one hair on your little one's head."

The last words he left with Gil that day were, "Son, promise me you will consider this. You have been blessed many times, almost as many as me. Do what you must do!"

He waved to Joseph as he was approaching with the team. Gil looked up at the sky for a long moment, took a deep breath and gave his father a sturdy embrace.

He promised him and said, "I will Father."

His father took the reins from Joseph to finish plowing the last row. Joseph mentioned to Gil, "He still likes to lecture, does he not?" Gil replied, "Our father is a wise man." Then he added, "We would do well to heed his wisdom."

Joseph replied, "And to heed less of his stubbornness, I suspect, as well." They both laughed in agreement.

Gil said, "It looks like we are going to get this field done today." They bid each other farewell and went about their work.

Joseph yelled to his nephews and waved. He shouted praise and encouragement for the stout work they were performing at their father's side. "You are good workers," he exclaimed.

Gil went to the team and resumed his plowing. He gave a gentle snap on the reins and the team set to their paces. The rest of the day passed and he pondered his father's words. Finishing the last row, he yelled to the boys, "Let us call it a day." He conveyed to his sons they had impressed his uncle and their grandfather with their performance in the field that day. "I am proud of all three of you!"

The boys looked up at their father; the two older boys had big grins on their face and said, "Merci."

Gilbert Junior was also looking up at him, his smile had a more questioning expression associated with it. Though one could detect a gleeful look in his eye along with dirt all over his face. He asked, "Me too father?"

His father laughed and lifted him high above his head. A huge smile appeared on his son's face; all the boys laughed. Gil exclaimed

Seeking to be Loved

in a loud, gruff tone, "Oui, you too." He patted the older boys on their head and said, "Well done." He added, "It is a lucky man who has such industrious sons."

After all were settled in bed for the night, Marilda readied herself for what she had hoped would be a peaceful night's slumber. Neither she nor Gilbert had gotten much rest the previous night.

Gil tended the fire in the fireplace and added a few pieces of coal to the large cast iron stove in the kitchen. It was similar to his parent's stove and was a wedding gift from her parents. It took four men to maneuver it into place. There were two fire boxes, a large one below the oven and one alongside, which was for baking. There were burners on top of the stove, with four burner openings on the surface with removable lid covers. A smooth cast iron surface separated them in the middle, where food items could be kept warm.

Once the fire was lit, the cast-iron body of the stove was an excellent source of radiant heat. Keeping the house warm and cozy once lit. Marilda used it for most of nine months out of the year. In the summer all cooking and heating water for baths and laundry was done on the patio. Gil had the foresight to construct a fireplace outside for such uses during the warmer months.

Marilda changed Phillip and carried him to the chair between his crib and their bed. She held him close and securely as he fed. Occasionally, they would make eye contact. Each felt the warmth of deepest regard, a pleasurable peacefulness. There was absolute trust and affection, a loving union shared between them. It is an attachment which only a blessed mother can experience, knowing she bore such a precious gift. A gift which was bestowed on her by the love of God and her spouse.

She brought it forth to the world. They share a link, a tie that only an infant can experience when it hears or sees the presence of its mother. Each child has their own special way of showing its excitement when acknowledging the one human being who showers and cloaks them in this holy blessed heartwarming love. It is

Seeking to be Loved

reflected not only on the face, the whole body rejoices when the infant senses his loving mother's presence. It really cannot be described in words, only acknowledged by the senses within the depths of our being.

This joy, warmth, security, and comfort is brought about by the purest, most enduring love of this mutual unity which a mother and child share.

This is the natural starting point, where an infant learns to love. It is learned by words, actions, and by something that cannot be observed, only felt. This is where the foundation of love is set; the base, the footer from where it grows. When the foundation is solid and unbreakable, love will flourish and grow, readying the senses within as one matures for another level. Each stage of life as one develops offers unique experiences. When one grows naturally and learns with proper guidance, they are prepared for the next stage.

Entering the room, Gil was struck by the radiant sight of mother and child. They were connected, nourishing each other with the food of life, body, and spirit. He smiled gently at Marilda, who possessed such a peaceful smile on her face. She turned her head ever so slightly to glance at him. Her gentle smile brought an instant calmness to his being. The world seemed still and peaceful. The room was filled with the warm glow from the fire and a candle. Their home was quiet and all the children were still and resting peacefully throughout the night.

The same was not to be true once again for Gilbert and Marilda's slumber. Their sleep was deep, and even though they were close together, side by side, neither noticed the tossing, turning, twisting and tension of the other's body throughout the night.

Gilbert dreamed of his father and brothers who were shouting, with fearful looks of horror on their faces. They shouted "Go, go, go," waving him away. He saw the landscape pitted and destroyed. He looked about his beautiful fields; he saw leafless, broken trees. His pastures were laden with debris. He looked to his left and observed what appeared to be grotesque humanoids. Some were bent over, others kneeling, while others rushed about spreading destruction. Dead animals and strange looking beasts gnawed and clawed at them. He recognized his own animals torn, bleeding and lame. He turned to his right and observed what appeared to be a team of horses. Their ribs were showing; they were covered with mud and blood from wounds of the whip. Their muscles were tense under the strain. The once noble animals struggled to move the load they were being forced to drag. Any reasonable man would know they could not possibly be able to bear. The load itself was some sort of machine that they were attempting to haul through knee-deep mud. He felt sorry for the beasts, as he thought of his own pride and joy, a pair of strong well-bred Percheron stallion draft horses. He stared at the animals and wanted to shout to the men who were laying the whip on them. His attention was drawn to the eyes of the horse nearest him. He stared intently into the pupils and saw fear reflected in them. He realized there was something familiar about the eyes of these horses. He thought again of his team that he harnessed each day. He raised the pair from colts, given to him by his father as a youth. He trained them to work side-by-side. They knew him, his voice, his touch and felt his care.

When they were in the fields they worked as one, all three of them. They knew his will and it became theirs. From the time they were foals, he fed, watered, and groomed them. He spoke to them as his friends and partners while he groomed and pet them.

He nurtured them, knowing one day they would be relied on each day to help him earn a living for him and his family. They were not just animals, beasts of burden; they were comrades, partners, and helpers.

The eyes he was looking into now were the eyes he looked into many times. He gasped at the appearance of these beasts. Everything within him revolted with agony, anger, and disgust. He

Seeking to be Loved

could barely look upon the sight, seeing these noble creatures treated this way.

In his dream he had to turn away, and as he did, he heard them neigh. He just had to turn back to see, for it was a familiar sound he had heard many times. A sickening feeling rose within him dropping him to his hands and knees. Staring at the horses again and looking deep into their eyes, he finally realized they were his own. It caused him to convulse.

After what seemed to be an eternity, he raised his head looking towards his barn and shed. Both buildings were destroyed. He was stunned with fear, thinking of his home and family. It overwhelmed him. He turned his head slightly to see what had become of the rest of his farm. Before his vision cleared and the scene around him came into focus, he heard blood curdling screams and crying.

His heart felt as if it were being torn from within his chest. The mist and smoke began to clear, he could see what he once called home, now a smoldering rubble. He recognized Marilda in the distance; she appeared ragged and worn. There were dirty children crying and clinging to her, their children!

The vision horrified him. He prayed this was a dream. He knew it was real, and this frightened him terribly. It felt too real and the vision was too clear to be a dream. He knew in his mind that it was real. He was panic stricken and bewildered. He felt a paralyzing inability to react to the situation at hand. His body jerked throughout the night.

He understood the phrase, "A bleeding heart." That was the feeling within him as he laid in bed enduring this fitful nightmare. It felt as though his heart was bleeding. He could literally feel the warm blood from his innermost depths pouring forth. He prayed for all this to end.

Nattie also dreamt throughout the night. In her dream, she awoke to a day that started typically, in the usual manner following her standard routine. She saw herself in the process of packing. To

Seeking to be Loved

her, everything seemed to be beyond reality. She kept wondering, "Where are my belongings?" The things so dear to her seem to be displaced, lost, or hidden, gone. It was as though they could not be found, and this made her anxious. For some reason she felt rushed, in a hurry to get away, to where or why she did not know?

She was confused and did not seem to know how to start, what to bring, and not a clue where they were going. She never felt so frustrated and indecisive. She was glad her children were there.

Finally, in her dream she regained her faculties. She slowly became confident with the help of the older ones. They would be able to help with what needed to be done. The older boys were outdoors doing the chores as she cared for the younger ones.

She was preparing breakfast, having just finished nursing Phillip. Suddenly the door burst open and the boys entered shouting. She could not make sense of what they were saying. She heard a loud sound as Ernest's body was flung forward, his arms flaring as he fell to the floor. She stared at the still body, lying on the floor, bewildered. Then she noticed a stream of blood poured forth from it. She was stunned for a moment. She instinctively yelled to the girls to get the children as she rushed to Ernest's lifeless body. Before turning him, she yelled instructions to the other two boys who were crying, standing beside her. She told them to grab provisions and to go out the back door. She shouted, "Run to your grandfather's house. I will follow."

In her mind she knew this was not real, it could not be real. "I must be dreaming. It has to be a dream. Oh, dear Lord, please let this be a dream; what shall I do?" Her mind was racing while she held Ernest's lifeless body in her arms. She was kneeling on the floor with his head laid across her thighs.

She heard loud sounds as though something heavy dropped on the house, then what seemed to be the sound of rain falling against the exterior of her home. It was the debris, the dirt from the bombs bursting around her house, causing the sound. Between the booms, she heard shouting and yells. Then what sounded like the rapid cracking and popping of new unseasoned wood in the fireplace. It was then she realized it was gunfire.

That thought brought her back to reality. She heard the baby cry. Instantly she thought, "Oh no, Phillip, we must leave." Only the love of the living and helpless child could draw her away from her dead son. Thinking of nothing else other than protecting her baby, she ran to the bedroom. She lifted Phillip, grabbing the blankets covering him and ran out the back door. She quickly looked to see if she could spot her other children, making sure none were left behind. She saw them passing over the ridge above her. She heard nothing from that moment on. As horrible as they were, she was able to block the sounds from her mind. Her full attention was on reaching the others. She was oblivious to everything going on around her. There were explosions, screams, the air filled with smoke and debris. She ran.

When she reached the crest of the ridge, she paused only a moment to see her children running in the distant valley. Without stopping, she experienced a moment of relief and she thanked God, knowing that they were alive and creating distance from the immediate danger. Time seemed to race even as she felt she was going in slow motion. She was running as fast as she could. Despite needing to catch her breath, she would never stop, until she reached her children.

Alas, she noticed she was getting closer. She could see the children rushing about the grounds of their grandparent's farm. They appeared to be looking for something. She thought of Gilbert. Where is he?

At the very thought of him, a deep ache within her heart overwhelmed her. She dropped to her knees still embracing Phillip and wept. She instinctively knew something terrible and tragic had happened to him.

"Oh, dear God, no, no," she screamed "Nooo!"

Her motherly instincts forced her to action once again. Never releasing, never letting go of Phillip, she rose to her feet and ran,

Seeking to be Loved

shouting for the children to come to her. When all were together, less Ernest, Mary uttered, "We could not find our grandma or grandpa or any of our uncles."

Marilda told them, "We must make our way to the village."

The children asked, "What about father?"

"He will find us. We must go!" Marilda said rushing them to the road. It seemed to be empty. No other people were to be seen. Where was everyone?

She wondered, "Why is everyone not rushing to town or trying to get away?" Houses and fields appeared vacant and lonely, void of life. They wandered past empty homes and buildings. They saw no one. No man nor beast, just emptiness, everything was so vague, surreal, and abandoned. It was so eerie and silent.

Marilda felt the same sensation as Gil; warm blood spilling from her heart when she thought of Gilbert and leaving Ernest. She had to erase the thought of her eldest son bleeding on the floor.

She walked the road leading to town with her children gathered closely.

It was the sound of the rooster crowing that woke Gilbert from his sleep. He quickly rose and thanked God. It was only a dream. The realistic lingering images troubled him. He pulled on his trousers and shirt, buttoning them as he left quietly and went outside.

Marilda also awoke suddenly. She was aware of Gilbert dressing. Instantly aware it was morning, and glad to acknowledge she had been dreaming. The realness of her dream worried her. She reviewed and processed it, lying there in her bed waiting for Phillip to wake.

She did not want to say a word to Gilbert. That was why she did not bid him good morning, nor kiss him to start his day. She was just thankful it was a dream. She had laid still until she heard Gilbert closed the door as he left the house. Then she began to weep. She was so thankful it was only a dream.

Seeking to be Loved

Both went about their day as usual. It was Tuesday and the children had school. Marilda hugged and kissed the children with a little extra passion that day. She sent them out the door and off they went. She was thankful to have the three younger ones at home with her. She hovered over them, nurturing the little ones more than usual. She showered them with hugs, kisses, and her precious love.

Marilda and Gilbert kept their distance from each other throughout the day. It was not until the children came home late that afternoon from school that Gilbert returned to the house. Once home the children as usual, wanted to share their studies. Along with their lessons and assignments, they discussed the biggest topic of the day at school, which was the possibility of a war with Germany. As they were preparing for dinner, Gilbert looked across the table, making eye contact with Marilda. They both recognized the uneasiness in their glance.

Ernest asked his father, "What would we do if there is a war? We are so close to the border. What would become of the farm and the land? Would we stay here? The teacher told us that there may be an evacuation."

Little Gilbert, looking at his father, asked, "Da dee, what is an evacuation?"

Gilbert senior said, "Did you not pay attention in class today, Gilbert?"

Little Gilbert shrugged his shoulders and shrunk in his seat at the table just a bit. Then their father explained, "It is when people leave their homes, their property and go someplace different."

Marilda's eyes opened wide with a startled gaze as she remembered her dream. She could vividly see herself and the children in her dream as they were racing to get away, trying to make their way to the village. She had a fretful look on her face, which Gil noticed, and it made him pause for a moment. He also reflected on his dream. No more was said while the evening meal was placed on the table. A blessing of thanks was offered, and they began their meal.

Seeking to be Loved

Finally, little Gilbert exclaimed, "I do not wanna evacuation. I would not know where to go!"

Mary Alice, his older sister, said, "We would have to go someplace far away and safe."

Blanche, who had just turned five, asked, "Will we go all the way to grandma and grandpa's house?" The older ones laughed, knowing it was less than 2.5 kilometers to their grandparents' farm using the road, a shorter distance if walking through the fields.

Gilbert jokingly said, "We certainly should all be safe there."

The day was ending and the children were tucked into bed for the night. Gilbert and Nattie sat on their front porch. Several uneasy minutes passed without a word between them. It was Nattie who finally broke the silence. She reached over and laid her hand on top of Gilbert's and said, "I had the most horrifying and realistic dream last night. I had such a fitful night sleep. The dream itself was so real, it was very disturbing. I was in a state of panic and did not know what to do. It was a helplessness I never felt before. It was like fear, frustration, panic, and confusion all at once. It was paralyzing."

Before she went further, Gilbert told her, "I too, had a fitful night. I was haunted all day by the visions of the most terrible dream I ever had in my life. It also seemed surreal." The lump in his throat caused him to stop and swallow a few times. Then he took a few deep breaths and another moment's pause.

Nattie waited for him to regain his composure.

"I was in such a state of panic, not knowing how to react. Nattie, I do not even know if I can describe it to you, other than to say it was the most horrific sight."

Silence filled the next few seconds as he tried to find the words. Words that would describe what he was experiencing and feeling during the dream.

Marilda squeezed his hand. She said with a determined firmness to her voice, "William Gilbert, I fear we must go. Something tells me we must go, far away."

Seeking to be Loved

She almost shouted as she squeezed the words out, in the most resolute voice Gilbert ever heard come from her. She stated, "It must be soon." She continued, "I know you love this land and your family. Your family has been here for generations. It is a good land, rich and fruitful. We have lived well here. With your hard work, this land provided for all our needs. All our beautiful, strong, and healthy children were born here. No matter how wonderful and how fruitful this land may be, it is not worth the risk." Now she had to stop. Through clenched teeth, near tears. "It is not worth the breath of anyone of my babies," she shouted at him, forcing out the words.

Gilbert understood. He felt the same way. All day long he feared what might happen. He weighed the options of how he could keep his family safe. He could come up with no answers that convinced him with reasonable certainty that he could keep his family from harm if there is to be a war. His heart, soul, and mind, were all telling him they must go. His first and utmost priority was the safety of his family.

Nattie repeated, "We must go." She turned to Gilbert and asked, "Where would we go? Where would we and the children be safe?"

Gilbert remembered the words his father spoke to him, yesterday afternoon. He told Nattie, what he discussed earlier with his father, when they met at the corner of their field. He said, "My father suggested the other day that we should go to Canada. The recent letters he had received from George, Frank, and Louis, (Gilbert's older brothers) stated that there are plenty of farms in the Québec Province of Canada. There is need of skilled farm workers and jobs can be found."

"Will a worker's wage be enough to support nine of us?" Marilda questioned.

Gilbert said, "If land is available to us, we can raise what we need, maybe sell the rest. At least we will have food to feed our young ones. These things have been going through my mind all day long."

Seeking to be Loved

Nattie agreed, "We will make ends meet. We will provide for our children. No matter where we are," she boldly stated. "The most important thing is that they are safe. I lost one child to illness. It was fate, God's will!

I will do anything in my power to prevent my children from dying at the hand of anyone in this world. I will protect them with my very life, before I would watch any one of them die at the hands of anyone. I am afraid for them, Gilbert, and us. We must go now, as soon as we can, before it is too late."

Gilbert squeezed her hand and turned to look at her. "I will go talk with my father and start making arrangements tomorrow. We may not have the argent(money) to pay for passage," he reminded her.

"We must sell our livestock to whoever will take it," Marilda suggested to him.

"The market will not be good at this time of year," he replied. "The land we will deed back to my father. It was his and should be kept in the family." Then Gilbert said to his wife, "Nat, you and Mary start packing what we will need to take with us. After chores tomorrow, the boys will pack tools and whatever will be useful on our journey west to Paris, then to the coast. We may even take what we can along with us to Canada. I will write a letter to my brothers before I go to sleep tonight. I will mail it as soon as we can get to the village, although we may be at their front door before the letter arrives, God willing! For whatever reason, if we get held up and must wait for passage, the letter will give them an advance notice of our arrival."

They both stood. Marilda, with tears in her eyes, embraced Gilbert. She began to quiver. Gilbert struggled to hold back his own emotions as he held her tightly against him. He assured her saying, "Nat, it will be all right and maybe one day we will return to the land of our fathers."

Seeking to be Loved

She released a sorrowful moan and cried even more. They maintained their embrace. She finally stopped after a few moments and regained her poise.

His right hand moved to her waist as they turned and walked through the door. Marilda went to the bedroom. Gilbert sat by the fire and wrote a note to his brothers, letting them know his plans. He wrote that they would be arriving as soon as they could obtain passage. He thought it would be nice if the letter reached them before his arrival. Although he hoped they would be there as quickly as possible, even before the letter.

Being the eternal optimist, Gilbert knew with determination and, yes, his stubborn nature, they could be there first. He knew he would push himself and his family to their limits. Or at least as much as Marilda would allow, he chuckled to himself. He reminded himself to consider the babies and the livestock and not force them or himself as much as he would like.

He reflected for a few moments on his past and family history, his heritage. He knew his nature and character was to stand and hold his ground at all costs, as his forefathers had done for centuries. Understanding his own pride and his ancestry, he thought to himself, "If I am leaving, what must other people be doing? They must already be seeking passage or have already gone on to safe areas of France," he reasoned. This sent a warning of urgency throughout his consciousness. Who would be left to buy his stock, his property, and items they could not take with them?

If many others are leaving; to whom could they sell their belongings? He became concerned whether he would be able to procure enough funds to secure passage for his family, and the cargo. He finished the letter, addressed, and sealed it, and placed it in his pocket.

He was too restless to go to sleep. He went to the closet where they kept their savings jar. He counted the contents, which totaled 455 francs. He had no idea what it would cost for passage.

Seeking to be Loved

The next morning he would ask his father if he knew of anyone in town who would be interested in purchasing farm equipment, livestock, or household items. He started packing things in crates and placing them by the front door. It was getting late, and he needed to rest. There would be much to do tomorrow. Not wanting to disturb Nattie, he decided to sit on a chair by the fire. He was still full of exhilaration, although his body was exhausted from the labor and anxiety of the day. Many things kept running through his mind. He was not aware when he finally, closed his eyes and fell into a deep sleep.

He dreamt once again of the devastated landscape. His mind raced from one scene to the other, just as the night before. Knowing it was a dream, he knew Nattie and he made the right decision. In his dream he turned his head. The scene was different; it was a sunny day. The sun was on his face as he walked toward its light, looking west. Though not yet on a ship or near the ocean in his dream, his olfactory senses smelled the saltiness of the sea. It was a calming dream, allowing him to rest easy for the remainder of the night.

It was Nattie who woke first the next morning. She opened the bedroom door and saw Gilbert sitting in the chair sleeping peacefully. She gently touched him on the shoulder, awakening him.

Smiling at him, she whispered softly, "I see you already started preparing for our journey." She noticed the crates by the door. She suggested, "We must keep our spirits up when the children awake. Let us make this an exciting adventure for them. I fear we are in for a great struggle."

Gilbert nodded his head in agreement. He told her, "Let the children sleep as long as they can. I will start the chores. We will not tend the fields today. After breakfast I will instruct the boys to start packing things that we will take with us to Canada or may sell on the way."

After breakfast he met with his father, and told him what he and Marilda decided to do.

Seeking to be Loved

    His father expressed his pleasure with his son's decision.

    Gilbert handed his father the deed to his property, the very land he had given him as a wedding gift, fourteen years ago. He asked his father if he would like to have his livestock or any of his equipment, or if there were any items within their home he wanted. "Anything you would like to have is yours. We wish for you to have it," remarked Gilbert. Next, he asked his father if he were aware of anyone, neighbors, or people in the village, that would be interested in buying any of their items that he did not plan to take with them.

    When he returned home, he began to look about the home and his barns for things he thought he would be able to sell. He contemplated what things people might want in the towns and villages they will be traveling through.

    "I will start loading the wagon with supplies for us and the animals," he told Nattie. I will corral the animals we shall take on the journey. Our first stop will be the village to sell what we can. Hopefully, we will sell them and some other items there, or wherever we can along the way.

    All the other items here and what is remaining of the herd and flocks, my father will gather later after we are gone.

    What about your family, Nat?"

Seeking to be Loved

Chapter 6 <u>The Journey</u>

  May 5, 1914. It was going to be a busy day. When the children got out of bed, they sensed the excitement. Nat had breakfast on the table as soon as they got out of bed.
  Ernest, Mary Alice, and Henry thought it was very unusual to have breakfast before chores. Young Gilbert and Blanche were delighted. Little Joseph William, who was not quite four years old, was starting his day normally, except something was different. As he put it, "There are too many people in the house." He was not used to so many people being around that early in the morning. Even Phillip, who just turned seven months old less than a week ago, had a different look in his eye.
  When Nattie lifted him from the crib, he seemed to have a wondering look on his face. She observed his expression for a moment. She sensed that he is aware that something was different. He knew something strange was going on. A mother and child with that special inherent connection can read each other's eyes and sense each other's emotions.
  Nattie held him up to her face and said, "You are the wise little one." Then she vibrated her lips on his neck and he giggled.
  The older children asked, "Why were the crates packed? Are we going on a trip?" Ernest questioned.
  Nattie spoke from the other room, "We will discuss it all when your father comes in. Finish your breakfast." She told Mary to do the dishes and for Ernest and Henry to go help their father.
  Gilbert instructed his sons to gather all the hand tools that could be packed in the large feed box and carry the box to the wagon. Gilbert gathered the sheep from the field. He would select cattle from the field and add the cow from the barn later. He and the boys would herd them to their fenced corral. His father and brothers would have the first option to pick animals they would like to keep. What remained would be used for sustenance during their travels or would be sold along the way.

Seeking to be Loved

Many thoughts ran through Gilbert's mind, the least of which was leaving the land that he loved. He knew the dream he had was a message, telling him it was time to go. He thought again whether he would be able to get passage on a ship. He wondered how long it would take to procure a way for him and his family. He questioned whether he would be able to afford the expense of a transatlantic crossing. He had no idea what the cost would be. He knew that with so many people departing, there may be a long wait. Dwelling on that thought brought to mind another dilemma.

Where would they stay if they had to wait? Would the wait exhaust all their resources in order to sustain them. Will he be able to provide food, shelter and lodging for his family? That thought led to the next question he pondered; would they be able to find lodging?

His imagination provoked thoughts of the holy family. On the night of our Savior's birth, there was no room at the inn. Finally concluding, "It will be a good test of our faith." He really was not concerned about food. They would bring provisions, as much as they could load, enough to last several weeks if need be.

He was pleased to see the boys waiting at the wagon, although no crate was in sight. He guided the livestock to the corral beside the barn. When Gil approached with the animals the boys help funnel them into the fenced area. After closing the gate, he looked around and asked about the tools and crate. Ernest mentioned it was too heavy to lift; it is still in the shed. His father said, "It needs to be loaded first."

He placed the chickens, ducks, and geese into the makeshift wooden transport boxes. He had constructed them years ago to take fowl to market. That would hold them in place as they traveled the countryside.

The girls were also busy packing blankets, clothes, and food for the journey. Gilbert thought, "How on earth will we put all these things into the wagon?" He wondered, "How can all this be loaded on the ships? Will we be allowed to load the wagon, carts and beast

Seeking to be Loved

on board?" He realized the silly nature of his thought. The shipping industry has transported all kinds of things all over the world for centuries. He told himself to put that worry out of his mind. "We will deal with that when the time comes." He sent the boys to get the rope from the storage shed behind the barn. He instructed them to get all they could find, we will need all that we have.

Entering the house, Gilbert felt a slight ache in his heart. The sight of everything packed, cupboards open and bare, the racks and shelves empty. Nearly the whole house was stripped. The girls were busy as bees, buzzing about their business. He was proud of his children; they seem to take all things in life in stride. He stood in the doorway reminiscing for what seemed quite a long time, although it was just a moment. He realized, "This is our home." Immediately his next thought, "This was our home." They may never see it again, at least not as it is.

Many memories flashed through his mind. He cherished each and every minute they lived in this bungalow. He and his family, loved this home and each other. He glanced at Nat. Their eyes met. They both recognize a sorrowfulness; no, it was more of a mournful sadness, in each other's hearts, reflected in their eyes. They were leaving their home, a place they loved, the birthplace of their children. There was a moment of unspoken recognition of the other's emotions. They both noticed a transformation in each other's gaze as they maintained eye contact. Both saw the reassuring light of confidence, confirming the acknowledgement that the right decision was made. They reflected on how much they loved the other, as the sparkle in each other's eyes reappeared. Neither said a word to the other and each went about their business without hesitation. No time to reminisce, no time to question their decision! It was time to move on. The urgency of it all was displayed in each other's directness of their actions.

Finally, Gilbert laughed and stated, "The wagon will not hold all these things."

"It will have to," Nat said.

Seeking to be Loved

"Well, we shall start loading and packing now. It looks like we will have a good day to travel." The boys helped him load the wagon with the heaviest things first. Things they would not need along the journey constituted the first layer. Gil harnessed and hitched the horses to the wagon while the boys carried out crates and boxes from the house. Gil inspected each to see which should go next. He made sure everything was secured for the long journey. He arranged items that would be needed daily for the next three to four weeks, placing them to be easily accessible. He did not want to repeatedly untie and unload to get clothes, food, and cooking utensils as frequently as they would be needed.

The poultry would be carried on small carts drawn by their ram and dam(mother goat).

Gilbert thought how they could be traveling, with such a load for such a great distance. Their wagon had never been so full or heavy, only when bringing hay from the field was it ever been packed higher. Nat would have to take the reins, with Blanche and Joseph on the seat beside her, and little Phillip in the basket at her feet. Gil and the others would have to walk, guiding their flock and small herd.

Gil thanked the Lord that they were all in good health, while tying the load securely. For he knew the journey would be long and trying on them, and they would face many uncertainties along the way.

Marilda told Mary to take Blanche and go to the wagon, and let your father know we are almost ready. Marilda then looked around, inspecting each room, making sure nothing needed was left behind. All she saw were empty cabinets, empty bureaus, and stripped beds. It was an emptiness she could see and feel within her being. For a moment, she noticed a thickness in her throat as her eyes blurred.

Gilbert appeared by her side, "The wagon is loaded, we are ready," he whispered. He placed his arms around her, "It is time to go. God blessed us with almost fourteen good years here."

Seeking to be Loved

Nat wiped her eyes and said, "Oui, he has. Let's go!" They walked out the door of their bungalow for the last time.

Gil informed Nattie, "You will need to drive the team." He assisted her in the wagon. Then handed her Blanche and Joseph, and took the basket containing their infant son, Phillip, from Mary and handed it to Nattie.

He yelled to the boys, "Get your walking sticks and the shepherd hooks, then open the corral."

Gil instructed Nat, "As soon as the animals start coming out of the corral, start the team. The animals will naturally follow as we guide them along."

The wagon started rolling, while each in turn glanced back at their home. One more visual reminder of the land they had lived and worked. One last look at the house, the home they made for themselves, the farm their family grew and thrived on. Ernest, Mary, and Henry looked forward to this great adventure. Their younger siblings seemed indifferent. It was just as any other ride to church, town, or trip to visit relatives.

For Nat and Gil, there was a sadness, although they were resolute, knowing they were doing what they must do.

The first stop will be Gilbert's parents' farm, it was just over the ridge and down the road. Everyone's level of energy was running high and the trek went quickly. His father saw them approaching from a distance. Gilbert's parents greeted them at the gate. As always, the young ones had difficulty containing their excitement and glee. Gil had to lift them from the wagon before they jumped off. As soon as their little feet touched the ground they ran to their grandparents. Hugging and laughing, Monsieur and Madame Guyon knew this may be the last time they would see their son, daughter-in-law, and the grandchildren. Gil walked to his father, before he could speak, his father said, "You are doing the right thing. Many have already left."

Gil asked his father if he knew what the cost for passage to Canada may be. He shared his concern about whether there would

Seeking to be Loved

even be passage available, with so many people attempting to leave the country.

His father was optimistic as always. "There will be passage. How long you may have to wait is another question. We would love for you to stay and visit. We know the journey ahead for you will be long, so you must not tarry with us. What will you do with the livestock?" questioned Monsieur Guyon.

Gilbert asked his father to pick what he would like from his animals. His brother Jean and sister Mary Clara heard the commotion and came to see them. His brother Joseph and his sister-in-law had just arrived to see him off as well. He and Jean looked at each other and said to Gilbert, "Father said that you will be here soon and on your way to Canada to join George, Frank and Louis."

Gilbert laughed heartily and said, "He is wise and knows us well, does he not?"

They told Gil their sister Marie would be disappointed, she would have wanted to be here to see you off.

Gilbert had not seen his sister for several months. "Please give her my love and tell her that she and Germaine are in our prayers always. We hope to stop and see them when we get to Metz. In case we do not, please give her our best regards. We hope to see all of you in Canada when you come to visit." They all laughed. Jean said, "Canada is a long way from here, Gilbert."

"Oui, it is!" Gilbert exclaimed.

Gilbert's mother went in the house with the children, followed by Gilbert's father. While Gil was still talking with his brothers, they returned shortly carrying containers of beverages and a basket of food she had prepared to give them for their journey. His father handed Gil an envelope.

Gil asked, "What is this?" He opened it and saw it contained l'argent and papers. He looked at his father and said again, "What is this?"

"It is for the livestock."

Gil replied, "Father, I owe you everything. I cannot take this."

Seeking to be Loved

Monsieur Guyon put an arm around Gil's shoulder. They walked away from the other members of the family.

"Son, you do not know what you are going to run into the next few weeks. With so many people leaving their homes and leaving the country, the cost for everything will be greater than you think. With your large family, you may need the extra funds to procure your passage. You must take it. We will not need it," his father told him. "Also, take your herd with you and try to sell it in the marketplace in each town on the way. Farewell my son, and may God bless you all and keep you safe. Let us join the others in the house."

Everyone had gathered in the kitchen when Gilbert and his father entered. Monsieur Guyon told Gilbert, "When you reach your brothers in Canada, tell them we love them very much, and that we hope one day we can see them all again."

"It will be a great reunion," his mother stated, and they all agreed. Each family member took lengthy looks into each other's eyes. To assure each of them would implant a special place in their memory.

All offered one another heartfelt handshakes, hugs, and pats on the back. Each knew much was not being said; that of which lies in their hearts. They saw in each other's eyes and felt what was not expressed.

Gilbert spoke, "I cannot thank you enough Father, for all you have done my whole life." He reminded him and his brothers that he left some livestock for them in the field to do with as they please.

His father said, "You have made me very proud."

They patted each other firmly on the back once more before releasing their embrace. His father shouted, "Be off with you then, and bon voyage." He laughingly yelled to his grandchildren, "You help your mother, father and each other. You will have a great adventure, until you are reunited with your aunts, uncles and cousins in the great land of Canada." They all hugged, embraced, and kissed each other once again and said goodbye.

Seeking to be Loved

Gilbert asked, "Where is Philippe?"

His father spoke up, "I sent him on an errand." He then whispered to Gil, "We sent him on, to inform Marilda's parents that you may be leaving and will see them soon."

They were off again, each in turn looking back and waving goodbye, until they were out of sight.

It was nearly noon as they approached their little bustling village. It seemed there were many people loading wagons, moving belongings, trading, and sending each other off.

Gilbert stopped at a butcher shop and asked the proprietor if he was interested in buying any of the stock.

The butcher laughed and said, "I am overstocked already. Many people have been selling their animals. I have no more room and no market for it to be sold, because so many are leaving our town and countryside."

He asked if he knew of someone that would be interested. He shook his head no. Not wanting to delay, they moved on.

"I hope to make it to the next village before nightfall," he told Marilda.

William Gilbert Sr., after speaking with Gilbert in the field the day before, had told his son Philippe that he wished for him to visit Marilda's parents. He wanted Philippe to inform Monsieur and Madame Berube, he suspects their daughter and her family would be leaving the country, and going to Canada. Therefore, they may want to visit or meet them on the way. He also told Philippe to plan on meeting them in the town of Thionville, and wait for them there. That is of course if Madame and Monsieur Berube wish to meet with them to bid them a farewell on their journey.

Philippe wasted no time. He saddled one of the horses and made his way to the Berube's home. His route took him 4km to Cattenom, another 8km to Thionville and 2km to the Berube's residence. It would be a good journey if all went well. They would surely appreciate an opportunity to wish their daughter and grandchildren farewell. Philippe arrived early in the evening. He informed Marilda's parents as his father had instructed. He suggested they meet Gil, Nat, and grandchildren in the town of Thionville, the following afternoon.

M. and Mme. Berube were not surprised. In fact, they were relieved that their only daughter and seven grandchildren would be in a safer place. They invited Philippe to spend the night and see Gilbert and Marilda's family off the next day. He agreed and thanked them. At the dinner table that evening, the Berubes made plans with Philippe to leave early in the morning and secure lodging for themselves and Marilda's family. Tonight, Madame Berube would prepare a feast sure to gladden their hearts and strengthen her daughters family. She knew they would be tired and famished from the haste of packing and the urgency of their departure.

Philippe informed them that finding lodging may be difficult. He explained that he saw many people loading wagons and preparing to leave. The roads were very congested.

Monsieur Berube said, "We will hope for the best." It was left at that, and they bid each other bonne nuit(good night).

The Berubes woke early to prepare food items and packed provisions for several days. Madame Berube had spent most of the night baking. She wanted to present a meal her daughter and her family would remember. She with the help of M. Berube and Philippe prepared all the children's favorite treats the night before.

In the morning, they packed that evenings meal, plus a hearty breakfast for the following day. Madame packed the children's special treats separately from the other provisions. For a moment, Madame Berube thought, what if they decide not to leave France? "What if they do not arrive as expected?" She asked her husband, "What will we do with all this food?"

He looked at Philippe, turned back to his wife, and said, "We will go visit them and have a great feast." The two men smiled and laughed. Madame was not so pleased, however, she was satisfied with his response.

53

Seeking to be Loved

Philippe mentioned to her, "We are confident they are leaving. That is why my father sent me. He is usually right about this sort of thing."

She said, "Well that is good enough for me! We must pack extra provisions for their grandchildren."

Philippe saddled his horse and helped Monsieur Berube prepare the wagon and harness his team. After they ate breakfast, they loaded the wagon with the food and quilted blankets she had planned to give them as gifts next Christmas. It was 8AM when they set off for the town of Thionville, where they would more than likely see their daughter and grandchildren for the last time. They were there by 9AM. Already the town was buzzing and the roads were busy. People were loading their carts and wagons with more than what they were designed to carry. In many cases, people were unloading to reconfigure the cargo an attempt to fit more onto a wagon already over laden.

Livestock were roaming about everywhere. They hope to procure lodging early before all the inns and boarding house rooms were taken. The plan was a good one, for they found there were as many people checking in as were checking out. The proprietor of the second inn where they inquired referred them to a boarding house to the west on the outskirts of town. Philippe told the Berubes, he would go to the east side of town and wait for his brother and his family. "I will return at sundown with or without them. I am sure they will be here before then, if they have no trouble on the way."

Going was slow for the young Guyon family. Marilda could not nurse and keep the team moving. The jolting of the wagon made Phillip restless, not to mention his hunger not being satisfied. Marilda decided to walk with Phillip, carrying him in the infant sling. She made the sling to carry him when she was doing chores around the house. This was much gentler and did not jolt him about. The steady pace and gentle sway of his mother's steps calmed him. He could also nurse comfortably when he needed to. Walking the last few kilometers before they stopped to rest the animals and let them

Seeking to be Loved

graze alongside the road helped ease Marilda's mind, and tension in her body.

Philippe had been waiting hours for his brother and his family. He found a large tree and rested under it, enjoying the shade it offered. He watched his horse graze beside him. He dozed on this pleasant, warm spring day.

It was late afternoon when he began to wonder what was taking his brother so long. Maybe his father was not correct, or they may have been delayed. Maybe Gilbert decided to stay, or not to leave yet. He dozed off again and when he awoke, he noticed in the distance a heavily laden wagon. He could barely count the number of people walking along with it. He thought that had to be his brother Gilbert and family.

He stood to get a better view and his eyes focused. He realized it was Gilbert and his family. He mounted his steed and sped off to greet his brother. Upon reaching them, he jumped from his mount and wrapped his arm around his brother's shoulder and reached Marilda's hand in his other. He explained that father had sent him ahead to tell the Berubes to expect your family today.

Marilda's parents are waiting for you on the outskirts of Thionville. Gilbert looked up at Nattie sitting on the buckboard, "Did you hear that?" She was thrilled that she would have a chance to say goodbye to her parents. From the moment they had left, she thought of them. She was experiencing deep regret, acknowledging that she may never see them again. She wished she had written a note and had someone pass it on to them. To express how much she loves them and would miss them so. She wanted to thank them for the life they have given her, and assure them she would never let their grandchildren forget them. Her weariness changed to joy and glee. Marilda could not contain herself. She hugged her children and told them that they would be seeing their grandparents. The older ones shouted, "Hourra!"(Hurray)

Seeking to be Loved

They only saw the Berube grandparents on special occasions. It always meant delicious food and treats, along with wonderful things grandma had made for them to enjoy and wear.

As they made their way through the town of Thionville, they were surprised to see the number of vacant buildings. Many businesses and homes were empty, with doors and windows left open. There were no signs of life in several dwellings. Numerous people were rushing about. In front of nearly every other building were wagons heavily loaded. They saw automobiles, which seemed even stranger to them still.

Monsieur and Madame Berube waited on the porch of the Boarding House, hoping any minute to see their daughter and beloved grandchildren. They watched travelers all day long, families carrying belongings to and fro. So many going to who knows where, to find a safer place to dwell. Monsieur Berube met people throughout the day, gathering news of upcoming events, what was taking place and the local gossip. The prospect of war still seemed a long way off. Nothing was certain, although the atmosphere was thick with fear and anxiety. There was a sense something terrible and tragic was about to happen.

Finally after hours of waiting they can see their daughter and grandchildren approaching. The Berubes left the porch to greet them while they were still nearly a half kilometer away. Upon reaching them, Marilda climbed from the seat of the wagon. Madame Berube was about to give her daughter a big hug when her daughter held out her grandson to her. She exclaimed, "Little Phillip." She had only seen him twice, shortly after birth, including last Christmas. She let out a big sigh, "Ahhhh," and stated how handsome the little fellow had gotten in six months. There was laughter mixed with tears of joy as her father hugged his daughter and shook hands with Gilbert. Monsieur Berube in turn, hugged all the grandchildren, admiring them and telling them how much they have grown.

Little Gilbert and Blanche asked in a questioning manner, "Grandpa, us too?"

Seeking to be Loved

Their grandfather laughed and said, "Most of all, you two have grown so much." He picked them both up and squeezed them with a great, loving hug. Monsieur Berube had made all the arrangements at the inn for the entire family. He even arranged for an assigned area where they were to keep the animals for the night. He told Gilbert, "I will show you where to put your livestock. I have received permission, so they can be kept close for the night."

Gilbert and the younger ones, who helped with the animals, followed him. They walked around the building. Behind it was a pasture and stream with good water for the livestock.

Gil asked M. Berube if he knew of anyone that would be interested in purchasing any of the animals, or if he himself wanted any of them.

Marilda's father looked down at the ground and shook his head no. Mentioning, "I have been observing people all day long buying, selling, and getting rid of as many things as they can. Everyone leaving is attempting to lighten their load. People are bargaining to procure needed funds for the train or ship to safer areas. It seems like nearly half the population in our area is heading away from the east border.

They are moving away from what may be a battlefront.

Gilbert asked, "Can you use any of them?"

His reply was, "I will think on it." He told Gil, "We already have all we need, although I may be able to convince Madame Berube to relieve you of a few geese or ducks."

Gilbert said he would have Ernest select one for dinner that evening.

His father-in-law held up his hand and said, "That has already been taken care of. Your mother-in-law has prepared a feast."

Gilbert laughed. "We all knew she would, if she had a chance." He added, "We are looking forward to it." They chuckled as they turned to walk back to the inn.

Marilda was so pleased the meeting had been arranged for her parents to say goodbye. She knew leaving now was the right decision. She thanked God for putting the pieces into place, especially for her family to visit with her parents one last time and tell them "Au revoir."

    May 6, 1914 - Madame Berube woke early to lay out another feast with Marilda's, the grandchildren, and Gilberts favorite breakfast items on the patio table to greet them.
    "It is like Christmas," Ernest declared.
    They thanked Marilda's parents and said grace. Then gorged themselves on all the wonderful foods that their grandparents prepared.
    M.(Mr.) and Mme.(Mrs.) Berube suggested for them to eat hardy and fill themselves for the journey ahead. "You will have a long day on the road and will have many more before you reach your destination." They really did not need the encouragement; their grandmother was a wonderful cook.
    Gilbert and his brother Philippe, along with the older boys, harnessed the horses and gathered the animals. He had sold the cattle to the keeper of the boarding house. He kept his best dairy cow to supply them with milk and byproducts for daily consumption to assist with sustaining the family on the journey.
    Marilda shared her and Gil's dreams with her parents. They agreed leaving for Canada was a wise decision. She cried as she told them how she will surely miss them so much. She repeatedly thanked them for everything they had done for her throughout her life. She expressed to them God could not have given her better parents.
    Her mother and father told her she was the blessing God had given them. To have a daughter as kind, loving and determined as she, was the greatest gift their Lord could have bestowed on them.
    M. Berube added to Mme. Berube's comment, "Headstrong and stubborn as well." They laughed through their tears. Then he finished the sentence, with Mme. Berube in chorus, "You have made us very happy and proud."

Seeking to be Loved

Gilbert entered announcing, "We have everything ready, except for you and the little ones."

Mme. Berube gestured to Marilda, "You get your things and the babies. Your father and I will gather and pack what is left here. It is for you to take on your journey."

M. Berube looked at Gilbert. He made a slight shift of his head to the left to suggest he come to the side, to speak privately. He told Gilbert about his conversation with several of his friends and merchants in town while waiting for them yesterday. He learned that many of the villagers were departing, as well as many living in the country. Many were abandoning homes and property, seeking safety in Paris and areas west and south. Many as well are leaving the country.

"I have seen this before, Gilbert. People act very strangely under these circumstances. They may do anything when they are afraid. It is as if they become godless people, seeking only to get what they can for themselves. Please, be vigilant. Keep alert at all times. Be wary of any and all who approach you. Always be hopeful for the best, however, always expect the absolute worst. Take nothing for granted. Be prepared to protect yourself, your family and belongings at all costs." He asked Gil, "How much argent do you have for your journey and passage?"

Gilbert told him we have 455 francs, plus what his father had given him, which may be a few hundred francs. "I have not counted it. Plus 55 francs for the three la vaches(cows) I just sold."

His father-in-law mentioned, "That may not be enough for your voyage, with all nine of you. Monsieur Goesson, who manages the bank, told me there are not enough cruise ships to handle the numbers of people that are seeking passage to the Americas and Canada."

He told Gil not to wait, because each day waiting placed him and his family in greater danger. Not from foreigners or the enemy, but from thieves and robbers that he would likely encounter. He explained desperate people can panic and become ruthless.

Seeking to be Loved

Gilbert could not imagine his countrymen and fellow citizens acting in such a way. It was beyond his reasoning. He had too much faith in his fellow countrymen to comprehend such actions. He thanked his father-in-law for the advice and promised he would be diligent in protecting his family. Gilbert could not imagine what his father-in-law said to be true of what they may encounter.

Monsieur Berube handed him an envelope and said, "Do not bother to open it now. It is just something I want you to give Nattie that will come in handy on your journey. Your mother-in-law reminded me to make sure she had it before starting off this morning."

"I will see that she gets it," Gil replied.

"We are ready," Nattie announced, carrying Phillip with one arm, and holding Joseph's hand with her other.

Mme. Berube said, "We have your lunch and dinner packed right here." They walked outside to the loaded wagon and carts.

Marilda decided to drive the team that morning, at least for the first few hours. She thought keeping Phillip in her sling and close at her breast would be more comfortable for him instead of bouncing and jolting on the floor the wagon. The sling would serve her better than carrying him like she attempted yesterday when she walked. She knew he would rest well after having nursed and tasting his grandmother's delicious porridge for the first time. Tasting foods was new to him at this delicate age. Marilda had thought, "This is a good time to supplement his diet with a little more than mother's milk."

They all hugged and kissed each other and the men shook hands. All bade each other farewell.

Gilbert helped Nattie up onto the buckboard of the wagon, then handed her the envelope her father had given him. He said, "This is from your parents."

Her father approached her and said, " No need to open it, at least not yet." He told her, "Just keep it in a safe place where it will not get lost. We thought you may need it for passage. I fear the cost

Seeking to be Loved

of the voyage may be more than usual due to the demand. If not, then you can use it to help yourselves get settled in Canada. I love you my dear."

"God bless you and save you and keep you safe from all evil, until we all meet again." It was a phrase Marilda heard her father say many times when they were parting from loved ones.

Gilbert gave Philippe a great hug. During the embrace he thanked him and said that he would miss him and all his family. He asked Philippe to give all his brothers, sisters, parents, nieces, and nephews his best and to tell them, that he loved them. Also, thank mother and father once again on our behalf, for all that they have done for all of us." Gil told him to be safe and his prayers would be with them all.

Philippe said, "And our prayers would be with you, my brother, and yours."

There was an awkward pause, no one wanted to leave. Gilbert finally said, "We must be off now." The Berubes and Philippe stood, waving goodbye until they could no longer see them.

Blanche and her little brother Joseph rode in the wagon with their mother and little Phillip. It was not long until they were out of sight of their grandparents and uncle. Young Blanche noticed her mother and gestured to Joseph, look at Ma mee.

Joseph was first to ask, "Why are you crying?"

Then Blanche, "Why are you crying Mother?"

Marilda was unsuccessful hiding her emotions and her quiet sobs. She took a deep breath and simply said, "I will miss your Grandmama and Grandpapa very much."

Blanche asked, "Will we see them again, Ma mee?"

Marilda just replied, "I certainly hope so my dears."

Blanche responded immediately saying, "That would be very sad not to see Grandmamma and Grandpapa anymore." Then she added, "Who would make the Mille-feuille, croissants and cream filled choux religieuse on special holidays?"

Seeking to be Loved

Marilda laughed, wiping her cheeks, and said, "I guess I will have to learn how to do it as Grandmamma does."

Blanche asked, "Will they be like Grandmama's!"

Marilda replied, "I could never prepare them as good as Grandmama."

They moved on in silence. With every crossroad they saw more people. Many families were on the move with their belongings. They all wondered where they could be coming from and where their final destination would be. Other than an occasional cart driver or person or two on foot, there was almost no traffic heading east. It was beginning to appear that a caravan was heading west and southwest to Paris.

Gil shared with Nattie that he had hoped to travel as far as Metz. It was approximately 35km from where they started from that morning. Progress was slow, although with less herd to contend with, it was easier to make steady progress. All was moving along well. Not much was said to each other throughout the day. It was as if all were in their own world of thought as they walked on. They all settled into a rhythmic pace with the other travelers. It was the steady, mundane, repetitive pace that gave each an opportunity to get lost in their own train of thought.

Gil thought about what may lie ahead. He reviewed the warnings of his father and father-n-law. He thought of the dangers and every possibility that could occur along the way.

Nat was comforted knowing Phillip was resting in the sling. He looked content despite the noise and active commotion of travelers. The sounds had to be so unusual to her infant's ears. Maybe it was the sound of her heartbeat that kept him calm. Every time she looked down at him, she had to smile. It made her feel at ease. At that moment, such a satisfying peace came over her. Seeing her infant son in such a comfortable state helped override her anxiety regarding the drastic undertaking which they were now involved. She wondered how difficult this could be on one so young. As soon as she looked up to check the road ahead, the apprehension

Seeking to be Loved

and uncertainty would flood back into her mind. She often gazed at the other two beside her. They alternated their position occasionally, from the seat to the floor at her feet in the wagon.

She wondered, "What must they be thinking about all this? Such an instant and complete upheaval of their young lives." They seemed so unaffected, she thought to herself. "How can this be? Just yesterday their little lives were so, so what?" she thought. "Common" was the word she came up with. "Yes, common."

They were comfortable in their home, the only home they had ever known. The days were the same to them, except Sunday, when they would attend church. Of course, holidays and the school days for the older ones must have seemed different to them. Maybe not, because that did not change their routine for the younger ones, only the older children.

What must they be thinking? They seemed to take the sway and bumps of the wagon, as well as the unusualness of the travel, in stride. They acted as if this was all so natural. Maybe it is the peace of God that these little ones' souls already possess. They are content to just be and accept what comes their way!

"Oh, Dear God, Merci so much for the fact they are insouciant (carefree). Merci so much for the peace you give me each time I glance at Phillip. Please let this peace guide and comfort me and all my children, along with Gil, on this journey."

She took a deep breath and let out a loud sigh of relief. She did not realize how loud it was, until Blanche and Joseph both looked up at her and started to giggle at the sound their mother had made. Nat laughed with the children.

Phillip opened his eyes as Nat glanced down to see what his reaction was going to be to this new commotion. Their eyes met, and his opened wide and the broadest smile came across his face. The joy in his mother's heart rose. She sighed again and exclaimed, "It is a beautiful day, my Phillip." She turned to the other two beside her and asked, "Is it not, my little ones?"

Seeking to be Loved

They shouted aloud with such glee, "Oui Ma mee." It was heard by all around them.

One passerby made the comment, "Now, there be a bonne couvée(happy brood)."

Ernest was excited about everything. He was absorbed by the new surroundings of the countryside. There were farms and homes, some great, some small, and he was fascinated by the new and old architecture. Every town, village and homestead was so interesting to him. It was a great adventure, with so many wonders to see.

Mary Alice was also thrilled about their journey. She was not as curious and as interested in every detail of the landscape, homes, and scenery. She seemed more concerned with what her mother was doing. She thought she should be in the wagon with the younger children, hovering over them and keeping them in line. She did not mind walking and occasionally keeping the lambs and goats, especially the kids, on the road and close to their mother. They were not yet two months old and so cute. The baby goats seemed to wear a perpetual smile adding, to their cuteness. She found it amusing when she would touch them with her staff to keep them close to their mother. They would perform a startled jump, let out a bleat and bump into the dam pulling the carte. It was comical and she had to giggle each time.

She took special delight when they were crossing paths with other young girls and boys her age. Her exceptional delight would change to contempt when noticing that mindless young boys passing by made rude noises at her.

She found it even more annoying when she stepped in something soft, warm, and fresh from one of the animals.

She enjoyed seeing the many magnificent château's. She wondered what luxuries might be within their walls. Her mind filled with thoughts of what life would be without all the chores young girls like her must perform. She imagined the girls living in those château's did not have to perform daily duties. Each time she would always come to the same conclusion, which was, "I think I would

Seeking to be Loved

much rather be living where I do. I like having an uncomplicated, dutiful life." That did not keep her from thinking, "I bet it would be nice to not have chores to do." She was always dreaming and imagining as young girls do.

"Oui, I like my life!" She had observed that her mother always seemed satisfied and happy with each day's toil. Her thoughts always returned to the comfort and security she felt within her own home with her family. Walking along, thoughts of sadness crept into her mind. She found herself wondering if she would ever go back home. Would she ever have a home similar to what she knew when she grew up?

It was the unknown that excited her and at the same time made her anxious. She had not yet considered what this new life might be like, especially in a new country, a foreign land.

What will the people be like?

Will the boys be like boys here, teasing the girls and being rough?

Would they be more genteel, or would they be barbarians, like her brothers? "Sacrebleu, I hope not!" She quickly glanced around, hoping she had not thought that out loud.

"Will they speak French?" she wondered.

"What language do they speak in Canada?" she asked her father, as she rushed up beside him.

Her father said, "Many will speak French. It may not be the French that we are used to hearing. They will speak French and English, since both nations have claimed territories in Canada for many years since its independence."

She asked, "Will we be able to understand them, and will they be able to understand us?"

Gilbert laughed, as did Ernest. He told her, "Your uncles made no mention of any difficulty understanding the language or getting along otherwise." His next statement was, "There is a common language throughout the world that many people acknowledge." Then he thought, here is an opportunity. He spoke loud enough for

Seeking to be Loved

the other children to hear. They perked up their ears; they know what is coming.

He began by stating, "The language that all people will understand is the one of kindness and consideration of one's fellow man. A language of honesty, sincerity, diligence and a willingness to help and benefit one another."

Mary Alice stated, "Well, it will be just like here in our area and village."

Her father replied, "People are people everywhere. The country will be similar. You can rest assured things will be different. As long as you are willing to do what is necessary to make your way and are considerate of others, you will get along just fine. Plus, you will have your aunts, uncles, and cousins. Some that you have never seen, so we will not be all alone."

Henry, overhearing some of the conversation asked, "How many of my cousins went to Canada? I can barely remember my aunts and uncles George, Louis, and Frank. Will I have cousins my age? Boys that I can play with."

"There will be at least five that I know of," Ernest told him.

Henry said, "Five," with a big smile on his face.

His father replied, "Oui, five, that are just about your age, within a year or two."

"Do you know the names, Father?"

"Well, your Uncle George has a son George Junior. Uncle Frank has two sons Gilbert and Richard."

Henry mentioned, "That is your name Father!"

Gilbert replied, "Oui."

Little Gilbert shouted, "It is mine, too."

"Is he named after you or grandfather?" asked Henry.

"His first name is Gilbert, it is my middle name. So, I guess you can say we just share the name," explained Gil.

"He could be named after me," suggested little Gil.

"Your Uncle Louis has two sons also, Armand and Louis, named after your uncle and one of your great uncles."

Seeking to be Loved

Mary Alice asked, "I know of three girl cousins my age, right, Da Dee?"

"Oui," he said. "Do you remember their names?"

"Oui, my cousin Doris, who is Uncle George and Aunt Cynthia's girl. Uncle Louis and Aunt Rachel have my cousins Delia and Yvonne. I cannot think of any daughters of Uncle Frank's."

"That is because they did not have any when they left for Canada. Who knows? They may have children now. We will find out when we get there."

Mary Alice was excited about the prospect of seeing her cousins and possibly meeting some new ones. "I love being around babies, even my little brothers and sisters." Then she added, "Sometimes." She started to skip, looked up at her father and said, "I cannot wait to get to Canada."

Gil laughed and said, "We have a very long way to go before we get there."

Henry asked, "How long will it take us to get there, Father?"

Gil patted Henry on the head and just repeated, "We have a long way to go." He then mentioned to all, "We will travel nearly 8000km."

They all repeated, "We have a long way to go."

Their father then mentioned, "If we are lucky, we will enter Paris in ten to twelve days, if all goes well. Then another six to eight days to get through Paris and arrive at Rouen, the city of bells which is near the coast of the channel.

"What is the channel father?" little Gilbert asked.

"It is the body of water, the ocean separating the west coast of France and the east coast of England. There we hope to get passage on a ship, going to the Americas and to Canada."

"Will it be a big ship, Father?"

"I expect so, Gilbert."

"How big are the ships?" asked Henry. "Have you ever been on a big ship?"

Seeking to be Loved

Gil told him, "Non, I have not. I suspect them to be very large if they are to make it across the great Atlantic Ocean."

"How big?" little Gilbert asked.

"All I can say is I suspect it will be as big as some of our barley fields at home."

"Wow, how can a big ship like that stay afloat?"

Gilbert laughed at the question and said, "It is all in their design. They are made to be on the ocean, as vast as it is."

"What will it be like being on the ocean, Father?" asked Henry.

"I have never been on a ship. I can only imagine it would be like floating on one of the ponds in our pram, except it will be like being on a floating village," explained Gil.

Henry's eyes widened as he tried to imagine that in his mind. A moment later he said, "That would be very strange."

Mary Alice agreed. "I cannot even imagine walking about on a floating village."

Henry laughed and wobbled as he walked along, pretending that he was walking on their little fishing boat from one end to the other. They laughed at his antics.

Gil told him, "You better not fall in. You will be left floating in a large ocean all by yourself. A big fish might swallow you up, just like Jonah."

Henry looked up at his father and said, "Maybe that big whale will swallow me up and take me to Canada, to spit me out." They chuckled again.

Then Mary Alice joined in and said, "It may just swallow you up and spit you out its other end."

Gil and Ernest laughed at her comment.

Henry was silent as he tried to figure it out, not quite getting the joke.

Marilda shouted back to them, "You all seem to be having quite a time back there." She had to turn herself around to see her entourage of family making their way along the road.

Seeking to be Loved

Gil shouted back, "We are discussing our journey across the great ocean."

She told him, "I think we will need to stop soon to take a break."

Gil agreed. "I have been thinking of all the food your mother has prepared for us all morning long. I think it is time to eat some of it," he shouted back.

The morning had passed quickly walking along the roadway. Nattie said to the young ones in the wagon, "We seem to have covered a lot of ground." She asked Gil if he had any idea how far they had traveled.

Gil said, "I will ask the next person we pass where we are. That will give me an idea how much further to Metz." He confirmed her initial statement. "I agree we have been making good progress. The morning has flown by. It will do us all well to get off our feet and find some shade and replenish ourselves. I have not heard much from those three little ones for a while." Gil asked, "Are they faring well?"

Nattie said, "Phillip has been quiet as a mouse, smiling and enjoying the sway of the wagon in his little sling. I need to change him. He must be hungry, plus he and the other two need to move about. A sign just ahead has the name of the little villages of Vremy 1.5km and Sainte Barbe 4km, printed on it."

Gilbert looked at the sun. It was very high in the sky. He stated to Nattie, "It must be just past noon. If we are where I think we are, we are making very good time and we are beyond the halfway mark to Metz. We will continue to Vremy and rest there. We will water the animals, let them graze and have something to eat ourselves."

Nattie acknowledged, "Oui, the children in the wagon need to stretch their legs and Phillip needs to be cleaned and fed."

"We all need a break to get off our feet," concurred Gil.

Ernest said, "I sure am getting hungry."

Seeking to be Loved

Mary agreed, "Moi aussi(me too)," and all the children, one by one, repeated "Moi aussi," "Moi aussi," "Moi aussi." Even little Phillip sounded off with a big "goo," loud enough for all to hear, to their surprise.

Approaching the town of Vremy, Gil asked the first person he came to where they could water their animals and let them graze.

The gentleman looked at them and observed their hoard, with a peculiar expression on his face. He asked where they were headed.

Gilbert said, "We are going to Metz."

The gentleman produced a questioning look in his eye. Gil knew what he was thinking before he could ask the question. Gil told him their destination was Canada. "We were concerned about the news of Germany and possible invasion," he told him.

The man's expression changed to that of acknowledgment and said, "Oui," in agreement. Then he proceeded to say, "You may have made a wise decision." He extended his hand and introduced himself, "I am Pierre Dubois."

Gilbert shook his hand. "I am Gilbert Guyon."

Monsieur Dubois exclaimed, "Ah, a farmer."

Gil responded, "Oui," and introduced his wife Marilda and his family.

Monsieur Dubois smiled and said to Gilbert, "We would be pleased to have you as our guests. We have a small patch of land where your animals may graze, alongside a small spring feeding a stream. There your animals can drink, and your family can rest. It is only a few hundred meters off the main road. Just take your next right. You will see a small stone bungalow with two goats tied out front. My wife's name is Charlotte. You can tell her that you met me, and I agreed to let you rest and water your animals. I will be along shortly."

Gilbert thanked him for his willingness to accommodate their request. The bungalow was easy to find. It was just as he had said, with goats out front. The little procession consisting of their wagon,

Seeking to be Loved

two carts and a small cluster of animals stopped in front of the house. Gilbert asked Ernest to unhitch the team from the wagon, as well as the goats from the carts. He approached Marilda to help her off the wagon. She turned to disembark, extending one hand, using the other to support Phillip in the sling across her chest. He said to her, "I will go introduce us to Madame Dubois."

As he approached the bungalow, Mme. Dubois opened the front door to greet them, asking if she could help him.

Gilbert introduced himself and asked if she was Madame Charlotte Dubois. She confirmed, "Oui, monsieur." He explained, "I just met your husband Pierre. He has graciously agreed to allow us to water our animals and let them graze, while my family and I rest and eat our meal."

She looked beyond Gilbert, noticing Marilda with babe in arms, and Mary helping the other little ones off the wagon. A big smile appeared on her face as she looked at Gilbert and said, "You have quite a load with you."

"Oui, madame," replied Gilbert.

In the background Ernest was holding the team, along with Henry and Little Gilbert carrying the crates of geese, ducks, and chickens. They stood ready to herd the goats and sheep. Gil asked Charlotte, "Where shall we take them, Madame?"

"I will show you; follow me." She turned around to guide them to the field behind their home. As they walked, she turned her attention back to Gilbert and said, "You help your wife and the young children, then come around to the back of the house." She waved to the others, "Follow me boys." She hurried to lead them to the field behind their home.

Marilda, Mary and the three little ones followed. Nattie reminded Gil as she walked past him, "Mother prepared us a basket. It is just under the seat in the wagon. Bring it along!"

Madame Dubois pointed to the small stream and told the boys, "The animals may graze on this side of the stream. As you can see, the grass is very lush and high. It is too much for our goats to

Seeking to be Loved

keep down this early in the year. God sent you just in time to shorten the grass and keep the pests and varmints from making their burrows and nests so close to our bungalow."

The boys graciously thanked Madame.

She turned and walked to Marilda and locked her arm around her elbow. She whispered to her, "You come with me." She walked Marilda into her home and asked where she was from.

Marilda answered, "We had spent the night with her parents in Thionville." She explained why they were leaving and where they were going. Marilda noticed how cool it was inside the home despite the lack of trees sheltering it. It felt good to be out of the sun.

Mme. Dubois gestured for Marilda to have a seat on a comfortable, padded armchair in the corner of her kitchen. "Let me help you with that sling and get a good look at this baby. You must be tired." She then asked, what time they had started that morning. "You must have left very early to come this far so quickly."

Marilda told Madame, "That chair looks inviting and very, very comfortable, however I think I would like to stand for now." She removed Phillip from the sling and handed him to her. Charlotte reached her arms to receive the infant.

She said, "It has been a long time since I held a baby."

Marilda asked, "Where would be a good place to change him and freshen him up?"

"Here, you take him. Let me clear the table," said Charlotte. She laid a large cloth over the table and Marilda proceeded to change Phillip. Charlotte said to her, "Let me prepare something for you to eat."

Marilda stopped her. "Non, non, Madame. My mother prepared us a basket, which I am sure they have already spread and are about to say grace over and devour. Will you please join us? It is the least we can do for your willingness to allow us to rest here."

Mary entered the doorway and knocked gently on the opened door. "Mother, lunch is spread and ready. We are about to say grace." Mary's eyes had not quite adjusted to the dim light inside

Seeking to be Loved

the house. She strained to see them. She recognized her mother and looked at the other figure standing next to her and asked in such a beckoning manner, "Will you join us Madame?"

The sincerity in Mary's voice was so inviting that Charlotte could do nothing but graciously accept. Although she knew a family this large would need much while they journey on the road ahead. "I have some cool goat's milk and fresh bread and cheese that I will supply." Before Mary and Marilda could say a word to refuse her offer. Charlotte stated, "And there will be no argument about it."

Marilda looked at Mary. "We cannot argue with our host." They both thanked her. Mary turned to exit. "We will be along shortly," her mother said.

Charlotte mentioned, "Come here, my dear, and take these cups." She asked Marilda, "How many do we need?"

Mary responded, "We will need eight, Madame, plus one for you and monsieur."

They enjoyed a pleasant lunch under the shade of a large yew tree. The young boys had a difficult time staying away from the creek. Like all children, they seemed to have boundless energy. Gilbert constantly warned them to stay off their feet and rest. They still had a long journey ahead, before stopping for the day.

Charlotte was very curious about the young family and had many questions. Her children had long since grown and moved away. She explained that she had only seen her grandchildren once. She enjoyed watching the Guyon children play. It was pleasant listening to their young voices, screams, yells, and the laughter as they frolicked. It seemed they had just finished their meal, although more than an hour passed.

Gilbert directed the boys, "Gather up the animals now and let us hitch the horses."

Marilda took the cue and instructed Mary to gather up the cups, pitchers, and utensils to return to Madame Dubois. She proceeded to pick up the blanket and repacked the basket with the leftover food.

Seeking to be Loved

Charlotte took the cheese which she had wrapped and handed it to Marilda. Before Marilda could say no thank you, Charlotte spoke. "You take this. We have plenty, and you may need some nourishment before you get to Metz."

Monsieur Dubois had turned and stood beside madame, after he had helped Gilbert hitch the horses. "There seem to be many on the move." He shared the news he had heard from his neighbors. There were many unsettling rumors they have heard from friends who had spoken with travelers from the east. Especially those from along the German border areas, they identified, it is there where tension is growing. "You may have left just in time."

Gilbert assisted Marilda into the wagon, then lifted the little ones up to sit beside her. She positioned the sling around her shoulder and neck.

Charlotte handed Phillip to Gilbert with a warm grateful smile on her face. She said to them, "I thoroughly enjoyed you and your family stopping here." She stepped back and M. Dubois placed his arm around her shoulder. They both wished them well on their journey and Godspeed to their destination.

Gilbert asked if he owed them anything, they just waived their hand and shook their heads.

 "Non, it was our pleasure to give you a brief respite."

Gilbert handed Nattie the baby and turned to shake both their hands. He thanked them again and gave them a blessing. "May God bless you and keep you safe."

Monsieur Dubois returned the blessing, "May he bless you all on your journey as well."

As they were Leaving M. and Mme. Dubois, Gil and Nat thanked them again for their hospitality.

Refreshed from the meal, being off their feet and resting in the shade, they were eager and energized for the rest of the day's journey. With any luck they would be in Metz before nightfall. They maneuvered back onto the main road. There were a few more wagons with families and travelers all heading west. The sun was

Seeking to be Loved

high and warm. Marilda took the sling off and laid Phillip beside his brother and sister on a padded blanket on the floor. She believed they both would be more comfortable during the heat of the day. He was starting to cling to her body before they had stopped. They both would be cooler, and hopefully more comfortable, with him at her feet.

At every crossroad they were joined by more travelers from the north and east byways, making their way westbound. Gilbert suggested that Ernest, Mary, Henry, and young Gilbert stay close. He instructed them to maintain the pace behind the wagon, and keep the animals moving forward in a tightknit formation. Soon it would become a great and continuous caravan on this road heading to Metz. "I can hardly imagine what it will be like when we get closer to Paris," he thought to himself.

They plodded on throughout the afternoon, moving steadily as more people joined the procession. Very little was said to the other families, except when they crossed paths, or others attempted to merge into the line of travelers. Glancing at others waiting on the crossroads or occasionally looking behind, one would wave to them acknowledging and indicating everything was all right.

The hours passed and the sun had risen to a point just ahead of them in the sky. Its light shone in their eyes continuously, now that the day was waning, and their path led them right into its glare. Marilda put a linen sheet over the seat for a canopy to shade the children. She had already noticed that Gilbert distributed hats for the young ones to keep the sun out of their eyes.

At the next crossroads there was a sign, 4.5km to Metz. Gil was pleased and relieved that they were making such good progress. Despite the increasing numbers of travelers along the way, it had not slowed their pace. They should reach Metz within the next two hours. He estimated the arrival time between 4:30 and 5PM. "It is good that the days are getting longer," he thought to himself. Maybe that would give them time to find his sister Marie's home before it got dark. He hoped that it would not be difficult, for he had never

Seeking to be Loved

been to such a big city. He was not wanting to show up too late, without warning or announcement at her doorstep.

Marie had often mentioned to all at family gatherings to come visit and bring their family. She always invited brothers and sisters to stay with her and see what life was like in the big city. The thought always seemed to be quite strange to Gilbert and the rest of the family, as to why Marie enjoyed the urban life. However it was always exciting to hear her tell stories of life in a large town. She and her husband Germaine had quite a different existence away from the family farm.

Living in the city was foreign to Gilbert and his family. He preferred life on the farm and the small village where they made their living. They knew no other way of life would offer them the same comfort and satisfaction.

A new excitement seemed to be growing within the children as the sun got closer to the horizon. They were just short of a 1/2km away when they could feel the busyness in the atmosphere. Approaching the city of Metz, they noticed smokestacks in the distance. There were strange noises, the sounds of factories. The young children wondered what could possibly be creating the smell. The odor was unfamiliar to anything they ever experienced in the country or on the farm. It was the unpleasant smell of soot and smoke in the air from the industrial furnace. Everything was different and exciting. The older children were most reenergized in this new strange environment. The younger ones were cranky from a long day and not being able to move about freely.

Gilbert began to wonder. "Who will I ask in a city so big that would know my sister and brother-in-law?" He remembered the address his father had given him. If he did not run into anyone that knew Germaine and Marie Moreau, maybe they would know the address.

Getting ever closer, they could feel the buzz of the city. It seemed to have a different rhythm all its own. That was the thought in Gilbert's mind, as he and his family approached the city limits.

Seeking to be Loved

Each recognized a strangeness and sensed it, though no one put it into words. They had no words to describe the stimulation created by entering an area, an environment so different to them. One could only acknowledge their senses were awakened and alert.

Ernest and Mary commented to each other about the people and the architecture. They were amazed, gazing at all the structures. "Look how close everything is, all the buildings are so crowded together."

The firm dirt road was now a cobblestone street. The sound of the wheels and hoofs of the animal's feet made a distinct and a rhythmic clatter. It also made the ride in the wagon a little less comfortable, alerting everyone to the change, and something was different and unique in this place. This added to the apprehension and waves of excitement running through their veins.

It was good that they were arriving in the early evening hours. Many had apparently left their jobs and were already heading home. The streets were busier than usual, more so than regular business hours. There were more people than they had ever seen at any given time in one spot in their whole life milling about.

The strange noises were deafening to them. It appeared the people of the town were not distracted or concerned with the sounds. There seemed to be a directness about the people of the town. The children looked around in awe of what they saw. Some buildings were four stories high. They appeared massive; larger than any structures they had ever seen before.

Gilbert surveyed the town looking for a place he thought would be good to ask for directions. They came to an official looking building. He stepped up to the wagon and told Marilda to stop. He would go in and ask if anyone knew the address or how they could find his sister. He knew nothing else to do.

Metz was a large city, housing more than 40,000 people at the turn of the century. Metz is an ancient city, once known as Divodurum, which was the capital of the Celtic matrices.

Seeking to be Loved

It was considered a strategic city where the junction of several military roads lead. It was a fortified city of great importance for travel and trade in the region. Metz had been a spiritual, intellectual, and creative mecca for centuries.

The children were amazed by the sights of the buildings, architecture, and steeples. Many could be seen from everywhere throughout the city. Gilbert entered the building, approached the counter, and introduced himself to the clerk and asked if he could help him.

The clerk asked, "How may I help you, monsieur?" Gilbert gave him the name and handed him the piece of paper with the address. The man looked indifferent and just shrugged his shoulders. "The name, I do not know, monsieur. The address I am fairly familiar with. Why, may I ask, are you looking for these people at this address?"

Gilbert responded, "This is my sister and her husband. We wish to visit them."

"I will give you directions monsieur. I must inform you, unless they have a stable, there will be no place to keep your animals overnight and they may be confiscated."

Gilbert asked him if there was a livery near this address that could house the animals overnight.

"Not that I am aware of. That is a residential area. I am not sure they will have one close to them. I can give you directions to that street. It will be easy, although it will still take you about forty minutes. He explained the directions to Gilbert.

"Continue on this road until you cross the bridge over the Moselle, approximately 1 kilometer. After the bridge, proceed a half kilometer or less. You will come to an open town square. To the far east of the square, the road will be heading northeast. The road you are looking for is Rue Louis Rossel. You will stay on it approximately 300 meters, then you will come to another bridge that you need to cross over. Take the second street on the right after the bridge. Continue until you see a stream confluence with the Moselle River,

Seeking to be Loved

about a quarter kilometer north. Follow the road along the river. Look for the signs for names of the streets. There will be seven, eight maybe nine streets, more or less. The good thing is you will be along the river, so follow the river lane. You will turn left onto the street you are looking for. Just stop at the number of the residence you wish to find."

Gilbert thanked him.

The man wished them good luck and said, "Au revoir(Good Bye)."

Gilbert replied, "Au revoir," as he left the building.

The children greeted him on his return from the office. "Father, look at all the buildings, look at the steeples. What a beautiful city. Are all cities like this?"

Gil and Nat laughed and said, "All cities are different, and some are even much larger than this."

The little one's eyes opened ever so wide and they looked at each other and said, "Ouah"(Wow)!

"Nous partons(Off we go)," Gil said as he lifted the children into the wagon and assisted Nattie. Then she gestured to Mary, who was holding Phillip, to hand him to her. Mary handed him to her father because she can not reach high enough to hand him to her mother.

Gilbert looked at Phillip as he raised him up. He was smiling at his father. Gilbert looked into his eyes and said to him, "You are quite the trouper, little man."

Nattie took him and snuggled him into her sling. Gilbert gave her directions. Off they went. Their little entourage seemed pretty conspicuous. However, the people they encountered paid no attention. In the big city this was a common sight. The Guyons were amazed by it all. They admired the buildings, shops, stores, homes, and businesses. It was new, different, and exciting, and they felt the energy of the city. There was a new vitality in their steps as they walked and looked about. *As* they approached the river, the old stone bridge was just ahead.

Seeking to be Loved

Nattie saw it first and turned slightly to the others and said, "It is in sight."

Ernest and Mary look at each other. Ernest said, "Let's go." He glanced at his father and asked, "May we, Father?"

Gil glanced at him, then the others, Mary, Henry, and little Gilbert. He could hardly believe the little fellow had kept up the pace all day long. He saw the excitement in their eyes. He quickly assessed the animals. They had remained in line trailing the wagon all day and probably would continue to follow what is in front of them with little guidance. He nodded his head to his children for them to go on, telling them to be careful and not fall in. "We will not be able to get you out," he said. Hoping those last words would put the fear of God in them, and keep them safe. He did not want to have to jump in after them.

They ran past the wagon. Blanche and Joseph looked at their mother and asked, "Can we go, too, Ma me?"

Nattie looked at them and kindly, but firmly said, "Non."

"Please Ma mee!"

Marilda said sternly, "I will have your father take you to see the river once we get on the bridge." That satisfied them for the moment. They were now standing on their tiptoes, trying to get a better glimpse of the bridge and the river as they got closer.

The city seemed to open up as they approached the bridge. It really was a beautiful sight. Nattie took a deep breath, looked upriver and down and saw the buildings and structures along its banks and the sky above. "What a wonderful sight," she thought. "How unusual it is in the city."

She shouted to her children to be careful and not to get too close to the edge of the rail. She observed Ernest, Mary and Henry leaning over the guide rail to look at the river. Henry was on his tiptoes leaning over the stonework. Her heart skipped a beat when she noticed little Gilbert trying to climb the edge. Just as Gil grasped him in his hands to lift him up in his arms, she let out a sigh of relief, instead of the shout that was swelling in her lungs ready to burst forth.

Gilbert explained to his children, "This is the great Moselle River. It is no larger here than it is in our little town, only 35km away. Although that is probably more like 50km by way of the river. It looks deeper with the built-up embankments."

Ernest, looked at him and questions, "This is the same river, Father?"

"Oui," he replied, "The Moselle flows through two countries and borders three. It starts in Germany, forms borders for Germany and Luxembourg, before flowing into France in the Lorraine region where we are from."

Blanche looked up at her mother and asked, "Can we get down? We want to get down Ma mee."

Marilda looked at Gil, who was holding little Gilbert, then turned her gaze to Ernest and asked if he would help the little ones down. As he lifted them from the wagon, his mother ordered, "You and Mary hold their hands." She warned them both not to let go of them, not for a second. She kept a watchful eye on everyone. It seemed all were oblivious of the traffic crossing the bridge.

One particularly large wagon was pulled by a team of four magnificent beasts. The teamster made them aware of their folly. The driver of the team shouted to her, "You are blocking the bridge and holding things up." She was startled by the gruffness of his voice, although it was not a malicious tone.

Marilda looked around. They were not impeding passersby. She shouted to Gil, "We should move on now and not take up space any longer on the bridge."

Gilbert agreed, and said to his children, "We must go. We still have to find your aunt and uncle's home and get settled in for the night." All happily went back to their assigned positions.

Ernest helped the younger ones up into the wagon and they proceeded.

Seeking to be Loved

Gil repeated the instructions to Nattie. "Next turn will be after the second bridge. Once we reach the square, we will look for Rue Louis Rossel." They found the street without difficulty and followed it across a small stream. Gilbert shouted, "Nat you will take the second right you come to."

She turned the team onto the road without noticing the name of the street. Gil shouted for her to start counting the streets they passed on the left. "We will follow the stream north." Everyone, except Phillip, started counting the streets as they passed them.

Mary asked her father, "What street are we looking for?"

Gilbert told her, "Rue La Maxe."

She replied, "We should be there very shortly then, Da dee?" I can hardly wait to see Aunt Marie and Uncle Germaine."

"Oui my dear." Then Gilbert added, "They will be very surprised. I hope it will be as pleasant for them as it is for us."

Ernest and Mary shouted out the names of each street, and the younger ones chimed in, repeating each name. It is all they can do to keep their gazes from being drawn to the river. Mary mentioned to Ernest and Henry, "The river looks so different with all the houses and buildings along its banks. It is quite interesting. It is so different from what we see."

The two boys agreed and little Gilbert wondered aloud, "Are there big fish to be caught in the river so close to the city?"

They passed the ninth street. Gilbert said to Nat, "It should be the next street or two." As the street signs came into view, Nat saw it first and said, "Ooh-la-la, here it is!" She turned the team to the left. "Let us all be looking for number 223, on the houses."

Gilbert thought the time was between 5:00 and 5:30. He wished he had kept his watch in one of his pockets instead of having Marilda pack it for safekeeping during the journey. He thought to himself, "I must remember to ask her where she placed it, so I can retrieve it and keep it with me."

While they made their way up the street, several people opened doors or peeked out windows to see what the commotion

Seeking to be Loved

was at this time of day. It was unusual to hear horses stepping on the cobblestones this late in the afternoon, not to mention seeing such a sight, a wagon so heavily loaded making its way on the street.

The living quarters and appartements(apartments) were joined together, with people living in close proximity, some with little balconies overlooking the street. The Guyons looked down the little allées(alley). All they see are little doorways, windows, and a cobblestone path. It is not much wider than their little carts being pulled by the goats. Even they might have trouble making it through such a narrow way. Intersecting before the next little allée, they are startled by a young man coming toward them.

He stated boldly, "This is unusual for this time of day, to see such a, such a," finally deciding on, "défilé(parade)."

They smiled at his comment. Gilbert took the initiative and asked the young man if he lived there.

"Oui!" the man acknowledged.

Gil next asked if he happened to know where house number 223 would be located. Before the man could answer, Gilbert asked if he knew Germaine and Marie Moreau. He told him, "I am her brother, and these are her nieces and nephews."

"I am sure they will be very pleased to see you. I happen to work with Monsieur Moreau. They live just ahead. May I escort you?"

Gilbert smiled broadly and reached to shake his hand, stating, "What good fortune to meet you. We will be privileged to have you guide us to their home."

"My name is Jim. It will be my pleasure monsieur. Just follow me, you are almost there."

For the first time all day, Gilbert thought how pleasant it would be to see his sister. He had never been to her home, and had not seen her since Christmas. She and Germaine always came home to visit for the holidays.

Seeking to be Loved

At the same time, Marilda had an uncomfortable thought. She knew how inconvenient it may be to have guest arrive unannounced on your doorstep. Not to mention at this time of day.

Jim, in a joyful voice, declared, "There it is, 223 La Maxe." He ran up the steps to a small patio, and bound to the front door and knocked.

Marie opened the door. She was surprised to see him. "Hello Jim, what are you doing here?"

He started laughing. "I am here to announce your guest," then he laughed all the louder. She knew him to be a prankster, so she could not imagine what was to come next.

Gilbert was walking up the steps. Marie looked beyond Jim, she shouted, "Gilbert!" She pushed Jim aside, nearly knocking him over. Shouting to her brother, "What are you doing here?"

Upon reaching the top step of the patio, Gilbert caught his sister as she flung herself into his arms. They embraced, wrapping their arms around each other. They laughed with joy at the sight of each other. Gilbert lifted her off her feet. Marie noticed the rest of the family at the foot of the stairs. She could not believe her eyes, as she saw all the children, then locked eyes with Marilda.

Marilda instantly felt at ease. She saw the welcome in her sister-in-law's reaction. She knew she was sincere when she recognized the joy in Marie's eyes. Marilda said to herself, "Oh, thank goodness." With the fatigue of the day and a rush of emotion, her eyes blurred slightly when she acknowledged Marie's pleasure at seeing them.

Marie turned to Jim, "Go inside and get Germaine. He is upstairs. Tell him we have guests. "Laughing, she said, "Tell him many guests!" She turned to Gilbert with a broad smile and absolute delight reflected in her expression. "Gilbert, finally my little brother comes to visit me. What a great day!" She grabbed his hand and rushed down the stairs so she could hug her nieces and nephews. Looking up at Nattie, she asked, "How is that little baby?" She noticed all the baggage and animals with them. She made rounds hugging each of her nieces and nephews in turn, and asked, "Are you taking a holiday, or are you moving to the city?"

Gilbert did not want to tell her they were on the way to Canada. He decided to wait until they were settled in for the evening before he explained to her and Germaine the reason they were there.

Germaine appeared with Jim by his side. His smile was broader than Marie's. He asked Gilbert, "Do you have a place to stay?"

Marie slapped him on the shoulder and said, "My brother and his family will be staying right here."

Germaine laughed, "Where will we put them all?"

"Anywhere and everywhere," Marie told him. "We will have to watch our steps, so we do not step on any of the children, for they will be roaming about the house and underfoot. You will have to watch yourself when you get up to go to work in the morning. You do not want to step on them. They will surely still be sleeping."

They laughed at Aunt Marie's comment to Germaine.

Germaine asked Gil, "How early this morning did you start traveling?"

Gill replied, "We started at Bouzonville, where we met with Marilda's parents and spent the night there. We left close to 8:00 this morning."

Marie and Germaine both stated, "Well you had quite the journey today. You covered a lot of ground, with wagon, carts and children in tow." Marie mentions, "You all must be exhausted and starving. Let us carry the little ones into the house."

Gilbert asked Germaine, "Is there a place to keep his livestock?"

Germaine informed Gilbert, "There is nothing close. I do have a brother that has a small farm. It is just a very short distance from here, less than a kilometer. He would be happy to board them for you."

Seeking to be Loved

Gilbert said to him, "That would be wonderful if he would. We will be happy to pay him for the board."

Germaine said, "Non, non, you are our guest, it will be my privilege to take care of that for you. We are honored that you are here to visit with us."

Gilbert bowed his head and said, "Merci."

Germaine made the suggestion, "First, let us get your things inside. Then you and I will take the animals to my brother's farm."

They all started to grab the things that they would need for the night. Nattie took charge of what would go in or stay on the wagon.

Gilbert asked Marie and Germaine, "May we provide you with meat on the hoof or on the wing?"

His sister and brother-in-law looked at each other, and Marie suggested, "A few ducks would make a wonderful meal for tonight's celebration."

Germaine told her, "I will slaughter them at the farm and bring them back. We will not be long."

"I will get other victuals prepared, while Nattie and the children are getting settled in and freshened up," replied Marie.

Germaine declared, "Wonderful. We will be off then."

Gilbert attached tethers to the wagon, to pull both carts along at a quicker pace than the goats would maintain independently. He then asked if Germaine could take the wagon, while he and Ernest herd the sheep and goats along the way. He knew the younger boys were tired and would not be needed. It would not be necessary to distract them from visiting with their aunt.

Jim had stepped back and observed the joyful meeting as a spectator. He now took his leave and told them he would be on his way. "It was a pleasure to meet you, Gilbert, and your family. Enjoy your stay." He turned to Germaine and said, "I will see you tomorrow."

Germaine asked Jim, "Is there anything that you need?"

Seeking to be Loved

Jim replied, "Non, I just showed them the way to your home, after they nearly ran me over coming out of the allée."
They laughed over the incident.

Gilbert revealed, "We were thankful for the near collision," and added, "It was a pleasure to meet you, Jim."

It was not long before they arrived at his brother's farm. Gilbert and his son saw to it that the animals were unharnessed and brushed. All the stock were watered and given plenty of hay and oats. Gilbert had two ducks pulled from the crate. He asked Germaine if he would slaughter them while he took care of the animals. Before he could respond.

Germaine's brother took the fowl and uttered, "I will have them ready shortly."

Before Gilbert, Germaine and Ernest were finished settling the animals for the evening, his brother had the fowl drained, dressed, and bagged for them to take home.

Germaine's brother handed him the bag, "They are fine fattened birds. You will dine well tonight."

Gil and Ernest looked at each other, wondering in amazement. He enquired of Germaine, "How did your brother, performed the chore so quickly."

Germaine declared, "My brother is a very skilled butcher, quick and precise with a knife." He muttered under his breath, although all heard, "I would not like meeting him in a dark allée at night." This teasing statement caused a bit of concern, before they laughed together, along with his brother.

They bid his brother bonne nuit. Gilbert let him know he will be back in the morning to get the animals.

While walking back, Germaine asked Gilbert if there was a purpose for the visit.

Gil said, "Oui, we are going to Canada."

Germaine had suspected as much. "We have seen many moving away. Some of our countrymen are angry at them for doing so. Your sister and I are glad that you are moving to a safer place.

Seeking to be Loved

Living so close to the border would be dangerous if war breaks out. Your sister and I have talked a lot about our concern for all of you and the rest of her family.

What have you heard? Being so close to the border, there must be many rumors about possible war with Germany?"

Gilbert explained, "The word is that war is imminent, though, no one is certain why. Many still have doubts, for there appears to be no apparent reason or cause. Being so close to the border, we hear many rumors and see more of what the German people are doing to prepare.

Their armament build up and fortification has been observed by those who trade and travel across the border. The officials say nothing to the French people. It seems a bit surreal. Everyone senses something is about to happen. No one in authority is telling us anything of certainty.

I guess when the time comes, they will let us know. My fear is that it will be too late, and many lives may be at stake."

"So close to the eastern border, you might be doing the wisest thing." Germaine continued, "What is the rest of your family doing?"

Gilbert replied, "They plan on staying."

"You, Gilbert, who love that area, working the land and raising stock. How is it you came to this decision? Here I thought you would be the last one to evacuate and leave the land."

Gilbert did not want to share the dreams he and Nattie had, they were too horrific. He simply stated, "I needed to protect my family at all costs."

Germaine agreed. "I certainly understand that. It had to be a very difficult decision for both of you."

"Oui, it was. We both knew it was the right decision for us. We pray nothing will come of all this talk and nothing happens. We hope it blows over and goes away, so all will be safe. Thus, life will go on as it has for the last thirty years or so. It was very difficult for Nattie and I to leave our families." He hesitated before saying, "The

Seeking to be Loved

decision has been made, come better or worse. My greatest fear is that we may not see our family again."

Germaine patted Gilbert on the shoulder and said, "We wish you well on your journey. We are glad that you stopped to see us. Maybe one day we will join you in Canada."

They turned to walk up the street to his house. The town was quiet, the sun nearing ever closer to the horizon. By the time they reached the steps to Germaine's patio, there was a calm peacefulness in the air.

When Germaine and Gilbert entered the house, all was quiet. They noticed little pockets of belongings and blankets laid out on the floor, little sleeping places for the children.

Gilbert said, "Look at all the little nests." Each had their belongings neatly packed beside them.

Marilda met them in the door to the hallway leading to the kitchen. She and Gilbert embraced.

Gilbert stated, "I see you had the children prepare their sleeping spaces for the evening."

Marie greeted them from the other room. "Everything was ready except the preparation of the duck." Germaine handed the package to Marie. She told the men, clean up. "We will prepare the duck for dinner. It will be ready shortly, so do not tarry. The children are nearly starving to death."

After dinner, the children got ready for bed. Ernest and Mary wanted to explore the community and town, as most teens and adolescents their age would. Marilda could tell by the questioning look on their face.

She knew that they would like to go out and explore the neighborhood. She placed her finger to her lips, to silence them. She whispered, "You two can join us on the patio," and winked. They understood their mother did not want to give them permission in front of the younger children. They know her ways nearly as well as she knows them. They glanced at each other with a smile on their

Seeking to be Loved

face and a gleam of excitement in their eyes. They nearly skipped out the door in delight to join their aunt and uncle on the patio.

Gil and Nat helped the little ones get ready for bed. They talked with their children, listened to their prayers, and kissed them good night.

They joined their hosts on the patio. Germaine had opened a bottle of wine. Dusk was easing into night and Marilda told Ernest and Mary, "You may only have about a half-hour to explore. Darkness is already setting in. I want you back before it gets too late. It is already difficult to see where you are going. It is easy to get lost in the city."

Germaine, impressed upon them, "This is a small and safe neighborhood, extending only a few squares(blocks) in each direction. It would be hard for someone to get lost." He recognized the look in his sister-in-law's eyes. She did not want him to encourage them too much. He quickly added, "The streets and allées can be like a maze. It is easy to get turned around and lose your direction, if you get lost, just scream the whole neighborhood will hear you."

Mary and Ernest both laughed and agreed to be back shortly. They descended the steps quickly.

Marilda cried, "Be careful." She looked at Gil, "I know we must teach them to be courageous and independent as possible. I worry about them in a place they are not familiar. Many things can happen."

Gilbert agreed. He knew she was trying to justify herself for letting them go, despite her motherly fears and always wanting to protect them. "You are a wonderful mother. I want them to be responsible for themselves as well. We will see if their excitement and curiosity overrides their sense of responsibility."

Marie and Germaine, chuckled and said, "That is quite a test for a young teen and adolescent."

"Oui" Marilda said, "We do not know what lies ahead. Each of us will be put to many tests on this journey. It is best to keep our wits

Seeking to be Loved

about us. There is a long road ahead and I fear great demands will be placed on everyone."

Germaine lifted his glass: "With that, let us raise our glasses in a toast. To a safe journey and voyage to a new life, in a new place and a new beginning. May God bless you, guide and protect you, until you reach your destination."

They raised their glasses and Gil said, "Cheers and may God bless my dear sister and you, Germaine, for accepting us so graciously."

"And so unexpectedly," Marilda added; they toasted each other, laughing.

The evening was warm and pleasant as they sat on the patio sipping wine and enjoying each other's conversation. It was always a pleasure to catch up on news from home and each other's lives. Especially now, with the uncertainty of war, and the knowledge they may never see each other again.

There was an occasional light breeze, with it the fragrance of many flowers blooming in window baskets. There was also smells of someone preparing a late dinner which added to the pleasantness of the moment. Darkness settled in. The glow from sparse pockets of light from windows and doors on the narrow streets and allees was barely enough to negotiate unfamiliar surroundings.

Gilbert realized several minutes had passed. He descended the steps. Upon reaching the street below, he could see two figures walking down the middle of the stone paved street. He turned toward the figures approaching and recognized the images and smiled. Thinking to himself, "They passed the first test."

He waited for Mary and Ernest, putting his arm around both. He asked if they enjoyed their exploration.

Mary was the first to answer. "Papa, the sunset was magnificent from the river. There are so many houses and buildings. They are all different, and there were so many homes with window boxes filled with the most beautiful plants."

Seeking to be Loved

"It seems funny," Ernest said, "There is no place else to plant. They do add color and fragrance, nevertheless what good are they? You can't eat them."

Mary said, "You boys, is that all you think about is eating?" She turned to her father. "The city is such a different place."

Gilbert smiled and agreed as they walked up the steps.

The two hugged their aunt and uncle and thanked them for a delicious dinner.

Marilda kissed them and told them to get some rest, they would be leaving in the morning.

Mary resisted the urge to ask if they could stay a few days. She sensed she should not.

Marie conveyed to Gilbert and Marilda, "You have two fine children," then corrected herself. "I mean seven."

Germaine asked Gilbert, "Where is your next destination?"

"We are heading to Paris and then to the coast by way of Rouen."

"Have you confirmed passage to Canada?"

Gil confessed, "We have not."

Germaine said, "As each day passes, I suspect there will be more people heading to the coast.

Paris is such a large city. It makes Metz, look like a tiny village. Just getting through it will be a test of your endurance and patience. Paris will be crowded and busy with people going about their business."

The Parisians may not seem as friendly as the people you are used to in the rural area you are from." Germaine paused to rephrase what he was about to say. "I assure you they are, and will be quite helpful when you approach them.

The route you are taking is definitely the shortest. My concern is, and you may have already considered it, stay away from the channel coast."

"Why?" Gilbert asked.

Seeking to be Loved

Germaine shared his thoughts, "If war is declared, I suspect the channel will be heavily patrolled by enemy ships. Thus increasing the danger and risk of safe passage even for the passenger ships. No one on land or sea will be safe."

Marie interjected, "We hate to see you go, although I am glad you and the children are leaving. I think you are wise to go early. We hope this all amounts to nothing and one day we will reunite with you and all our brothers and sisters." She looked at Germaine and stated matter of factually, "We may holiday one day with you all in Canada."

Gil grinned. "A great holiday that will be, and we look forward to it. What an exciting time that will be for all of us. We must make a pact today. Once we reach Canada and get ourselves established, you both must come and visit."

They raised their glasses in agreement.

Germaine continued his previous thought. "It may be too early to point this out and may or may not be of much concern. If things change over the next week or so, you may consider going southwest or even south to Nanres or St. Nazaire. Those ports may offer a safer starting point for your voyage, although a much greater distance to travel. No one knows what to expect.

"Oui," Gilbert replied, reminded of the words of his father-in-law. "We must expect the worst and hope for the best."

"That is a good philosophy," Germaine agreed.

Marie said, "Oui, we have all heard that many times growing up."

Germaine declared, "It is getting late. I must be up early so that Jim does not get to work before me. Plus, you must be on your way before the roads become crowded with the days business and travelers."

Gil and Nat thanked their hosts for their hospitality and gracious welcome during their unexpected visit.

Germaine assured them, "I will not wake you when I leave. It will be very early." He offered God's blessing and speed on their

Seeking to be Loved

journey. His final question to Gil was to ask if he had any family or other connections between Metz and Paris. Or to the West or Southwest?

Gil smiled and said, "Only about 8000km to the west."

Germaine chuckled and replied, "Oui, and they will not be much help getting you through Paris or to a port city. I do have a good friend in Paris. I will write a note for you to give to him. Who knows? He may be of some assistance."

Nattie and Gil shared their appreciation and bid them bonne nuit. They retired to the room his sister Marie had prepared for them. Nattie had already placed Phillip on a big cushion next to their bed. He and all the children were sound asleep. They both fell asleep quickly, it seemed even before their heads touch the pillows. Nothing disturbed them throughout the night.

Gil was in a deep sleep, and started to dream. He began to see scenes from his first dream of the horrible landscape that laid before him; the destruction and beaten animals. He quickly forced it out of his mind.

Another vision replaced his dream. This time he found himself in a big city, where dirty people were grabbing at him, his children, and their belongings.

He quickly told himself this was that same dream. He then replaced his thoughts, with today's pleasantries. He smelled the roses his sister had placed in a bouquet on the table. He could smell the sweet fragrance of the flowers and the aroma of a meal roasting. He felt the gentle breezes carried through the allée to them as they sat on the patio earlier that evening.

The next thing he knew it was morning. Phillip let them know it was time to wake. He thought it was still in the middle of the night until he opened the door of their room and saw light shining in through the front windows and door.

Marie was already awake, and Germaine had long since left for work. Bidding Gil good morning, she gestured for him to sit and

Seeking to be Loved

have something to eat and drink, before he and the boys go retrieve the wagon and animals.

He asked her what time it was.

Marie said, "Huh, let us just say these are bankers hours, not that of farmers."

Gil laughed at her comment and said, "The city life has ruined me already."

Marie noted it was 7:30 and she was glad they all slept well. The children have not stirred yet, despite Germaine having to step over them when he left for work. She told Gil, "It is amazing they are sleeping so well on the hard tile floor".

Gil divulged to his sister, "Marilda always sees to the comfort of our little ones."

Marie smiled and said, "She made cute little nest for them to rest in."

"She is such a wonderful mother," replied Gilbert. "It is certainly her calling. Her mothering and protective instincts are uncanny; for which now we journey.

"I will wake up Ernest and Henry so they can come with me to get our wagon and carts."

She said, "That would be a good idea. Have them come eat now, with you."

Gil woke the boys.

Ernest questioned, "Is it morning already?"

"Oui," Gil replied. Aunt Marie has breakfast prepared for us. Then we must get the animals, load up and be on our way. So let us get ready to go! Wake your brother."

When the boys got to Germaine's brother's farm, Gil was pleasantly surprised. He had not expected to see the horses already hitched and the carts loaded. Upon seeing them coming up the road, Germaine's brother, who had been sitting on his front porch, rose to meet them by the wagon. "Germaine stopped by on his way to work earlier this morning and asked us to ready the wagon, to assist you on your journey. The milk is in a pail, it is under the seat in the

Seeking to be Loved

wagon. You can leave the pale at Germaine and Marie's place, I will get it sooner or later."

Gil was very grateful the cow was milked and all the animals hitched and ready. The kindness he and his family had received the last two days touched him deeply. He shook hands, thanked him and they were off.

When they got back to his sister's, Marilda, already had the children dressed and ready to go. Gil was amazed they were ready, thinking they could not have been gone for more than an hour. They reloaded the wagon with their overnight belongings. then bid farewell to Marie, with hugs and kisses, thanking her for such a wonderful visit, even though it was short. They told her they would look forward to her and Germaine, coming to visit them in Canada.

Marie waved goodbye, she reached one hand into her apron pocket. She felt the envelope, she was to give to Gilbert. She ran after them, and handed it to Gil. "This is to give to Germaine's friend in Paris. He may be able to help. With any luck, you will be there within a week. If you wish to find him, give him the letter."

"Germaine request he assist you and your family with setting up the voyage. He may also be able to help with housing if you need to stay in Paris. Germaine is sure that he can and will be of benefit to you, if you need it." She gave him another hug and wished them a safe journey. She shouted to her nieces and nephews, "I love you all. Obey your parents." She also reminded them to give her love to her brothers and sister-n-laws, their aunts, uncles, and cousins in Canada. They all promised they would.

Gilbert was concerned about the late start. He hoped to make it to Conflous-en-Jarnisy today. He knew with each day's travel and the closer they got to Paris, the slower their progress would be. The weather was pleasant, and everyone's spirit were high. It was good to see his sister and bid her farewell. He hoped one day they would be together again. The day was uneventful to his surprise once they left the outskirts of Metz. There seemed to be as many people coming toward them heading east as there were leaving.

Seeking to be Loved

Gilbert was comforted observing people going in the direction he and many were fleeing from. Sensing the urgency of the imminent danger this country may be facing, may not be as immediate as many thought. At the same time, in the back of his mind he remembered the vision of his dream and its brief reminder last night.

The day progressed with the usual stops to water the animals and let them graze, and so they, too, can rest, nourish, and refresh themselves.

May 7, 1914. Another day has passed. They found themselves traveling once again alongside the pastures of a lovely countryside. There were newly seeded fields on either side, just west of the town Conflous-en-Jarnisy. They had covered the distance they had hoped to travel that day. People were pulling to the side of the road to stop for the evening. Gilbert thought it was necessary to find a landowner and ask for permission to spend the night on their property. He quickened his pace to catch up to Marilda in the wagon. He shared his thoughts and she agreed. They would stop at the next bungalow they see.

Marilda, having a vantage point, mentioned to Gilbert, "There is a small farm not too far off the road ahead on the right." He nodded and motioned for her to turn onto the pathway leading to the residence. The family waited as he inquired of the owner, permission to stay for the night.

Gilbert walked toward the house and noticed a man coming toward him from the bungalow with something in his hand. Closing the distance between them, Gilbert noticed the man did not look friendly. He was carrying a pitchfork in his hands as if it were a weapon. Gilbert stopped as the man continued to approach. Gil took off his hat and asked the man who owned the property.

The man shouted, "I am he."

Before Gilbert could say another word, the man bellowed, "What do you want?"

Seeking to be Loved

Gilbert holding his hat in his hand, explained to the man. "We are looking for a place to rest for the evening, where we may graze and water our livestock."

By the humble tone of his voice, the man's anger was defused. The man was silent for a moment. He glanced past Gilbert and saw Marilda holding Phillip, the other two at her feet. He looked beyond to see the other four children keeping the animals confined to the road. The property owner, maintaining a scowl on his face, glared at Gilbert. He finally barked, "Since you are the first to ask, I will grant your request."

Gilbert thanked him, extending his hand, and introduced himself. He asked where he could water his animals and allow them to graze. He noticed the man's eyebrows rise. Gilbert quickly added. "If it is not too much trouble."

Gilbert also asked if there were any chores or work he needed done. If he and his sons would be allowed to do it, they would be obliged to do so.

"If that will help make up for any inconvenience this may cause. Is there anything we could do that would be of assistance to you, monsieur?"

The man was taken by surprise. He sensed sincerity in Gilbert's request and the fact that he was willing to do something in return. The man said, "You may stay." He instructed Gilbert. "Move everything behind our barn, over there," pointing to his right. "You will find a fine grassy field and a well."

He explained to Gilbert that he was the first to ask permission. He had become angry over the last two weeks, with people just stopping and spending the night on his property without asking. "They leave their fire pits and waste. I have to pick up after them. Next night, the same thing. Each day there seems to be more and more people and families passing by. I understand they are concerned. Nevertheless, people should not lose their respect for one another, especially their own countrymen."

"You sir, and your family are welcome to be our guest."

Seeking to be Loved

Gilbert expressed his gratitude once more. He turned and waved for Nattie, to come forward.

Once everyone settled for the evening, the man and his wife came and introduced themselves. "My name is Victor, and this is Priscilla Belizile."

Nattie smiled and introduced herself and her children.

Priscilla ask if she could hold Phillip.

Victor said, "Our children live down the road and Priscilla is getting ready to be a grandmother."

Nattie looked at her with compassion and congratulated them. She then expressed her appreciation to the couple for allowing her family to stay on their farm.

Victor suggested they stay in the barn and sleep in the loft. The children shouted "Oupi"(Yahoo)!

They asked their mother, "Ma mee may we?"

"Oui," said Marilda.

Victor mentioned, "I think you will find it most comfortable."

Gil asked, "What may we do for you while we are here?"

Victor spreads his arms, gesturing, "You can see the fields are planted. We have everything in order for the season. If you will just leave the area how you found it, that will be enough."

Gilbert could see Victor kept his farm in order. He persisted, "We will be leaving early. If there is anything you would like for us to do before we go, we would be happy to. Please let us know."

Priscilla handed Phillip back to Nattie and wished their visitors a good night and a safe journey to wherever they were going.

Marilda thought it odd neither Madame nor Monsieur Belizile had asked where they were from, or where they were going, or why.

It did not matter where they were from, why or what they left behind, or who they were. They understood if war did occur, everything would change. Nothing would be as it was before. What would be important is only what lies ahead.

Seeking to be Loved

When all the children were asleep, Gil mentioned to Nattie that it was odd that they were not more inquisitive about them.

Nattie said, "I had thought that myself, earlier. From what you told me about the people coming through and stopping on their property, they must have been resentful with good reason. From what I have already seen these last few days, there will be many more people traveling through in the days and weeks to come. How could they keep up with them all? Especially if many, or should I say most, do not even make an effort to speak with them.

"Gilbert, you are a good man. People see that in you. It is in your actions. That is why I married you. Your parents raised you well, and they instilled in you a sense of responsibility and respect. Not to mention your diligence and willingness to work and provide. We are blessed. I can think of no other man to be an example to our children. They are lucky that you are their father. I only wish and hope they will learn such things from you."

Gilbert said, "Well Nattie, the same goes for you. We must teach our children to be diligent and respectable and to always Seek First the Kingdom of God. All else will fall into place." He kissed her good night.

May 8, 1914 - The day began with an overcast sky. Gilbert woke the older boys and they got the animals watered and ready, while Nattie prepared breakfast. As they are making their way down the path, they looked back and saw the front door open. Victor and Priscilla waved goodbye. They shouted, "We wish you well and may God bless your journey. Good luck to you all."

Victor intentionally delayed his morning chores in order to allow them to prepare themselves and be on their way. When he opened the door to the barn, he saw that everything was swept and stacked neatly. The mangers were full of hay, the troughs full of fresh water and the stalls were cleared of animal waste.

Seeking to be Loved

Today's journey would be a long one for the Guyons and they were glad to be off early. They could see why landowners were dissatisfied and angry. Many were camping alongside the roads and sprawled and scattered in nearby fields.

Gilbert thought to himself and told his children as they walked along, "You must always make an effort to find out who owns the property before trespassing." He also told his children, "Wherever you go and wherever you may find yourselves, always strive to leave the places you tread better than how you found them."

They hoped to make it at least as far as Haudainville, which was close to 23km, by early afternoon. He hoped the weather would hold, although he could smell the rain coming. He shouted to Marilda to stop, and had Ernest and Mary to get coats and hats for everyone.

He untied the canvas covering the load, then attached two poles up over the seat. He stretched the canvas over Marilda to shelter her and the young ones from the rain. He told Marilda the road would be miserable when wet and muddy.

On the way again, it was not long before the anticipated rain started sprinkling down upon them. It became a steady rain and heavy at times. Many that had not already started, decided they would just stay put and wait out the weather in their pitched tents and shelters. Marilda was glad that they were on the road and had a good meal early. She was not looking forward to stopping and attempting to remove items from the wagon and prepare a meal in the rain. Phillip, awake and alert, comfortably swayed in the sling hung across her shoulders.

She sang songs, to the children all morning to keep their spirits up. She thought this would be a good distraction from the rain since they could not enjoy the scenery due to very limited visibility. She thought to herself, there was not time to consider weather conditions before leaving the farm. Although the fact is, that would not have made any difference, even if they had. There was nothing they could do about it, except, endure and go on.

Seeking to be Loved

She was thankful it was not any worse than what it was for this time of year. She hoped it would stop soon. She was glad the little ones were comfortable under their little shelter. She could only imagine how muddy and wet Gil and the older ones were.

Her thoughts began to consume her and the singing stopped before she realized it. She began to think of what may be up ahead. Not just the muddy roads and swollen streams, there are more and more people on the road each day. She thought about what her sister and brother-in-law had said of Paris and other large cities.

She wondered, "Where and how will we feed and rest our animals?" She thought about the ocean passage. With so many people evacuating and migrating to other areas, how slow would progress be on the highways? Will the distance they create each day between the eastern border be enough to keep them out of harm's way? Will people be civil? From what she gathered from Monsieur and Madame Belizile's comments, they would not.

If we got passage on a ship, how would she and her family tolerate being at sea for three or four weeks, or longer? She recalled stories of crossings from her grandparents. It took months to sail across the sea. Their food supply would not last that long.

"What would we eat? The animals? I must not think too much. Things are different now." She had heard, ships were faster, relying on steam instead of sail. She was not sure how long it would take a ship to cover 8000km.

She had heard of seasickness, though did not understand how it occurred and its symptoms.

Blanche asked, "Why are you not singing Ma mee?"

Nattie did not realize how consumed she was in her thoughts. She decided they would just have to cross those bridges when they come to them. Then she began to sing "Frère Jacques."

The steady rain, showed no sign of letting up. The morning passed with only one stop for relief. Nattie asked Gil if he wanted to stop to eat.

Seeking to be Loved

He said, "Have Mary grab a few things for us to snack on as we continue to walk."

Stopping in the rain would just slow progress even more, and everyone, man and beast would get cold. Since they were already so wet. He decided it was best we keep moving until they were ready to stop for the night. Then they would change into dry clothes. He had Mary, Henry and Gilbert take turns riding on the back of the wagon. This gave them a rest from walking in the muck and assisting with pushing the carts through the muddy road. Which was getting too difficult for the goats to pull on their own power. They needed to keep the carts moving along. He knew it was tiring work and they would need to take frequent rest.

By midafternoon, the rain was letting up and the clouds were breaking. The sun's rays and the blue sky boosted their morale. The sun started to warm their faces and a steamy mist began rising from the ground, as well as from their wet bodies. They decided to remove their jackets and hats. The Guyons and all their layers of clothing were soaking wet. As their clothes began to dry, their feet became heavily laden with mud. The sun was evaporating some of the moisture from the mud. Which made it a stiff, sticky paste.

Each step made a suctioning sound, when lifting their feet from the muck. Every step was a grueling and very laborious process.

They were disappointed for not having seen any signs for Haudainville as of yet. It would be nearly another hour before they realized they still have another three kilometers to go.

At this pace, Gil estimated it would take two hours. Making the day a nearly an eleven-hour march, most of which was through the mud. He wanted to plod on until 6:00 that evening. Then it would be time to look for a place to stop for the night.

Gilbert observed how weary the children looked. He knew they all needed to stop soon. He started looking for a place that may offer them shelter, as well as grass for grazing and water for the animals.

Seeking to be Loved

He shouted to Nattie, suggesting that she start looking for a place that would be suitable to stop for the night, even if it is before Haudainville.

He could see his family and the animals were near exhaustion. It would be best to find a place to rest and replenish themselves. For he knew not what they would face each day, and what they must endure. He knew it was imperative to keep his family healthy.

Another grueling hour passed, all Marilda could see was pastures and seedling crop fields ahead. She can see no houses or farms, only travelers, setting their camps along the road for the night in wet, muddy fields.

Gil and Nattie noticed an outcropping of trees in the distance. She can make out a long, lone path leading to the grove of trees. There were no houses near, that could be seen.

Gilbert hoped there would be a spring of water nearby. If not, at least the trees would offer some shelter from the weather. He yelled to Nattie to turn off the road when they reach the path. It was close to 400 meters to the outcropping of trees, from the road. They could not locate a water source. He thought that was unfortunate for the animals. There was little to browse on; only leaves from the trees and bushes.

At least the path was not muddy. It was still packed firm, there had been no traffic on it that day.

Gil gave the boys instructions to unharness the horses and goats from their wagon and carts. He told Nat, "There may be a homestead over the crest of the ridge, Ernest and I will go see. Perhaps there is a stream they could not see, where he can at least water the animals, or a field. We will be back shortly." He and Ernest began to herd the animals down the path.

Nattie and Mary Alice started preparations for the evening meal.

Crossing over a low ridge, which was less than one hundred meters further down the path, they saw a home. Just behind it, a swollen stream ran swiftly. He noticed there was lush green grass growing around the house and outbuildings. Upon seeing the sight before him, a smile crossed his face as he turned to his son.

Ernest mentioned, "It is a beautiful spot Father. I hope they let our animals graze."

Gil looked to the heavens and gave thanks silently, "Dear Lord, merci for guiding us here. May these people be as gracious as the couple we stayed with last night."

Gil did not notice any movement, which he thought it a bit odd. Plus the fact on such a damp day, smoke should be rising from the chimney. When he got to the door, he knocked, waited a moment, then knocked again. He told Ernest to go around to the back of the property and check the outbuildings. Gil tried the door, it was locked. He looked through the windows, there was no lights, only darkness. He could not make out much, the curtains were drawn. He just assumed no one was home.

Ernest came back and told his father, "I looked in all the buildings, and they were empty. I saw no animals. They were well furnished, although I saw no one, man, or livestock."

Gilbert thought, "Maybe this little farm has been abandoned. The owner may have left this home just as we have. Let us water the animals and then will let them graze on this field."

He and Ernest walked back to the others. Gilbert mentioned, "Maybe the owners of this property had just gone for the day. We will see them when they come home. If so, we will tell them what we have done and ask them permission to stay on the property for the night."

Ernest shared with his father, "It would be nice to sleep in the barn, or even better yet, in a bed in the house."

Gilbert smiled. "Oui it would, although without permission we must not."

"What if they are gone Father? Who would know? Who would care?"

Seeking to be Loved

Gilbert placed his arm on his son's shoulder as they walked toward the others. "Son, God has provided us with water, fresh tender grass for our animals, and a nice group of trees for shelter. We must be grateful for what has graciously been offered to us. We should not expect, or want, more than what we need."

Gilbert's mind and conscience battled. He knew a warm fire built in the hearth, making for a warm cozy house, would be much better than sleeping on damp ground, under a wet canvas shelter. He was taught growing up, that one must always treat one another and their property with the utmost respect.

The battle in his mind was over when he realized that his prayer just moments ago had been answered. He will neither ask for nor expect more. They were led to water and a sheltered area. Before he and Ernest reached their camp, he thought to himself once again, "Merci, Lord."

When they reach the others, Marilda asked Gil to start a fire, if he thought it would be all right. "Did you find anything or anyone?"

He responded, "Oui, an abandoned home." Then he thought building a fire would be a good idea. Knowing that everything was still wet and damp, he began looking about. He noticed there were several hemlocks in the grove, causing him to think; God always provides.

He knew the resin in the twigs of the hemlocks would ignite even if damp and would burn with much heat. He instructed the children to gather and break off all the dead branches they could find under the pines.

He turned to Marilda and asked her if they had any dry blankets. She responded, "Oh, oui. Would you mind getting them? I am taking care of Phillip. They are in the trunk."

Gilbert took his pocketknife from his trousers after opening the trunk. He used it to scrape off some of the lint from the blankets until he had a fluffy handful. He then looked for a safe place to build a fire and a fairly dry spot. He asked Blanche to hold the lint gently and make sure it did not get any drips of water on it. He collected the driest twigs from the growing pile. He arranged the first layer flat on the ground with space for air to come underneath them. He then proceeded to build a little lean-to with thin, dry twigs. He gestured to Blanche to come over to help him. He instructed her to place the lint very gently inside the lean-to.

Blanche thought this was great fun. She had an important role in this process, as she carefully placed the lint inside the little twig shelter.

Gilbert struck a match and the lint ignited immediately. He blew on the flame and the hemlock twigs quickly started to burn. They all were very excited to have a campfire. The thought of a nice hot meal and they would be able to dry their wet clothes pleased them all. Everyone's spirits were high, they were warm, had hot food in their bellies, and the family safe and sound.

May 9, 1914 - Gilbert was awakened early by sounds of the birds chirping in the trees. He rekindled the fire. The crackling of the flames woke Marilda. She immediately looked at Phillip, who slept between her and Gil, then glanced at the other children all still sound asleep. The sun had not yet risen. Gil wanted them to rest as long as they could. He lifted his finger to his lips, gesturing to Marilda with a near silent whisper in her ear, to let them sleep.

She smiled and nodded. She placed her hand on little Phillip's chest. She thought to herself, "As soon as his little eyes open, he will see his loving mother smiling at him. What a wonderful way to start the day." Watching him sleep, she noticed he looked so relaxed and content. "Yet, my dearest, you are so exposed. You have not the comfort and security of our home, nor your crib. You, my little one are sheltered only by my adoring love." She thought how peaceful Phillip looked, despite what he was going through so early in his life. She thought, "He does not know anything different. He is too young to have concerns about any of this. Other than being fed, clean and comfortable, he should not have a care of anything."

Seeking to be Loved

Gazing at him, she wondered, "What is he dreaming? What is he thinking? Does he dream?"

His little face twitched, wrinkled and his face changes. "He must be dreaming," she thought to herself. "By his expressions, they must be pleasant dreams." Her heart was gladdened. She laid her head down next to him, and closed her eyes and fell back asleep.

She felt a speck of warmth on her cheek. Even in her sleep she knew that its source was not from an object. It was such a comforting warmth. She traced the warmness, as it moved across her face, then to her forehead. It made her smile.

She realized it was a ray of sun, and refused to open her eyes or to awaken. She enjoyed the comfort of her sleep and the warm kisses offered from that beam of light slinking through the trees. She is aware it is morning and it is going to be a beautiful day.

Phillip was awake, his little eyes followed the ray of sunlight on his mother's face. He reached out to touch the spot of light on his mother's forehead. His touch was so gentle, with such innocence. An ecstasy of pure love completely engulfed Marilda's entire conscious and unconscious being. She was instantly wide-awake; her eyes wide and bright, gazing directly into Phillip's. The broadest smile came across his face when she opened her eyes. She swore she could hear soft laughter from the child. Heard not with her ears, it was from within the recesses of her being.

So powerful was the emotion that moment brought forth, she could not speak. She could only be still and relish the moment. For during that moment, nothing else in the world mattered. Just the love between a mother and her baby.

She kissed his forehead and said, "Je t'aime my little one."
He squeaked, laughed, and kicked for joy!

On the road, as each hour passed the mud became firmer. The ruts were great, and baking into the road. This made it difficult for the animal's footing. Their objective for the day was to reach the town of Clermont-en-Argonne, a 34km distance. Gil believed this

Seeking to be Loved

could be accomplished without too much difficulty if the weather held, on that pleasant spring day.

Everyone appeared to be in good spirits. Despite being in the elements last night. All appeared to have a good night's rest. He thought perhaps it was because they were all huddled and snuggled together next to the glow and warmth of the fire. The coziness allowed them to fall into a deep, peaceful slumber.

Time passed quietly with each kilometer. The scenery consisted of rolling hills and pastures with only occasional houses and small farms. The clusters of homes close together could scarcely be called a village. There was an occasional "Bonjour," from passersby or folks waving as they strolled pass people who were working in the fields. Other than that, not much was said amongst the group. It was a steady march onward.

Marilda wanted to walk with Phillip after being in the wagon all day the day before. Mary was glad to take the reins. Gilbert suggested that he carry Phillip in his arms to allow Nattie to walk freely. Plus, he wanted to carry his son, it broke the monotony of the walk and the constant herding of the animals.

Phillip seemed to enjoy being in his father's arms. He liked being in an upright position. It was quite a change for him compared to the swinging and swaying of the sling, where he spent the last three days. He seemed to absorb all that was going on around him. He continually pointed at things, Gilbert knew not what.

Marilda noticed him looking about and gently pinched his cheek and said, "You are such a little inquisitive one." He smiled broadly at the feel of his mother's touch and the sound of her voice. He made a sound, "mmmma."

To Gilbert, it sounded like a humming but ended differently. He looked at Nattie and said, "Did you hear that?"

"Hear what?" questioned Marilda.

"He said Mama. When did he start saying that?" Gilbert asked.

She said, "I have never heard him say it."

Seeking to be Loved

Gilbert turned Phillip in his arms as they were walking, to face him and looked into his eyes. He told his son, "Say Mama." Phillip smiled and just cooed. Gil repeated his request, Phillip just smiled.

Marilda repeated to Gil, "He did not say, Ma mee," and she pinched Phillip's little cheek again.

Phillip repeated, "mmmmma."

Gil said, "See, he did it again," as he handed Phillip to her.

"I heard it that time." She reached to take him into her arms and gave him a big hug.

He giggled and repeated, "mmmmma, mmmma."

"Oui, my little one, I am your Mama." Marilda, proud as a peacock, shouted to the other children. "Phillip just said his first word, and guess what it was?"

They asked, "What, Ma mee, What did he say?"

"Ma mee, of course!" she replied. The family laughed, and a few wondered, what he would say next. They all started repeating their own names. Each of his brothers, Ernest, Henry, and little Gilbert, took turns walking beside him encouraging him to say their name, as well as his own.

Little Gilbert was so funny. He kept asking him, "What is your name, Phillip? What is your name, Phillip? Phillip, what is your name? say Phillip."

Phillip looked at him in a most attentive and peculiar way. It was almost as if he was noticing him for the first time. Little Gilbert kept bouncing up and down to get closer to his face. Phillip found this quite amusing and laughed every time he jumped close to him.

Gilbert said to Nattie, "He seems to be a happy little fellow. The traveling must agree with him." He thought to himself, "This is the start of a wonderful day."

After they walked a kilometer or so, Phillip had fallen asleep in Marilda's arms. He was becoming dead weight. Gilbert reached for him and Nattie was more than willing to let Gil carry him. Gilbert was quite pleased with Phillip cradled in his arms. He glanced down occasionally to see him sleeping soundly. He asked Nattie if she was ready to take the reins again.

She replied, "I think I would like to walk a little longer. It feels good to be stretching my legs."

He asked if she was getting hungry and wondered if the children were as well. The sun was high in the sky, making it near noon.

She said, "I am not, but now that you mention it, I am starting to feel a bit hungry."

Henry overhearing, cry's out, "I am starving."

Gil shouts to Mary, be looking for a place to water the horses and grounds where they may graze. Preferably near a residence, he added.

She shouted back to him, "Look up ahead poppa, on the left."

He glanced ahead to the left, it looked to be an ideal spot. He cried out to Mary, "Pull the reins left when you get there." There are several men working in the fields. Once the wagon turned and came to a stop, the men peered at this strange convoy coming off the main road.

Gilbert noticed them looking at each other. They stopped what they were doing and huddled together. He had Mary hold the team, handed Phillip to Nattie, and started walking toward the men, and they to him. He introduced himself and asked permission to rest here.

The older man asked, "How long?"

Gilbert replied, "Just long enough for them to rest and prepare some food."

The men looked at each other suspiciously. Gilbert asked if they had a spring or stream, where he may water their animals and a patch of grass for where they may graze.

The oldest gentleman stated, "We have a well you can use to draw water for your animals. We have our animals grazing in the field beyond the ridge, as you can see these fields are for crops." He

Seeking to be Loved

did not offer the field, on which to allow his animals to graze. "I can have my son bring you some hay; it will cost you a franc."

Gilbert agreed to the price and thanked him. By the time the animals were watered and eaten most of the hay, they had finished eating their meal as an hour had passed. Gilbert asked the man, if he knew how much further it would be to the town of Clermont-en-Argonne?

He replied, "Sur 15km"(About 15km).

Gilbert thanked him and bid him, "Au revoir.

The man told Gilbert, "Take the remaining hay, you paid for it. You may need it for your animals later."

Gilbert told Ernest to stack it on the wagon and cover it with a blanket, then tie it off, so they would not lose any. He assisted Nattie on to the wagon, he mentioned to her that they made good progress today. If the afternoon is as good, they should reach their destination around 6PM.

Nattie stated to him. "That will be good, our journey is just beginning, and we have such a long way to go. We must not be hard on the children."

Gilbert agreed, then reminded her, "These Guyons, are a hearty bunch."

"Oui," she concurred, "She reminds him, they do not have their beds to rest in at night. The repetitive drudgery of walking such long distances each day, will take a toll on all of us."

Gil harked back, "The boys are used to working in the fields and walking great distances even on loose soil. They proved themselves this spring. Although I agree, the journey will be long, and it will be tiring, I fear the worst is yet to come."

Ten kilometers to Clermont-en-Argonne, the sign said. Gilbert thought, "We will be there earlier than expected." The road is not as rutty as it was earlier in the day. As they draw closer, the terrain became more hilly. Clusters of houses are nearer and more frequent.

"Five kilometers to Clermont-en-Argonne," Marilda shouted.

Seeking to be Loved

Ernest and Mary, were getting excited. They pointed out the hills in the distance, they asked their father, "Is this a big village we are going to?"

"Non, although it is a very well-known town. They have a monastery there and the eglisé(church) named for and devoted to St. Anne."

"Who is St. Anne, Papa?" asked little Gilbert.

Before Gilbert's reply, Mary explained, "Saint Anne, is the mother of the Blessed Virgin Mary."

Little Gilbert asked, "You mean Jesus' mother?"

Mary and Ernest state simultaneously, "Oui."

The young Gilbert asked, "Will she be there?"

Mary laughed, "Non silly, the eglisé is dedicated to her."

Their father interjects, "She is known to be there, in spirit. There have been many miracles performed there."

Little Gilbert ask, "Will we see any miracles Papa?"

Gilbert said to him, "It is a miracle you were born."

"It is a miracle that we are going there," Ernest added.

"It is a miracle were going to Canada", Mary said, and laughed. "Plus it is a huge miracle, that I put up with you three boys."

Henry retorted, "It is a miracle we put up with you." All the boys laughed. Mary just stuck out her tongue at them.

Little Gilbert asked, "Will we be able to see the eglisé? Can we go in?"

Then Ernest made the suggestion, "Maybe we can leave Mary and Blanche at the monastery."

Little Gilbert asked his father, "What is a monastery?"

His father explained, "The monastery at Clermont, is where young ladies devote their life to serving our Lord and those within the community. It is a life of devotion, a very honorable life and one that benefits many. It is a life, in which one must be willing to make great sacrifices to pursue."

"What does sacrifice mean?" asked the boy.

Seeking to be Loved

Gil thought a moment to think of the right words to share. Words that will help his young ones understand the importance of sacrifice in one's own life. **"Sacrifice, is when you are willing to give up certain things that are important to you, for the betterment of others. When you love someone or something, you are willing to give up many things."**

"Why do we have to give things up, if we love somebody?" little Gilbert, questioned.

"It is not a matter of having to, it is a matter of wanting to," said Gil.

"Why would anyone want to give things up," the inquisitive little fella asked?

Mary said, "You told us Papa, to never ever give up?"

"Oui" he replied, **"You should never give up, and sometimes that is the sacrifice we must make. To not give up, even when it would be easier if we were to do so. When things get difficult and it does not seem like things are ever going to change in our life. When we must endure injury, insult, indignation; we must always remember there is tomorrow. And with each tomorrow, there is new hope. There will be other opportunities to make things right or better. For when there is hope, we know things can improve, for ourselves and others. If we are willing to make the effort, take the time to do what is necessary, and that which is right.**

When we learn to love others as ourselves, sacrifice for one another becomes a way of life. Which makes life better for all. Our Lord and Savior Jesus Christ, taught us how to love unconditionally. The fact that no sacrifice was, or is greater than to love one another, despite differences. Love is the ultimate sacrifice," explained, their father.

"So, sacrifice is a good thing," right Papa?

"Any sacrifice made earnestly and/or done unselfishly is a good one, and a righteous act. By living and working to improve yourself, and showing others how they can do the same, benefits all."

Seeking to be Loved

"We work hard don't we, Papa?"

"Oui, and that means you are making sacrifices each day. That will be helping you and me, your mother, brothers and sisters."

"I like sacrificing, Papa." little Gilbert exclaimed, with excitement!

His father laughed.

His older brother Ernest told him, "Why don't you make a sacrifice right now, and be quiet." They all chuckled, except for little Gilbert.

Gil patted him on the head and simply says, "We must march on."

The sun is getting closer to the hilly horizon line. Gilbert knew they must be getting close to the town of Clermont, Marilda shouted back to him, "There is a sign up ahead at the next crossroads." Drawing ever closer, she made out the print on the sign, she shouts back, 3km. Then she exclaimed, "I am ready to stop."

"I think we all are," Gil replied.

Ernest adds, "You can say that again."

Gilbert estimated that it must be close to 4 o'clock and reminds himself, I must find my pocket watch and keep it with me. Forty minutes later they see the sign Clermont-en-Argonne, all are aroused by seeing the village. It is more than just a village, maybe somewhat bigger than their little town. The first thing they see is the steeple of St. Anne's church. To the young children it seems like a great cathedral. They all asked, "Papa will we be able to go in that big eglisé?"

Gilbert said, "Eglisés are always open."

Before he can finish his next statement; Marilda, interjects, "We must go in to request of the mother of our Holy Lady, the mother of our Savior, to guide us and protect us on our journey."

Little Blanche looked up at her mother and said, "Oui Ma mee." The excitement was heard in her voice and seen in her eyes.

Seeking to be Loved

There are many people that have already stopped, from their day of travel. They have already set up their little camps on the roadsides. It appeared haphazard, as they camped wherever it suited them, before entering the town. Gilbert stopped at the first sizable building. It appeared to be some sort of business the door was locked, it was getting late. Gil knocked on the window. Someone came from inside and unlocked the door. He addressed Gil, "Monsieur how may I help you."

Gil asked, if he knew of a place they could stay for the night and graze the animals and set up camp with his family.

The proprietor looked at him a bit odd. "It is considerate of you to ask. For days now, many have come and camped, nobody asks, they just set up where they please. Thank goodness they stay out of the way. The man reflects for a moment, then confided there is a nice field near the monastery.

Gil asked if that happened to be near St. Anne's Église?

"Oui Monsieur, it is a short distance, as you can see, we are a small town. I believe the sisters would be able to accommodate you and your animals."

Gil was given directions; he thanked him, and returned to the others.

Marilda with Phillip in her arms told Gil, "I need a moment to finish changing him. The other children are very hungry."

Gilbert mentioned the monastery is just down the street to the left. They may be willing to accommodate us for the night. I was told they have a small pasture for the animals. Gilbert noticed the look in Marilda's eyes, he knows she is contemplating about something. "What are you thinking Nat?"

"I was just wondering; the monastery may have a place for the nuns and sisters to bathe. Maybe they would allow us to take a bath. How wonderful it would be to set in some warm water and wash. We all need a good scrubbing and cleansing. Let us keep our fingers crossed, in hope they are willing to accommodate such a request from strangers."

Seeking to be Loved

Gilbert said, "I did not think of that, surely, they do. The only question being, are they willing to let us." He reached his arms for Nattie to hand Phillip to him. "I will carry him, it is nice to hold him in my arms so he can look about."

"Good idea, which way do we go", she asked while reaching for the reins. "Where should I aim this fine team of stallions."

"Just down the street, take the next left."

The children looked around with excitement. They catch the eyes of the townsmen, and women carrying their baskets full of provisions. Going home to prepare the evening meal for their families. Some of the shops, restaurants and bakeries are still open. Two men sitting at a table outside, the one nearest them raised a glass of wine at us as we passed by. They seem to be enjoying the little defile. Marilda turned the team, and noticed just to the left of the same square a large building with fields in front and to its sides. Reading the sign, she acknowledged, this is the monastery. She has never been to one nor, her family, she was not sure how she should present themselves. Then she thought, I will leave that up to Gilbert, he has been the spokesman for the family all along.

Gil told the children to keep everything close, I will go knock on the door. He saw no one, though he was impressed observing how well everything is groomed. There seemed to be a peaceful silence surrounding the property. He tapped the heavy metal ring on the door, he can hear the echo of footsteps inside. A few moments pass, he can hear someone walking toward the door from within. The door opened, and he was greeted with the words, "Good evening monsieur, May the Peace of God be with you. How may I help you?"

He introduced himself to the young woman. He made his request known, that he and his family are in need of a place to camp, feed, and water their animals for the night.

"Un instant s'il vous plaît(One moment please) monsieur," she closed the door. He can hear the footsteps walk away. He looked back at those in the wagon. He shrugged his shoulders and flared out

Seeking to be Loved

his hands. Marilda and the others observe him questioningly. He heard footsteps again, this time it sounded like many returning to the door. It opened, a middle-aged woman dressed in full habit, looked at him and beyond, taking note of the family and all their belongings. She introduced herself as Sister Marie. She looked at Gilbert and said that your request is not common. She asked how long do you plan on staying?

Only to early tomorrow morning," said Gil.

"Insolite en effet(Unusual indeed)," she exclaimed.

"We cannot turn you away, it is not our custom to do so. There is a trough just behind the building where you can water your animals, they may graze in the pasture beyond. You will be able to see a small barn in the back just beyond the trough. That is where we keep our animals. You may board your animals there if there is room. If not, please tie them so that they may not get loose and trample the grounds and garden."

He bowed his head in reverence to the sister. He then asked, "Is there any way that he and his family can be of service to you, my grace?"

She looked at him, "We will consider that. There are always many things we have need of assistance with. I will come back and meet you and your family later."

Gilbert said, "Merci," as she turned and walked back into the building.

Marilda suggest to Gilbert, "It may be best if you lead the horses. I would not want them to tear up any of the plantings that they have around the building and grounds. It is so well-kept." She thought to herself, simple, well-kept, and clean, she acknowledged there is need for reverence here. She directed the children to be quiet and respectful as they proceeded around the structure. There was a courtyard behind the main building, and the outbuildings. The little barn that housed their two cows, goats, and a few chickens, would never accommodate their animals. Beyond the barn a hill rose

Seeking to be Loved

not much higher than the big building itself. Examining the area, they noticed the property sets at a vantage point over the little town.

Ernest asked his father where the horses were to be placed.

Gilbert scanned the grounds, he can see there is no fenced area. We will tie them in the pasture over there. Ernest unharnessed them and walked them to the field.

Gil has Henry and Mary take the carts into the barn to unharnessed the goats and take them to Ernest. He will tie them near the horses, I will lead the cow.

Nattie had already began to unpack foodstuffs for dinner.

A few minutes later, Sister Marie and a few of the other sisters, dressed in their habits appeared. Following the nuns were several younger ladies. The girls were wearing similar colored gowns, it seemed the entire monastery was approaching them. Marilda, could see the joy in their eyes as they looked at her children, especially the younger ones and baby, Phillip.

These women and girls have devoted their life to serve God and their communities. They have vowed a virtuous life.

Marilda knew, because of her own motherly instincts, that the sight of children, especially an infant, could not help arouse the interest of their paternal instincts. She has Mary gather her siblings. Marilda introduced herself and all the youngsters according to their age.

The young nuns and girls appeared especially interested. They seem unable to keep from touching them. They placed their hands on the heads and shoulders, of the children. They all waited to take turns holding Phillip in their arms. He seemed pleased to let them, showing no signs of discontent. The sparkle in his eyes and smile on his face melts the hearts of each one as they hold, hug, and pass him to one another. They laughed and giggled. Many of the nuns and girls stated to Marilda, what a wonderful disposition this little boy has.

When Gilbert and Ernest return from the field they can hear and see all the cackling and laughter of the women folk. Ernest

Seeking to be Loved

looked at his father, Gil nodded his head slightly learned toward him and stated, "Women," they both chuckled.

Sister Marie breaks away from the crowd and meets Gilbert. She made a request of him. "We do have one small favor, if we may ask it of you." She looked at Ernest, "And you young man. We have had a leak in the roof, we think it is coming from one of the chimneys. We have pitch and tar, we are not sure how to get to it, or how to find exactly where it is leaking. Do you think you could help?"

Gilbert nods and asked her to show them where it might be. "It should not be too difficult to find. Do you have a bucket? We will fill it with water, then show us where you think it is leaking and we will test the area. That should allow us to observe where it may be coming from."

Sister Marie said, "We do, come let me show you." She guided him into the monastery and walked them upstairs to show him where water is causing stains and dampness.

He asked if there is an attic, and a way to get to it and to the roof up above.

She guided them to a narrow stairway. When he opened the door there is no light in the attic. He asked the sister if they had a lamp or a lantern and she said, "Oui, I will be right back."

While they are waiting Gilbert and Ernest's eyes had already adjusted to the darkness and they can see. At least enough to make their way over to where the chimney came through the floor and rose through the roof. Examining the rafters and floor area, they notice the stains caused by water. They looked up and they can see light coming through the roof. Gilbert said to Ernest, "This should be an easy fix. Finding it is usually the big problem."

They can hear the sister's footsteps, and met her at the door. Gil told her the area causing the leak had been located.

"Oh good," she said, and handed him the lantern.

They packed the openings with fibrous material from inside the attic first. Gil told Ernest we must now get on the roof and pack from above then seal it with the tar. They asked if she can show them a way to the roof?

She just shrugs her shoulders, "I do not know, where it would be."

Gil knew there must be a bulkhead somewhere in the attic. He took the lantern and searched the rafters until he found a framed section between them. He had Ernest hold the Lantern, as he unhooked the latches and pushed the cover up off of the hatch. Lifting it clear, he laid it aside. Then grabbed the edges and he pulled himself up onto the roof. Ernest handed him the packing and tar bucket as well as the trawl, which he will use to apply the tar around the chimney. It did not take long to seal to the cracks. When he finished he told Ernest, "That should take care of it nicely."

They stood and noticed a magnificent vantage point for viewing the countryside from the top of the monastery. The sun had just disappeared behind the mountain to his left, behind the building. It was casting shade onto the building. Looking north, then East, the sun still bathed the pastures and agricultural land, they traveled earlier that day. The sky was a brilliant blue with irregular puffs of clouds scattered here and there. It made for such an interesting image. The waning sun highlighted the verdant fields under the blue sky.

He took a deep breath and they lowered themselves through the opening. He replaced the lid, latched it securely and mentioned to his son, "Job well done, let us clean up and have dinner." Coming down the stairs, they met sister Marie. Gil explained what he did and assured her, it should not leak, at least not from that spot any longer. He asked what he should do with the tools and bucket as he handed her the lantern.

She directed him to take them into the shed near the barn. She thanked Gil and Ernest, declaring it is nice to have men around for such labor.

Ernest took a deep breath expanding his chest. He thought to himself proudly, that this was the first time anyone ever refer to him

Seeking to be Loved

as a man. Before they walked away Gilbert asked Sister Marie, the best way to get to St. Anne's Eglise, and an appropriate time to enter. He mentioned to her, after they have their evening meal, he would like to take his family there for devotion.

She is pleased, to hear that they are willing to devote time to the honor of their matron Saint. She turned to him and offered in such a pleasant voice. "We will be very pleased to take you there. If you like I will have one of the sisters meet you in a half an hour, to guide you and your family. It is very close and easy to get to, just around the corner really. I know the sisters would thoroughly enjoy assisting you. It will give them an excuse to spend a little extra time with the children. That is something we do not see much around here." She said, then turned and walked away.

The timing was impeccable, just as they were finishing their dinner and starting to put things away, a young girl not much older than Mary, approached them. She was not dressed in a habit, she wore one of the common gowns. The dress of the day of those who have not yet become nuns. She walked to Gilbert and introduced herself. "I am Angeline, sister Marie asked me to take you to St. Anne's."

The children are delighted, to have someone so young to guide them. It took only a few minutes for them to be ready. The evening was pleasant and clear, as they walked on the cobblestone streets of the little town leading to the church. They had many questions for Angeline.

Marilda asked if she lived in Clermont. "Were you born here?"

She said, "Non."

Mary asked, "Then where were you born?"

"Relms," she replied.

Marilda, mentioned that is not too far from here. What made you decide to come to the monastery?

Angeline identified I really did not have a decision in the matter. From what I have been told, I was only three years old, I barely remember anything about coming here. My father died and our mother could not take care of us.

"Us," Gil questioned.

"Oui, I had two brothers and another sister. We were all very young, the oldest was only seven years old. From what I was told the older ones went with aunts and uncles. I being so young needing care and supervision was sent here to be raised by the sisters. My mother went back to her parents, my grandparents. I was told, due to her grief she came down with the consumption, not long after our father died. It may have been a year or two, when my dear mother went to rest with our father.

"Do you ever see any of your family?" he asked.

"Oui, I do occasionally, usually at holidays they either send for me, or they come here to visit."

"Do you wish to be living with your family?" Marilda asked.

"I love my family very much, the sisters and the other girls here at the monastery, are my family now, I love them also. I believe my mother made a wise choice. She must have known I would be well suited for this life."

"You are a remarkable young lady Angeline, wise beyond your years," said Marilda. She gazed at Mary and Blanche, and asked if they would like to live in a monastery.

Blanche shouts, "Oui!"

Mary delayed before she replied. When she made her response she said, "I would have to look into it a little further. We did have a nun at Sunday school last year from a monastery. She explained to us about life there. It sounded very interesting, and a wonderful opportunity for many to devote their life to God."

Gilbert thought as he heard the words come from his oldest daughter's lips, "She is growing up." He whispered to her so only she could hear, "Well put Mary, very diplomatic."

Angeline pointed ahead as they walked along the paved path leading them around the hill that cast a shade over the walkway.

Seeking to be Loved

Now you can see St. Anne's. It is bathed in the light of the setting sun.

Henry and Blanche shout, "Woo," simultaneously.

Angeline revealed, "It is grand, although nothing like some of the big cathedrals in Paris. This is modest, compared to those."

"Have you ever been to Paris?" asked Mary.

"Only once, some of the sisters and I went on a pilgrimage there."

They walked up the stairs, Gilbert stepped to the front to open the door for his family. They enter and after blessing themselves at the font placed in the entry hall of the church, made their way to a pew.

The illumination is breath taking, observing the glow of the magnificent stained-glass windows. Many of the windows are representative of Saints and of course, St. Anne herself holding the blessed mother as a babe. They all follow the lead of their father and walked towards the altar. He stopped to kneel before a pew, then stepped aside and gestured to his family to enter. They each kneel facing the altar, made the sign of the cross and took a seat.

Once all are seated, Gilbert knelt to pray, the rest of the family followed his lead. Gilbert, in prayer, thanked God for a safe journey so far and the kindness that people have shown them. He offered thanks for the opportunity to be here, at this moment. Making a sign of the cross, he sat back onto the pew. He silently stepped into the aisle and bowed towards the altar.

He walked to the apse on his right. He is drawn to the statue of Saint Anne, staring for a moment before he lowered himself to the kneeler.

While kneeling he knows what is in his heart. He is not quite sure how to put it in words. He is uncertain whether to ask of God, once again the request in his heart. Or should he present his petition to St. Anne. He wondered how to ask and to who. He always had prayed directly to God, in the name of Jesus Christ, our Lord and Savior.

Seeking to be Loved

History has taught him, as well as experiences from people around him and scripture, that God has charged his angels and saints with duties to bestow graces on the faithful that request them.

He knelt before St. Anne's statue, he felt ignorant, a bit foolish, and indecisive. He is confused, he knew what to ask, and has already. So, why was he drawn to this Saint, to ask once again? Finally, he proceeded to ask the Good Saint Anne, to guide and protect his family on this journey. He glanced up at the statue, tears began to run down his face, the instant he began to make the request of St. Anne.

The Good Saint, who prayed many years for a child. She was barren well into her old age before she conceived. She loved her daughter Mary, she vowed before her conception, if God would grace her with a child, she would dedicate the child back to the Lord. The Good St. Anne, consecrated her only child to the Lord. The very child God had chosen, even before her birth, who was to be destined to be the blessed virgin mother, of our Lord and Savior. The Good St. Anne, who waited so long and so patiently, was rewarded with the grace of giving birth to the purest human being to be born to the world. She was so full of love and devotion, she had no choice but return the very gift, God had given her.

Gilbert knew how much he loved his own children and family. He could not imagine anything within this world that he would be willing to trade for anyone of them. He thought, "How pitiful I am, compared to you St Anne. For you have loved more perfectly than I can ever possibly. You had faultless, and absolute trust in our heavenly father. You returned your most precious gift, to God. The purest and most blessed to be born of man/woman, could only be conceived in such a pure vessel. Saint Anne, you gave the greatest gift the world can produce. The vessel that would bear our Lord and Savior. The entire human race will forever be indebted to you.

It was only his soul that could reach out to Saint Anne, to convey what his mind and body could not. To protect his love one's,

Seeking to be Loved

and to see them through this journey, no matter how trying and difficult it may become.

Gil felt shame, and disgrace. He could not imagine making such a sacrifice as the Good Saint. The realization of his unworthiness, to even ask for assistance and protection, caused him to feel even more ashamed. Words cannot enter Gilbert's mind, nor come forth.

He is being overwhelmed, by a flooding of his senses. He felt a warmth and a comfortable firmness. It was as though a force completely caressed every inch of his being, inside and out. It felt as though the heavenly father and the Good Saint are embracing him, his entire body, mind, and soul all at once. He knows how much he loves his own. It is pitifully pathetic compared to what he is experiencing at this moment. He could not speak nor register a single thought. Nothing can describe this adoration being given to him by our Lord and good saint.

Gilbert was oblivious to his surroundings during his meditation. He finally realized where he was when his prayer was complete. He regained his senses and his composure. He said to God, as well as St. Anne, "Merci".

When he stood up and looked around, the church was empty, and it had gotten dark. The only light was that of the candles, lit in front of the statues of the Blessed Saints.

He did not realize how much time had passed, he blessed himself, left the church and made his way back to the monastery. When he got back, he went to his wagon, no one was there. He went to the barn, neither did he see anyone with the animals. As he came out of the barn, he noticed Angeline, walking toward him.

"You are looking for your family Monsieur Guyon, they are all inside. They all had baths and are resting well."

"What time is it?" he asked.

"It is just after 10PM."

"You mean, I was there for more than three hours."

Seeking to be Loved

"I do not know how long you were there, monsieur. We left after about 30 minutes. I gave your family a tour of the church and the grounds. Your wife peaked in just before we left, to tell you we were leaving and to come back, when you are ready. She told us you were still there and that we should leave you."

He said, "I could have sworn it was only a few minutes."

She mentioned sometimes when we are deep in prayer, time alludes us, it may seem to stand still. God does not consider time, it is as though God is timeless. It is a reality that we cannot comprehend. For we only think and perceive time in minutes, hours, days, months, years, and lifetimes.

Gilbert listened in amazement, thinking to himself, how can such a young child, be so wise?

She ushered him into the room where all his family were sound asleep on cots. Marilda and Phillip, were asleep in the only bed. Gilbert nodded and thanked Angeline.

Her only response was, "Sister Marie told me, to mention breakfast is at 7AM. Please be our guest."

May 10, 1914 - Gilbert was the first to wake, he scarcely remembered placing his head on the pillow. He slept so soundly; the others still were. Phillip was the next to wake, Gils movement must have caused him to rouse. He slept between his mother and father that night. Phillip looked up at Gilbert and said, "Mom, Mom." Gilbert smiled broadly and shook Phillips little belly gently with his hand.

"Oui, it is you who is making that Mama sound." That had caused the awakening of Marilda. Gilbert kissed her good morning and whispered, "Your son is calling you. Listen to him!" Gilbert, putting his ear close to Phillip.

Phillip said, "Mom."

"You want your Mama?" he asked!

Phillip smiling turned his head slightly towards Marilda and said "Mom."

Seeking to be Loved

She picked him up smiling and said "Oui, I am your Mom." Then vibrated her lips on his neck, which made him giggle. She whispered, "You need changed and you must be hungry, little one."

Gilbert said, "I will get dressed and get the livestock ready." Looking at Marilda he mentioned, "That girl Angeline, is a remarkable young lady."

"Oui she is," replied Marilda.

He glanced around the room and said, "Look at this". He noticed everyone's clothes they had worn since they left his sisters in Metz, were clean and folded at the end of each bunk. We were lucky to find this place. He said, "Angeline told me, they would have breakfast at 7AM and we are to join them. You must go ahead and wake the children, so they can get their things packed and themselves ready and have this room in order and as clean as we have found it, before we go to breakfast."

After a modest breakfast, all in the monastery had gathered around the Guyon's wagon and carts, to bid them a farewell and safe journey. The mother superior graciously expressed her gratitude that the lord brought them here, when they were in need. She had been concerned for a long time about the leaks in the roof. She was certainly glad it was finally fixed properly. All the sisters and students said their goodbye's, and assured the family they would include them in their prayer and partitions to the Good Saint Anne, to protect them.

Angeline stepped forward and whispered something to Mother Superior, who looked at her and nodded.

She approached Marilda with and object in her hand. It was wrapped in a hand-woven doily. It had a five-centimeter crocheted lace around the outer edge and short-knotted tassels to prevent the exquisite work from unraveling. She handed it to Marilda imparting, "I want you to have this and take to Canada. If you happen to go to America, you must take it with you there."

Marilda inquired, "What is it?"

Seeking to be Loved

All the children and Gil, gather around to see what was wrapped in the cloth.

Angeline said, it is a vase. It was twenty centimeters high, ten centimeters wide at the base narrowing to 3cm at its neck and flaring out to four at the top crest. It was my mother's flower vase, she told them. It was given to her the day of my mother's birth, by her grandmother, it was made by her mother. It was filled with the peonies that came to bloom the day she was born.

Marilda, immediately handed it back to her, "We cannot accept such a precious personal gift."

Angeline refused to take it back from her. The young girl continued to explain, each spring my father would cut the fresh peonies on the morning of my mother's birthday. I can remember, though I was very young, he would let me select the flowers to place in the vase.

Marilda, was bewildered why Angeline wanted them to have such a beautiful personal piece. She finally spoke, "So, you really mean, that it came from your Great Great Grandmother?"

"Oui!"

"Did she make it," she asked while examining it? "Or." Before she could utter the rest of her statement.

Angeline interjects, "I was told she had made it, from what I understand, she was a very talented potter."

"Is this her name?" Marilda asked, while turning the piece upside down.

"Oui, madame! Eleonore Barineau"

The colors were brilliant shades of blues and greens. Greens covered the base and randomly rising as the base narrowed. The blues intermix until the neck forms. It flared out near the top and becomes blue as a magnificent sky, on the clearest day. At the top just inside the rim are various shades of white. The glazing of the vase was brilliantly clear and shiny. When the sun alighted on it, it reflected the light as if it were actually rising and radiating from inside the piece. Marilda is transfixed, as she slowly twirled it in her

Seeking to be Loved

hand to the right. Watching the sun as it appeared to be moving across a landscape of the vase. She happened to think, it is moving to the west, just as they and many families were.

Unaware of the pause as she appeared dazed, Gilbert asked Nattie, "Are you okay?"

Angeline sensing the awkwardness, spoke to break the uneasiness of the moment. "When my mother was about my age, her mother taught her to weave, embroider and do fine needlework. She learned and excelled at it, along with other artistry. She made this doily just for the vase. It rested on it while displayed on the hutch in our dining room."

"Why are you giving it to us and not keeping it? This is to precious, you must keep it," replied Marilda.

Angeline continued, "My mother always dreamed of going to America. She spoke of it often, I was very young, yet I remember her saying it. Poppa would say to her; 'You have big dreams.' This is the only thing I have of my mothers."

Marilda, stopped her in mid-sentence and said, "Your mother would want you to have this." She attempted to hand it back to her.

Angeline peered into Marilda's eyes. "Last evening at St. Anne's, during my adoration, to the Good Saint. The thought occurred to me, you should take the vase with you. That way the only part of what I have, from my dear mother, will get to America. It was as if, she was telling me to give it to you. That by doing so, it would have a safe passage, and would fulfill my mother's dream."

As soon as Angeline said the word "America," an odd sensation had come over Nattie. Her first reaction was to tell her we are going to Canada, not America. Before she could speak; everything had come to a complete stop. There was no sound, it was as though all came to a halt, time, even life itself ceased. How odd, she thought to herself. I have never had this sensation before.

She wanted to tell the girl, we are not going to America. We may never go to America. Without making a sound, she realized her head was slowly shaking side to side.

Seeking to be Loved

- Was it her attempt, to say no, we cannot accept such a precious gift?
- Could it be she is trying to understand what this strange, yet, somehow familiar feeling, sensation, awareness of going to or being in America, had brought on.
- Or was she attempting to reject, refuse the inevitable? She wondered why, but could not even imagine, due to the oddness and confusion going on inside her brain.
- What is this that is sweeping over me at this very moment? She wondered to herself, it seemed like much time had passed.
- Could it be she is attempting to deny what her subconscious already knew?

She refocused realizing she was still looking into the young girls' eyes. All the while, she had not missed a word, of what Angeline had expressed to her.

Angeline finished her statement, adding, "The Good St. Anne, was letting me know it would be safe on the journey. She assured me, that you and your family would be also. You see, you must take it, so all of you will be safe."

At that tears ran freely down her cheek and dripped off the smile she could not keep from her face. She could not possibly say no to Angeline.

Mary and Gilbert admired the artistry of the vase and doilies', and expressed how beautiful they were.

Gilbert thanked her and assured her it will always be given a place of honor, wherever they will be and reside. He looked to the mother superior and asked if it would be proper to embrace this dear girl.

She smiled and simply stated, that would be totally up to Angeline. Who opened her arms wide for a hug.

Marilda, and all the children gather around for their turn to hold close, this remarkable young lady whom they just met. Who had been so kind, and who now entrusted her most precious worldly possession to them.

Seeking to be Loved

Marilda can tell by the expression on Angeline's face, when Gilbert hugged her, that she dearly missed her own fathers loving embrace. She let all the children hug and thank her as she held Phillip. When it was her turn, Angeline, placed her hand ever so gently on Phillips head and kindly said, "Bless you little one, on your big journey." While Marilda wrapped her free arm around her, giving her Blessing to her as well.

Gilbert, request their address, so they may write.

The head mother simply told him; "We accept mail only from the diocese. We are committed to our daily duties and to what good we can do each day as it presents itself."

Gilbert's responded, "And you do that so well. We will never forget your charity and we will keep you in our prayers."

She expressed to Gilbert, "For that we all are very grateful."

As they leave, all kept turning to wave and repeat goodbye.

Nat is still pondering, the very odd sensation she experienced, when Angeline mentioned America. She could not help wondering why, or where such an odd sensation came from and for what reason.

It will be another long day of travel. Gilbert thought, if the traveling is good and the road not crowded with evacuees, he would like to make it to the town of Chalons-en-Champagne. That would be over 50km, he also knew anything beyond half of that would also be a good day. His sense of urgency to create distance between them and the east border of France returned.

Things were just beginning to stir in the town of Clement. Workers and business owners began to open shops and start their days labor. He was glad to be getting an early start before the streets got too busy. The day was magnificent, the air fresh and sweet, it passed without incident. Not much was spoken, Gilbert, assumed all were still dwelling on the brief stay at the monastery. He thought, what a privilege it must be to live such a sacred life. For people to toil each day and devote their entire life to our God and Creator. How peaceful it must be, to not have all the worry and anxiety associated with life, family and making a living.

- Do they not worry about war, or what is going on around the world?

- What must it be like to be living in peace with your existence?

Gilbert thought about the Scripture, where Jesus is telling the apostles, **"Peace be with you, My peace, I give you."** He thought, is this true, can there be peace? He thought of his experience kneeling before St. Anne's statue. He knows there can be.

He snickered to himself, acknowledging that as far back as he can remember, stories of his father, his grandfather, his great-grandfather and great great-grandfather have all fought battles for France. Even before France was a country, the old stories he heard about the Guyon Clan.

- A fiercely independent bunch, where does the fighting end?

- Where is the true independence? He thought to himself, we fight in battles from birth to death.

- Where is this peace our Lord and our Savior offers us?

His thoughts focus on Angeline. Is she content? "Oui."

He dwells for a moment on how peaceful she appeared to be. Especially at a time when girls her age are just full of themselves.

- Has she found this peace? She must have, how wonderful that one so young can possess, what so many cannot find!

- How can one accept the peace that our Lord and Savior speaks of? Peace, Gilbert thinks to himself, lies within each one of us, it lies within our soul. He could feel his emotion welling inside him, his eyes blurred.

- "Why can I not accept this peace you offer?

- Why Lord, do we struggle?

- Why do we think of so many things that bring anxiety into our life?"

When the reality is almost always those things never come to be. He made a decision then and there as he walked along, deep in his own thoughts in silence. I will accept this gracious gift, that our

Seeking to be Loved

Savior gave to each of us, residing deep within us. He will do whatever he must to teach his family about this same peace, that is bestowed upon each of us.

He thanked God for this revelation, he asked the Lord to help him, to put it into words, so he can share it with others, especially his love one's. To guide them in the understanding of this gift of peace.

The sign at the last crossroad intersection said 20km to the town of Chalons–en–Champagne. The sun was now leaning on the western horizon. Another 2 1/2 to 3 hours it will be dusk, he thought to himself. Gilbert could hardly believe the day had passed so quickly. He shouts to Nattie, for her to keep her eye on the lookout for a good place to stop for the evening.

Young Henry, told his father, "I sure am getting hungry." It sounded like an echo canyon, as each of the children in turn repeated the phrase.

Nattie, shouted back to Gil, "All I can see to the horizon is fields and pastures."

Gilbert suggest that they stop for a brief rest and nourishment, for themselves and the livestock. They had not stopped since they resumed walking after lunch, which he estimated probably was four hours ago or more. He was not sure of the time, it seemed to pass quickly today. He reminded himself to ask Nattie to unpack his watch when they stop for the evening.

Nattie agreed she thought that it would be a good idea to stop. She and the little ones needed to stretch their legs and move their bodies. They cross a bridge over a small stream, they decided this would be a good place to repose. There is grass and water for the animals. It looked like a peaceful place to rest themselves as well.

They will resume travel after the break until they find a good place to rest for the evening. Gilbert suggest that Nattie, be looking for lush green fields and a place with water would be ideal.

"I know Gilbert, I know", she turned to look at him quite queerly. Then stated to him matter-of-factly, expressing in a sarcastic

Seeking to be Loved

tone, "I know what to look for Monsieur Guyon, you failed to mention a place with some shade!"

Gilbert laughed and said, "You are right Madame Guyon." They passed several spots that would have been good. However, could see no farmhouse where the owners might reside. Even though others were stopping and setting up camp for the evening. They decided to find a place where they may ask permission. The sun had faded over the horizon and they knew they traveled over 12km. The last time they saw a sign, it identified 10km to their destination. Gilbert suggested that they should stop soon whether they can find the property owners or not.

She agreed and pointed out to Gil, "Look up ahead as the road curved. There where you see the trees, maybe a good spot." From her vantage point it appeared that they may be a spring or pool of water. Thinking out loud; she said, "That may be a good place to call it a day and to stop for the evening."

Gilbert looked and agreed.

The night was uneventful, all rested well after a long day's travel.

May 11, 1914 - They were awakened by unusual sounds, at least unusual to them, the last few days. It was the sound of voices, heavily laden wagon's, horses snorting and the strange sound of machinery. As they had camped close to the byway, that evening. The machinery sounds were produced by automobiles, a rare and very unusual site. They may have seen only one or two in their lifetime, usually on Sunday at church, when visitors attended service. This morning they have seen three within the first 25 minutes of waking.

Gilbert was usually one of the first to rise, and start the day. This past week he and his family were normally on the road by this time. Therefore, the sights and sounds that woke them seemed very strange. The machinery and loud voices, shouts is what broke the silence of the new day. Until just a few days ago, the usual and

Seeking to be Loved

expected morning sounds they awoke to were the chirping and songs of birds. Or their own animals and the gentle sounds of their parents' voices, that arose the young ones in the morning. The sun had already rose in the eastern sky as the highway was getting busy with people heading to the town of Chalons-en-Champagne.

It is a busy town of fair size, with an interesting history. It was a town that stood its ground in many conflicts and battles. It was here where one of the greatest barbarian rulers, Attila, king of the Huns, was repelled in his quest to assail the Roman Empire. Thus, stopping the advancement of the Huns in Europe. Much later in the 12th century Chalons's citizens with local militia twice repelled the English.

The church of Notre-Dame-en-Vaux, located here has had marvelous stained-glass windows installed nearly 400 years ago. Gil divulges to his children, one of them is of the great St.-Jean-Baptiste. There is some connection there to their family.

Gilbert does not know the details to share with his children. Although he has heard many stories from his father about his descendants. One of his great grandparents had shared the name of the great Saint.

"When we bless the food that we are about to receive this morning we must petition the great Saint, to guide and protect us on our journey. Whether he is one of our ancestors or not, he will be one of our patron Saints, of who we will request protection and guidance while we travel."   All agreed with enthusiasm!

Little Gilbert burst forth stating with glee, "We will have a safe journey with all the protection of so many Saints." They smiled, and laughed, confident of their saintly protection. Then they devoured their breakfasts and are in good spirits after a deep and restful night.

Gilbert said, we should make Epernay, easily today if all goes well, maybe much further. They will take the road that follows the Marne River. This should give them ample opportunities to stop for rest, water and give the animals good grazing. Once they had passed

Seeking to be Loved

through Chalons, the road was not quite as busy, until it neared noon when they were approaching the outskirts of the day's destination. With each intersection more people were joining the caravan. After they had stopped to rest, refresh themselves and fed the animals they decided to continue at a comfortable pace before retiring for the evening. Creating more distance between them in imminent danger. Throughout the day they overheard much talk of the impending doom of the villages on the eastern border. They heard many discussing and debating about Paris and its outskirts. Where would be the safest place if war broke out. While others stated, there is no place in France, that will be safe.

France always seems to be a gateway, to the conquering of Europe. Whether it be countries to the east, south or across the channel East and North. He heard many discussions of the proud patriotism, that has been this lands heritage for hundreds of years and occasional shouts of, "Vive La France."

Each time upon hearing it, his pride would swell within him and only for an instant would he doubt and question his decision. Whether he made the correct one by removing him and his family. Yes, it was for only an instant. For the love and protection of his dear ones, he would swallow his pride. He would not be in a restful state of mind until he finds what they seek. That of which would be a safe haven.

Eight kilometers to Damey, they began seeking a place to stop for the night. Preferably a place close to the Marne River. If they can find an area along its banks with easy access to water for the animals. Hopefully, it will be a peaceful place to spend the night, that is where they will choose to make camp.

They reached an intersection of roads heading to Damey, it took them further away from the river. They decided to stay on the route in hopes that the river would bend its course and they would once again be on its bank. It did, as they approached the town of Villemongeois.

Seeking to be Loved

    Marilda, noticed what appeared to be an ideal spot. A pasture followed the bend of the river. They found no houses of which to inquire permission to camp, near the immediate site. Gilbert confirmed the spot looked fine and suggested that she lead the team on the trail leading into the field. She drove the team to a small clearing on the riverbank without any plantings, just a few trees.

    Gilbert asked Ernest to climb the tallest tree and to see if he could determine which way to direct them to the nearest house or dwelling.

    Ernest located a small bungalow and barn, south of the road they had just come off, estimating probably a quarter kilometer off the roadway. He suspected it was about equal distance from their present spot as it was from the road.

    After they watered the horses, Gilbert placed a bit on one and rode bareback to the house. A young man met him as he entered through the gate. Gilbert asked who owned the land down the road along the river?

    The young man replied, "The land belongs to us, it has been in my father's family for over 300 years."

    Gilbert introduced himself and explained, "I have come to ask permission to stay on the property tonight by the river."

    The young man stated, "That would be up to my father, he is in the barn milking."

    Gilbert dismounted, and asked if he may speak with him?

    The young man directed him to follow him. Entering the barn, it took a few moments for his eyes to adjust, after coming out of the sunlight. He was struck by the familiar sweet smells, of grain, hay, fresh milk and yes, even the cow manure. They were smells that were so familiar and even though it has only been six days, he had missed the routine of the farm.

    The young farmer nudged Gilbert on his shoulder, pointing to his father sitting on the stool, milking one of the herd. He walked

Seeking to be Loved

over to his father and told him, this man would like for his family to stay near our fishing spot along the river.

The man without interrupting his milking rhythm, asked how many are in his camp?

Gil said, "My wife and I and seven children."

The man replied, "You can see the fields have been seeded and are beginning to sprout. If you swear to do no damage to the fields, you will be welcome to stay. Keep your brood on the grass patch, down by the river, just around its bend. You will find a field of fresh grass, for your horse to graze. You are welcome to let it feed."

Gilbert told him, a have a team of two, a cow, 2 goats, a few sheep, and fowl.

"The field will support them, you will see. Monsieur, I warn you keep them tied. If there is damage done to the crops, I will expect payment for what would be lost."

Gilbert agreed to the terms.

The farmer simply turned his forehead still leaning it on the cow, noticing the pale was nearly full he said to his son, "Get another bucket."

Without looking up, he said to Gilbert, "You will find the fishing is very good at that spot. May you have a restful evening."

Gilbert thanked him, as he left the barn. He could not wait to get back to his family. The thought of having fresh fish for dinner sounded quite appetizing. He knew that would excite the entire family, especially the boys, when it came to catching them.

Upon returning to his family he wore a solemn expression on his face. Making them wonder whether the news was bad, and they were going to have to move on.

Marilda finally inquired of him what was wrong, wondering whether he received permission to stay or not.

Although he tried, Gilbert could no longer keep a straight face. A large smile slowly appeared across his face. Followed by loud laughter, as he looked to the sky. By this time, the whole family had gathered around him. He said. "Oui we can stay, we can graze the animals."

Leaning forward looking at each of the boys, then said, "We can fish for our dinner. The landowner told me, where we are (he is pointing to the river), right here at this very spot, this bend of the river, the fishing is excellent."

A concerned look came over Ernest's face, as he mentioned I did not think to pack any of our fishing poles.

Gil smiled and said, "I always keep some tackle in the toolbox, that would serve nicely. If you, Henry and Gilbert can find some nice straight branches."

The boys look at each other with excitement, little Gilbert shouted, "I am going to catch the biggest one."

"I hope you do, if it starts to drag you into the river we will grab and hold on to you and pull you and that big ole fish in. Then we will give that fish to Momma, she will cook it, and we will dine like kings and queens this evening.

First, we must get the animals settled for the night and guide them to the pasture. Let us take them down around the bend of the river to drink, so we will not disturb the fish at our campsite.

Once the animals were tied off, they return to camp. He sent the boys to find branches that would serve well for fishing poles. He prepared the gear, tying on hooks to line and attached it to the poles as each of the boys handed them to him. Then he sent all the boys on a mission to gather bugs, crickets and to look under rocks for worms. They soon had one of his buckets filled with a variety of insects, grubs, and worms. Ernest lifted the lid to show his father.

Henry said, "The fish should be interested in at least one of these." They certainly brought back a great variety of bait to choose from.

Their father suggested they all try a different bait to start with. Once they saw what the fish preferred, that would be the bait of choice. Fishing was slow initially, once the sun cast shadows on the river the fish began to bite more readily. They soon had more

Seeking to be Loved

than enough for dinner. While they were cleaning them, Marilda suggested if they keep biting and the boys keep catching, she will smoke the extra overnight. That would preserve them and supplement their supplies for their journey. She added, "You never know what tomorrow will bring."

Gil thought that was a wonderful idea. He looked to the boys, and asked them, "Do you think we can catch a few more fellows?"

Little Gilbert was the first to respond shouting, "We can catch a whole wagon full."

His mother smiled, "If you can catch that many, I will have to give some to the man who owns this land as payment for his generosity."

Gil looked at Nat and said, "That is a wonderful idea. It would be a great way to repay him for use of his land." He admits, "Your seasoned smoked fish is a delicacy, I am sure very few have ever experienced, outside of our little town."

Nattie, produced a quirky confident looking grin on her face. With a cocky expressive tone in her voice said to Gil, "You and the boys catch them. The girls and I will season and smoke them." She suggest to Gil, "If you can find some apple trees or cherry trees, smoke from their wood will add flavor to the fish."

"I have seen a few on the way to the pasture, I will go gather some now," replied Gil.

He knew the boys would much rather fish than do another chore. He instructed them to go catch some more and to be careful, keep an eye on their little brother. Ernest and Henry agreed they would.

Gil had gathered enough dry branches and a few of the bare green ones from the apple trees. While he was tying them to carry back, he heard shouts and screams. He ran to the riverbank, to see what was causing the commotion. Not being able to see up around the bend, he quickly followed along the riverbank. He heard splashes, thinking one of them must have slipped into the river. By the sound of panic in their voices he knew something was wrong. He ran toward the sight. He heard Ernest, shouting to his mother. Who was already bedside them on the river. "We cannot see him anymore!"

Gilbert stopped to scan the river. He saw in the slow-moving current, a wake with its point coming down stream, slightly to river left. He knew something was being pulled from under the surface of the water. "What could it be?" His first thought was either fish or turtle. The next thought was something big was dragging his youngest son through the water. He dove into the river, anticipating the direction it was dragging him with the current. When he surfaced, he saw the direction of whatever it was had changed its course. Whatever was dragging him through the water, had swerved just above shoals in the middle of the river. He swam as fast as he could. The rivers current forced his son onto the rocky shoals. Gil is slipping and stumbling to get footing but was not able. Not until he found himself in water shallow enough for him to gain footing, was he able to stand. Now on his feet, he was able to see his son on the shoals rocky bottom, which had trapped and held little Gilbert securely. He observed his son struggling in an attempt to stand. He was unable to establish his footing, just as he could not an instant before. Gil was frantic as he ran through the shallows, to get to his son.

Gil observed the death grip, his son had on the branch he was using for a fishing pole. As he got within arm's reach of little Gilbert, he noticed the strain on his sons arms. What it was that was on his line was stretching them to what appeared to be twice their normal length. He reached for him, grasped his hands around his sons waist, and lifting him right out of the water.

His son shouts, "Let me go father." Being held securely in his father's arms, the branch broke. Gilbert squeezed and hugged his son, who was gasping for breath.

Little Gilbert can only muster the words of anger, "It got away."

Seeking to be Loved

Gil was lost for words. He was just thankful he was able to retrieve his son from the river. Once he calmed down, he heard shouts from the riverbank just up above them. Asking, "Is he all right? Is he hurt?

"He is okay," Gil shouted! He made his way through the shallow shoals to the bank, they rushed down to meet him at the shoreline. As soon as he reached the bank of the river, Nattie, grabbed her son from Gil's arms.

As soon as he is secure in her arms, she said, "Oh Non, where is Blanche, Joseph and Phillip?"

Mary spoke up, "I told them all to stay right where they are. I told Blanche and Joseph to watch Phillip."

"Get to them right now," ordered her mother.

Gil said, "We will all join you."

All little Gilbert can talk about was that big fish.

Ernest sarcastically told him, "It is always the big one that gets away."

His father mentioned, "I think that fish caught you, I am glad that you got away." The children laughed.

Marilda sternly retorted, "It is not a laughing matter. Your brother could have drown in that river. I do not see the humor in that."

Gil knew not to say a word, just to agree with her. He knew it could have very easily, turned out disastrous. Once again in the silence of his heart and mind, he thanked God, for helping him save his son.

He told his family, "We all must be very careful, we all must be looking out for one another continuously, not just on this journey but always. Anything could happen to anyone of us at any moment. It is just but for the grace of God, that we make it through each day. I do not want to see anything happen to any of you. I would not want to lose any of you to the river or anything else. We do not want to see any of you get lost or hurt, in the cities we will be entering, nor the great ocean, we will be crossing.

Seeking to be Loved

Each day we will travel to areas we have never been. We know nothing of the people we will be coming in contact with on this journey. We may face many challenges before reaching our destination. There will be many places where getting lost or separated from each other will be very easy. Let us all make a vow right now to be on the guard and constantly be looking out for one another."

When they got back to the camp, Nattie was relieved to see Mary with all three children. She went over and hugged each one of them. She suggested that Gilbert start a fire right away, to dry their clothes. She too had become sopping wet carrying little Gilbert.

After dinner when all have had their fill of fresh fried fish, the first rack of fish was drying and being smoked by the fireside. They sat by the fire, listening to the fish stories of the boys. Gilbert made each one in turn starting with himself, going from oldest to youngest of his family, take the vow, he spoke of at the river. The vow was that each one from this day forward would be constantly on the lookout for one another at all times. Each in a solemn tone did so, a promise to one another, to be always vigilant and aware that anything could happen at any time anywhere. All promised and solemnly swore to look out and protect one another always.

There was silence around the campfire.

It was Gil, who finally broke the silence. "I wish I knew what it was that caught Gilbert. Did anyone see it, he asked?"

Ernest and Henry both replied, "We did not see a thing. All we heard, was Gilbert, shout woooo and a splash. By the time we turned our heads to look, all we saw was the ripples in the river where he went under and then the wake it made going out to the middle of the river and then downstream. We started shouting immediately, not knowing what to do."

Ernest told his family. "I wanted to jump in after him. I did not know where to go, he was underwater, we could not see him. I just started yelling for help."

Seeking to be Loved

"It was a good thing you did," said his father. "It was important to alert all of us quickly. It was fortunate the shoals were so close to where you had been fishing. It helped that the current was strong enough to keep Gilbert's momentum going downstream, so he could get stuck and lodged in the shoals."

"Maybe that big fish knew if he could get that line caught on a rock, it may snap it and get away," said Henry.

"That must have been a smart fish," said Blanche.

Henry commented, "They do live in schools."

"It is no wonder they are smart," replied Blanche.

Little Gilbert spoke up, "I was not going to let that one go. I told you I was going to catch the biggest fish."

"Oh yeah, well where is it then?" Questioned Ernest, "If it gets away, you did not catch it."

"I did not let it go, it broke my pole," was little Gilbert's defense.

"Well, you did not catch it then," said Henry, "And that is that."

Marilda spoke up, "Enough of this fish talk. You all did very well catching so many. We should not go hungry for the rest of this journey. Now it is time for you all to get some rest, get under your blankets."

Gilbert agreed and reiterated their mothers instructions, for them to get some rest.

Nattie and Gil sat by the fire tending it, smoking the fish. She said to Gilbert, "You need to get some rest, you have been on your feet all day long."

"I will sleep here by the fire with you," he said and kissed her. With his head close to her side, she gently rubs her fingers through his hair.

"Why did he not just let go of that fishing pole?" She whispered to Gil. He could have died, over that fish. It was horrifying. I was in such a panic and fear. I would say, I was almost in a state of shock. I am so glad you reacted so quickly. Why did he not just let go?"

Gazing at the fire, his only reply was, "Sometimes you just cannot let go, no matter how much you want to."

She said, "I would let go in a heartbeat. I would much rather let go, than allow myself to be dragged underwater. No way, no fish, no anything is that important."

For a moment they were silent.

Gil replied philosophically, "In life, one is faced with many situations where it would be easy to let go. Yet one just refuses, something inside tells you, you must hold on. Through thick and thin no matter what the outcome."

- "Why is that?" she questioned.
- "Why do men think like that?
- Is that why there are so many wars?
- Do people think they have to hold on to things, or take things? And are willing to die, for that?
- Why can we not, just let go, of certain things?
- Why must we struggle and risk our very life?
- For what, to hold something or get something that is going to get away, and is going to perish one day, anyway?"

"I wish I knew Nattie. I guess, it is just in our nature."

"Why? We are not holding on to what we had!"

"In a sense we are Nattie," said Gil.

"What do you mean?"

"We are making this journey to bring our family to a safer place. For fear of the potential loss of one of them, to something that we are not even sure of."

"The war," she whispered. "We are given up everything we have in this world," she said.

"Non," Gil replied. "We are preserving and holding on with our dear life, to the most precious things we have."

"Our children," she whispered. She leaned over and kissed him on his forehead, whispering, "Je t'aime."

Seeking to be Loved

May 12, 1914 - Gilbert woke to the sound of the fire crackling, he had slept well. Apparently, the children had also, they were still sound asleep. Although Nat, only dozed off occasionally throughout the night, was still sleeping lightly. Gils movements woke her.

She checked the fire as she did all night, assuring the fish would smoke evenly and dry thoroughly. She did not feel that tired or sleepy especially after the scare that she had. She also attributed it to riding all day in the wagon and not getting the exercise that the others did. The little naps she took throughout the night, left her refreshed.

She worried about Phillip, which also kept her awake. She wondered how he will endure such a trip, in the coming weeks. At this point he seemed to be faring well, and is comfortable. She knew it had to be hard on such a young infant. She wondered about her own milk, knowing that if she does not keep her body refreshed, in good health, she may not be able to produce enough to nourish him. She whispered to herself, "It is good that he is starting to take other foods to supplement his diet."

She smiled as she thought, "He seemed to thoroughly enjoy bread dipped in cow's milk mixed with a tad bit of honey. She snickered to herself, as she considered, who wouldn't."

She was actually glad she had the fish to dry, it kept her busy and from excessively worrying. It would have been an awful long sleepless night if she had nothing to do.

Gilbert stood up and kissed her and bids her good morning.

She responded the same.

"I will check the animals and take them to the river to drink," Gil said.

"I will start breakfast, I will not wake the children until you get back," replied Marilda.

"After they eat, I will have them pack everything up and to get ready to leave. We will be heading to the town of Dorman's,

Seeking to be Loved

today. We should be there in a few hours. That is if nothing impedes our travel. From there I would like to get as close to Château Thierry, as we can before stopping for the day. That will be close to 50km." He realized that may be unreasonable. "It is a lot to expect, if we can get close that would be a good days progress," said Gil.

"From Chateau Thierry, how far is it to Paris," Marilda asked. She handed him a bowl of the dried fish. This is for you to bring to the landowner."

He replied, "Nearly another hundred kilometers, four to five more days of travel, if no unforeseen delays; three if we are lucky."

She explained, "We have nothing else to wrap the fish in. Mention to him, his wife will have something to transfer it into. Please be sure to bring the bowl back."

It was noon when they reached Dorman's. Gilbert knew at the pace that the people were moving on today's migration, they would be lucky to get within 15km of Château Thierry today.

They would spend the night camped near a small stream just off the road, just east of their destination they had set for the day. Near the village of Chierry and camped along the Ruisseau de Chierry, for the night. The evening and night were uneventful. The only disturbance came, twice during the evening. Angry villagers had been shouting at trespassers. We could only make out, that someone was accusing someone of stealing or taking something that did not belong to them. We were glad we stayed a distance from any of the property owners. Gilbert, was feeling guilty, about not seeking out the owner of the land they camped on. It had been very late, they were weary, from the long day.

May 13, 1914 - When Nattie woke, Gilbert was already awake, lying silently beside her. He whispered, "Bon jour," and kissed her lips.

She asked, "How long have you been awake?" Before he could answer, she mentioned, "I cannot believe Phillip, slept through

Seeking to be Loved

the night." She turned her head to look at him. His eyes were wide, bright, and alert. He smiled broadly when their eyes met. Marilda reached to gather him into her arms, "Someone else is awake. Father like son," she whispered in the sweetest most lovingly voice she can muster. Which brings delight to both Phillips and his father's heart, both smile ever so broadly when they hear the familiar sound of it.

Nattie tends to Phillip, Gilbert gathers his things together in the dark. He tugged on his boots, and buttons his shirt. He began his morning routine of chores, feeding the animals while the children slept. He did not mention to Nattie, the concerns he felt and pondered all night long. Many things had raced through his mind, brought on by the commotion. He feared the anticipated difficulties they may face ahead.

They are maybe two, three or more days from Paris. The masses joining the caravan at each intersection adding to the pilgrimage to the capital city, was unnerving. Gil was wondering with uncertainty, the nature of man. Thoughts of the warning from Marilda's father, kept his mind busy. He was having difficulty comprehending what one might do when fear and panic are the rule of the day. He busied himself physically, he was glad to have chores to do to break his chain of thought. The thoughts that kept awakening him during the night. He was glad Phillip was awake, so he did not have a chance to share his own concerns with Nattie. He knew he did not need to worry her any more than she may already be.

While watering the stock, there was not much commotion. A dog barking in the distance, as the day was starting to get lighter, the sun had not quite risen on the horizon.

He looked up as he noticed movement, there was something a few hundred meters away. He watched as a person came into view, walking towards him. He noticed that he was carrying something. A man with an aggressive gait, walking in his direction. He was close enough to make out the image. He had something under his arms

Seeking to be Loved

and a mallet in his hand. It was apparent this man was approaching him. He had a cross demeanor on his face.

Gilbert nodded cordially to him, when he was close enough to hear, using a quiet humble voice. Gil bid him good morning, the man squared up with Gilbert.

"You are on my property? What are you doing here?" The man questioned Gilbert. "You did not ask permission to be here."

Gilbert can see the tension and anger in the man's face, it was inherent in his voice. Gil understood this is the landowner, he bowed his head, and stated he and his family are travelers and they only wished for a place to spend the night.

We are not familiar with the area. We did not know who owned this property. I was not sure who to ask and it was very late. We did not want to disturb anyone. If this is your land, I apologize for not asking your permission. It bothered me all night that we stayed here, without your consent. Gilbert's words and humble speech diffused the man's anger.

The man was not quite sure how to respond, he was expecting more confrontation. He can only utter in a gruff voice, "I hope you do not plan on staying."

"I apologize, and let me graciously thank you, for allowing us to stay here last night. We will be on our way as soon as we can gather our things together, and I feed my children. If that is agreeable to you?" stated Gil.

"Oui, as long as you will be off my land soon. I do not want people destroying my property and stealing from my family."

Gilbert told him we hope to be on the road before the sun rises.

"Be sure that you are," the man stated. He turned and walked away.

Gil observed the man hammering signs on all post and rails that were around the front of his property. The print read "Aucune Intrusion,"(No trespassing).

Seeking to be Loved

When Gilbert returned with the team to the camp, Marilda had asked him, "Who was that man?"

He is the owner of this property. Many people must have been stopping here to camp. Like us, they may have not asked for permission. He also seemed concerned and fearful, probably because of damage and or thievery. We overheard some of that last night. Gil wanted to share with Nattie, the things he was thinking all night preventing him from sleeping soundly. Something told him to keep those thoughts and fears to himself. He mentioned to her, we cannot remind ourselves or the children enough. We must always be alert at all times. Always vigilant of each other's care and safety. It seemed like the more people we run into and more congested the roadway gets, the more trying our journey becomes.

She said you are right, we must instill in all of our young ones to look out for one another always, not just on this journey. I suspect the more crowded it gets, the more alert we must be. Let us keep an eye on everyone. Not to mention keep an eye out for others, we must be leery and weary of all on this trek.

Gilbert studying Marilda's eyes, "You are a wise woman and such a good mother."

She laughed and said, "After eight births, one gains some experience and with years hopefully wisdom." With that she paused, with a muffled tightness in her voice quietly whispered so only they can hear. "We must not take anything for granted on this trip or for now on."

Thinking to himself, "Such a beautiful, intelligent, caring and wise woman." Gil kept his word, they were on the road before the sun appeared on the eastern horizon. They were glad to be on their way early; they had the road to themselves.

The Guyon's observed many still in their camps. Some in tents, some slept in wagons, some underneath them. Soon people were everywhere on both sides of the road.

An uncomfortable feeling kept coming over Gil. He brushed it off due to the lack of sleep. Despite what little bit of restless sleep he

Seeking to be Loved

had gotten that previous night, he knew it was something else. The children did not have much to say, they just seemed preoccupied watching the people as they passed by. In those early hours, the traffic got heavier and heavier, as more people joined the caravan. As the day progressed the caravan became a train of people. Most in wagons or driving heavily laden carts of all sorts and being pulled by all manner of beasts. Some being pulled by the people themselves. A few sojourners were carrying just what they could on their backs.

Henry mentioned to his father after they passed a family walking on the edge of the road carrying their possessions. Those packs are so big how can they carry them Papa? How could they carry them all day long?

Gilbert said to Henry, "Some of those packs are bigger than the people carrying them."

A thought occurred to him, something his father shared with him many years ago, although it seemed like it was just yesterday. He realized this is an opportune time for another lesson for living life. He spoke loud enough, so all his children could hear.

"We all have our loads to bare, in life. We must always do what we can when we can. I want each one of you to know, you must always be willing to bare your own load. Living will require us to bare many different loads throughout life. For example, your chores, who does more you or your brother Gilbert?"

Henry speaks up first, "I do way more than him."

Ernest added "And I do way more than you."

His little brother looked at them oddly, then at his father. Little Gilbert wanted to say something, but, had no defense.

Gil continued, "You are older and stronger. You proved you can do more. You also started out doing just as he is. When you were able to do those chores well and efficiently, you were given greater duties and responsibilities. When our load gets greater, God gives us the strength and knowledge we need to move on. We find ways to do more important things."

Seeking to be Loved

Henry who is closest to his father, figured it out. He said, "So that is why, you had Gilbert doing my job in the field and now I am helping Ernest and using the tools. That is why you drive the team pulling the equipment."

Little Gil spoke up, "That is why I am picking up stones."

"Oui, and as we learn to do our chores, lessons in school and we learn more, we are giving new duties and responsibilities. Sometimes in life our load may seem too much. We see only what is in front of us. Just like when we get up in the morning, we have many daily chores and with each season additional things that must be done. It is never ending, we wonder how can we do everything in the time we have.

Many things will try to stop us or slow our progress, weather, equipment breakdowns, trees falling in our fields, animals or we get sick. It seems we will never be able to catch back up. No matter how difficult things may seem to be at times, you will be able to bare it and get through. It does not matter where you are or what your circumstances may be. Life is full of difficulties, trials, tribulations, and opportunities. When we accept it as part of life, which it is. When we understand everything whether it appears good or bad, is a test that has been presented to us by God.

With that we also know by not giving up or giving in to anger and frustration, we will deal with each issue and do what is necessary.

The lord always provides new ways to get us through, to bare the load he gives us. As well as joy and satisfaction when at the end of the day, when we acknowledge we did what we could. We carried our load this day, without compromising our integrity or our dignity. It is the loads we place on ourselves that can be the most damaging."

"What do you mean Father?"

"That is a lesson for another day," said Gil.

Little Gilbert asked, "What is dignity Papa?"

Gil without breaking stride, picked him up to carry him. In a bold voice he spoke to his children as they walk along. Dignity is a

Seeking to be Loved

state of mind. When you have a proper pride and self-respect. When you know in your heart and mind, that you are honorable, noble and you respect yourself and others. One projects it in his or her appearance, mannerism, and actions.

What is noble Papa?

Gil laughed. "Noble is an interesting word. It has many meanings. One noble was a form of gold currency/argent in England. A noble, may be a title of someone who is high ranking in your country. What I want each and every one of you to know as to the definition of noble is this.

To be noble is to have great character, having and always showing high moral qualities and ideals.

I wish for you my dear ones, to always be noble, to always have great dignity and be of good character. Promise me this, he looked at Ernest, expecting a response.

Ernest acknowledged and said, "I will Father."

He looked at Mary, "I will Papa."

Then Henry walking beside him, he said "I will Papa." Before he has the chance to look at Gilbert, who is still in his arms, he shouts out, "I will too Papa. I will be the most noble of all."

Gilbert squeezed him in his arms, laughing he said to his son, "I bet you will, you will be the noblest of nobles."

As they walked along for a few moments in silence.

Ernest broke the silence, as he exclaimed; "If that would be the case, you would be like Joseph, in the Old Testament."

Gilbert comments, "That is a good analogy, Gil is not the youngest in our house, but one day he may be noblest of nobles."

Mary said, "I cannot imagine myself bowing down to him."

Ernest, Mary, and their Father laughed, Henry and little Gilbert were not quite sure what to laugh about. Not being familiar with the story of Joseph, the youngest son of Jacob in the old Testament.

They made it through the town of Château Thierry before noon. It was fun crossing over the Marne river twice, large bridges such as those they crossed were a novelty and the source of excitement for the young ones.

Going through the towns large and small was always interesting and exciting for the children.

On the island was a busy community, just thinking people lived and worked on an island in the middle of a river was a novel thought-provoking experience. It was interesting driving their wagon, carts and walking the animals through the town of Château Thierry.

Gilbert hoped to make it to Montréuil-aux-Lions today. He now had his doubts, due to the slowed progress of the mass of people. So many family's on the move. They still had nearly 25km to go, it did not seem likely they would make it today.

Everyone's energy was high including his own despite the restless sleep. Other than stopping to water the animals and give them time to graze, he suggested to Nattie, they eat on the move. They decided to stop only when it was necessary. He suggested that he lead the team when she needed to change Phillip, so they would not have to stop.

Marilda, thought that was a good idea and identified that I will take turns having the children ride in her place. I will walk and carry Phillip in his sling. Giving those that are walking time to rest.

Gilbert said, "That is good thinking, to get them off their feet for a while."

Progress being slow, they averaged just a little over two kilometers an hour. Because the constant contact and close proximity of all the travelers, there was never a dull moment. So many people and their belongings traveling in one direction. There were the occasional onlookers and people coming toward them on the other side of the road going about their daily business. The hours passed so did the kilometers. By late afternoon many were stopping for the day, the highway became less crowded. Fewer people and families blended in at the crossroads, 10km to Montréuil-aux-Lions. Gilbert estimated it being close to 5PM by the position of the sun.

Seeking to be Loved

Thinking to himself, I must remind myself to find my watch. It will help me keep better track of time.

He asked all the children how they were doing and holding up, as well as Nat. All said they were doing fine.

Nattie identified walking felt good, especially after riding so much the last two days.

Gil suggested that they continue another two hours on the road. He reasoned now that it is less crowded, they should make better time and hopefully get within five or 6km of the destination. After an hour, Nattie was ready to take the reins of the wagon and ride with the younger ones and Phillip.

Gilbert suggest she look for a good place to stop, with pasture and water for the night. There were plenty of pastures, but no streams, springs, or ponds along the route for several kilometers. They were tired, the sun was nearing the horizon in the western sky facing them.

Gilbert was getting concerned, the animals needed water as well as they themselves needed to stop, it is getting late. The countryside was magnificent farmland as far as they can see in all directions. There was no one else on the road. All had set up camps for the night. He asked several campers if they had a water supply close by? The only response from them was, "Non". The people were short, not very friendly with their greetings or response.

The Guyon's pace had slowed again, this time not because of traffic on the road, but fatigue. He apologized to his family. He told Nattie, "We have to keep going to we find a water supply. she knew that. I pray that it will be soon, at the last crossroads the sign said 2km to Montréuil-aux-Lions. That was long ago."

The sun was now at the horizon, casting the last of its glow on the land. The various shades of green in the pastures presented a magnificence array of vivid colors enhanced by the weaning sunlight. It was mesmerizing, observing the last rays of sun reflecting off the outcropping of tree's before dusk. It was a needed distraction from their plodding along, in their semi-conscious state of mind. No one

Seeking to be Loved

spoke for a long time, it would have taken too much energy. Just marching along and Gil could only imagine, how weary his family and beast must be.

Marilda broke the silence, "There seems to be a small farm, up on the left."

"We better stop there, they should have a water supply that we cannot see. A pump, or a well, something," said Gil.

"That crossed my mind also," she agreed.

It seemed some spirit and a little bit of life came into each. As each had a comment, starting with Mary saying - "Thank God," Ernest - "Amen," Henry - "Praise the Lord." Little Gilbert was sleeping in his father's arms, Blanche, Joseph, and Phillip all sleeping on the floor of the wagon, under the buckboard.

Marilda turned the wagon on the worn path, leading to the house.

Gil was glad that it was fairly close to the highway. He handed little Gilbert to Ernest. Then walked to the door and knocked. The master the house opened it. Gilbert removed the hat from his head and introduced himself.

"Who is at the door A.B.?"

Gil heard a woman's voice from within ask the man.

"Strangers," the man replied, "It looks like he has a whole hoard of young ones with him."

"It is late you must invite them in." The voice replied from another room.

A. B. stared at Gilbert, and asked, "What is it you want?"

Gilbert explained, "We and our animals are in great need of water and rest. Would you be so kind to direct us where we may find water and a place to camp for the evening?" Gil heard the voice again.

"Why have you not invited them in?"

"They need rest and water, and a place to stop for the night." The man shouted back.

Seeking to be Loved

Gil observed the woman approaching from behind the gentleman. He stepped aside to allow her to see Gilbert standing in the doorway.

"You look tired and hungry. How many are there of you?" She asked in a demanding tone.

"There are nine of us Madame."

The man and woman look at each other in an awkward and amazed glance. She ordered her two sons to go out and help these strangers and care for their stock. Then she invited them into their home. She called Merriam, you come to the kitchen and help me prepare some food for these people. Gilbert recognized a young woman's voice reply, "Oui Mama."

The man looked at Gilbert then said, "She has spoken. Let me help you with your gear."

The woman nearly pushed A.B. out-of-the-way. She walked to the wagon to greet her guests. She is amazed and gasp when she eyed two sleeping infants. A young man holding another sleeping in his arms and near him two other children standing next to the wagon. She said, "You all must be exhausted, where did you come from? How long have you been on the road? There have been so many travelers!"

All before Marilda could say a word, all she can blurt out was, "Bless you Madame for your willingness to let us stop here."

The woman assisted Marilda from the wagon. She was not aware there was a baby sleeping, in the sling slung around her shoulders. "Let me get a look at the little darling," she asked as she lifted the cloth covering the child. "What a peaceful content little thing." She got up on the tiptoes to see the others sleeping on the floor. She exclaimed, "The poor tired darlings!"

She ordered her sons to help with the animals, even though they have already initiated the task.

Gilbert stepped forward suggesting to the boys as they pass by him walking to the horses, "They need water more than anything. Is there a place we can water them?"

Seeking to be Loved

They already had begun to unhitch the team, going about the task. Although quite young they are able and knew exactly what to do with all the livestock.

"In the house you all go." The woman said to Marilda and her children. "It is so late to be stopping, you all look so tired."

Marilda said, "We had hoped to stop much earlier than this but could find no place where we can let the animals get a drink."

"Oui," replied the woman, "There are no good streams or ponds anywhere near the roads for many kilometers."

Marilda, in agreement said, "That we well know."

The woman told Merriam, to heat up some cider, glancing over her shoulder at all the children. You better prepare it in the big pot.

Marilda said, "Water will do just fine."

"Non, you need something more nourishing, something that will put life back into those bodies of yours," she said. "Now, let me take that young one from you. You and the children go clean up there at the pump, right outside the back door, you go on." The woman helped her remove the sling, as Marilda handed her the child briefly to rearrange her dress.

Merriam got a few towels and handed each of them one as they passed through.

Little Gilbert was still asleep in Ernest's arms. Finally, he is awakened by the commotion and the crisp volume of the woman's voice, shouting out her orders. Still clinging to Ernest's as they were walking through the kitchen.

Merriam turned around with towels to hand them.

Ernest's and Gilbert's eyes opened wide, they are bright and seemingly bulging out of their sockets. As they acknowledged Merriam's attractiveness.

Ernest thought, "She must be about my age."

She looked at him, handing him a towel and directs him to the pump out back. "Go through that door, you get that cute little

159

Seeking to be Loved

boy and yourself cleaned up. We will have cider ready for you when you come back inside."

Ernest was tongue tied. He wanted to say something that would sound intelligent. Something that would cause her to think well of him. Nothing comes to his mind, the awkward moment which was only a few seconds seem to paralyze him for a long time. He just stared at her and took the towel and said, "Merci." Wishing he could come up with something else to say.

Mary is marching the others right behind him. Merriam hands her a towel as well. "What a fine bunch of little ones," Merriam proclaims to her. The younger boys Henry and Joseph, even at a young age acknowledged the beauty of this young girl. They stared at her, turning their heads to look over their shoulders as they pass by. Mary had to push them from behind out the back door. She handed Mary another towel, noticing how dirty the boys were, as they passed. She is followed by her mother holding little Phillip.

Merriam observed her mother carrying Phillip. "What a beautiful little baby," she said.

Marilda told her, his name is Phillip, he is seven months old.

"May I hold him," she asked as she glanced very briefly at Marilda, handing her a towel. Her attention is focused on the baby being held in her own mothers arms.

The woman looked at Marilda, she nods her head in agreement. The woman said to her daughter, "I will prepare some food while you hold him."

Gilbert joined them at the pump to wash and freshen up.

Marilda said to him, "We are fortunate once again to find such a pleasant family who are so willingly inviting us into their home. God is truly guiding us."

"Oui, I to believe that." They are speaking to each other so the children will hear. "There is no doubt, we both knew from the dreams we both shared the night before we left. That the Lord was letting us know it is time to leave."

Mary asked her mother, "What dream did you have mother?"

Seeking to be Loved

Marilda glanced at Gilbert, she knew what he is thinking, for she was also. They did not want to scare the children, by sharing the visions that were presented to them, in their dreams that night. She merely said, "We both had a very similar dream that we should leave and take the whole family to Canada. To join, and be near your aunts, uncles and cousins there."

"Do you believe that it was God's will?" Mary asked.

Nattie glanced at Gil and he replied, "We both are sure of it."

Ernest said, "It was certainly very sudden, usually we discuss things like trips and visits to relatives with each other. We usually are forewarned, plus have extra chores to do to make sure the animals will be cared for by other family or friends."

Marilda once again glanced at Gilbert and expressed to Ernest the dream was clear to both of us. The decision was made in our minds even before we woke up that following morning. We both just knew the message was made known to us that it was time for us to go. They left it at that, she could see Ernest and Mary were not quite satisfied with the explanation. Their mother recognized they still had a questioning look in their eyes. It may have been the fatigue of the day's journey, that kept their inquisitiveness in check. Instead of the usual barrage of questions. As with all healthy young minds they are full of uncertainties and questions, especially at their age.

They were tired, hungry, and ready to stop for the day, actually more than ready to stop several hours ago. It may have been providence which kept them going so far this day and to this place.

When all was settled for the evening, the thought came to Marilda. Today's journey was likened to that of Moses, the leader of the Israelites through the desert. The day was so long, although the pastures they had been passing were green, unlike the desert. No surface water was anywhere in sight, for hours of travel. They were tired and weary. It was just but for the grace of God, that this one spot appeared. It was like they themselves, as was with Moses, from the book of Exodus, were being led through the desert. Then this place, just appeared before them.

Seeking to be Loved

God is faithful, to those who persevere during life's trials and tribulations. He will always provide for their needs in ways more abundantly than one expects.

She whispered to Gilbert, who was falling asleep. "Oh, I am sorry dear, I did not mean to wake you."

"What is it Nattie?"

"I was just thinking about the day."

He started to focus, "Huh, What?"

"I kept thinking, how it seemed like today's trek was never going to end. What kept coming to mind when we were so exhausted, it was as if we were wandering in the desert with Moses."

"Ah huh," mumbled Gil.

"We were traveling and generally not knowing where or what to expect. Concerned, worrying as the ancient Hebrews were, thinking where is this man going, where is he taking us. The thought occurred to me, for hours there was no water for the animals to drink. No place to stop for the evening and then this place appeared. Providing us not only with water, food, and shelter as well.

Out of nowhere this gracious family welcomed us and offered us more than we were looking for, with compassion and generosity."

All of a sudden Nattie was understanding the very words she was speaking. God, truly was guiding and providing for their needs. The realization overwhelmed her senses. She thought all we had to do was be persistent and patient. She became aware of the depth of her gratitude, at that moment. Knowing the Spirit is guiding her family, filled her with thankfulness and appreciation. She felt a humbleness in her heart, she could not say anymore. She could only squeeze Gilbert tight as they laid on the floor. She heard Gilbert's snore, she kissed him on the cheek and in a barely audible tone whispered, "Sleep well mon chéri(my darling)." She rolled to her opposite side, wrapped her arm around Phillip.

He is lying beside her, his eyes wide and brilliantly alert and full of life. She kissed him on the top of his head and whispered, "Je t'aime my sweet child."

Seeking to be Loved

"Mmommm," she heard him say!

"May God bless you and always, guide and protect you, no matter where you are and no matter where you travel in your life my dear one." Then she whispered, "Merci, Dear God."

May 14, 1914 - It is Thursday, before dawn lighted the morning sky, there was busyness within the household, each going about their daily chores.

When Gilbert woke, he was embarrassed, it was already light outside and the sun had already risen in the eastern sky. His stomach growled the instant he smelled sausage cooking and bread baking. He quickly rose, dressed went to the kitchen. He felt very awkward, he did not even know Madame's name. He failed to ask her last night. He felt rude and ashamed of himself.

He greeted her with, "Good morning madame." He asked for her forgiveness.

"My forgiveness, for what, Monsieur Guyon?"

He apologized for not knowing her name, explaining he had failed to ask her last night.

She laughed, "You were so fatigued and your family. Monsieur Belizile and I were amazed you had traveled as far as you did, in one day. With all you have with you, especially with those four little ones. It had to be a miracle! I was surprised you knew your own name, monsieur."

"It is funny you should say that. Marilda and I had discussed that before falling asleep last night. It had to be providence truly, that had guided us here, to this place, and to you Madame Belizile. He had to be looking out for us, we were fortunate to follow the guidance. How may we thank you, for your kindness and generosity?"

Madame Belizile said to Gilbert, "It was a blessing to be able to share what we have with a family so diligent, that came so far. It was a joy to hear the voices of little ones and to cradle that baby in my arms." She glanced at Merriam, just entering the kitchen, and

Seeking to be Loved

said, "That is the first time my daughter had an opportunity to hold a baby."

Merriam spoke up with such a gleeful tone and said, "What a beautiful child. He is so happy and alert, you can see the love in his eyes, when you look at him. How can such a young one endure such a long grueling day and be so pleasant?" She wondered in amazement!

Gilbert said, "He has a very loving mother."

Madame Belizile informed Gil, A.B. and my sons are outside. You may wish to join them, they are likely to be in the barn. Tell them breakfast will be ready in twenty minutes. The time she gave, as always was exact to the minute.

The routine of life on their farm does not vary much. Gil knew that all so well! He joined the men in the barn. Their whole family seemed to work as a unit, with all the duties and responsibilities. It is as his own family and their way of life. No matter what the day brings, the consistency and ritual of their life varies little. They are happy with the routine of life. That is apparent by the graciousness and matter-of-fact attitude they have. Gilbert walked to the barn to meet up with M. Belizile and his sons. He recognized the look of satisfaction in the expressions on their faces, confirming his thought.

Gil sensed the solidness of this family. It showed in their commitment to each other and the life they live. He is aware how unshakable their existence, and the stability of this small unit of people. Who are so willing to accept what comes their way. To generously share their blessings with others. He too is thankful, for being guided to this family on their journey. "Good morning Monsieur and garçons(boys). How can I assist you this morning?" The men shook hands.

"You already have M. Guyon."

Gilbert, looked questioning at M. Belizile.

Understanding the look on his face, by reading Gil's expression and the look in his eye. He began, "Your children brought a great joy to my wife and my daughter. I guess it is always in a woman's nature to be around young ones. They do need something to nurture, take care of and mother. We have the farm and the animals."

They chuckled, knowing it must be true, babies have a way of bringing joy and a lightness to everyone's heart, especially women folk.

Gilbert thanked him, "What can I do to help you Monsieur?" Gil gazed around, "Your cows have been milked." He realized how late it is in the morning; it was in his nature to ask. "Do you have chores my sons and I can help with?" He observed his own cows' udders needed to be relieved. He thought offering the milk to them would be a good gesture of their appreciation.

"Are you in need of some extra milk, M. Belizile?" After he said it, he felt silly asking a dairyman such a question, but it just came out.

The kind man responded by stating, "Oh Madame Belizile, will find some use for it, nothing ever goes unused here." He motions to his son, "Get one of the pails you just cleaned and give it to Monsieur Guyon, so he can bring it into the kitchen, when he is finished milking.

"Oui, Papa."

I will have the boys draw plenty of water for your animals in the meantime. He then asked about his fowl; are they in need of feed and to roam.

They are indeed, said Gil, "They have been only brief moments for them to do so the last few days."

"We have a high fenced area, I will have the boys let them out in there, before we go in for breakfast."

"Merci, we are indebted to you sir."

"Just good animal husbandry," A B replied. "They will scratch out and find what they need to keep themselves healthy."

When the men had finished the chores, the meal is ready. She had the food on the table as they enter.

Seeking to be Loved

After breakfast they loaded the wagon and readied themselves to continue the trek. It would be another late start; at least they are refreshed and at ease. Gil thanked them for their hospitality. They have been nursed from their weariness, not only of bodily and mind, their spirits as well.

Gilbert asked M. Belizile, if there was anything, he could offer him in return for he and his family's generosity.

A.B. responded, "You gave us your milk and you gave our hearts joy, that is enough. We wish you well and a safe voyage to Canada and safe travel to get you to the port of your departure." Looking beyond Gilbert towards the road, he said, "The roads and highways will be crowded today as you can see."

They shook hands and said their goodbyes.

Merriam came running from the house and approached Ernest. She handed him a piece of paper. Then kissed him on the cheek, and shied away, looking at the ground.

Gilbert glanced at Marilda and quietly said, "That was an interesting peck."

Ernest's eyes widened, and once again he is confounded, not knowing what to say. He just smiled broadly and let out a quiet chortle and said, "Ah, Merci."

Merriam shyly asked if he would write her and tell her about his journey.

Ernest clumsily mustered the words, "I will," looking at the piece of paper, she just handed him. It included her name and address.

M. Belizile exclaimed, "Oui, spring is in the air."

The adults laughed, and bid each other farewell. While making their way to the road M. Belizile asked them, "Where will your plan of travel take you today?"

Gil, turned around, walking backwards away from them replied, "We hope to make it the Trilport." Although in reality he hoped todays goal would be to make it as far as Meaux. This would

Seeking to be Loved

be an easy traveling day and a fair distance from Paris, he estimated about 40km.

A.B. turned to Madame, "They will be lucky to make it that far, with the road so heavily traveled today."

Mme. Belizile shouted, "You will be in our prayers!"

Nattie, turned her head, waved, and shouted, "And you will be in ours, Merci, Au Revoir."

They were able to merge amongst the travelers with the sun at their backs. They can see clouds in the distance sky, ahead of them. They can only hope for continued fair weather while they are on the road. The first half of the day's travel was consistent with no delays, as they made their way through this agricultural region. All noticed the towns were not quite so distance from each other, as they have been when they started their trip. The open landscape is giving way to more small villages. Many separated by just a few kilometers, some alongside each other. You exit one, with a sign announcing entry to the next town.

Ernest made the observation to his father, "There is no space between these villages. Only a sign marking the boundary and letting you know you are in a new town. That is the only difference between one and the other, except their names."

Gilbert explained, "The closer we get to Paris, the more populated it will become. By tomorrow or maybe the next day when we reach Paris, we will travel for several days and not see any pastureland or open space. The great city will be nothing but buildings and houses as far as the eye can see."

"Father, have you ever been to Paris?" Mary asked.

"Non he replied, I have only heard stories from people that have been there."

"I can hardly wait to see such a big city," Mary said.

"Me to," said Henry.

Little Gilbert with excitement in his voice, exclaimed with a shout, "Me too!"

Seeking to be Loved

    Ernest just said, "Oui." His mind is still on Merriam. He wished he had thought of something important or special to say to her. He kept thinking of the words that he would have liked to have said. He realized it was an opportunity missed and gone forever. Yet something different happened inside him, he is not sure what or why. In his mind, he committed himself to write them in a letter when he figured it out. He told himself, I will put these thoughts to words, then send it to her. The feeling he has, is a strange one. Quite different from what he has experienced before. He has a great desire to say many things to her. Yet he does not know why, he only has known her for a few hours.

    He thought, I can only count two words I said to her. I wanted to say more, I just could not think of what. He believed there must have been some attraction, she must have sensed it also. "Why would she have given me her address. She does not know me from Adam." Yet there was something, in the way he felt about her; he knew it the moment he saw her. He cannot get her off of his mind. All he knew was at this moment, this morning as they walked along, there was something strange that he was experiencing. Something he could not explain, a yearning deep within his being and he was not sure why. He rehearsed words and actions in his mind, of what he would say and how he would act, if he were to see her again. As he was doing so another part of him was thinking.

    "Why do I feel like this?"

    "Why do I even care, you will never see her again." Even as he said the words, in his mind's eye he could see her face and his heart ached. "This is so strange," he thought.

    He tried to understand the feelings within him. He recalled the moment he saw her. "I was so tired. I did not want to move, then seeing her in the kitchen, instantly I was wide-awake. The moment before I looked up at her, my arms were so tired from carrying Gilbert. I did not even realize I was still holding him, until she mentioned it. I could not even feel my arms, nor feet on the floor, it was almost as though I was suspended.

Seeking to be Loved

She was so cute, and I could not think of anything to say. Oh, I was so stupid, I must have looked as stupid as I felt," he thought to himself.

He could see the sweetness in her eyes, and he heard a confidence and directness in her voice. When she told him what to do. Then he thought, "Who needs anyone telling you what to do, anyway? I have got to think of something else. Look at all the travelers, all the different houses and shops. Stop thinking about Merriam."

He only experienced limited success for a few minutes, or should I say relief, for a few moments. He continued to dwell on his own awkwardness at such a crucial moment, at least it seemed crucial in his mind. "I wanted to say something, but what and why?" He again, reflected on the moment he first saw her. "I know I opened my mouth, it felt like something was in my throat. I could breathe, I just could not speak. It was like my mind was numb. It was like something came over me and dumbfounded me. I remember the energy, I remember an excitement, I even remember thinking this is different.

I never felt like that before, even the other day with Angeline. She was a very good-looking girl, kind, sweet and so smart for her age.

No one has ever made me feel like this. I wonder if I am in love with Merriam. I wonder, how do you know if you are in love?" He looked over at Mary, and knows he loves his sister. He glanced at his brothers and his father and beyond to his mother on the wagon, "I love them too. They never make me feel like this."

There is an emptiness in his stomach, it's not hunger, it is more like a tightness. A feeling of wanting something terribly and not knowing what, or how to relief it.

"I do not know if I like this feeling," he said to himself.

"I have to just start thinking about something else."

Gilbert noticed that Ernest was deep in thought. For a moment he wondered what it may be, then he realized. "Ah oui, the

Seeking to be Loved

peck on his cheek." He let out a chuckle. Little Gilbert and Henry who are walking beside him, look up at him and ask, "What is funny Papa." Their father just said as he glanced over at Ernest, "Ask your brother," and chuckled again.

Ernest just replied in a perturbed tone of voice, "I do not know what is so funny... "

Gil suggest, "Ernest, maybe we can talk about it later if you like."

Mary and Henry looked at each other, then their father, then at Ernest, "Talk about what?" she asked.

Ernest hesitated a moment, then simply stated to them, "I have no idea."

Progress was slow today, at least it was steady. They did reach Mary-sur-Marne and crossed the Marne River, by midafternoon. Trilport just under 12km away, would make another extremely long day. Gil suggested to Nattie, any time after the next couple of hours if you find a place to stop for the night, we will make camp. With the dense population in this region within the outskirts of Paris finding a place to stop with pasture may be difficult. A few hours pass, several travelers have stopped for the evening already. The animals had recently been watered. They took advantage of the fountain in the last village they came through 30 minutes ago. Mary and Nattie switch places, Gilbert carried Phillip, as Nat walked beside them.

Mary read the sign at the next crossroads, "The sign reads it is 5km to Trilport, Papa."

Gilbert glanced at Nat and said, "That is good." Then shouted back to Mary, "Keep an eye out for a good place to stop for the evening."

"What would be a good place?" she asked.

He quickened his pace to catch up to her, to avoid shouting. "A good place is one that would have water close by and preferably shelter and a grazing area for the animals."

Seeking to be Loved

"Okay Papa, I will be looking for such a place."

Gilbert returned to walk with Nattie again. "She handles the team well," he said to Nat.

"She is your daughter Gilbert."

"Well that explains it then."

Nat looked at Gilbert, "What will we do with the animals and all these things, plus the wagon, if they are not allowed to be on the ship? Do you think they will let us take all of our belongings with us?"

"I also pondered that question many times in my mind the last few days. I do not know if they will, if all these people are wanting to take all their things, I do not see how there will be room on the ships. They will surely be overloaded with just passengers and what they can carry aboard in their hands and on their backs."

She asked him, "What will we do with all we have if in fact that ends up being the case? What can we do with all our thing?"

"I do not know Nattie, I hope we can sell it, although everybody will probably be trying to sell what they can. Which means we probably will not be able to get much for it, even if we can find a buyer for things we cannot take."

Marilda thought for a moment, then told Gilbert, "I will start making a priority list. If worse comes to worse, we will know which things we will take, which things we will leave. That is if we cannot sell them."

"That is a good idea Nat, you might want to discuss that with the older children as well. It will allow them to start thinking, in advance of the things that are most precious to them. More importantly we must consider what would be necessary and needed.

I do hate the thought of just leaving our things on the dock or street, although we might face that possibility."

Rounding the bend of the road, Mary can see the river again. There is also some grassy areas, near a small village up ahead. She shouted to her father, "This looks like it may be a good place to stop Papa, look up there on the right."

Seeking to be Loved

Gilbert looked beyond the team, and said to her, "This looks like an ideal spot, good observation my dear." They pulled off the road, the path led to a little homestead on a rise just above the riverbank. A quaint little bungalow of a home, with two wide steps leading to an open porch running the entire frontage of the house. The front door was large almost oversized for such a small house. He noticed the lush green fields and a small garden alongside the home. He walked alongside the wagon to Mary at the reigns, he instructed her to ease the team to a stop. "I am going to see if anyone is home."

Observing the architecture, he assessed the home although small, had a very quaint look about it. He ascended the stairs and he noticed that it looked like a fairly new home, recently built and very well constructed. When he came to the door, he can see through the glass side panels, a young woman approaching. Before he can lift the heavy brass knocker, she opened the door. Gilbert suspects she is probably in her mid-20's and with child.

"What can I do for you Monsieur?" she asked.

Gil introduced himself and made his request. He sees a young fellow tagging along behind her, he looked to be three to four years old. The young woman looked beyond him, she saw the family, their wagon, and carts.

"This I cannot grant you monsieur, my husband is not yet home, I expect him shortly. I cannot say whether or not you may stay, only he."

Gilbert said, "I understand." Then he asked, "Would we be allowed to water our animals if we take them around back to the river?"

"Oui monsieur" she replied. "Please avoid the garden for the sprouts are just starting to peek through the ground."

"Merci Madame, we will guide them carefully."

The Guyon's were allowed to stay for the night. The animals grazed on the lush grass in the field above the river. It was a beautiful piece of land, Gilbert estimated only about three acres

Seeking to be Loved

from the road to the river. He knew the young couple were not farmers. The fields had not been plowed for many years, nor grazed upon, just a small vegetable patch. A small bungalow of a house, with a basement exposed only from the back under a covered porch. It matched the porch on the front entry of the house, except being off the ground due to the slope of the land where the foundation lay. The porch must offer a very nice view for observation of the river, thought Gil. They would be able to take shelter under the porch, for the evening, if need be.

Marilda, was sitting on a bench under the porch near the basement door, admiring the view. The sun was setting to their left, it cast magnificent shadows over the river and lush green field. She was mesmerized by the sparkling and glistening of sun beams on the rippling water's surface of the Marne river. Watching, as it reflected the last rays of the setting sun. She patted the bench gesturing for Gilbert to come sit down with her, to admire the view.

He sat beside her and agreed, "It is a magnificent scene is it not?" It was peaceful, they watched their children running and playing in the field below. It reminded them of sitting on their own porch during the dwindling light of day. Observing them play in their own field with the river in the distance. Gilbert heard Marilda make a muffled whimper, he turned his head to see her face. She brought her hand to her mouth.

"What is it dear?"

She only shook her head no.

He said, "It reminds you of our home."

Now both of her hands are covering her mouth and tears ran down her cheeks. She nodded her head in confirmation.

Gilbert placed his arm around her shoulder and scoots closer.

She turned her head to his shoulder and sobbed. The reality struct her, a sadness, a bit of remorse and grief of leaving their home. The life, their life, her life, home, land, and the beloved country, all she ever knew. Somehow she knew she would never be back.

Seeking to be Loved

Gilbert's heart ached hearing her cry. He asked God for words to comfort her, none came. He can only whisper a prayer in his mind, "Dear Lord comfort her, continue to guide and protect us on this journey. Give me the words that will set her at ease."

Her sobbing stopped, staring at their children. Who now were also sitting in the field below them looking toward the river. He whispered to Nattie in a consoling tone in his voice, "We knew we had to leave."

She confirmed with a nod, and she lifted her head from his shoulder. She sat up and continued to watch the children and view the scene around them.

Gilbert had noticed earlier, after they watered the animals, there were trenches starting to form on either side of the house. There was no drain to divert nor displace the water from the roof. He also noticed a pile of gravel overgrown with weeds on either side of the building. He knew the owner or builders of the home left an incomplete job.

He is aware of the importance of drainage, to divert water away from the home. It is vital to maintain integrity of any structure. Water must always be diverted away from the home. He suspected the new homeowners being young maybe inexperienced, did not understand the nuances of maintaining the structure. He confirmed his suspicions when shaking hands with the young man when he came home from work. His hands were a bit small and soft, not calloused from manual labor. He decided at first light the following morning when he heard sounds of the homeowner awakening, he would mention he and his sons could correct the problem. If he would like for them to lay in a basic French drain. It being Friday, his planned destination would be Meaux, a very early start would not be necessary.

May 15, 1914 - Gilbert was awoken from the stirring sounds within the home. When he opened his eyes, he was surprised that it

Seeking to be Loved

was still quite dark. He waited several minutes until he heard bothsets of footsteps from within the home, he decided to tap on the door.

The door opening slowly and cautiously, he was greeted with a "Bon jour, M. Guyon. Is there something I can do for you?" the young man asked.

Gilbert said, "I beg your pardon monsieur, I do not wish to be disturbing you so early in the morning. You have such a lovely home, on such a scenic plot of land. I have noticed something that you may or may not be aware of," Gilbert paused.

"What is it Monsieur Guyon?" he ask.

Gilbert explained his observation.

The young man acknowledged, then commented, "I have always wondered why those piles of stones were left there. Oui, they were there when we moved in," he told Gilbert.

Gilbert suggest that he and his sons, can dig a trench and fill it with the stones. He explained, "I am sure that was the intent of the gravel, this will help divert the water running-off the roof. It will stop water from pooling along the structures foundation and limit erosion as well." Gilbert could see delight in the man's eyes momentarily, then what followed with a look of disappointment.

The young man mentioned, "My wages are very modest despite the long hours I must work. I would not be able to pay you for the work."

Gilbert's only response was, "You already have. Do we have your permission to start?"

The words he heard Gilbert speak, did not sink in. He sensed an air of gratitude in Gilbert's voice and observed in his expression. The young man was not used to hearing, nor recognizing such sincerity, in peoples voices.

He refused Gilbert's offer and said, "I must get myself ready for work." Then he closed the door.

Gilbert thought about the young man's response. He knew there was something he was not saying or understanding.

Seeking to be Loved

    The young man's wife kept a close ear to the conversation. When he returned to the kitchen, she was there and had resumed busying herself with preparation of their breakfast. She looked at him queerly, then questioned him. "Why did you not take him up on his offer?"

    He looked at her, "You know we cannot afford their help."

    "It sounded to me he was willing to do it without charge. For us allowing them to stay on our property."

    "Are you sure?" he asked. "Who would do such a laborious job and not expect to receive a wage?"

    "I am certain of it; did you not hear him? When you mentioned you cannot pay, his response, was, "You already have."

    "Oui, I did hear that! It just did not make sense to me. To think that he would be willing to do it for nothing. Out of his kindness?" He stated and laughed at such a foolish thought. He looked at his young wife, with an inquisitive expression on his face. He stated to her, "You know there was something in his eyes, I noticed when he was speaking to me. It was something different, I was struck by it. It was like an earnestness; I really do not know the right word to put on it. Although there was a sense of trust, maybe. I really do not know what it was. All I do know is that, I have not experienced it very often dealing with people. If ever, and it struck me in a peculiar way."

    His young wife suggested to him, "You should speak to that man before you leave this morning, to confirm what it is he would like to do. If it is his way of returning a gesture of kindness, you must give him the permission to do so." She told her husband, "If the work is completed, it may help preserve our home and get rid of those unsightly mounds. You worked long hours to save enough to build us this home. I would hate to see damage occur that can be prevented."

    "Oui, you are right my dear, I will talk to him right now." Before the young man left for work, he spoke with Gilbert.

    Gilbert showed him the area that was washing out, and how it was pulling the ground and fill away from his foundation. He also,

Seeking to be Loved

showed him the piles of rubble, which were on either side of his house. He explained, what he and his sons will do and assured him that it would not be very difficult, nor very time consuming. Then they would be on their way this morning.

The young man expressed his appreciation. Although he had doubts the job will be completed. They both thank each other and shook hands. The young man walked away half pleased, not wanting to get his hopes up. He believed the reality is the work will not get done. He thought to himself, M. Guyon will start the work, then tell my spouse he found something much worse. This will be leading to an excuse that more work would be necessary. Well Monsieur Guyon will not pull one over on me, he exclaimed to himself. I will send them packing as soon as I get home this evening.

Gilbert shouted to the young man, "God bless you and protect your family monsieur." When he noticed him leave, for what he assumed was his place of employment.

Gil woke the two older boys, and set them to work on the trench. While Marilda prepared breakfast. After eating, Ernest hitched the team, the girls repack and loaded the wagon. Gilbert, Henry, and little Gil finished digging the drainage ditches. They shovel the stones in and smoothed the fill dirt.

Gil and Nat took one last look to admire the view. A pink sky and its colors reflected on the river beyond the lush green carpet of the fields. They started on their way acknowledging that they have been fortunate once again, to have another pleasant and restful night in such a peaceful spot.

They were getting a late start, as they approach the highway Gil observed the long line of travelers. Gilbert led the team walking in front, hoping someone will allow him to merge in without disrupting the caravan. He gestured to those coming toward him on his left, that he would like to enter in. In hopes someone would slow their pace leaving a gap to allow him to enter. He told the children and Marilda, "If someone lets us in move quickly. Hasten the pace to

Seeking to be Loved

merge in without delay or disruption of the other travelers." He knew any hold up may anger some.

He waved and gestured to the people approaching from the east. When one finally acknowledged him and returned a signal to proceed. Gil noticed the man leading his team, slowed his wagon just a bit, creating a slight gap. He shouted for his family to move quickly onto the road. In the few moments of time that had passed, there was a 30-meter gap. Marilda snapped the reigns. The team was quick to respond, pulling the wagon into the space. Gilbert and Ernest position the children and their carts and herd the livestock in trail following closely behind the wagon. The gap closed quickly.

Gilbert, turned to the gentleman driving his team behind him, thanked him for letting him and his family enter the line of travelers.

The man nodded and smiled.

It was not long, as they followed in line with the caravan, maybe an hour before they cross the river. They saw the sign for the town of Trilport, a quaint village. Crossing the river once again as it meandered through the countryside.

Later they entered the town of Meaux, Gilbert estimated the time to be between 1:30 and 2PM. Once again, he reminds himself, I must get that watch when we stop for the day.

Meaux, is a large city supporting over 30 thousand people, there is much grand architecture. Gilbert explained to the children, that walking on the cobblestone streets is easier for us. He conveyed to those walking close to him, it is not good for the animals. He is not sure the effect it may have on their hooves. He explained the horses should be fine, with shoes protecting their hoofs.

The rhythmic, clop, clop, clop sound of metal shoes on the horses hoofs against the stones mixed with all the other noise of passersby, was a symphony of rhythm. The loudness of the rhythm, along with the human activity going on about them in the city, heightened their awareness and increased their excitement. They marveled at the many buildings, there design and workmanship.

Seeking to be Loved

    They could see the bell tower of the St. Etienne Cathedral. This Grand structure was centuries in building. Gilbert thought it would be good exposure for his children, to see the results of such magnificent craftsmanship. The work was created by great artisans that he had heard so much about. He wanted his family to witness such things, whenever the opportunity presented itself. Such as this work produced by skilled masters of their trade, from all over France who labored in its construction. It would be a good experience for the children, and a shame to pass by. Thinking as he often did about the future of his young ones, he decided to stop.

    He wanted to expose them to as many things as possible to give them a broad awareness of the world around them. What better time than now when an opportunity presented itself.

    He debated with himself briefly. The practical and driven part of him, told him we should press on. His next thought was we will never have this opportunity again. He is willing to move on. Then the reality struck him. Their children may never see such things again. He shouted to his spouse, "We will rest here." He wanted his family to be exposed to the vast options available to them. He would like such things to inspire and help them to understand there are many ways to make a living. Each individual has gifts to develop and share with those around them.

    It is his desire to learn from, and use each opportunity when life presents it to them. Also, encourage his loved ones to explore the many options and possibilities that abound in this world. He hoped by exposing them to such things, would open their young minds. So, they might wonder and will seek their own gifts and talents, that our loving Lord in Heaven bestowed on them. He has always known, probably from his own father and mother's teachings, the world has much to offer and so little time to appreciate it.

    Although they rarely left the small community, where they grew up. His parents never failed to speak to them about the wonders of the world and the glories of heaven. They took every opportunity to point out good workmanship. It did not seem to

Seeking to be Loved

matter what it was. It may have been the construction of bridges, homes, barns or even a well-constructed fence. It may even have been needlework, someone had done or pastries in the shop.

They would also, with the same observant eye point out deficiencies, when someone did not put forth their best effort. They would take the time to explain, how this may cause a problem later, do to such flaws. His parents would explain to them, shortcuts and not correcting mistakes will cost you more in the long run. This is especially so with the construction of buildings, furniture, and clothing.

He smiled, thinking of his mother and how many times she told them when she instructed her children in the needle crafts; "A stitch in time saves nine."

His father's constant reminder, "Do it correctly the first time." Even if it meant starting over. "It will save you time, damage due to the poor workmanship, expense and trouble for having to redo it later."

Sound advice and good lessons to learn early in life. To be patient, observant and willing to learn from the experience of others. Thus, when your time comes, your skills will be honed, your service will be sort after. You will bring honor to your name, comfort to your family, and food to your table. He would always say at the end of it all, "Even more importantly, to always do our very best, no matter what our circumstances. It will be pleasing to God."

Gil also knew it would behoove him and his family to daily pray, and give thanks, for allowing them to safely come thus far. Also, to continue to ask for safety during the miles and days ahead, until they reach their destination.

Gilbert quickened his pace to catch up to Nattie. He shared his thoughts, she agreed. Although he sensed a bit of apprehension in the manner and tone of her response.

"Shall I turn off, before we go too far beyond the church?" she asked questioningly.

Seeking to be Loved

"Why not turn off on the right, we are only a few streets from the Cathedral." suggested Gil.

Marilda gave a quick firm pull on the right reign, the team responds crisply. The children and the carts followed behind her.

"Continue for a few streets and then turn the team right again. That should bring us back into view of the steeple, so we can determine which way we need to go next," instructed Gil.

Marilda acknowledged his instructions, she looked back to see if the children are still following her lead.

Gilbert's directions landed them in a large town square, not far from the Cathedral. Marilda spies a large open area just ahead on the left, she slowed the wagon just a bit. Then shouts to Gilbert, I will turn left here and as she does, immediately in front of her, to her amazement is the magnificent cathedral. It is imposing; the team comes to a halt independently of Natties command. It was as if they too were struck with awe, as well. Or maybe they had another force directing them and controlling the reins. She is amazed at the size and beauty of the structure.

Blanche, is the first to say something, "Oow-La-la, Ma mee look!"

Ernest can be heard from behind say, "Look At That."

Blanche, unable to contain her excitement, shouted to her mother, who is beside her, "Can we go in, Ma mee?"

"I think we all will be going in," she told them, glancing down at Blanche.

Gilbert had Ernest and Henry secure the carts and the animals to the wheels of the wagon. He surveyed the area looking for a fountain or trough, to water the animals. Seeing none he approached Nat, as she is gathering up Phillip and the other children. He took the reins from Nattie and tied them to the brake lever. He will take the animals and find a place to water them, while the others go into the Cathedral. After he helped her down from the wagon, he attempted to assist Blanche. Who insisted she climb down from the wagon herself. He directed them all to stay close to their mother and their

Seeking to be Loved

sister Mary. Joseph is ready to jump just as Gil turned around, he flung himself off the buckboard into his arms. Laughing, Gilbert handed him to Ernest. He told him to keep a hold on his hand.

Nat extends Phillip to Gilbert, she lets him know this little one needs to be changed and fed before we do anything.

Gilbert reached his other hand to assist Nattie.

She said, "Keep him for a moment, I will get the things I need."

Gilbert told her, "I will stay here while you and the children go in. He reminds them all to stay together. I will wait until you are finished looking around and the children have said their prayers. I will go inside after you come out. I do not want to leave our things unguarded. While you are doing that, I will ask about a place to water the animals and where they might graze. I will meet you back here."

Nattie collected the things she needs. She also gathered something for the children to eat and handed the food to Mary; so she can distribute it to her siblings.

I have heard many things about this cathedral, Marilda conveyed to her children. She shared what she knew of the history of the church with them. They made their way up the steps of St. Etienne carrying Phillip in her arms. Upon entering the Cathedral, they had to look up, then around in both directions as they slowly step forward to the water font.

Marilda dipped her finger in, she blessed herself and Phillip. The others follow her example. All the while glancing in every direction in awe, of what they see. The beautiful ornamentation, the transepts appeared to be fine lace, though they were craved from stone. The work and its surface were finished so smooth and ornately with such detail you had to touch it to know it was stone. All the stonework and the carvings were done in similar manner. Everywhere they looked the church is adorned magnificently with sculptures and monuments.

Seeking to be Loved

Mary, whispered, "It is beautiful, everything is beautiful, even the light coming through the windows is Au-delà de la beauté(Beyond beautiful)."

"Oui, it is," Marilda replied; then remembered she needed to care for Phillip. She asked them all to follow her to find a place they may go freshen up. A place where she can privately change, clean, and feed their little brother.

Ernest mentioned he noticed a sign to the left of the entry when they came in.

Once they had all finished their prayers and were satisfied, they had explored every nook and cranny they prepared to leave. She gathered the children together and they went out to meet their father at the wagon.

Gilbert had questioned many of the passersby whether a stable or livery was close. He found out there was, as a gentleman explained to him, you must be a guest of the hotel that runs them in order to keep your stock there.

When Marilda and the children get back, she described to Gilbert, how magnificent it is inside.

She informed him to where the privy room is. Gilbert asked Ernest to stay with his mother and Phillip. The others he asked if they would like to go back in, they all shout, "Oui Papa."

Blanche with excitement told her father, "I have to show you the windows and the statues and the beautiful paintings Da Dee."

"Let us go then, you must show me, my dear."

She grabbed him by the hand attempting to drag him up the steps.

Mary and Henry were both explaining to their father everything they have seen inside. Once inside they directed him to the water font, to bless themselves again as is customary when entering a holy place. He dipped his finger to touch the water and made the sign of the cross on himself.

He was admiring the architecture as well as the fine workmanship. There is a constant buzzing in his ears. It is all the

Seeking to be Loved

children speaking at once, to come here, look here, look there, come see this. He was glad to see such excitement on their faces, and hear the glee in their voices.

Gilbert explained to his young ones, "This is the largest Gothic Cathedral in France. The organ was completed in 1627, by the best organ builder in the country."

He himself marveled at the arches, and transepts connecting the support columns. He told his children, "The intricate designs on the support columns look like the finest lace work your grandmother has ever made. Yet, it is carved and polished stone. The work was truly and still is a devotion to our heavenly father."

He reiterated to his children, what he has encouraged them at every opportunity. "We must always do the absolute best job we can, with every undertaking we have set before us. When you commit yourself to such a standard, God will guide you in your work. Perfection is not an should never be the goal, for nothing is perfect accept our heavenly Father. We will only confound our self and not accomplish much. On the other hand, Never be satisfied with mediocrity, just do your best. Know your limits and with each project, or endeavor you set out to do, challenge yourself and your skills will improve."

Looking at the workmanship, it is hard to believe, one can possess such skill.

The light shone through the stained-glass windows, in such a manner that it not only glowed on the altar, it illuminated the entire church. It is such a holy glow, when one is engulfed by it, you cannot help feel humble and want to express adoration to our Lord.

One begins to consider how insignificant we are in the scheme of things. While acknowledging each and all have a mission on earth. One cannot help but wonder of what their own will be.

- For what purpose could God possibly have in mind for each one of us?
- For what reason were you brought here into this world?
- What purpose in Gods design, and plan, are you to do?

Seeking to be Loved

When they returned, Marilda told Gil, "I overheard the conversation you had earlier, with a gentleman. The window in the room where I had changed Phillip was open. You must have been close to it." She asked him, "Will we be staying in a hotel?"

Gilbert looked at Nattie, with an odd expression on his face. He then reads the stalwart indifference in her expression. The children were listening now and overheard this bit of conversation. Wondering and hoping to experience a night in a city hotel. They look at each other with smiles and enthusiasm.

Gilbert all the while is thinking, and admits, "It would be a good respite." He weighed the options heavily on his mind before he had returned after speaking with that first gentleman. He had already decided; they should be traveling on. Maybe we can find a place to stop near a church just outside one of the nearby towns, closer to Paris, he conveyed to Nattie.

They both looked at the children, and noticed the anticipation, and excitement leave their expression.

As they proceed through Meaux, Gil questioned his decision. He contemplated; they would have to backtrack at least 2km through a town they are not familiar with. That would have been the closest Hotel with a livery, from the Cathedral. Then travel 2km again on foot to explore the town, then back to get their belongings. Repeating again as they head west out of town. He decided all that extra walking, and the fact that it would not shorten the distance to Paris, would be a greater hardship on everyone. Adding to his decision, was the unknown factor of the cost and schedule of the voyage. He believed it best to continue to make westward progress with as few delays as possible.

Gils greatest concern is the cost of transporting his family and belongings. He has no idea whether or not it will be within his means. No one yet in all the towns they had traveled through seem to know what the cost would be. He suspected when he gets to Paris, they will be able to find out and secure passage there. Even though Paris is not a port city, surely, they have many connections to all the

Seeking to be Loved

ports on the West Coast. Unless there being some unforeseen delay, they should make it to Paris in two days without much difficulty, for it is a little more than 40km away.

They proceed on their way, leaving the town of Meaux, the first sign they see, is Claye-Souilly, 15km. There the Guyon's stopped briefly to water the animals from a stream running alongside the roadway. Gil thinks it must be nearly 4PM or later. He realized there is no way they can cover the distance he had hoped to travel today. Many have already begun to set up camps for the night off the road. Allowing the few travelers that were still on the roads to move on at a steady pace.

Marilda driving the team, looked down at Joseph and Blanche on the floor of the wagon. Both with their backs leaning against the brace of the seat, they looked tired. It appeared that Phillip is dozing off, with his head lying on his brothers' lap. Joseph has his little hand resting on his brother's shoulder. Marilda observed, Joseph looked quite pleased, that his little brother chose him, on which to rest his head. She smiled ever so lovingly at the three of them.

She tapped on the back of her seat, to get Gilbert to look. With her head turned, she can see she has his attention. She waved her hand gesturing him to come forward. He reached her with a few quick strides.

Marilda mentioned to him, "The children are very tired, look there." She nodded her head toward them.

She told Gil, from her vantage point, "It just looks like pastures as far as I can see to the horizon." Then she asked, "How are the others holding out?"

Gilbert suggest they go a little further, maybe an hour or so. He reminded her, "If you see a good place to stop, pull off and we will camp for the night." Slightly over an hour passed, it was a pleasant evening. They still had not found a suitable place. Almost all the other travelers had pulled off the road into vacant fields.

Marilda, can see in the distance a little village, she estimated it being at least 2km away. The children had awoken from their nap.

Seeking to be Loved

She knew Phillip would be hungry and needed to be changed. She thought about calling Mary to come take the reins, then decided not to. She thought the team tracked the other wagons, matching their pace and not drifting to either side. Gilbert trained them well. She thought with so few travelers on the road, she would place the reins on the rail of the buckboard. She experimented for a moment. They kept their pace, and maintained a good distance with the wagon ahead of them, as she thought they would.

She lifted Phillip from the floor to the seat beside her, checks and quickly cleaned and changed him. She placed him in the sling around her shoulder allowing him to nurse. Phillip staring at his mother's face reached up to touch her chin. She has a hard time taking her eyes off him, both are transfixed on each other's gaze. They both seem to be in a blissful state, there is no other sounds, no other world around them. There is a warm, soft tenderness felt between them, it is as if there is an aura engulfing both during these moments. A mutual adoring pledge, of love and absolute trust, that only a mother and child are privileged to experience.

When it is time to reposition him, she set the reins at her side. Then lifted him up out of the sling, repositioning it on her opposite shoulder. He burped and smiled, as she replaced him in the sling. She leans forward slightly to give him a kiss. He uses both hands to touch her face. One touched her lips and she kissed it. The other hand he placed on her nose. He then reached it up and patted her forehead. She kissed him once more and lets him resume his dinner.

Looking up she noticed they are approaching another small village. Drawing near, she can see a sign at the crossroads, she cannot yet read its print. She mentioned to Gilbert, "There is a town up ahead. It may be another half kilometer."

A few moments later, she is able to read the sign, Charmentray, is the name of the little village. She does not need to ask; she turned the team to the left at the crossroads leading into the little village.

Seeking to be Loved

Gilbert estimated it being 6PM or later; "This is a good time to stop he thought."

Mary, Ernest, and Henry had been walking for two hours or more. That is after, they had heard their father, tell their mother, "Maybe another hour or so."

Mary comments, "I hope we are stopping here for the night; it has been an awful long, <u>Or so</u>." She always had a keen ear and was usually quick to repeat any contradiction in her father's speech.

Ernest and Henry both add "Me to," looking at their father.

Gil said, "Oui it is time, hopefully this will be a good place to stop. We have had another long day."

Little Gilbert who is in his arms, is quick to add, "It was a good day, Oui, Papa?"

Gilbert said, "Oui it has been, a wonderful day fils(son)."

Marilda knew just what to look for, there is a grazing pasture right next to a canal. She gently tugged the reins, the team turned right onto the path leading to a house, close to that spot they wish to camp for the night. Once in front of the house, she pulled the team to stop.

Gilbert instructs the children to keep everything close together until he speaks to the property owner.

He looked up, a gentleman is coming from the house, he had a questioning look on his face. Gilbert taking off his hat introduced himself to the gentleman. He asked him if he is the property owner.

"I am monsieur."

Gil made his request, if he would be so kind to let them camp overnight, water their animals and let them graze.

"I am John, oui you may water the animals, although I must charge you a small fee to let them graze and camp."

"What will be the fee?"

"Two franc's." he told Gilbert.

Gilbert stated, "That is very reasonable. Where would you like us to set our things?"

Seeking to be Loved

"I will show you, follow me. You must keep track and care for your stock. I cannot afford to lose any young crops. You will be held responsible for any loss or injury they, or you, and yours may cause."

Gilbert thought, as John is leading him to a place to camp for the evening, "He must have had some experience with travelers also. It seems likely, being this close to Paris and having such sprawling pastures and fine planted fields. Plus, the fact there was not many options for people to spend the night, at least from what he could observe. Many may have taken advantage of the open land and may not have considered all the work necessary to prepare and seed the fields properly.

A small family and a few animals could easily destroy an acre of crops in an evening. Thus, weeks of one's labor is for not, which could mean and economic lost for a season to a farmer."

Gil thanked him, reached in his pocket, and pulled out a few coins and handed John two franc's.

"Merci, if you have need for anything, just knock on the door," said John, as he walked away.

Gilbert turned to look over the property, the children having heard the arrangement already know what to do. Ernest is on his way to unhitch the horses and goats. Mary had already started to unload some things for the evening, from the wagon. Marilda is tending the young children. Henry, leads the cow to the designated grazing spot, and little Gilbert feeds the fowl.

Gilbert recognized, we are becoming a well working unit on the road. This family has adapted well to the routine of traveling. "We are efficient nomads', traversing the French countryside." After a little more than a week, he is proud of his family.

They had a restful night. The boys attempted to catch fish in the canal, they were unsuccessful.

May 16, 1914 - When Gilbert and Marilda woke, they discussed the progress of their journey. Gil mentioned to her, "We will get an early start, then find a place to reside the rest of the day."

Seeking to be Loved

Marilda, mentioned tomorrow is the Sabbath day. Gilbert nodded his head in confirmation. They both look at each other and said, "A day of rest." They smile at each other and embraced.

Gil said, "We will attend a service, then find a place to spent the day."

John came out to see the Guyon's off. Gilbert asked if there was a church where they may attend service.

"There is, and it is about equal distance from here to Meaux or to Claye-Souilly. Which way are you going?"

Gilbert told him they are heading to Paris, and then on to the coast.

John replied, "You may want to attend the église(church) Saint-Etienne, in Claye-Souilly, it will be on your way. It is only about 12km maybe a little more. They will have services every hour until noon on Sunday.

Gil told John, "Monsieur we visited the Great Cathedral of St. Etienne in Meaux."

"Oh, oui it is a magnificent église. The one in Claye-Souilly, is our St. Etienne it is near the canal, a little église, not the same one. There are many églises named for the Great Saint."

Many people were on the road that morning, travelers seemed a bit more frantic and argumentative. Progress was slow and trying on one's patience. At times all were at a standstill, covering the nearly 12km was a struggle and took all day.

Claye-Souilly, is a small commune in the country not far outside of Paris, a quiet and peaceful community.

They find the St. Etienne Église, it was late in the evening. Gil asked the Priest if he knew of a place they could camp for the night. The Priest suggest right here, "We have a little space in the parish house, although you are welcome to camp on the grounds. There is tall grass behind the parish for the animals and a trough to get water. Bonne nuit monsieur if you are in need of something come knock."

Seeking to be Loved

May 17, 1914 - The Guyon's quickly gathered their things before the service, so not to take up room on the grounds. They attended mass and were preparing to leave.

Gilbert expressed to Marilda, this would be a very appropriate place to rest and recuperate before we go into Paris.

The parishioner who had parked his carriage next to their wagon asked them, "Where are you from and where might you be going?

Gilbert told him, "We will be going to Canada to join my brothers."

The older gentleman asked Gilbert, "Where do your brothers live in Canada?"

Gilbert said, "They live in the city of Québec."

The gentleman extended his hand, "I am Herbert Goulet. I have two sons that also live in Québec. They have been living there in Canada, for the last three years. You should find many a good opportunity there."

Gilbert nodded in response, "We hope so." He did not want to tell the man is real concerns for leaving. Although it does not seem to be a mystery, why so many are migrating these days. Gilbert asked Monsieur Goulet, if he knew of a place he and his family can rest for the day, before making their way to Paris tomorrow morning.

Monsieur Goulet observed Marilda holding Phillip and Joseph in her arms. He proceeds to tell them, "My farm is less than one kilometer down the road. It is in the direction you would be heading if you are going to Paris. We would like to welcome you to spend the afternoon and night with us. We have a good pasture and a spring of pure sweet water. We welcome you to recuperate there and would be delighted if you did." The man looked to Gilbert, waiting for him to respond to his offer.

Gilbert turned his head and smiled at Marilda, and said aloud, "It appears the Lord has blessed us again."

Marilda nods her head, looked at Monsieur Goulet and said, "He has sent us another Saint."

Seeking to be Loved

Madame Goulet is standing next to Gilbert, she nudged him in his side with her elbow and said, "Ah, he is a far cry from that, I am no angel either." They laughed at her comment.

Monsieur Goulet jokingly said to his wife, "We still have time to achieve that my dear." The Goulet's focused on Gil and Nat and said to them, "We would enjoy having you stay with us and watch your children run about. We have not seen our grandchildren in three years."

The Guyon's followed them to their small farm. It was quaint, well kept, everything appeared to be in order and in its place.

M. Goulet suggested to Gilbert, "Let me show you and the boys where to take your animals. There are post in the field, to tie them while they graze."

Madame Goulet took Marilda by the arm, "I will show you, the girls and the little ones where your rooms will be."

Marilda halts herself, from the tugging of her hostess.

"Madame we cannot impose on you. You have already been kind just to allow us to rest here."

The woman tugged her on, "Do not be silly." she exclaimed. "We are privileged to have you and your family as guests. This is a rare treat for us. Our home feels empty since our sons have left. We very seldom have visitors. I am excited to be cooking for a family."

Marilda, again expressed her desire not to impose or be of any burden to her. "We do not want to take advantage of your hospitality."

"Don't be silly," repeated Mme. Goulet, looking reassuringly into Marilda's eyes, and expressed with a corrective tone in her voice. "All the way home from church, I had been thinking of the things I would like to prepare for you and your family. Now you must allow me this little pleasure." She proceeded to the entry door to her home.

"Oh, Non Madame," Marilda retorted to the woman!

Madame tugged again and turned her head to look at her guest. She reached for Joseph, picked him up to carry into the house.

Seeking to be Loved

She squared up with Marilda once again. This time with a stern mothering expression, and postured her stance, as to say, this is the way it was going to be. Then she stated, "You are our guest, and that is that."

Marilda lowered her head to look at Phillip. He was glaring at her. He to seemed to have a questioning and similar look of sternness in his own eyes. She thought for a moment, then softly said to him, "You are taking sides with Madame."

Madame Goulet said, "See even the little one knows."

Nattie sighed, and said to Madame, "We will accept your graciousness under one condition."

"What is that my dear?" she questioned.

"It is that we may assist you in whatever preparations that will need to be done."

"Fair enough," said Madame. "It will be a pleasure, having help in the house and kitchen."

After lunch, the adults retired to the back porch. The children explored the small barn and outbuildings. They just frolic most of the afternoon.

Gilbert asked Monsieur Goulet, about any news he may have heard on the matter concerning the eastern border and their neighbor Germany?

"Only what you probably already know," was his response to Gils question. "I would say, you would be more familiar than I. You living as close to the border as you were, you may have a better feel and understanding than most people. More so than we do here this close to Paris."

Gilbert explained, "It was a concern and a major reason why we decided to join my brothers in Canada."

Monsieur Goulet told Gilbert, "You have too much at stake, to not have ventured this long journey. You have made a wise decision. Your duty is to your family first above all else." Then he began to back up a bit, first to God, then to family, third to your countrymen, "Vive la France." They chuckled, the patriotism of the homeland, is felt within them both.

Gilbert's next concern is about passage for his family. He questioned M. Goulet if he knew anything about intercontinental voyages.

M. Goulet said, "Only what my sons have arranged."

Next Gil inquired, "Will we be able to obtain passage in Paris? What did your son's need to do, or did they have to go to a port city? What about cost, do you have any idea what it would cost to transport a family and the belongings that you see we have here?"

"Oui, oui and oui," said Monsieur Goulet, "You should be able to make all your arrangements in Paris. I can give you the address of the shipping company that my sons used when they went to Canada. Cost, that will depend on how you wish to travel. My sons took a standard cabin, which was 476 francs for four of them, 3 years ago."

He noticed the look of concern that came over Gil's face. He asked if he was not feeling well?

Gilbert thought for a moment then said, "I am fine. I was just thinking we may not be able to afford passage."

Monsieur Goulet told him there may be other options. Possibilities that the common person may not be aware of.

"My son wrote in the letter, he sent to us a few years ago, he could have saved a lot of argent. If he was aware that they have rooms below deck, on most of the ships. They may be noisy, very cozy, and close to the engine room. The rooms may or may not have a porthole, because many of the little quarters are below the waterline. He had heard from others who were assigned those small cabins, they were dark and uncomfortable. They were very petite, humid, and stuffy compartments.

My son entered one of those cabins. A man he met on the ship during their voyage was staying in one, with five strangers. He showed him his room one day. My son explained in the letter; the room was no more than 1.5m wide by maybe 4m long. They had a locker separating the racks for sleeping, stacked three high against one of the walls. The cost was much cheaper, than the standard fair.

The man noticed Gilbert's eyebrows rising, as Gilbert's spirit lifted once more.

He asked about storage of baggage and placement for the animals.

Monsieur Goulet said, "Unfortunately I have no information about that." Looking at Gilbert, he realized that his guest missed the point, and started shaking his finger at Gil.

Then he continued to describe what his son wrote about the room. "The cabin was damp, as well as everything in it. The muskiness, you could feel, as soon as the door opened, even before you entered. The smell was repulsive, musky, old sweat, bowels smells.

He mentioned that his son wrote, there could not in any way be an accurate way for him to describe it. The memory of it he said in his letter, caused him to convulse.

Looking at Gilbert, he shook his finger at him again and said, "There is a price for everything, and for everything a price."

Many of Gilbert's questions had been answered, some were not. He still had concerns that weighed heavily on his mind. They still had a great distance, another 10 to 12 days travel ahead of them to get to the coast. That is if there are no great delays in Paris, or any unforeseen mishaps. Thinking out loud, he mumbled to himself, there is still the dilemma of transporting the belongings and the livestock.

Monsieur Goulet shared with Gilbert, "You may want to sell everything you have accept the clothes on your back. Keep only the bare necessity of items you can carry. I have seen hundreds of people and families heading east to Paris and on to the coast. I am sure many of them are seeking transport, it could be a long wait for you. The cost of waiting as well as the voyage can be very expensive."

Seeking to be Loved

He recalled an experience as a young man during the Franco-Prussian War in 1870-71. We the French army were defeated.

I have seen and heard many stories of families attempting to escape the German army, many could not. Many stayed wherever they could find space to place their belongings. They were everywhere, on the side of roads, fields, or any place they were able to squeeze into. Many waited months, no one was allowed to stay in any spot very long. They lived where they could, until forced to move by the authorities. They were nomads in their own country. Some had been forced to move moments after settling into a spot and setting out their belongings to rest.

Like you and your family they were traveling along the southern and west coast, and shorelines, waiting and hoping to obtain sea passage to the America's.

They stayed until their resources had run out. I guess it was a blessing, a treaty was signed. Much of the occupied lands were returned, some were not. It had to be a great hardship for many. I remember my father telling me, many died from starvation and exposure.

Monsieur Goulet stopped for a moment in deep thought. He was shaking his finger near the side of his face close to his own temple. He shared his thought to Gilbert, you may want to keep in mind when seeking passage, look to ships that transport only freight. It may be an option, they may offer passage for your family, although I would expect accommodations to be very basic. I do not know what can be done with the livestock.

Marilda appeared on the back porch and handed Phillip to Gilbert. She said, "He was looking for his father." She turned to go back into the house, and mentioned to him, "Please have Ernest bring the milk into the kitchen when he is finished. We plan to have a treat for dessert."

Gilbert held Phillip at arm's length, wiggling him side to side, until he started his funny gurgled laughter.

Seeking to be Loved

Marilda peeked her head partially past the door as it is closing, to observe father and son laugh at each other's antics. She reminded Gilbert, to keep an eye on those children, "You remember what happened the last time they were fishing."

Gilbert glanced towards the canal, he was not concerned for the older children. Blanche and Joseph are his immediate concerns. They had been playing at his feet, just off the porch the whole time. He smiled at them, they were engulfed in whatever they were exploring in the grass.

The Guyon's and their host had a wonderful meal on a makeshift table setup on the lawn. They enjoyed each other's company. The setting of the sun marked the closing of another Day. The soufflé Marilda had made with the sweetened whipped cream topping was an unexpected treat, it made the meal seem like a holiday.

Gilbert thanked the Goulet's, for such a pleasant Sunday afternoon. The information, advice and allowing us this respite, and of course the wonderful meal.

Madame Goulet said, "It was your wife, who prepared most of it. I just enjoyed the conversation, along with having a few other women in the house. This has been a great day for us, because of you. We would appreciate it, if you would stay a few days longer, to rest yourselves."

Marilda thought a few days off the road would be refreshing. Alas, she expressed to Madame Goulet, "It has been a splendid visit, and the pleasure would certainly be ours if we were to stay a little longer." She reached for madame's hand, she understood the genuine nature of the woman's suggestion. Nattie told her, "We must be on our way." Nat and Gil said in unison, "It has been a blessing to us that we have met you both."

The Goulet's reply, "It has been a pleasure that you and your wonderful family shared a day with us."

Gilbert had asked if there was anything, he or his family can do for them.

Seeking to be Loved

"Oui there is, you can see to it that the letters I will give you tomorrow before you go, get to my sons when you get to Canada. I request you not to place it in the postal until you get to Canada. I am concerned about any transatlantic postage making it in a timely manner without getting lost during this great migration of our people, especially if war develops any time soon."

Gilbert assured him that he will wait until he gets to Canada, to put it in the proper postal.

"If you just so happen to meet my sons, expressed to them we love them, and miss them very much." Monsieur Goulet made the request of Gilbert, with a slight tremble in his voice.

They all helped clean up, the ladies started on the dishes, while the men dismantled the table. They carried the chairs and table into the house, then checked on the livestock. Gilbert told his children to thank the Goulets, and get a good night's rest.

Nattie was holding Phillip, who was nearly asleep in her arms. She and Madame Goulet joined the men on the porch. The sky was darkening. The sun had long since set over the horizon, the first few stars were beginning to appear.

Gilbert inquired once again if there was anything that they could do for them to repay their host's generosity.

He shook his head no.

Madame expressed, "What a pleasant day it had been for us. I had a feeling going to service this morning that this was going to be a special day. You and your family have made it so, it will be one we will always remember. It has been so nice seeing the motion of children at play. It was a pleasure hearing voices of people, having company, conversation, and assistance with daily task. Oui, your family made this a special day for us. To be able to share this time and the good things that we have with others is a blessing. As sojourners you and your family have made our hearts, and soul savor this day."

The Guyon's knew by her tone of voice and words she selected that they were spoken from her heart.

Seeking to be Loved

Nattie reached her free arm around Madame's shoulder and whispered, "Merci, you both are angels."

May 18, 1914 - They rested well, Gilbert and Marilda were woken by a heavy rain, falling just above their heads. They slept on the loft, in the Goulet home.

Nattie whispered to Gilbert, "What are we going to do?"

"We will wait until it gets light, then we will see what the day has in store for us," was his reply.

She then leaned over to see Phillip, snuggled under a small blanket in the little cradle, the host provided. M. Goulet had made it for his sons, and hoped to one day, have it used for his grandchildren.

Gilbert climbed down from the loft and left the house in silence not wanting to wake the children, or anyone else in the house. He slowly closed the door behind him gently stepping onto the porch. It was still dark. He heard a whisper.

"No need to get yourself soaking wet." The rain had not stopped yet.

Gilbert whispered, "Oui, the spring rains have returned."

"You should wait until it stops, there is no sense starting out wet and staying wet all day long."

Gilbert admitted, "You are right, we have experienced that, just a few days ago." Gilbert started walking towards the steps of the porch, to tend to his animals.

Monsieur Goulet whispered again, "The animals are fine, I have already checked them. I believe you will have a good day traveling to Paris. If you wait until the rain stops, and the road dries. Although it may be slow going, there is always a lot of people coming and going on Monday. The roads will be heavy with travelers and locals going to town carrying out their business."

"Are you familiar with Paris monsieur, its streets, and places in the city?" Gilbert questioned.

Seeking to be Loved

He explained, "I had been there several times, but non. You should get very close to the city today, even if you get a slightly late start, you are only 34km away. If lucky you will make twenty five of them. You will have difficulty finding a place to stay as you did here. A place with fields will be nearly impossible the closer you get. You may want to stop once again at some of the farms, or parks as you start closing in on the city. You will not make it through the city in one day. You will need to find shelter and a livery."

That reminded Gil of another question, he wanted to ask Monsieur Goulet. "Would you be in need for any of our fowl, goats or sheep?"

"We have no need for the sheep or the goats, fowl always are good to have available. Eggs, meat and keeping insect pest out of the garden. What would you like to get rid of?" asked M. Goulet.

"The chickens are good layers, even amongst all this traveling I would like to keep them. The ducks and geese you are welcome to."

"Well name your price, Monsieur Guyon?"

"A franc for each duck, two each goose."

"That is not a fair price Gilbert, I will take two ducks and two geese and give you ten francs, or no sale."

Gilbert suggest he pick the ones he would like to have. Then he changed his mind, "I will get them for you." Gil will select his best birds from his small flock, and leave them in the man's barn. Gilbert suspected, from the charity in Monsieur Goulet's heart, he would have selected the scrawniest birds of his flock.

The early morning spring rain had not done much damage to the road. It was already drying as they and many other travelers are on their way. A sign at the first crossroads read, Villeparisis 5km. It did not seem long before the next town, Livry-Gargon 7km. The villages and towns were becoming clustered closer together. Stops were becoming much more frequent, with people entering and leaving the roadway.

Seeking to be Loved

It seemed to be a constant buzz of noise, people talking, dogs barking and other sounds that none of them can describe. These sounds are unfamiliar to their ears. Neither of them ever heard such strange sounds before. It was clatter and banging, industrial sounds of factories, the roar of machinery and backfiring of those new automobiles. They were not sure what was causing many of the unusual and unnatural sounds they were hearing.

The only familiar overbearing noise, they recognized was the clanging of the trains steel wheels rolling on the tracks and the whistles they blew. Even they who were from the country, the remote agricultural areas/departments of France, were familiar with those sounds.

It was already late afternoon, by the time they got to Livry–Gargon. The area almost appeared as an oasis amongst this heavily populated department of France, which they are traveling. Gilbert mentioned to Marilda, it would be a good time to stop, rest and water the animals. They were all too, ready to get off the road. Despite being well rested, the strain of stopping and going as well as the slow-moving crowds of travelers impeding free flow of their progress fatigued them. It took a toll on everyone's patience.

The town was well-suited its name. There were many places that look much like small farms, surrounding and within the town. They were livery stables and small grazing fields. It was stationed an easy day's distance from Paris. It was apparent the industry of this hamlet was to cater to farmers and herdsman. Giving them an opportunity to rest, feed and replenish their stock as well as themselves before the final trek of their journey. When bringing their flocks and herds to the capital city. To supply its needs and the cities and towns surrounding it.

As soon as they pulled off the road, they were greeted by several representatives. Each offering friendly greetings and services, guaranteeing the freshest feed, greenest pasture, the purest water and comforts for man and beast. Gilbert was quite pleased with his decision to stop here.

Seeking to be Loved

Marilda, caught on very quickly, this was going to have a price. She suggested to Gil, to make sure to ask what the price would be. They discussed the options they heard presented to them and concluded they must not assume anything, and ask upfront what the cost would be for each convenience. They wanted nothing more than to take care of their immediate needs.

They were naïve, thus suspicious of those who had nothing better to do than provide conveniences to weary travelers livestock. Each were assuring that what they are offering is better than all the others. Promising to fatten your stock for market, to get you the best price per head. To say the least, they were uncomfortable with the arrangements being offered to them. They decided only to let their animals rest, graze, drink and relieve themselves. The cost being 10 centimes per hour for four-legged animal, they were glad for not having more of their herd with them. The two legged were the only ones that were allowed to relieve themselves without charge. With nine of them, they were thankful for that.

Two hours later, they harness the horses and goats to their assigned wagons and carts. On to Bondy, another 5+ kilometers closer to their destination. They have already made the decision to get as close to Paris as they can today.

Gilbert had spoken with several people at the livery. All had good things to say about Paris. Several people also have warned them to be wary and diligent. They spoke of the street urchins, these little fellows will distract the friendly traveler, while their cohorts rob you. Others have mentioned that the element is everywhere, especially where there will be masses of humanity gathered.

Most of the travelers heading west have already stopped for the evening. It seemed the eastbound traffic has increased slightly. Gil suspects they are workers heading home after a long day's labor. The sun is getting low in the sky as they approach the outskirts of Bondy.

He noted it is another industrial town and suggest to Marilda, who was at the reins, to start looking for a place to stop for the

Seeking to be Loved

night. He reminded her, if she sees a church, to stop there. He would inquire of the priest of a place to lodge.

Mary Alice has been noticed by several of the young men. Some boys standing on the side of the street, others passing on the road. She felt the gaze of their eyes, and heard the mumbling of their crude comments along with an occasional whistle. Mary only being twelve years old is tall for her age, her womanly shape only slightly beginning to blossom. She is uneasy with the attention, as she found it so crassly given.

It is flattering, she shyly acknowledged to herself. Although she is very uncomfortable receiving it. Her eyes give the slightest glance in the direction where the taunting originates from. When they know they got her attention, she can hear the whispers, and then the laughter. This embarrassed and infuriated her, yet she relished the attention, I am sure any young girl might.

Of course, her father and older brother noticed as well. Ernest is angry by the lack of respect being given his sister.

Her father noticed the role his daughter is playing, with her modest flirtation. He tolerated it, until he recognized the role she played, that which was her reluctance to ignore the taunts.

He simply mentioned to her, "For many young lads it does not take much encouragement to cross the line of respectful, to disrespectful attention given to attractive young ladies."

She understood the chastisement, of his words and teaching, as yet a lesson of conduct. She knew her father's way, of teaching lessons of morality, without dictating, accusing, or threatening the recipient of his comment. She knew her parents are observant, and always take advantage of every opportunity, to instruct appropriate morality. As well as, institute respectful ways to respond in certain situations. They point out lessons to learn and have always done so. She has even found herself doing and saying the same things to her younger brothers and sister.

She recalled a few times when her mother unbeknownst to her, overheard her correcting younger siblings. When she finally

Seeking to be Loved

acknowledged her mother was present and observed, she recognized the look of approval on her mother's face, and a smile of satisfaction.

It made her feel very proud of herself, and good inside. She wondered why it always feels good within ones being, when one does the correct thing?

Still hearing the jeers and the whistles of the passing young men. She is deep in thought, thinking how she liked the attention the boys and young men are giving her. She also realized they were giving it to all the young ladies, ahead and behind them also. When she finally acknowledged that realization, she thought, "What stupid boys. What fun can it be taunting the pretty girls?"

She caught herself in her vainness. Her immediate thought was of self-chastisement, "Oh, so, now fille, you think you are a pretty fille attirante(attractive girl)?" She thought it is very presumptuous and conceded, to be thinking of oneself in that manner. She reminds herself to ask Ernest for his opinion, later.

She decided, she will just enjoy the walk along the streets as they pass through, listening to the sounds and enjoy the sights.

Marilda spots a high steeple and gets Gilbert's attention, who has been carrying little Gil on his shoulders.

He acknowledged and signaled with a gesture of cocking his head to the left, suggesting that she turn. Gilbert rushed ahead to stop the oncoming traffic. Marilda turned the team onto Avenue Pasteur. They head towards the steeple. After a few hundred meters, they come to a square outside of St. Peter's Parish.

Gilbert has his family stay together with their belongings. He made his way into the church. He blessed himself with the holy water. He noticed a handful of people kneeling in silence, there is no priest.

He is drawn to the statue of St. Joseph carrying the infant Lord and Savior, Jesus. Taking a coin from his pocket, he placed it in the donation box. He kneeled to light a candle. He began his prayer, "In the name of our Lord and Savior Jesus Christ." He made the request of St. Joseph, To guide and protect his family. "Dear St.

Seeking to be Loved

Joseph, God in heaven, commissioned you to guide and protect our Savior. Please watch over us and guide us on our journey. For it was you my dear St. Joseph, who was selected and entrusted from all mankind to protect the Holy Family, and all family's on earth. You were born to guide, and protect our incarnate Lord and Savior created to save the faithful here on earth. He knew his prayer was already being answered when he heard footsteps from the altar area. One of the priests was preparing for the evening service.

Gilbert approached the priest and introduced himself and made his request known.

The priest smiled and told him that there is an elderly gentleman Monsieur Mordeaux. "He owns a small farm less than a kilometer north west of here. He comes to service every day. He will be here shortly for the evening mass. His wife died last year, he has not missed a mass since. I am sure he will be happy to host you, maybe, he will enjoy the company. Will you stay for mass?" the priest inquired.

"We would enjoy that father. All our belongings are just outside. I believe I should stay with them, my family will attend."

"Let us go see." said the priest and he positions his hand behind Gilbert's left elbow and leads him down the aisle to the entry. They both turned to face the altar and the crucifix, they kneel and make the sign of the cross before exiting the chapel area.

Gilbert led the way to where he had entered.

Upon seeing the menagerie of wagon, carts, beast and seven young children with Marilda. The priest said to Gilbert, "I see what you mean."

Gilbert suggest he and Ernest stay with the belongings, while the rest of the family may attend the service. They are glad to do so, to sit and rest their legs. Not to mention hear the word of the Lord, and sing praise to him. It was always a comfort and pleasure.

The priest told them, "I will speak to Monsieur Mordeaux before the service. I will mention to him, I would like to talk with him after the mass. To make sure he delays his exit, so I can explain your request, and introduce you. I am sure he would like to accommodate your request."

"Merci, father." replied Gilbert.

After the service, Monsieur Mordeaux sat alone. Marilda and the children were the only others left in the parish. The priest had gone for a few minutes to he changed his vestments. He took a seat beside Monsieur Mordeaux, and explained why he had him stay.

They both turned to the right, and look over their shoulder, to see the family sitting across the aisle three rows back.

Marilda managed a small smile, then she noticed a smile cross the man's face, he nodded at her. She tilted her head in recognition.

The priest and the old man knelt, made the sign of the cross facing the alter. The priest ushered him to meet Marilda and the children in the pew where they were sitting.

Just as the priest predicted, Monsieur Mordeaux was pleased to have guest. He introduced him to Marilda, and the children. Blanche and Joseph were asleep on Mary's lap, using her thigh as a pillow. Phillip was sleeping in his mother's arms.

They gathered outside the church, where Gil and Ernest awaited them. Gil introduced himself, and expressed his gratitude to monsieur Mordeaux, and the priest. The Guyon's followed him through the town's streets to his home. He seemed to know everyone he met and crossed paths with as they walked along. Upon arriving at his home, he stepped ahead of them to open the gate to his plot of land. He warned them to be careful, the gate is narrow. Once everyone is in, he closed the gate and latched it. He suggest to Marilda, go into the house with the little ones, he would join her soon. "I will show your husband to the stables and the well. Then I will come show you where things are placed inside, and to your rooms.

Marilda disembarking from the wagon, directs Mary and Blanche to get the basket with the day's provisions. Overhearing her, as he was directing Gilbert where to take the animals.

Seeking to be Loved

He shouted to her, "S'il vous plaît(please), s'il vous plaît, do not bring anything in to eat, you will keep your provisions. I have more than enough, my wife and I preserved enough for years to come before she passed away. Since she is gone, I eat very little, I need to get rid of as much as I can. I will never be able to eat it all, and I do not want to store it very long."

"That is very kind of you monsieur," she said in reply.

"You go in, I will be right there," he said.

Marilda and Mary entered the home of the old man. It has not been well kept. Everything was in its place, it appeared not to have been touched, dusted nor swept for a long time. Marilda carrying Phillip, looked at Mary who was carrying Joseph. They both knew what the other was thinking. "We have cleaning to do!"

Marilda let out a little sigh, "It should not take long to dust and wipe every surface. I will take the children and let them sleep on the couch. While you ask Monsieur Mordeaux for a bucket of water," she told Mary. "I will start to dust, when you get the water, follow me with the bucket and wipe everything I clean off. Then we will go into the kitchen and clean, as we prepare dinner."

Monsieur Mordeaux guided Marilda to the pantry, which is well-stocked. Next he ushered her to the smoke room, where he is curing meat and sausage. He explained he has the best sausage in town, you can ask anyone. He selected two of them, grabbed another and mumbled to himself, "This will be plenty."

He suggested to Marilda, "Please pick out what preserved vegetables and fruits, you and your family would like from the shelves."

He started preparing the dinner, Marilda request that she do the cooking. He explained you are my guest.

She insisted, and he contently conceded to her affirmation. She and Mary continued cleaning the kitchen, he does not object. He smiled to himself and whispers under his breath, "They are just like you, Mon Chéri(My Darling)." Looking up as if he were speaking to his wife in heaven.

Seeking to be Loved

"They must have everything clean and spotless."
"Did you send them, Mon Chéri, my dear one?"
"Did you think, I needed a woman's touch, around the house?"
"Sacré bleu, you are always right!"

His eyes filled with moisture. He missed his lifelong companion. He and his wife had been married for 57 years, ever since he was 18 years old.

May 19, 1914 - It is early, they and the old man have there early morning rituals and routines. They are used to getting up before dawn to start the day. When they are ready to start making their way to Paris, Monsieur Mordeaux, presented them with a very large saucisson. He told them, "This will keep you strong for your journey."

Gil offered to pay him.

The old man told Gilbert, "I have no need for l'argent now. There is nothing that I need, and there will not be many days of my life left, before I will join, Mon Cheri." He pointed and looked to the heavens above.

All the Guyon's, bid him fair well, and, thanked Monsieur Mordeaux. Gilbert offered the old man his Blessing, "May God bless you, monsieur."

He replied to Gilbert, "He already has my son, he already has, many times."

They are pleasantly surprised at 6:30AM the streets are still virtually empty. Only the bakers were busy, they smell the delicious satisfying aroma of fresh baked bread and pastries. It is not long before they felt the sun on their backs as they make their way to Paris.

The sign at the crossroad read, Parc La Villette. They are just northeast of Paris; it is too early to stop. Since the day was hot, they decided to rest for a while. It would be a good time to let the animals' repose, drink, and graze.

Seeking to be Loved

The park was quite extensive with plenty of places to rest in the shade of the Plane trees massive canopy. There were many fountains, where they could water the animals. It was shortly after mid-day, when many travelers stopped to take their break, and to rest. The Guyon's decided they would move on, and make it to the outskirts of Paris before they stop for the evening.

The topic of possible invasion and the war with Germany, was everywhere. Gilbert took advantage of the time they spent at the park to talk with many of the people nearby. He noticed a man sitting not too far from them. The man had the familiar look of a mariner. He was wearing a watch cap and a p-coat, despite the warmth of the day. Gilbert approached him and introduced himself. He asked if he might answer a few of his questions. The man nodded and said, "Oui monsieur."

Gil explained what he was planning to do, that is to obtain passage to Canada for his family.

"Oui," was the only thing the man said.

Gilbert asked, if he knew what he would need or must he do to obtain passage for he and his family, as well as all their possessions?

The man explained, it has been a long time since I have been out to sea. Although, I will tell you what you will need to do monsieur. He proceeds, "The office Des Longitudes, in the heart of Paris, it is along the Seine River." He told Gilbert, "It is there you can get any and all information. If you have questions, there you can get them answered."

Gil asked, "Will that include fair, passports, proper papers, passage, ship assignment and boarding place and time?"
Then added, "Which port and what company we may contact?"

"All your questions will be answered there, Oui."

"How do we get there?"

The man laughed and said, "There are many ways to get their monsieur. I think the best would be to take Avenue de Flandre, south to Rue du Farbong Saint Martin, to Rue de Turbigo. There you will

Seeking to be Loved

run into a Église, Saint Eustache. It will be on the other side of the river, from there at the river you will be able to see it."

Gilbert thanked the man and wished him a good day.

The old sailor waved and wish to them, "Bon Voyage."

Gilbert thought they can be there easily in three hours. He was not realizing the extensiveness of the traffic on the crowded streets of Paris, during the late afternoon, early evening hours.

He thought how lucky they are, being so close to Paris. His concern now was focused on where his family could spend the night in safety, and a place to keep their animals.

The city seemed to buzz with much excitement. There was so many people, unlike what Mary experienced the day before no one seemed to notice her. Everyone seemed to be in a hurry and about their business, on their own mission. The children could not help noticing all the beautiful architecture. Many of the buildings had a grandness about them. Shops were everywhere on both sides of the streets, many side-by-side.

Blanche riding in the wagon sitting next to her mother, ask "Why is it, there are so many stores Ma mee? Who can use so many things?"

Ernest and Mary noticed the fashion and dress, of the young men and ladies. They were amazed people were wearing such clothes on an ordinary day especially during a workday. It looked as if they were wearing their Sunday best. They thought to themselves, surely there must be a very special occasion. Maybe a holiday, they were not aware of is being celebrated in Paris.

They can no longer see the sun, even though it was still the light of day. The streets were narrower the buildings were higher. All Gilbert knew, is that it was getting later in the day. Once again, he reminded himself, I must get my watch and keep it in my pocket.

They had been on Rue de Turbigo for only a few minutes when they see the magnificent, Saint Eustache church. It seemed to be rising right in front of them. It appeared, that this road runs right into it. The closer they get, the more they can see its magnificence.

Seeking to be Loved

It was truly a masterpiece of Gothic architecture. It is one of the largest parishes in all of France. It has a grand cut stone courtyard, and a large park beside the south side of the church. They are all anxious, anticipating going in to see the inside of this magnificent structure. They can hear the organ playing, they knew it must be the middle of the evening service.

Gilbert suggested to Nattie, she and the children go in. He and Ernest would stay with the wagon. He reminded Nattie, to make their request known, to one of the priests.

Marilda guided the children into the church and had them dip into the font to Bless themselves. They are awestruck, if not more so than they were when they entered St Anne's and the other St. Etienne parishes they have visited.

The sound of the organ and its vibration is not only heard in their ears, it was felt as well. The tunes resonated a deep pulsation within their bodies. They stare about them in amazement. The whole interior is aglow from the many candles, and the light still pouring through the magnificent stained-glass windows. It is caused by the sun casting its waning light of the day. There is a flickering of multicolored beams coming through the many windows, lighting the entire chapel. The sound of the organ was engulfing; it was more than perceiving the sound of the music. The sound was inside and you became part of it. Only now they are aware of other sounds mixed with the organ. The sound of chants and singing, how angelic and magnificent the sound.

Henry asked, "Is it the heavenly host we hear?" Partially joking and serious at the same time, in his utter amazement. It would be impossible not to be moved by the sound and the site, they all beheld at that moment. It was almost as if the music was penetrating the fibers of ones being yet, at the same time spewing outwardly from the depths of the soul.

Marilda, turned Phillip in her arms, facing him away from her so he can observe the spellbinding sight. She can feel his legs kicking. She watched his arms moving, and his head in motion looking about.

Seeking to be Loved

She hears the soft joyful cooing sounds he is making, despite the loudness, and vibrations of the organ. As she hears his voice, the sounds of her son, all else is barred for the moment. She realized how in tune she is to her youngest babe.

This I suppose is the same instinct in every living creature. As it is on a distant island shore covered with tens of thousands of cow seals and their pups, or, penguins and their chicks. Even with all the deafening sound about them the parent and child, recognize one. So, tuned in to their own infants bark, or chirp, and no other, they hear and find their own amongst thousands.

- Is it only instinctive with a mother and infant, this sacred bond?
- Is it a built in homing device that locates, nurtures, secures, and recognizes its own, when it may seem an impossibility?
- Or is it more than that?
- Is it a love so pure and uninhibited, harboring no preconceived expectations?
- Is it a sample of the gift given us?
- A love, that just exist in its most perfect form?
- Love that makes possible the seemingly impossible?

Marilda motioned her children to a pew at the rear of the church. They quickly realized that they have entered during the closing hymns of the service. Once the procession of the priest's pass, she had the children remain in their seats. Meanwhile, she quickly went to introduce herself to the pastor, who was positioned to meet with his parishioners as they exited. She presented her request to the priest.

He opened the door to see Gilbert and her son at the far side of the courtyard. The Priest suggest she have a seat with the children. I will come to you after the congregation has exited.

He came back to the pew and all were asleep, except for her and Phillip, who was patiently waiting to be nursed. The Priest

Seeking to be Loved

motioned to Marilda to stay there. He whispered, "Let the children keep their rest. I will go meet with your husband."

He approached Gilbert. Gil greeted him and introduced himself, and his son Ernest to the priest.

"I am Dominique," said the priest. "Now how may I help you?"

Gilbert explained the purpose of their journey, and they are in need of a place to spend the evening. He inquires if he knew where he can board their animals.

"It is truly Providence, that must have led you here, to our Élgise of Saint Eustache! We happen to have a stable underneath the north wing. We are the only église in all of Paris, maybe all of France, that has one within the parish. Let me show you, we will have plenty of hay and water for your animals. The space will be crowded, all the stalls are filled with the steeds of some of the wealthy parishioners."

The priest explained, we have a hostel here, although by this time of day it is usually filled beyond capacity.

Gilbert made a request to the priest, "If it is not troublesome, or inconvenient father, we can sleep in the stable. We will be happy to do so, we are farmers." Then he said, "That would be much better than sleeping in the streets or the little park beyond the courtyard. It is starting to look like we may be having some inclement weather this evening. We will be very careful not to disturb any of the other animals, in fact we will be happy to assist in their care while we are here."

The priest glanced at Gilbert in a questioning manner. Then asked him, "How long is it you plan on staying?"

Gilbert replied, "Only as long as it takes to obtain whatever papers we need and to procure passage to Canada. I know little of the matters, my hope is that we can be on our way by noon tomorrow."

"I too know nothing of such matters," stated the priest. "I do know from experiences shared with me by parishioners when they travel, it may take days. Sometimes weeks to get the proper papers.

Seeking to be Loved

If you are not from this area/department, where they can immediately access public files to prove your residency. It could take a long time, the agents must verify and confirm what you are saying, is true. You may need to see a magistrate to assist you. That also may take days, weeks, sometimes longer."

"I am afraid we can ill afford either of those options," stated Gilbert. "Will you pray for us father?"

"I will," replied Dominique.

Marilda approached them with the children nearly clinging to her.

The priest motioned them to follow him, he led them to the north wing. There he guided them through a narrow allee to get to the stable entrance. It took an expert teamster to maneuver through the allee with the wagon. The Priest motioned to the Guyon's, to stay here. He knocked on a small door, there was a delay before it opened, and he entered. A moment later the two large doors swing open, exposing a well-constructed support structure for the magnificent chapel above. Between each major support, were large stalls, that housed some splendid horses. There was also an area where just carriages and buggies were kept. Many were outfitted with luxurious seating and decor. The priest introduced them to the stable master, Monsieur Poincare, and the boy John B. He seemed pleased to have guest, and welcomed them.

Monsieur Poincare inspected each beast carefully as they proceeded by him to where he had them stop. There he examined them closer, lifting each leg of the horses, cow, goats, and sheep. He looked at their hoofs and feet.

He complimented Gilbert, on the care and condition of his animals after such a long journey. Gilbert took in a deep breath, expanding his chest with pride. Knowing that despite the length of their journey, and the long days, he had not neglected the care for his stock. He knew his father taught him well. He in turn, by example and deed, was also teaching his children to care for what they have, with all diligence.

Seeking to be Loved

    The priest excused himself, explaining to Gilbert, he must go. Letting the Guyon family know, Monsieur Poincare and John, will now show them around. They will see to it, that you have what you need.
    Gilbert asked Dominique, if he knew about the Office Des Longitude, and its location.
    "Oui," it is very close just on the other side of the Seine River." He told him, "All you need to do is crossover the old Stone bridge and you will see it. You will get all your questions answered there. You may even possibly get your papers. I do not believe they sell passage, although they can direct you to the various transport and shipping companies close by."
    Gilbert, Ernest, and Henry quickly focus their attention, caring for the animals. The stable boy assisted them, he is thrilled to have company his age. Other than the daily contact they have with those who own the animals they board, and more often, the owner's coachmen. They have few visitors. No one has ever stayed in the stable with them.
    Marilda, Mary and Blanche gather the things they need for the evening and preparation for the evening meal.
    John cannot stop talking to them about all the horses and who they belong to. He shared his speculations of the people who own them. Imagining where they live and what their lives may be like. He was inquisitive about the Guyon's, asking them many questions about where they are from, living, and life in the country. He always wondered what it was like.
    His existence was that of a stable boy, that was all he knew. He often dreamed what life outside the stable, or, city is like. He had only his imagination, he has never known anything else. He never met anyone who lived outside the great city of Paris. Only the stable, and the city immediately surrounding it, and the parish itself was what he has known.

Seeking to be Loved

He can only imagine what a countryside would look like. His only conception of open land is that of the small parks just beyond the church.

Of course, he took every opportunity showing off his strength and knowledge of the immediate surroundings, to impress Mary Alice. Not wanting to make it look to conspicuous, he attempted to avoid eye contact with her.

She noticed his glances, for her eyes have been following him as she is trying to concentrate on assisting her mother and watch him at the same time. He is strong for a city boy, she is not impressed. Her brothers are as strong as any boys their age, and can easily out work most.

A short time has passed, they are joined by two of the nuns, who Dominique has requested that they assist them. The Nuns were dressed in the typical habits, the only apparel worn by their order. They approach Marilda and asked, "Madame Guyon, how may we be assistance to you?" They introduced them self only as sisters of Saint Eustache, one sister does all the speaking.

Marilda is very gracious, she told them, "We are in need of nothing."

The sister asked if she may show her to the wash area and latrine?

Marilda is quite pleased that they have an area to wash and relieve themselves, she responds, "Oui my grace." She, and the girls and two youngest follow the nuns to the back corner of the stable. Opening the door, they find the stone spiral staircase. It made two complete spirals to reach the next floor. They opened the door and passed through, into another level, and are led down a hallway. To the right were a line of windows letting in the fading light of the early evening. It illuminated the long hallway. They can see light coming from the buildings below and beyond the windows, in the shadow cast by the great cathedral.

Blanche said, "Look at all the lights Ma mee."

Seeking to be Loved

Mary commented, "I never seen so many all at once, in one area."

The sisters giggled, one opened the door to the left and motioned for them to go in. It was a large open room which had seven small stalls, each had a paneled door. On the wall opposite the stalls, were seven basins on a table. At the end of the table where the basins were set, was a hand pump. On the floor beside the pump, were stacked seven wooden buckets.

Marilda looked at the sisters, and exclaimed with wonder, "A hand pump inside?"

"Oui madame!"

Marilda, is impressed, the children do not know what to think!

Marilda had an idea what the pails were for, to pump water into and carried to the basins, so they can wash. Something told her she might want to question the nuns about the pails use, just in case.

The sisters giggled again, the one who did all the speaking nodded to the other. Who then proceeded to the buckets, acted like she was pumping water into it and carried it to one of the stalls. When she opened the door Marilda and Mary recognized what it was for. They looked at each other in agreement, with a grin.

Mary Alice looked at her mother and whispered, "We could have used this luxury at home."

Marilda agreed, nodding in confirmation.

Blanche also understood, and stated to her mother, "I need to go now."

The nun who had not spoken a word asked, "May I pump the water into the bucket for you?" She did and placed it next to the stall Blanche had entered. She used her foot to slide it underneath, she heard a little voice say, "Merci."

The sister spoke, "Would you please follow me." She ushered them back out into the hall, where they proceed a little further. By now they can smell the delicious smells coming from the kitchen. They are led into a dining area, it is very simple, tables, benches with

Seeking to be Loved

a cooking area off to the left. This is where the nuns prepare their meals. They informed Marilda, that we have already finished our evening meal. Sister Elaine, is baking bread for you, and shortly a soup will be prepared for you and your family.

Marilda, is humbled and embarrassed by the graciousness, and the hospitality being shown them. Holding Phillip in her arms, fatigued and weary from their traveling. She is grateful for the treatment she and her family are receiving. She placed one hand over her mouth, she is being overcome with emotion.

The nuns noticed she was close to tears, and attempted to comfort her. "Madame you must not be sad."

Mary asked, "What is wrong Ma mee?"

Marilda shook her head side to side. After a moment she finally told the nuns, how thankful she and her family are for being led here to them. She shared with the nuns, how kind and generous so many have been to them on their journey.

The nuns both at the same time stated, "Our Lord is always willing to provide for those that trust in him. It is God's will, we share what we have with whoever we can, when the opportunity arises. We must go now to evening prayer. Can we show you back to the stables?"

The other nun whispered in the vestal's ear.

"Merci, for reminding me sister."

There was one more area they wished to show them. Exiting the little dining area, it is just the next door down.

"Follow me please." Opening the door, they see a long narrow room with small beds, not much bigger than a cot. Each with a blanket and a pillow. A hook on the wall, at the head of the bed was used to hang the nuns' habit. A crucifix hung over each of the cots, and underneath several are small trunks. There are several barren hooks and beds with the crucifix over them and no trunk underneath. The sister mentioned that you may sleep on these while you are with us.

Seeking to be Loved

The sister said, a candle is lit until 10PM each evening. The candle then is extinguished for the night. That is when we retire from evening prayer. Only you and the girls, and, of course the baby would be allowed to sleep here. The men are not allowed. Monsieur Poincare, will show the men where they will take care of their needs and rest."

The sister reiterated, "We must go now, please make yourself comfortable, your dinner will be ready in just a few minutes. You may want to tell your men."

When they got back to the stables, they told the men folk about their brief tours of the washroom, dining area and where they would be allowed to sleep.

Gilbert suggested to Nattie, "We must hurry to clean up, so we do not keep them waiting. It would be rude of us not to be prompt, when they are demonstrating such wonderful and gracious hospitality."

Nattie agreed, the women gathered their things and went upstairs. Meanwhile Gilbert, Ernest, Henry, little Gil, and Joseph followed John and Monsieur Poincare, to where the men wash and dine. Gilbert is concerned about leaving all their belongings. Monsieur Poincare assured him everything will be safe, the doors are bolted, the stable is closed for the night.

The dinner was simple, it consisted of soup and bread. It was delicious, and they were thankful for it.

They returned to the stable, the men and boys checked the animals. The sun has yet to set, although the weaning light is about gone. Night is beginning to settle over the great city of Paris. Ernest asked his father while returning from the dining area, if they may walk about the streets of Paris, before they go to bed for the evening.

John B. overheard and expressed he would be delighted to show him around this part of town. Being a young teen, he was familiar with the city streets, and he liked being out at night.

Seeking to be Loved

Monsieur Poincare, with a peculiar look on his face said, "Where you would be taking them my boy, may not be the best places for them to go."

"I would just take them to the area down by the river and along the boulevard. It is grand and open their, and there will be establishments open for another few hours, some much later," John said, with a grin.

Ernest and Henry looked at their father and made the request, "Can we go father?"

"We will wait to see what your mother has to say. We all had a long and trying day, and I am not sure what tomorrow will bring."

When they finished looking after the animals, Marilda and the other children were there waiting. They had their evening garments and things set out, ready for bed.

Ernest made his request known to his mother.

Mary Alice quickly agreed with the suggestion.

Henry, then Blanche, and little Gilbert, despite his fatigue were excited about the prospect. Joseph is asleep on a soft blanket covering a pile of hay and Phillip quite content in Natties arms.

Gilbert asked John, "How far is it to the river?"

"It is only about two squares Monsieur."

"Maybe we can take a leisure walk to the river, we can be back in an hour," Gilbert decided.

Nattie uttered, "I will keep the two youngest with me, I do not want them to be disturbed, I will stay here. While you are taking care of business tomorrow. Maybe then, I can take the family on a little walk myself."

"That sounds like a good idea," said Gilbert.

Mary had her bedclothes already laid out to take upstairs to the girls sleeping room.

Gilbert told her, "We will wait for you here, we will not leave without you."

"I will be back in a moment Papa," she exclaimed with a exhilarating tone to her voice!

Seeking to be Loved

    The children and Gilbert, are excited about being in their capital city, and seeing some of the sites. The evening sounds are quite different, than what they are used to. It is much quieter, than it was during the day. It is dark between the buildings and along the streets, although there are gas streetlamps illuminating areas along the way. It is interesting to see the storefronts and restaurants, with the lights glowing from them. They can see the people sitting, talking, laughing, and dining inside. Occasionally they hear music, as they pass by, along with laughter and the hum of voices having conversation. It is not long before they can see the openness, as they approach the great waterway of the Seine River.

    Gilbert asked John if he is familiar with the Office des Longitude. He explained the directions that the Priest Dominique, had given him.

    John replied, "I can take you there."

    Each noticed the multiple warm colors glowing just above the buildings. The western sky, as they reached the waterfront was ablaze. They were able to view great stretches of the city to the Northwest and Southeast along the Seine river. The clouds that were rolling in reflected the rays of the setting sun, which had just dropped below the horizon. It was a pleasant seen, coming from amongst all the buildings.

    They thought the sun had long since set. It was the shadows cast by the buildings that caused the darkness earlier. Now standing in the open, there is still the last remaining light of day fading as the sun had just disappeared from the vista. There was a sense of freeness in the atmosphere of the city. It was not the same sense of freedom, or, feeling of independence they would get when looking out over the Moselle River, from their home. It was more like an energy, that caused the excitement. Maybe it was just the newness of being in such a crowded area where buildings, houses, shops, and stores were all around. It seemed to spark, and ignite the senses of the children. Although Gilbert thought it was interesting, he was glad that he did not live in the city. He wondered what it will be like when he meets his brothers in Québec.

John guided them along the river to the old Stone bridge. Once on the other side of the Seine, they walk east for 200 meters along the street with the river to their left. John pointed to the building he believed M. Guyon is looking for. He had passed it many times, never giving it notice before.

The Office des Longitude, Gilbert locked into his memory the names of the streets, and its location. He did not want to have to trouble anyone tomorrow trying to find it. They cross back over to the north bank and follow the street west. Making their way back to the church and stable. They hear the clock chime as it struck nine.

John had to knock very loudly several times. He can hear Monsieur Poincare coming to the door. He asked, "Who is it?" He confirmed it is John, before he unlocked the door. He greeted them and asked if they enjoyed their walk on the streets of Paris. He questioned John if they were bothered by anyone.

"Non, I knew where to take our guest to avoid being harassed by them," he replied.

Monsieur Poincare wrapped his arm around John and looked at him. The expression on his face was of a nurturing, proud father gazing at a son. "You should know, what they are up to, you were one of those rascals."

Gilbert asked, "Are you referring to the street urchins, we have heard much about them, and been warned to be leery of them, monsieur?"

M. Pioncare and John both chuckled, then he said, "And that is what they are, urchins, spiny little devils. They will steal the shoes off your feet, and get everything in your pockets before you even realize you have been robbed.

It is a good thing, you got here when you did. They will be out all night. Then they will be harassing many of the people in the morning, as they are drowsily going to work and going about their business in the markets. Before they retire, to hide in their holes, all

Seeking to be Loved

day resting, counting their lute. They know when people have the (he rubs his fingers together, to insinuate argent, francs), in their pockets or purse. They do not care who you are either; whether you are the mayor or even their own mother, it matters not to them."

Gilbert suggest to Mary Alice; she and Blanche go to their mother for the night.

John enthusiastically said, "I will show them to their quarters."

Mary shyly looked at her father, while she was reaching for Blanche's hand.

John guided them to the spiral stairs. He reached back and told Mary, "Take my hand." He has been waiting all night to hold it. He attempted to do so several times while they were walking. He intentionally inched his way closer to her with each step while they were on the streets. Occasionally brushing his hand ever so gently against hers. She not recognizing his intentions, just gently created more space between them as they walked along.

His hands felt like her brothers, firm and strong. Although, there was something different in the touch. It made her heart flutter a bit, she liked the sensation that seemed to move through her body as much as in her mind. With each step up, she had to be aware of her right hand holding onto Blanche's, who followed behind her. She thought to herself, this is a good thing. If I did not have Blanche's hand in mine, I may feel as though I were adrift. She had never walked holding hands with a boy, other than family members.

With each step, John became ever more aware of the gentle tugs on his hand. Excitement loomed in his mind, thinking she also wanted to delay their ascend. Each step, each slight tug caused his heart to race. He noticed a lightness in his step and an unusual warmness in his heart. John opened the door, never letting go of her hand and gently guided her through. He points with his left hand the way to go down the corridor, blocking the door with his body.

Mary can see the candlelight glowing from the room at the end of the hall.

Seeking to be Loved

He said, "I am not allowed to be here. You must go the rest of away on your own." His hand opened slowly, letting go of hers. He is uncertain of what to say to her, other than, "Bonne nuit." He allowed the door to close behind him. Just before it closed, he looked back and whispered, "I will see you tomorrow."

Mary Alice turned to look at him, nodded her head, just as the door closed.

He walked back down the stairs to the stable.

The quarters and sleeping space for the stable man and lad were cramped. There was room for two bunks, a small table with a basin and a bucket they would use to draw their water from the hand pump. It was located just outside their room in the stable for their use, as well as the animals. There was also two good size wooden chest where they kept their personal belongings.

Monsieur Poincare had suggested to Gilbert, they could sleep in the hay loft or pitch down some hay to lay on. They did the latter, explaining they can cover the hay with their quilts. In the morning they would use the hay to feed the animals. It was not long before Gilbert and his sons were sound asleep.

Little Gilbert's last words before he dozed off were, "I never slept in the stable under a église before."

Seeking to be Loved

Chapter 7 The Arrangements

May 20, 1914 - Monsieur Poincare was up early as usual. He knew which horses needed to be ready for their masters, or coachman, and the time they would arrive for them.

Gilbert bid him, " bon jour," then proceeded to assist him in feeding the horses and seeing to his own animals. At the direction of the stable master, John began to roll out the carriages and place them between the stables. M. Poincare had everything well-organized, knowing the routine of each coachman. There would be no delay when they came for their steeds. Each will have their carriages or buggies ready for them. When the last one had pulled away from the stables, Monsieur Poincare was ready to take a break. He asked Gilbert and his sons to join him and John for breakfast in the men's kitchen. They were happy to join them; the morning chores had worked up their appetite. On the way, Gilbert asked Monsieur Poincare when would be a good time to go to the Office des Longitude.

Monsieur Poincare, told him they will not open the door until 9AM. He met Dominique in the men's kitchen, and once again expressed his gratitude. He asked him, if he knew of any procedures that were customary for such business as his. What he should bring with him to obtain passports or proper papers for he and his family?

All Dominique could suggest was proof of your citizenship if he had that, would be helpful. Also everyone needing papers, must be in attendance. Otherwise you may have to make another appointment. They must verify the number of papers that are needed to be issued to the proper individuals. In this case you and all your family members. They will also inspect each of you to assess your health. If there are signs of illnesses, diseases, or other conditions they may not allow you to obtain passage.

Many nations do not allow anyone with sicknesses, or disease to enter their countries. There is concern and fear of spreading the illness. That may cause weeks, if not months of delay.

Seeking to be Loved

A ship delivering its cargo with sick passengers, may not be allowed entry in the harbors and ports. Loss can be great and severe for all involved, it is good they have such practices. It can save the lives and the livelihood of many.

We have learned from the missionaries, years ago when setting up missions in undeveloped countries throughout the world. There have been entire tribes of indigenous people, in remote lands, and on islands who were completely wiped out. From diseases and contaminated goods brought in from other countries. Not to mention boarding ships where many people are crowded together, where illnesses can spread quickly. An epidemic on board would ruin the company's reputation. Ship captains are notorious for not allowing sick people or animals on board. I apologize M. Guyon, I do not mean to be spreading such gloom. Hopefully, your family are in excellent health, and will remain so throughout your journey, until you reach your destination and beyond. It appears you and your family are in good health.

Gilbert thanked the priest and asked, "Would you please pray for us?"

"I most certainly will," he replied.

After breakfast, the Guyon family gathered at the stable. All were clean, dressed, and ready for the day. Uncertain about what it may bring, all had their own itinerary. There was a steady drizzle of spring rain, that had persisted since early morning.

Monsieur Poincare, suggested that they get there early, knowing the rain may delay the masses somewhat. If they are at the front of the line, they will not have to wait long in such inclement weather. You will be ushered in and taken care of first, thus avoid the long waiting lines.

Gilbert told him, "I was thinking the same thing, merci monsieur, for reinforcing my thoughts." Gilbert, turned to Nattie, inquired if she had packed anything that may prove their citizenship. "Do we have any documents that may have our names on them?"

Seeking to be Loved

    He had wished that he had foreseen the need of such things as birth certificates. That his father and mother may have had and her parents as well.

    She said, "Oui, I know exactly where I packed them. We will need to unload a few layers of items to get them. I remember my father gave me an envelope, as did yours. They both told us Gil if you recall, 'You may need these'."

    "Get those as well, I will look for something to cover us to keep us all dry. We will have about five squares to ride and a little over a two hundred meters to walk." Gil mentioned.

    Poincare always alert of what is being said in the stable. Thought if he had anything, they could use to keep dry. The rain appeared to have picked up a little more and showed no sign of stopping. He knew everyone had come for their carriage, all were picked up. The carriages owned by the église, came to mind. He asked Gilbert if they had a parapluie(umbrella). They will need them for walking about, on such a raining day as today.

    Gilbert verified they do not.

    "I will request permission to use the parish carriage to transport you and your family to the Des Longitude. If they give us permission, all will be solved. If the answer is no, then either John or I will take you. That way you will not have to worry about leaving it unattended and blocking the street. It may take me twenty minutes to get permission. May I suggest M. Gilbert, you go on ahead and get in line, to take your place. The line can be awfully long and trying on one's patience.

    I will bring the rest of the family, either with the carriage, or John will walk with them to meet you there. If indeed we are granted use of the parish carriage, by the time we harness it and get there an hour may have passed. They will be opening the doors in a half hour; you may want to hurry on your way."

    Gilbert was thankful for Monsieur Poincare's advice. He went on his way quickly, wanting to place himself first in line at the door. When he came to the steps leading to the building he realized that

Seeking to be Loved

he should have left long before. Despite the rain, there was already several people waiting. He took his place in line and started a conversation with the person in front of him. All those overhearing the dialogue turned to say, "Oui, my family also." Confirming which Gilbert had already known, many people are seeking transport to foreign countries. All wanting to get their family's out of harm's way.

The talk, quickly turned to the anticipated and upcoming war. One gentleman said, it is inevitable. He declared it has already been confirmed, though he had nothing to substantiate it.

The door finally opened and people filed in. The narrow hallway directed them to a man at a booth who asked them their business. He handed him a card, and directed him to another room. A gentleman at the door checked their card, then pointed to specific desks. Some are ushered to a room beyond the door to the left. Others directed to take a seat where they were to wait for an agent to come get them.

There was at least twenty-five people in front of Gilbert. Some had their families with them, some were couples, some as Gilbert, came alone. After all the desk were filled, it appeared that he would be next in line.

He was concerned how his family would get through. Or, if in fact, he needed to have his family present.

How would they know where I am?
Would his agent allow him to go look for them?
Could he bring his whole family in?
Would one of the gentlemen in uniform, who is directing people where to go, be sent to find them?
Would he lose his space if he does not have everything that he needed with him?
What if he and his family do not have the correct papers?

There are too many unanswered questions, going through his mind. He decided to approach the man who directed him to his seat and pose the question to him.

Seeking to be Loved

He addressed the man in uniform, "Excusez-moi monsieur, may I ask you a few questions?" The uniformed man responded by simply saying, "That would be up to your agent." Then he looked away to direct the next patron.

Time dragged on, he had been waiting at least an hour. "I need to find that watch."

He began to wonder, there must be a lot of things to cover with each case. His wife and children should be here by now if they were able to get through the line. Before he even finished the thought, he heard a familiar voice. He looked up, to observe his family walking toward him. They were stopped by a gentleman in uniform. Gil noticed words being exchanged between him and his wife. He thought, "She is a determined woman, she will not be denied." He grinned and chuckled, knowing that these gentlemen will not stand in her way.

She noticed Gil, and pointed for the gentleman to look at him. He turned his head in my direction. He turned to her, nodded, and she stepped forward with the entourage proceeding towards him.

They embraced and kissed, Gilbert hugged all the children and kissed Phillip on his forehead.

Moments later they are escorted by a clerk to another room. A gentleman waiting in the doorway ushered them to a desk. The agent shook Gilberts hand and stated his name and title.

Gilbert introduced himself and his family. The agent gestured for them to have a seat. There were only three chairs at the desk. He told the children, they may sit on the floor or he points to a bench along the wall. The bench was longer than any church pew they have ever seen, it stretched the length of the room.

"What is your business that brings you here?" inquired the agent.

Gilbert explained, "We are seeking passport to the Québec province of Canada to join my brothers."

Seeking to be Loved

The agent said, "Good luck monsieur, you and many others are leaving France, in this troubling time." Observing the size of his family, he stated, "I can see why."

"What is it you need from us?"

Gilbert told him, "I have never left France, I have never been this far away from my home. I am not sure what questions I need to ask, or what I must do before my family and I can obtain passage to Canada."

The agent explained to them, "If you are a citizen in this country you must make a decision whether your plan is to return home to live, or, whether you are to denounce citizenship."

Gil and Nat look at each other, he shrugged his shoulders. Then he turned to the agent and asked if he could please explain.

"Oui, it is mainly a tax issue. If you are just visiting and plan to be back within a year, all you need is papers of transport, stating your reason for leaving the country. If you are taking, he looked at the children then continued, the family, and your belongings with you, my guess is you plan to take up residency in another country. Be that the case, you must fill out forms for any land or property you are leaving behind. Stating, who you are leaving it to, or, if you are transferring it to the state of France. That way Monsieur, you will be taxed properly, or not at all. The appropriate parties will be responsible for the property."

Gilbert mentioned to the agent. "I gave the deeds of my land and property, to my father. It was his before he gifted it to us on our wedding day."

"Did you fill out any paperwork, any forms verifying this," the agent asked?

"Non, I did not know I needed to." Gil thought for a moment and mentioned, "My father must have divided the land legally. The land was given to us in the form of an official deed."

In that case it is a simple thing to take care of. He reached into his desk and pulled out a form. Please fill this out for me. The agent reached into another drawer of his desk and retrieved another

230

and handed it to Natalie, and asked, if she would fill out this one. Instructing her to place all the names of the children on it, in addition to hers and Monsieur Guyon. This form identifies who will need papers. There is also a section to declare all the items you have with you in your possession, you plan to take with you. He identified, all the items will be inspected, not by us, by whichever company or transport service you utilize. They are required by law, when someone is leaving the country, they must inspect everything they are taking with them. It is precautionary to make sure nothing harmful will be coming in, or leaving the borders of the respected countries.

    Marilda, looked over and assessed the form. It will be quite simple to complete. "There would be not enough room to identify our belongings," she mentioned to the agent.

    He smiled and told her, "You can be general in your responses, example kitchen items, clothing, tools, etc."

    Gilbert interrupted and asked, "What about animals such as horses, cow, goat and sheep?"

    They do not need to be added on this, that will be determined by the veterinary inspector, and the other inspecting agents, at the transport companies. We are mainly concerned about people and things we would include within baggage, that is not apparent or visible.

    Gilbert handed the agent the form.

    Upon inspecting it, the agent asked Gilbert, "Is your father here?"

    "Non," Gilbert replied.

    One of two things must happen then, explained the agent. One we would have to get your father's signature, to verify his agreement. Or we can have you fill out another form, verifying if your father does not agree or cannot be found by such and such a date the land will be transferred to the state of France.

    "What do you mean, such and such a date?" Gilbert ask.

Seeking to be Loved

The date is within a five-year time frame. If there is no verification by either party in this case, you, or your father; the state will take over the property. At which point he, or you, can no longer reclaim it. The property must be verified by you, or the current property owner. That is the person you have transferred it to, within that five-year time frame. At the end of that time, whoever is identified on the form will be responsible for any unpaid taxes. If the state has not received notice on part of the property owner, by the end of that period and the tax on the property has not been paid, the property will at that time belong to France.

Gilbert nods his head in understanding, to him it sounds reasonable enough. He is silent, his face looked troubled, he is having difficulty selecting the words he wanted to say. He is reflecting on the images of his dream. Acknowledging the fact that his father and the rest of his family, may be fatally harmed. He shared his thoughts to the agent, if in such a case, something would happen to my father, what would happen then to the property?

The property will be inherited by the eldest male in the household. Then to the eldest male relative of the original landowner. Let me once again state, it must take place within five years from this date.

He looked at Nattie and told her, "I am going to complete this form. Surely within five years, we would have time to contact Papa."

The agent intervened, "We will be sending a copy of this to your father. He should receive it in a few weeks. So, oui, you or he will have plenty of time to make an alternative decision if he does not confirm or accept property back in his name."

Gilbert glanced at Nattie and then at the agent and said, "Well I believe that sounds reasonable."

"That will conclude our business here except for one thing. That would be a small processing fee which will cover the postage and this time spent. That will be Fr.10 please," said the agent.

Marilda whispered in Gilbert's ear, suggesting that he get a confirmation, a copy of the forms and receipt of the payment.

Seeking to be Loved

Gilbert expressed this matter of business to the agent.

"Oui, of course," the agent replied. He pulled a tablet from his desk and a official seal. He stamped the two forms that he and his wife just completed. On the form he outlined the transaction, the fee paid, dated, signed it, and handed to them. Now you must take these down the hall. The men in uniform will direct you where to go. There you will fill out more papers for yourselves in each child, it will be pertinent information. The names, department in which you and they live, the address or addresses of their residence as well as other information. They are very easy forms, each must be completed thoroughly monsieur.

Then you must wait for the doctor, he will inspect; (the agent paused to rephrase his statement, not wanting to sound rude, as if they were meat, or produce), I mean examine you. To make sure you have no illness or diseases. If all is well, he will sign your papers and that is all you need. He stood up and said, "Good day Madame, Monsieur," shook their hands and pointed the direction they need to go.

Gilbert thanked him. "May I ask one more question?"

"Oui."

"Where may we obtain passage? Is there any place close by, where we can obtain transport, on a ship leaving for Canada? A company where we can purchase space to take us to Canada?"

The agent told him, "We do not do that here. There are several transport agencies, and shipping companies along the river. They can arrange your transportation. The closest is a little more than a kilometer down river, there will be many for the next few kilometers from that point on monsieur."

Gil inquired, "Do you have any recommendations."

"Non monsieur there are many; let me suggest to you, be very explicit about what you are asking for, especially if you have animals, you are going to transport. Many companies will charge extra and even more for large animals. For animals take more care than passengers, they must be fed, cleaned constantly, and looked

Seeking to be Loved

after. Also, be sure to ask how much baggage will be included when you purchase your tickets. You may find out, that you pay extra for cargo.

There is no regulation on cost.

The agent obviously has a conscience. He expressed to the Guyon's the cost of transport may vary greatly from one company to the other. You may want to check with a few different companies to compare. You will find several starting at about 1km downriver and they will be on both sides of the river. I would suggest take time and compare cost from several companies and inquire about other fees monsieur. Make sure you have letters signed when you receive your tickets that verify what it is you will be allowed to transport. Ay, I believe that is all I can suggest, Good day to you, and your family!"

Gilbert showed his papers to the man in uniform who directed him down the hall. "You will see a door that will say examination, enter there. Show your papers to the secretary. She will let you know what you must do next."

They waited their turn, when the doctor is ready to examine them, he checked their papers. He handed them to the nurse, assisting him. He directed Gilbert, "Take your sons into the room on the left, take off your garments. I will meet with you in a moment." He looked at Marilda and pointed to the room on the right and said, "That room is for you madame and the mademoiselles, please do the same." He told them, "The baby should stay with the mother."

The examination is brief but thorough, He checked all the extremities, every inch of the body for wounds, infections, and disease. He checked for lice, fleas and other fauna pest and parasites. He listened to the heart and the lungs. He told Gilbert, "You have healthy sons, you and the boys may get dressed." He directed them once dressed, please go wait in the room they just came from.

The doctor upon examining Marilda and the girls, said the same of them. "You have a healthy family madame. He mentioned to her, "Your son is quite a pleasant young lad."

Seeking to be Loved

He wrote approved, signed his name, and dated all the papers. He instructed them to take these to the secretary on the way out. "She will stamp them and give you your verification papers as well." He wished them good luck wherever their travels take them. They thanked the Doctor as they left.

Gil, paid the examination fee, and received their papers.

Both Gilbert and Marilda were relieved, they were not sure what to expect. They were glad that the whole process went smoothly. Gilbert counted their blessings, so far on their journey they ran into no difficulties.

The rain persisted, it was a wet walk back to the stable at Saint Eustache. They discussed whether to attempt to pack their belongings and start making their way west. Gil believed they should gather their belongings and travel along the Seine. Visiting the shipping transport and passage companies, in hopes to obtain passage. Gilbert discussed with Nattie, how this would save probably 8 to 10 km of travel on foot. Plus they would not have to repeat it again when they leave to continue their journey to the coast.

Marilda suggested that we pray on it, and ask the priest if we see him. They heard a clock strike one. "You see it is already afternoon, we need to eat first. It may be best to wait to tomorrow."

Dominique noticed the family kneeling in one of the pews in silent prayer. He quietly took the seat behind them and waited for them to finish their meditation. He knew they must have a concern, so he waited patiently behind them. The last finished, and sat back onto the pew bench. It was then he placed his hand on Gilbert's shoulder and asked, "How did your morning go?"

They were pleased to see him and told him so. Gilbert shared the conversation he had with the agent and what transpired at the Office Des Longitude.

"Oui," then a thought came to Dominique. He made it clear, "I have never been on a ship, some people in my congregation have. A parishioner told me this morning, they are very busy. He works for a shipping company. He told me, people are seeking transport, more

Seeking to be Loved

and more each day to procure passage. I have heard from some of our parishioners who are experienced travelers, they say, late afternoon is the best time to avoid crowds. Most companies close at 5PM.

You may want to go an hour before they close, it may not be as busy then, the line should not be as long." Once again, he paused a moment before finishing his statement. "These times are different."

Gilbert asked the priest, "What do you think?"

Dominique smiled and pointed to the crucifix, and asked Gilbert, "What does he think? What has he placed in your heart?"

Gil looked at Nattie, then he told her and Dominque, "I think I should go now, this afternoon to find us a ship and obtain our transport."

All the children except Phillip said, "I want to go, may I go with you."

Dominique laughed, "I believe you have your answer."

"Father, you and your parish have been so kind, I am embarrassed to ask."

The priest stopped Gilbert in midsentence. "Please take our carriage. You must spend one more night with us."

Little Joseph said, in a most excited voice, "The sun is shining through the beautiful windows."

The drizzling rain had stopped, and the sky was clearing. The sunlight coming through the windows filled the interior of the chapel area with a magnificent display of multicolored light.

Dominique looked at Gilbert, "You have another confirmation of your decision. I will see you at the evening meal and hopefully you will be back before the mass. I will go inform Monsieur Poincare, to request that the carriage be available to you for the rest of the afternoon."

"Bless you father, merci. May I ask you, how you knew what was really in my heart? For my thought was sincere, although an impatient one."

Seeking to be Loved

Dominique looked to the alter, and said to Gilbert, "His plan is always better than ours. He knows what is in our heart and mind. We hear both, we must learn to listen to one. The one which is best for us, may not be the one we think we want."

"But, how did you know what we needed?"

"I am learning to listen, as well as respond to his will." He glanced again to the alter. "You see, when we do that, we cannot be wrong."

Gilbert said, "Mais."(But)

The priest said in anticipation, "There is always a joy and peace in our heart, when a correct decision is made in kindness." He knelt toward the alter, made the sign of the cross, turned and walked away.

The men hitched the horse to the carriage. Marilda prepared them a lunch to take with them. They enjoyed their lunch, while riding along the streets of Paris. Gilbert has no trouble getting to the Boulevard along the Siene River. The afternoon sky was a brilliant blue with only a few traces of clouds left from the rain earlier in the day. All of Paris was bathed with a bright afternoon sun. It made the city appear even more alive, with energy and life.

The trees are displaying their new leaves. They are glistening in the sun, from the rain drops not yet evaporated.

Gilbert, Ernest, and Henry are riding the buckboard although such an elegant carriage the front seat can hardly be called a buckboard. They are looking for shipping company signs on the buildings.

Marilda is in the back of the carriage with Mary, who is holding Phillip on her lap. Blanche between them on the seat, little Gil and Joseph on the floor eating their lunch. She was taking in the sights and scenes of the city along the river on the left, and the buildings and shops on the right. The excitement of being in Paris, on a wonderful spring day is hard to contain. Heads turned from one side to the other. One child points to something that caught their eye

Seeking to be Loved

and shouts for everyone to see. Then another on the opposite side of the carriage, yelled, "Look you must see this."

Everything was so new to them, they wanted to take it all in. The unabashed excitement of the children, kept Marilda's head spinning. For several moments she had not even realized that Phillip, was in her arms. Mary had passed him to her minutes ago. He too can feel the energy and saw it in his mother's face, as he stared at her. He extended his hand to touch her chin. Her attention is drawn to him, looking at her child, as usual eye contact made the rest of the world disappeared.

She is yet again mesmerized, as she recognized how magnificent and wonderful this child is. The smile on his face engulfed her. The joy reflected in his eyes, when he is in her arms penetrates every aspect of her being. He held his tiny fingers of both hands against her chin, at that moment nothing can disturb them. Nothing else can enter the radiance of their connection. Its locked and nothing can interfere externally or from within.

Gilbert noticed a large crowd outside one of the buildings. As they approach, they read the sign out front, Transatlantique-French line. He rolled past several storefronts when he noticed another crowd, the sign Compagnie Generale, it has a sailing ship below the name. He recalled what the Priest Dominique, told him about showing up in the late afternoon. He decided to continue on, to see how many other shipping companies he may find. They traveled nearly another 2km, finding many companies such as White Star line, Societe Generale De Transports Maritime, Cunard Line, Vapeur Cyprien Fabra, Canadian Pacific Line, USS United States Line, Compagne Francaise, Compagne Nationale de Navigation, etc...

They made their way down the Boulevard and cross over the next bridge. They worked their way upriver, from the south side. People had carriages stopped by the wall overlooking the river. He decided to do the same so the children can get out, stretch their legs, and walk awhile. He and Nattie discussed the options, as the children explore the area along the river.

Seeking to be Loved

He mentioned to Nat, two companies stuck out in his mind, the Cunard Line and Canadian Pacific line. Both, seemed to be well established companies. He decided he would start with those and Nattie agreed. Gilbert asked if she still had all the papers. "Oui, plus the envelopes our fathers gave us."

He helped her into the front of the carriage. He wanted to review all the papers and count to tally their savings and what their fathers had given them. They sat close not wanting to chance, losing any funds by passing it back and forth and to do so discreetly.

The envelope from his father included his personal and demographic information. Also, the certificate of confirmation from Eglise Saint Michel and Fr.300. The envelope that was from Marilda's parents contain the same information for Marilda, plus Fr.800. They nearly fainted when they counted her parents' gift. Gil looked at Nat and said, "This with our savings, plus what we may sell, if we can, may give us anywhere between 1700 and Fr.2000. Surely, this will be enough to allow us passage to Canada." They had never imagined seeing or having that many francs at one time in their hands.

He called to the children to come back to the carriage and take their seats. He asked Ernest if he would like to take the reins?

"Oui father," he nearly shouted; hardly able to contain his excitement. For him, guiding the carriage through the streets of Paris, was an opportunity of a lifetime.

He handled the team well, and Gilbert complimented his son. He told him to pullover on the river side of the Boulevard just outside the Cunnard Shipping Office. There is no crowd outside, although he was able to see through the windows. Inside there were still a number of people.

When he entered the office, it is a buzz of noise and some angry outburst. He picked up on the hostility immediately.

"This is an outrage," he heard from one side of the room.

"This is highway robbery," he heard from the other.

Seeking to be Loved

"Piracy is what it is," he heard, not recognizing what direction it came from. For it set off an outburst of many mumbles and groans of disagreement, from all over the room by the patrons.

A Teller shouted above the crowd noise. "May I help someone here?" Gilbert raised his hand and approached the counter. Someone passing him comments, "You best have a million Franc's, mon amie(my friend)."

Gilbert stood before the counter, which is chest high. There are cast iron rails with an ornate crown at the crest rising nearly a meter above. A crown spans the gap where the tellers perform their public business and serve their customers.

Gilbert stepped forward; "Good afternoon sir. I want to get passage to Québec Canada, for myself and family. There are nine of us, including my wife and I. The children range in age from seven months to thirteen years old."

The teller asked, "What would be your request for a departure date?"

Gilbert is taken back for a moment by the question. He said, "As soon as possible, monsieur."

"What port would you like to depart from monsieur?"

"We were planning on going to Le Havre," conveyed Gil.

"Very good monsieur, we do have ships leaving from that port every 14 to 16 days. The next one will leave in three days."

Gilbert thought a moment, then realized that would be extremely difficult for them to cover 100 to 130km (not knowing the actual distance), in that amount of time. He asked, "What is the distance to Le Havre?"

"It is exactly 197 kilometers from here."

Gilbert is stunned for a moment when he realized his estimation was that far off.

The teller explained to him, they leave on schedule. The next transatlantic to Canada will be in approximately seventeen days from now. Gils next question was about their belongings. He reviewed what they have with them, a wagon, two carts. We plan on selling

Seeking to be Loved

the carts and some livestock if we can. I would like to take the horses and cow with us.

The teller informed him, that it is customary for them to transport livestock. "Unfortunately, under the current circumstances we are facing, we are not able to do so on our cruise liners. Baggage including the wagon we can load and secure on board. The animals, non, non-Monsieur," he said while shaking his head.

The next question Gilbert asked was, "Do you have separate liners for freight only? If you do, could we transport them on those ships along with my family?"

He told Gilbert no one has ever asked him that question. I must talk to my Directeur. One moment please.

The teller returned with the Directeur(Director). Gilbert explained his dilemma, and his request. The directeur asked Gilbert if he would show him what he wished to transport.

Gilbert explained to the directeur, all their belongings are in the stable at Église Saint-Eustache.

"Ahh Dominique; I am familiar with the priest, I attend mass there and grew up in the church. Monsieur, your request is possible, although it is unusual. To have the passengers and cargo on a freighter, is a very unique request. I must see what you have, then contact the captains of our three cargo freighters. They will be able to tell me whether this is going to be feasible. I must tell you, the accommodations will be very crude for you and your family, to say the least. The voyage will be prolonged a few days compared to our new passenger liners."

The directeur made the suggestion that he meet them at St. Eustache at 5:30PM. He told Gilbert; "I must see for myself what it is you wish to transport. Then tomorrow I can contact the captains in the morning and have an answer for you by noon." They shook hands and said, "Au Revoir."

Gil left the building and crossed the Boulevard to the carriage. He noticed it is abandoned, he looked over the wall to see his family on the deck below, looking at the river. He whistled, and

Seeking to be Loved

waved to get their attention. He motioned for them to make their way up the steps.

Marilda asked him, "How did it go, do we have passage?"

Gilbert told her, "Non, it sounds somewhat promising, we will know tomorrow. We will meet with the directeur after mass. He must see what we wish to transport. We will take him to the stable tonight."

Let us go to another company, the Canadian Pacific lines and transport company. Although late in the day, a few minutes after 4PM there were still many there as well. Once he finally met with the teller, he was told they could not accommodate the animals at this time. The teller explained they do have designating compartments for the transport of animals on their new ships. He explained to Gilbert, we have these accommodations, however we have been instructed, they are only to be used by human passengers until further notice. I am sorry monsieur, but I will be happy to sell transport for you and your family.

Gil asked the teller the cost of passage from Le Havre to Québec Canada?

The teller presented the price to Gil. "That is Fr.280 for each passenger, the infants fee is the same. This is third class only monsieur."

Gilbert ask, "What does third class mean?"

The teller stated only that there are no luxuries.

Gil assumed a cabin to be a small compartment or one of the open stalls, normally used to transport animals. He considered, we do not need luxuries.

The teller in an attempt to influence Gilbert, and make the sale immediately, commented; "Once you are on board you will not spend much time in the cabin. Our ships are new and swift, you can be to Québec in 7 to 8 days and that is including the stop at one port of call South Hampton, England. The whole ship is modern, all accommodations are adequate."

Gilbert does the math quickly in his head, realizing that it will take all or more money than what they have. He thanked the teller and stood to leave.

"Monsieur, monsieur what about the tickets?"

Gilbert turned his head slightly to the teller and said, "I cannot make the decision yet, merci."

The teller raised his voice to Gilbert, "You must, the cost may be double tomorrow!"

"Non," Gilbert said to him. When Gilbert returned to the carriage, Marilda can see by the expression on his face it did not go well.

"What did they say Papa?" asked Little Gilbert.

"Oui, Papa," queried Blanche.

The older children had no need to inquire, they also read the expression on his face. Gil tried to smile, as he climbed into the driver's position of the carriage as he snapped the reigns. "We will know something this evening," he finally stated. They returned to the stable, it was already after 5PM. He suggested to Nattie, we and the children should attend the evening mass. He asked them to pray for each other and all their family they left behind. "We must also, pray for passage to Canada as well."

The Directeur Monsieur St. Claire, had arrived at the stable and met with Gilbert and monsieur Poincare. He exchanged greetings with the two men. Gilbert guided him to their belongings. St. Claire explained to Gilbert; he was confident the new freighters they had just added to their fleet should be able to accommodate them. He reiterated the accommodations will be the bare minimum and will lack comfort.

Gilbert was glad to hear they could be accommodated. The question in the back of his mind, was the cost.

Monsieur St. Claire asked Gil, "Where are you and your family residing?"

Seeking to be Loved

Monsieur Poincare said, "The femmes are staying in the nun's accommodations. The garcons over there," he said with a sigh pointing to the hayloft.

Gilbert told St. Claire, "My Family are attending the service upstairs, would you like to meet them?"

Monsieur St. Claire pulled the chain of his pocket watch for a peek. Which reminds Gilbert, "I must find mine."

He suggested to Gilbert, "Maybe we can get there before communion!"

"Shall we join them." They made their way up the stairs to the chapel area above. After the mass, Gilbert introduced his family to Monsieur St. Claire.

The priest Dominique had taken note of their meeting. He waited for them as they finally made their exit. "Ah, Monsieur St. Claire, I see you met the Guyon's."

"Oui father," he replied.

Dominique knew that the shipping companies are marking up the cost two to three times higher. In some cases, even more, than what the average cost for transatlantic transportation had been just two months ago. He has had several parishioners of his congregation share their experiences, as well as their anger expressed in the confessional. He looked directly into St. Claire's eyes and said to him, "I sincerely hope you are taking care of our guest and his family's needs."

"Oui father, we are doing everything we can to accommodate them."

Dominique, still looking into Monsieur's St. Claire's eyes, and extending his hand to grasp and hold his hand. Mentioned to him, "We are our brother's keeper."

The words struck him oddly! At first the sensation was just an instant of blankness. As if the words were just sound. The next moment was a tingling and he noticed the fine hair all over his body was standing up. Next followed the meaning, it was strange, it was

Seeking to be Loved

not coming from the brain, it was more like a consciousness growing within him. "What is this?" he thought.

A message was appearing in his mind. No, it was not a message, it was more of a resolve. He determined at that instant; he would put this family on a transatlantic transport. At the most reasonable price his company would allow.

St. Claire turned to Gilbert and his family and cordially expressed his pleasure in meeting them. He told Gilbert, "If you come to my office at 9AM, I should have answers for you then." He turned to Marilda, and he was struck once again. This time by the most innocent, loving, trusting look from the little boy in her arms. His eyes caught Phillips, as the child turned his gaze from his mother to M. St. Claire.

The moment he spoke to her, an unusual warmth filled his heart. It was such a pleasing sensation, he felt it on his way home. It remained with him all that night and into the next day. He was pleased knowing he was going to do right by a fellow countryman.

The next morning, he spoke to three of their ships captains, each was apprehensive. They realized, this is just another of the company's many unusual requests that had been coming to them.

One captain informed St. Claire, other than normal provisions that will need to be listed on the ship manifest. He would need to add hay, feed, and straw etc. for the animals. Plus, another additional nine people.

St. Claire told the captain, six of the children are under 12 years of age.

The captain also mentioned, "We have only one spare room, with four bunks."

St. Claire told the captain, he will inform them of that fact.

The Capt. also reminded St. Claire, that he nor his crew can be held responsible for their personal safety. We can, and will secure the belongings and the animals to the same degree as always. Though the passengers we cannot be held responsible.

Seeking to be Loved

Each crewmember has his duties and responsibilities. We are not a cruise liner; this is a Freighter designed for and crew trained to transport cargo.

We will instruct them on all necessary safety precautions, unlike the beast, and the cargo we cannot tie people down or lock them within an area. Though that is a thought you should consider. It will be easier if we would do so and less troublesome on all of us, the captain remarked to St. Claire.

St. Claire reassured the captain, all will be conveyed to them. I think you will like this family.

"Landlubbers!" exclaimed the captain. Then replied, "We will leave in four days. I must know no later than 4PM this afternoon, if we are to board them. That will give me three days to get the extra supplies loaded. I will also need to know what their actual charges will be from the company."

St. Claire told the captain to wire the total cost for the animals and include the extra expenses.

The captains reply was, "I will have them ready within the hour." He reiterated once again, "I must have confirmation from you, including what the company's charge will be. I must update my log and ledger before the crossing."

"I will wire you as soon as all has been confirmed and paid in full. If they do not secure passage with us, I will inform you of that as well by the time you designated," replied St. Claire.

Gilbert was waiting at the door of the Cunnard Shipping Company when they unlocked it for the days business.

Monsieur St. Claire noticed him immediately, he was the first who walked through the door. He waved him over to his office, "Bon jour monsieur." He informed Gilbert that he had spoken to the captain. I am waiting for his response, and we should have it within the next 30 minutes. At that point we will be able to determine the details, including the cost.

Gilbert told M. St Claire, that is my biggest concern. Especially after he heard the comments between, he and Father Dominique.

Seeking to be Loved

"Monsieur Guyon, let me assure you that the cost of your trip will be no more than what the company allows."

Gilbert brought up the comment he heard from the priest. "It sounded to me like the company allowed three times the cost, more in some cases than what it was two months ago."

"May I call you Gilbert, monsieur?"

"Oui," Gilbert replied.

I have already spoken to one of the owners. He continued, since you will be not transported on our regular cruise line, but a cargo vessel, he has given me permission to only charge you the standard passenger fare for third class accommodations. That is the best I can do. I am waiting now, for a wire from the captain letting me know the cost of the cargo and the animals. At that time, I will be able to give you a total cost for you and your family.

Gilbert ask St. Claire, "What will the third-class fare be?"

The passenger rate for third class accommodations, is Fr.302. Would you like for me to add that up for you Gilbert?

"Non monsieur, that is Fr.2718 for my family alone." Gilbert had completed the calculation in his brain.

"Oui monsieur, keep in mind there is still the fee for the cargo and your animals. We should have that information any moment now. I was told by the captain this morning they will be leaving in four days." He observed a concerned look and Gilbert's face, it almost appeared as if a look of fright had come over him. "Are you okay Gilbert?" he asked.

Gilbert took a moment before he replied. "Our existing funds will not support the passage for my family, not to mention the cargo and animals. Plus the fact we cannot get there in four days. We would have to walk day and night, without stopping to be there in time."

Both men have a pondering look on their face, they were in deep thought.

Seeking to be Loved

The realization struck Gil, there is no way possible. Even if he sold everything they owned, they would still not be close. Only his prize Percheron Stallions may get them the funds necessary.

Always the businessman, St. Claire is the first to speak. He said, "There are ways, you can get to Le Havre on time. One is a train, you would be there in a few hours, the other is a barge. We transport goods from Paris to the ports, every few days, it would only take two days. Once the barge starts its journey to the harbor it does not stop. They have no worries about highway travelers or other things getting in the way. However monsieur, I understand your dilemma, even those options have cost."

Gilbert questioned St. Claire, "Do you know of any other possibilities, other options that could help him to get his family to Canada?"

St. Claire's expression changed again, to a more blank look on his face. A few awkward moments passed.

Gil was first to speak. He mentioned, "My family and I would be willing to work. If there is work to be done during the transport, could we sign on as workers. We can perform any kind of job. We can surely do some kind of ship maintenance or whatever work is needed. We would be happy to perform any duty. My sons and I, even the younger ones are used to working in the fields. My wife is an excellent cook, my daughter's assist her or they can clean."

He noticed the deadpan look on St. Claire's face; causing Gil to think his request was not an option.

One of the owners happened to be walking by St. Claire's desk and overheard the conversation. He stopped, standing a few meters behind Gilbert. He waved to catch St. Claire's attention, and motioned for him to come join him.

St. Claire excused himself. "I must meet with the owner."

A few whispers are exchanged between the men. All Gilbert could hear was murmurs as they walked away.

The company owner told St. Claire, "We are running a business here, we cannot afford to have everyone sign on or even

Seeking to be Loved

question such a possibility. We will have every vagabond, and his family crowding our decks. Getting in the way of paying passengers, and crews on board our ships. We are here to sell passage, to move people, and cargo at a profit, might I add.

We are not a charity. Get rid of him, as soon as possible. You are to avoid any further conversation on the matter. Other patrons might overhear. Get about your duties, selling transport space to the people that are willing to pay for it."

"Oui Monsieur, I will sir!"

St. Claire turned around to go back to his desk, he felt his heart shrinking within his chest. Then the words of Dominique, echoed in his mind. He can also see the most sincere, kind, and trusting look on the little child's face. He said to himself, as he envisioned the child in his mother's arms, standing right there before him at this very moment.

The words echoed from his depths, from where he was not certain. He heard the phrase, it is penetrating his entire being, "We are our brother's keeper."

The feeling appeared again as it did last night. The words were not in his thought, it was present in his being. His chin rose as he walked around the corner of his desk to sit back down.

Facing Gilbert, St. Claire had a smile on his face, as he knew and was willing to accept his fate.

Gilbert observed an vacuous, yet inscrutable appearance in St. Claire's eyes. What he assumed had been exchanged, he did not anticipate any good news, he was braced, to hear the inevitable.

One of the message carriers approached St. Claire's desk with a wire from the captain, he handed it to him. He excused himself again from Gilbert for a moment, as he read the wire. It read, (Monsieur St. Claire, as to our conversation earlier. The expense would be an additional Fr.350 for the animals, Fr.25 for wagon and other baggage that needed to be stowed away, Fr.3 per day per person for provisions equaling Fr.270 - total Fr.645.)

Seeking to be Loved

St. Claire excused himself, he wanted to wire the captain back immediately. He explained to the captain, to go ahead and prepare for them. He took a deep breath before his next statement. Then told the telegraph operator to add this, "I would like for you to hire them on as crew members if it is at all possible." He informed the captain; two men can perform heavy labor. Two women can cook and clean, two others can perform cabin boy duties. He waited for the response; he knew the captain is expecting to hear back from him. He would not have to wait long.

While he lingered, the thought occurred to him; they have a barge carrying coal to the Le Havre shipyard. It is scheduled to leave either late this evening or first thing in the morning. It depends on how quickly the captain can complete his loading and obtain provisions.

Suddenly, he is aware that the barge would be there in two days, from the time of its departure. He thought, "This could work."

I must contact that captain, right away to see if he is willing and or able, to board the extra cargo and people.

If so, Gilbert's family and belongings can ride the barge to the coast. He knew that they could sleep in cargo beds, if need be, or even stretch out on the decks. He really was not concerned about the people. The river travel is calm, and they can rest on the way. His question is whether the captain would allow the animals, on board.

He is pleased with himself for coming up with that idea. He said to himself, "I am a genius." His next thought, "Or an idiot, I may get fired." Then the inner voice repeated: "I am my brother's keeper."

Within minutes, the captain responded to his wire.
- What the hell, are you people doing?
- We have enough duties and responsibilities. We do not need to train a bunch of landlubbers.
- They better be here one day before departure, or we will leave without them.

Seeking to be Loved

St. Claire has the telegraph operator wire back to the captain.
- They will be arriving on a coal barge in two days.
- It is scheduled to leave tomorrow morning.
- I will have them report to you when they get there.
- Please have a crewman meet them, when they arrive so they will not hold you up, trying to find your ship. St. Claire ended his message with, - Happy Sailing.

Thinking as he went back to his desk, what and how to discuss his plan with Gilbert.

The captain read his message, and grumbled out loud, "Happy sailing, My ass."

St. Claire tapped Gilbert on the shoulder and motioned for him to come follow him. They leave the building and proceed across the street, down the stairs and walked a short distance to a loading dock. He approached the barge and a crewmember, requesting to speak to the captain?

Moments later Capt. Bogart appeared. He nodded, in acknowledgement to the crewman, for St. Claire's request to come aboard his barge. The captain bellowed to St. Claire, "How may I help you Monsieur?"

St. Claire asked permission to come aboard, to speak with the captain.

The captain obliges, and said, "You may board." He met him at the gangway.

He introduced himself to the captain, while Gilbert remained on the dock. In a dignified voice, he presented to the captain his title; Directeur of Sale Representative, for the shipping company Cunnards. The ownership of this vessel, on which we are standing.

The captain wanted him to get to the business of his boarding and replied bluntly. "I am aware who owns this vessel, what is it you wish to discuss, monsieur?"

He explained to the captain, "We been instructed to sell passage anyway we can, to people wanting to leave the country. We have been ordered to make as much money," (he paused briefly to rephrase) "Aaaahh, sales for the company as possible. Before the government takes control over all our vessels." Another pause.

The Captain said, "I am listening."

"We are attempting to arrange transport for this man and his family, to Le Havre. His supplies consist of a wagon and two horses. He plans to sell his other livestock before boarding.

We would like to sell space for his equipment and his family, on this barge. We are making arrangements for them on one of our transatlantic ships, that is leaving Le Havre. It is one of our freighters, which is leaving for Québec in three days from tomorrow morning. We know you are scheduled to leave either late tonight or early tomorrow as soon as your cargo is loaded. Of course, captain it is up to you, who have the ultimate control of your vessel."

The captain was processing the proposal.

St. Claire stated, "The way I see it captain, you will be doing the company and your countrymen a great service." With that said, St. Claire kept his fingers crossed behind his back and whispered in his mind, "This is up to you Lord."

"If you are willing captain, we will have him bring his items here and board as soon as you agree, and we can finish our paperwork." Captain Bogart was about to respond, when St. Claire mentioned, "No provisions are needed, all we want is to transport them aboard your barge, that is all." He stated in hope the captain, will consider them no burden to him or his crew.

The captain reminds St. Claire, "They will lack comfort on this vessel for those two days. We may be able to shelter the family in one of the holds if it rains, not the beast or wagon. Those will be secured on the deck. Other than that, we can promise nothing except, they will be to Le Havre on time. That is if, there are no unforeseen difficulties. If they agree and you give them their boarding passes, they must be here no later than 6PM this evening. You better make that 5 o'clock, we would like our crew to have everything stowed and secured before dark this evening."

Seeking to be Loved

St. Claire thought, that should give us a few hours, which will be ample time.

"One other thing Monsieur St. Claire, we cannot be held responsible for them during those two days. Nor time they may be associated with any business this vessel may experience from the time they board, until the time they disembark in Le Havre. If they are not here by 5PM our supply holds will be secured and locked down. At that point we can load nothing else. If they still wish to come after that time, they can bring only what they can carry on. The only entry and exiting of the ship will be done by a narrow gangway for our crew."

Through this whole ordeal Gilbert is wondering, how his family will fair, if this comes about. Two days of rest on the barge will do them good. He wondered how his prize Percheron's will fare on a barge or the ten day crossing. They are not used to being confined for that amount of time, the animals nor his family. I will have to buy feed from the church, to supply the horses for two days. I will have to find a buyer for other livestock, monsieur Poincare, may have some information or ideas on that matter or maybe Dominique.

He is aware, this is for not. Alas, we might as well face reality, this barge will cost plenty in addition to the freighter. I explained that to St. Claire, I told him we cannot afford even the passenger fee on the ship.

I will hear him out. Gilbert knew the cost will exclude them. What next, Lord???

St. Claire shook hands with the captain and assured him he will have them show up with their boarding passes. "I will stress to them, they must be on time and have their papers ready, along with everything we agreed that they can take on board. Bon voyage, captain."

St. Claire and Gilbert, discuss details on the way back to his desk. Monsieur St. Claire gave Gilbert the figures. The captain's fee for the stowing the animals and equipment are nonnegotiable, the two horses and the wagon. He explained anything else that cannot

Seeking to be Loved

be carried on, if they cannot store in the wagon, would cost them more. It would increase the figure, we just stated. The figure the captain gave me was Fr.645 and that included hay and straw. Since you are not taking the passenger steam liner ship, I am allowing you the third-class charge per person. I will issue this at the fees we had established last year, at the end of 1913."

Gilbert questioned, "That will be?"

"Fr.173.6 Monsieur, that is the best we can do. I may lose my job by offering you this. You have just two days to get there, I have arranged transportation as you know with the barge docked below. It will be in Le Havre in two days cruising down river, that will get you to the freighter hours before it is scheduled to leave the harbor. I have to show a sales receipt for the Captains log covering this additional transport, from here to the coast."

Gilbert has a look of uncertainty, St. Claire picked up on it immediately. Gilbert looked up at him and said, "Monsieur St. Claire, you are truly kind, you for no reason are putting your job in jeopardy. You have done more than reasonably expected to accommodate our needs, which I am grateful. I am not sure we would be able to accept your kind offer. Maybe if I can sell my animals, we will have enough francs to cover the fee.

Being in a strange town, I do not know a butcher or anyone else who may buy our livestock. At this very minute, I am not sure if that will provide us enough funds to cover the cost."

Even St. Claire is astonished; he cannot believe the words coming out of his mouth. Even though, he is hearing himself pronounce them. "You are going to Québec."

The barge charge for your cargo, including your horses Fr.15. The charge for you and each family member will be Fr.10 per day. You will be cruising two days before arriving at the coast. A total of Fr.195, that brings your entire total from here to Québec - Fr. 2393.4.

Gilbert's face became ashen.

Monsieur St. Claire asked, "Is there something wrong?"

Seeking to be Loved

"Monsieur we are short, even with this charge by nearly Fr.800. I will sell our livestock, for whatever we can get; I am afraid we will still be short."

"How short?" asked St. Claire.

"We barely have enough to cover the freighter fee, we have Fr.1555.

"That will not cover the cargo and horses." mumbled St. Claire, as his mind raced.

He told Gilbert, "We will come to an agreement."

St. Claire commenced to write down figures. He started by deducting fees for the five oldest, who will be assigned work duties. If no meal fee for the five working, he reviewed in his mind as he reached for another piece of paper and his pen. He jotted down some figures, then crossed them out and started again.

He looked up at Gilbert, with a smile on his face and his eyebrows are high. Finally, he said, "I think we have it."
Passage fees for the youngest four not including a daily meal fee totals fr.694, plus cargo and horses fr.645, totaling fr.1339 for the freighter crossing. The barge transport fee fr.195 totaling fr.1534.

That is what you will be charged, assuming the captain will sign on five of your family as laborers."

Gil questioned, "This will include transport of my family, all of our belongings, my team of horses and livestock?"

"That is correct," St. Claire then said, "Non livestock, only your horses." St Claire instructed him, "Gather your things, meet me back here before 4:30PM, you better make that 4PM. I will need to complete your passage papers and orders for Captain Trudeau."

Gil does not know what to say to St. Claire other than, "Merci, merci monsieur." He is still uncertain, the numbers are not adding up, in his head. Also, the fact it is dependent on the captain's decision. Gilbert kept repeating in his mind as he walked back to the stable, beneath Saint Eustache, "Merci Lord, for getting us this far. Merci Lord, your graciousness and care is beyond what we deserve."

Seeking to be Loved

It is quickly approaching noon; Gilbert must hurry back to the stable. Marilda and the younger children will need to get things ready. I need to talk to Dominique, and monsieur Poincare at once. Maybe they are aware of a market for his animals.

He is so excited he can hardly contain himself. He nearly ran the 2km back to the stable completing the distance in record time. He almost did not even notice Marilda, and the children, in the park beside the church, as he was passing through it. He was not aware that they were there. It was Ernest, who noticed him first, and shouted, "Papa". The whole family recognized his excitement and wanted to hear the news. He hurried them to the stable as he explained.

He sent Mary Alice, to find Dominique. She is to request he meet her father in the chapel, or wherever he would like as soon as he can.

Gil asked Poincare if he was aware of any market for his animals. As Poincare was giving it thought, Marilda overheard, and walked over to Gilbert.

She told him, the nuns were very pleased an expressed their gratitude to have fresh milk and eggs each day. With it and the cream, they were able to expand their daily diet and use it for many other recipes.

"They rarely can prepare such things we take for granted each day. Gilbert, it has been so heartwarming, to see how delighted they were each morning and afternoon. They have been so kind to us. We should give the cow to the church if they were willing to take it."

Gilbert liked the idea, although he is concerned, the cow will bring the best price. He knew they will need every extra Franc for their passage.

Poincare heard Marilda's comments, and he agreed. He mentioned, "Yesterday and this morning, the change in the diet was excellent. The custard, pudding and pastries were heavenly and very rare around here, I might say."

Seeking to be Loved

Marilda said, "Gilbert let us leave the chickens here as well. All the birds seem to be laying in abundance, they are quite happy here." she laughed.

Gilbert is thinking that they could bring at least two francs a piece or more here in Paris.

Mary Alice was returning; they can hear her footsteps as she was running down the stairs. They turned to see her, she was opening the doorway. It took her a moment for her eyes to adjust, from the bright sunlight coming through the windows in the stairwell to the dimness of the stable. When she noticed them, she said, "Papa he can see you now. He said he will meet you in the chapel."

Gilbert kissed Marilda and told her, "I will be right back. You must start getting everything ready; I will be back shortly."

Dominique was sitting in the chapel, he greeted Gil with a smile. "I can see by the look in your eyes, and the excitement in your daughter's voice, that Monsieur St. Claire, must have dealt fairly with you."

"Oui, more than fair. Father, I am afraid, we still have some dilemmas."

Dominique expounds, "There is no dilemma, that our Lord cannot overcome. Do you mind sharing it with me?"

"I am afraid our funds are still a bit shy, of what we are going to need." The priest raised his brows. Gilbert knew that he is thinking M. St. Claire, may not have dealt fair enough with him. Gilbert immediately praised Monsieur St. Claire, for his efforts and how kind and considerate he had been. He described what he was doing for them.

The Priest began thinking a bit more highly of St. Claire. Gilbert stopped for a moment, his train of thought had changed. It was almost as if someone whispered in his ear, "I am my brother's keeper!"

The Priest asked Gilbert, "How may I be of assistance to you?"

He heard the phrase again, it is generated internally, "I am my brother's keeper!"

Seeking to be Loved

Gilbert responds, we need to get rid of our cow, goats, sheep, and our fowl. He hesitated for just a moment before he spoke, he knew he needed more argent. "We would like to give them to the parish." He immediately thought, "What am I saying, Why did I say that?"

The words just came forth. The instant they did, he felt a peace within him. A peace that could not be described, he felt weightless. He looked down at himself to make sure he was still in contact with the floor. Suddenly all the stress, all the anxiety, all the tension, all the concerns, he had been harboring for days vanished. He thought to himself, am I really standing? I feel so light!

The priest's noticed the transition of his appearance. It was truly a transformation in his being. He not only sensed it, he seen it before his very eyes. He knew it was the spirit, the Holy Spirit, working within him. He had to stifle his first reaction. Which was one of charity and he knew also, one of pride. He wanted to offer to pay the market price for his livestock. Recognizing the spirit at work, in the transformation within Gilbert, he knew he must not interfere with God's will. Even though he wanted to assist this man and his family any way he could. He knew he must accept the gift, as a gift, and do so humbly.

He expressed to Gilbert, extending his hand to grasp Gil's, "This is most gracious of you." You have already made many, within these walls in the few days that you have been here much happier. You and your family have blessed us.

Gilbert has one more request for Father Dominique. "Will you pray for us father, for a safe journey?"

Dominique replied, "I already have, I will continue."

Gilbert added, "Will you pray for our family and all the families traveling, and those staying in all of France?"

Dominique replied, "I have been, I will continue." He then said, "Monsieur Guyon, what do you think brought you here to our gates?"

Seeking to be Loved

Gilbert remembered the words Dominique spoke to him when they first met in the courtyard two days earlier. "It was providence, that brought you here."

How true his words have proven to be!

"I must go now father, merci, God Bless you and be with you always."

"With you and your family as well." Dominique said while making a sign of the cross in front of Gilbert, who's head is bowed. Sending him off with a blessing, "May God Bless you, Save you and Keep you away from all evil."

Gilbert turned and started walking away. The Priest said, "Merci, to you and your family for gracing this parish for two days, with your presence here."

Marilda and the children were ready when Gilbert came back down to the stable. She had a basket of food prepared for him. She and the children had already eaten their lunch. Ernest and John the stable boy, were harnessing the horses and Henry was preparing the carts.

Gilbert told Henry, to take the harnesses off the goats. They and all the other livestock will stay here, only the horses will continue on with us. Place the tools and the provisions that you have been carrying in the carts onto the wagon, under the buckboard. That is the only place there is room. The carts and the crates with the fowl are to stay here as well.

"Are you sure Gilbert?" asked Monsieur Poincare.

"Oui." he replied.

Marilda, hugged him from behind and whispered to him, "You are a good man, Monsieur Guyon."

All is ready, they said their goodbyes, and thanked Monsieur Poincare and John for their kindness and assistance.

Leaving the stable, John walked with them until they turned the corner. He gently reached for Mary Alice's hand. She stopped for a moment, and turned to him, he kissed her.

Seeking to be Loved

She blushed, and looked down.

He just said, "Au revoir."

She nodded shyly and walked to her family. Upon catching up to them, she turned to look at John. She smiled and gave him a slight wave of her hand.

When they reached the dock where the barge was moored, Gilbert gathered their papers and savings along with the financial gifts from both their parents. He and Marilda, counted it the total sum was fr.1555, plus a few centimes. They were still not quite sure they were going to cover the cost.

Gilbert started to second guess their decision not selling some of the livestock. Every little bit would have helped and a little extra may be needed. Gilbert asked Nattie to gather the children. He then asked all to bow their heads, he said to them, "Let us pray for God to intervene, to help in any opportune way that our heavenly father sees fit to allow us passage."

After their prayer request, Gilbert added, "Lord, it is your will not ours, we wish to follow, just show us the way." He took what he had, crossed the street, and climbed the steps to St. Claire's office.

He did not know God, had already manipulated all the necessary circumstances.

St. Claire, motioned to Gil, to come forward, as he ushered another patron on his way. He grasped Gilberts elbow to guide him to the seat at his desk. He is preparing to show Gilbert his final figures.

Gilbert stopped him and in a humble, serious tone, told St. Claire, "I am sure we are short of funds."

St. Claire stops abruptly, "How short?" he asked. "You had Fr.1555 this morning."

"The total you gave me Fr.1534, you said, was for the 4 youngest."

"Ouiiiii," St. Claire drawn out the expression, "Your point monsieur?"

Seeking to be Loved

"Our funds are not enough for all our fares," Gilbert responds.

St. Claire showed Gilbert his fees and orders. He is smiling broadly, one could not help noticing the elation in his eyes as well as his gestures.

Gilbert thought that was odd, due to the circumstances. "What about the rest of my family?" asked Gil.

I assumed the captain would sign you on as crew. Crew do not pay a passage fee, they work and do assigned duties. Room and board are provided in their contracts with the company. You, your wife and four oldest children are to be considered crew.

St. Claire is explaining to Gilbert what he must to. After he handed him the bill of fare. He started fumbling and leafing through files in his desk draw. Then handed them to Gil, to fill out.

Gil, upon examining the bill, does not know what to say. He can barely utter a sound. He then managed to ask, "Is the amount correct?"

St. Claire pulled several forms, from the files he had in his desk draw, and handed them to Gil. He explained, "You gave me an idea this morning. I discussed it with the Captain once you left. That you and your family can work aboard the freighter during the crossing, he is to sign you on as work crew. Your wife and daughter will cook, clean and your younger son serve as cabin boy, at the captain's disposal."

He did not tell Gilbert, that his suggestion to the captain was more accurately a strong recommendation from the company.

The captain is lord of his ship, no one gives him orders as to how to sail or run his vessel. He was thinking as he is speaking, wondering, how this can be seen as pleasing to the profit driven owners of the company.(?)

The captain will assign whoever you complete an application for, to duty on the ship. I suggested to the captain you and your oldest son are able to do manual labor. Your wife and oldest

Seeking to be Loved

daughter can cook and clean. The two younger sons can serve as cabin boys.

Gilbert asked, "What do cabin boys do?"

"They usually do simple task for captains or officers on the ship. Things like shine shoes, polish brass, keep officers' rooms and areas picked up, usually quite simple task."

"What about the three youngest? Someone will need to watch them," questioned Gilbert.

"I will leave that up to you and the captain, as to what to do with work duty scheduling." He explained to Gilbert, "A third class fare will need to be charged for the three little ones. I have decided there will be no food/provision charge for them. As part of the crew, the rest of the family will have their meals provided."

Gilbert knows they have enough provisions, to support the little ones. There is enough for his whole family under the new circumstances. Phillip for the most part is still nursing, so that should not be an issue.

"Monsieur St. Claire, how can I thank you?"

"Gilbert there is no need to, it is I who should be thanking you! You know up until two days ago, I was miserable and wretched. I have had everything I needed and wanted. My only concern was to make more money for the company and henceforth myself. Please do not get me wrong, I love my family as well as my job, it has provided well for us. Unfortunately still there was something not right in my life, something was missing. Life has to offer one more! I did not know, what that more was. Until Dominique, mentioned that familiar phrase. I heard it many times before, it just never had the impact that it was intended to.

I will never forget the look, the expression on your youngest one's face. There was something in his eyes, that brought that phrase to life ("*I am my brother's keeper*").

It struck a chord within me. It was a revitalization of my soul, a refreshment of my mind and spirit."

Seeking to be Loved

  He stopped in the middle of his statement and reflected on that very moment, an evening ago, in the entry hall of the church.
  Then he uttered the words; "Helping my fellow man." Saying and hearing himself speak them, brought another surge of energy and contentment within M. St Claire.
  "You Gilbert and your family renewed my life. You brought joy and love, Oui love, back into my life and my world! That is the best, biggest bonus/reward, I could have received."
  He allowed Gilbert time to fill out the forms, passenger information and work contracts. When Gilbert was finished, St. Claire reviewed the papers, which were completed in duplicate. "Gilbert, may I have you sign and date them here."
  St. Claire reviewed the copies and gave Gilbert his set. "Show them to the captains of the barge and freighter, at the appropriate time upon boarding. They are your passes and your orders. The orders you must never refer to as orders, they are request."
  "The captains take orders from no one on their ships, not even the company owners. You must always refer to them as requests if you are asked or questioned by the captain. They have big egos, no one tells them how to run their ships."
  "I understand," said Gilbert. "May God bless you and your family Monsieur St. Claire!"
  "And yours Gilbert," St. Claire returned the blessing!
  "I understand you and your family will be leaving this evening or early tomorrow morning, Bon voyage my friend!
  Monsieur Guyon one more thing, you and your family must work very hard and be no trouble to the captain or crew. My occupation and career with the company may be: non, will be at stake."
  He collected the fee of fr.1534. He doubled checked the paperwork to make sure both copies had been signed and dated properly. He shook Gilberts hand and said, "You must go now, farewell on your voyage."

Seeking to be Loved

Gilbert, nearly crushed St. Claire's hand while he thanked him.

"It was my pleasure to serve you, monsieur!"

Being the responsible agent for his company. He brought the receipt and fees to the owner on duty. He explained to his superior, his reasons for making such an agreement. Being careful not to mention his emotional, nor the spiritual motives, for conceiving such a contract.

He explained the standard fare was not possible for them. With Fr.1555 to their name, they were going to leave our office. I did not want to lose a customer and the Fr.1555, which was about to walk out the door. I did not want to forfeit space on our cruise liners, that many would be willing to pay full price. Or that which maybe inflated, or should I just say, the elevated fee which is now the going rate.

Our ships are always in need of maintenance, he reminds the owner. The barge and the freighters can almost always find some corner or space on board for animals or objects that can displace them self when needed. They can be moved on command, requiring little extra work for the crew. Unlike cargo that is secured and in place until it is removed by the crew, or the longshoreman, at the ports of call.

The owner listened, smiled once he realized the extra Franc's, are to be made without extra space, or expense, on behalf of the company.

"You are to be congratulated, St. Claire on your quick innovative thinking, and your salesmanship."

His boss instructed him to outline this procedure, he will set up a meeting with all the other directeurs and agents. He wanted to share this stroke of genius, and implement it immediately. He stood up and walked around his desk to shake St. Claire's hand, and patted him on the back, as he guided him out of his office.

Seeking to be Loved

He asked St. Claire, "How soon he could have this outlined?" in reference to this new sales option.

St. Claire said, "I will start right away and should have it finished before I leave work tomorrow." He looked straight into his bosses' eyes and said, "We are our brother's keeper." He turned and walked back to his desk.

He heard his boss mumble, "Oui, so we are. We are our brother's keeper! Especially, when there is profit to be made."

St. Claire then heard the door close behind him.

Seeking to be Loved

Chapter 8 Seine River cruise

Gilbert was standing on the dock with his family and he request to see the captain. He was granted permission to come aboard. A crewman led him to the captain's quarters. He introduced himself and handed his papers to the captain. They were quickly reviewed; the captain then ordered the escort to bring the family aboard and load the cargo. The captain informed Gilbert that his prize Percheron horses must stay on the deck.

"They should be fine for two days," said Gilbert.

The captain explained to him, "You must have someone responsible stay with them around the clock." He firmly stated to Gilbert, "The deck must be kept clean of animal waste at all times. I will not tolerate horse manure and urine on my decks. You and your family will be responsible, and will maintain a constant watch and clean the deck at every incident, is that clear, Monsieur Guyon?"

"Oui Captain," Gilbert replied.

The Captain has his first mate instruct the family as to the safety protocols. The captain adds, "My crew nor I must never see any of your family within two meters of the side of the barge." He informed them, that if one were to fall overboard, cries may not be heard due to the engine noise and the paddlewheel splashing.

He explained, "If someone did notice a passenger or crewman overboard and informed the captain immediately, stopping the vessel would take several minutes and two kilometer's distance. The victim may be lost forever, or may be run over by other vessels."

The first mate reiterated the captain's command and elaborated with his explanation. He is assured he had instilled sufficient caution and fear in each of the Guyon's. He told them that ample precaution must take place even with supervision. It must be the responsibility of the family, for their crewmembers have their own duties to perform. The Seine River, from Paris to the coast, is terribly busy, with much traffic.

Seeking to be Loved

The crew had stowed and secured the wagon on the open deck.

Gilbert and Ernest guided the percherons to the area the captain had designated. They roped off a small area barely large enough for the horses to stand side by side. To prevent much movement on part of the animals. He shared with Ernest, "It would be like an open stall for them. Not much room to move about, but plenty of fresh air."

The first mate showed Marilda and the children to their quarters. It was slightly less than two meters wide, three meters in length, with one small window. They were two double bunks built into the walls, that were slightly under two meters long and not much more than a half a meter wide. There was approximately a little more than half meter space between them to walk. There was barely enough room to move between them, to get into the bunks.

Marilda, Phillip and Joseph would share one, the two girls another, Henry, and little Gilbert another. Gil and Ernest will switch in and out of their bunk at night as they take turns keeping watch over the horses.

The door into the cabin was at the center of the inner wall of the vessel, opening into the cabin just wide enough to clear the entry. They were open storage shelves built into the walls that made up the extra meter of space forward of the bunks as you enter the cabin adjacent to the door. The space was compact, cozy and quite stuffy. When two people were standing there was barely enough room to move.

Marilda thought cruising on the river would be much better than a continued forced march. Her family had fared well, she knew it could very easily have gone bad. She was glad not having to keep contending with all the other travelers. Their legs, feet and bodies needed the rest.

The first night, sleep was fleeting from approximately 1PM on. That was when they finally disembarked. The engine was placed in gear and the steam powered vessel started its journey towards the

Seeking to be Loved

coast. The rumbling of the paddlewheel's, blowing of the ships whistle rang throughout the night. Once underway the noise soon became a soothing splashing sound, similar to that of a river's riffles and rapids or that of waterfalls.

Once they began making their way, it was only the disruption of the vessel's whistles that kept waking them. The vessels sounded their whistles signaling their presence to the approaching vessels passing by returning the gesture. It was that which startled them throughout the night until wee hours before dawn.

Gilbert and Ernest took turns watching the horses keeping them at ease throughout the night. It was the sound of their familiar voices, and occasionally petting, that allowed the pair to stay calm. The motion, noises and sounds were strange and unsettling to man and beast, who are not familiar with travel on the river. Gilbert took the first watch, Ernest the midnight and Gilbert again the early morning. They followed the crews four hour watch relief schedule.

It was interesting to watch the horizon, and the dark silhouettes of the landscapes on either side of the river. as they passed through towns and villages. The night had an unusual quiet and stillness about it on the river. Despite the repetitive drone of the engine and splashing of the paddle wheel. It was strange and at time a bit eerie, the night possessed a mystical nature. Maybe it had something to do with one's body moving along while you are motionless. Watching silently while everything around you appears and disappeared into the night.

You watch as the vessel flowed past each town and various landmarks in the dark of night. You know there are many things to see, but you are unable to see them. Some you are made aware of and were vaguely distinguishable by the lights that flickered from buildings and homes. Some visible only by the moonlight and the shadows they cast.

Ernest's, mind started to wander after two hours of watch. He found himself starting to understand and experience what his father and grandfather spoke of over the years. Attempting to share their wisdom. Some of their phrases were becoming clearer in his mind, as he was mesmerized by the passing scenes and constant rhythm of the engine and splashing wheel.

- "Life will pass us by, when you are still too long."
- "You may have many seemingly good ideas at night. When things are not clear. You must wait until the light of day to expose what you could not see."
- "Things are not always what they appear to be."
- "There is a whole world around us, yet we are lucky to get a small glimpse of it in our lifetime."
- "We never know for certain what is ahead."
- "We never see the whole picture."
- "We never know where life is going to lead us. All we know is what we leave behind."
- "We want to see, do, and know everything."
- "We do not want life to pass us by."
- "One wants to experience all life has to offer."
- "When one occupies oneself in such a manner, they may miss, ' **What it is, they have to offer life'**."

Ernest stood up to pat the horses. His heart is racing as his mind still wonders about all the places they passed the last few hours. What treasures they and the rest of the world can offer, and the meaning of his thoughts.

The horses are content, and their bulky bodies warm. He rubbed his hand over their necks, muzzle, and foreheads.

His mind settled the moment he felt their smooth coats. He sensed the comfort of being connected. He stood at their heads rubbing the cheeks of each. He recognized in the big eyes of the beast, a peacefulness. He whispered to them, "You labor each day, and you are well cared for. Each day is similar, each week the same and it only changes with the season. Are you not bored?"

Both shake their heads side to side, and neigh.

Ernest laughed, and asked them, "Why not, is it because you do what you have been intended to do? Or is it because you were trained for what you do? Is it because your labors provide for many, is that the reason you are so content?"

Both shook their heads up and down, and neigh.

"Well, I to must find labor where I also can benefit many. So, I can be warm, well cared for, at peace, and content with my life."

The night passed. It was not long before the sun lightened the landscape before it rose over the horizon behind them. The ripples on the river started reflecting the golden glimmer as the water became a sparkling carpet, that the barge plowed through.

May 22, 1914 - Marilda and Phillip were the first to greet Gilbert, in the morning on the deck of the barge. Gilbert turned to meet Nattie, he embraced her and gave her a good morning kiss. He turned his attention to Phillip, who possessed a look of wonder and inquisitiveness of his new surroundings.

She said, "He must feel the vibrations in his little bones." They looked at him and see he is smiling with his happy face. It seemed to enlighten and brighten the whole area around him as well as the hearts of those near. Nattie, gently pinched his cheek and said, "You know we are talking about you sweet child." His grin gets even bigger and the sparkle in his eyes even brighter, if that could be possible.

Gilbert asked her if the children were still asleep?

She acknowledged they were. She shared her concerns about their welfare and wellbeing. We have all had so much excitement and experienced so many new thing the last two weeks. Everything is happening so quickly. Now the noise and vibration of the vessel's engine, made it hard to settle oneself to sleep.

"Let them sleep, they have no chores to perform, let them rest as long as they can. Who knows how busy we will be in a few days."

Marilda reached for Gilbert's hand, her knees buckled. Her head drops to one side and her body became limp.

Gilbert wrapped his arms around her and Phillip as she collapsed. He eased them both to the deck of the barge.

Seeking to be Loved

The incident was observed by the ships pilot, he suggested to the first mate, "Go and assist them, or, should I."

"You keep the wheel," orders the first mate. "I will check on them."

The sudden action and Gil's reaction, startled Phillip and caused him to cry. His father supporting him firmly against his mother, with such a tight grip, squeezing them together. The child, in such a brief moment transcended from the warm, firm, comfortable support he felt against his mother. To a sensation of falling in midair. The sensation change was instantaneous, to a powerful quick near suffocating grasp from his father, before being lowered to the deck. The cry was from the sudden surprise and fear.

Gilbert quickly assessed Phillip, holding him in his arm against his chest. He reached to brush the hair from Marilda's face. He asked his wife, if she was okay, there was no response. He noticed she was breathing, as the ships mate arrived at his side.

The First mate asked if she had been sick. He grasped her hand and patted it, in an attempt to arouse her.

Gilbert kept calling her name, then said, "Non, she appeared fine a moment ago."

She rolled her head side to side, and opened her eyes.

Gilbert exhaled a sigh of relief. He asked her if she is ok? "You were just standing here, then you collapsed, fainted."

The Mate assisted her to a sitting position.

"I remember we were standing here talking and that was all, what happened?" she asked.

"Do you feel all right?" Gil questioned.

"I think so, I do not feel any different. I must be more tired than I thought," she replied. "I am not sure how much sleep I actually got the last few nights. It was very stimulating for all of us, especially the children. We were all cramped so close together in the little room it was hard to sleep."

The First mate told them, that he has seen this many times before with crew members. Especially those not yet seasoned, it is usually the first time out. He explained, "I believe it is the motion of the barge. It does not roll like the ships at sea. Seeing things pass on both sides of the rivers shore, while you go about your business, may cause people to lose their equilibrium. Especially when you are standing still, yet you see objects out of the corner of your eyes passing by on either side of the river. It can make you feel dizzy. It gives you a sensation that you are in motion when you know you are not. It generally comes on very suddenly and seems to happen most often shortly after someone has awoke. If they immediately go out onto the deck to walk about. You should be fine, after you watch the shore for a while. You will get familiar with the vessels pace, as you adjust to the movement before you walk the decks.

It would be a good idea not to be carrying anything, especially an infant or child, when you first come out on deck."

"Oui monsieur, I can see why," remarked Marilda.

"May I assist you to your quarters, Madame Guyon?"

"Oui, merci," she and Gil uttered to the mate simultaneously.

Gilbert told Marilda, "I will keep Phillip with me. Have Ernest come relieve me at 8:00 to watch the team. I will bring Phillip in with me since he has calmed down. The moment he heard your voice when you woke up, he stopped crying."

Nattie was resting when Gilbert brought Phillip to her. They both rested well while he nursed.

Gilbert slept for an hour and a half before the other children started to wake one by one. They all wanted to go on deck, Gilbert advised against it until they all have had breakfast. After their mother's experience, he wanted them to be fully awake for several minutes before going out on the deck.

Mary cared for Phillip the rest of the day while her mother slept, except when he was hungry.

Gil and Marilda both felt much better by the evening. They both needed a day's rest. Cruising on the river was very relaxing and quite interesting. They passed numerous cities, small towns and villages and some grand estates. The cabin served adequately as a private sleeping and nursing quarters.

Gil and the children enjoyed floating down the Siene River. They passed many magnificent castles and homes in Givery, Vernon, Les Andelys and Caudebec. They floated past Great Cathedrals, Saint Martin of Triel-Sur-Siene in Rouen and Honfleur. They marveled at the steep banks and out cropping of rock cliffs near the towns of Freneuse, Les Andelys, Saint-Aubin-les-Elbeuf. There were many islands the barge floated by during the two-day progressing toward the ocean on the Seine. Several clustered near the town of Poses. The river and scenery fascinated they Guyon's. The many ruins, along the banks of the great river, were interesting to observe.

May 23, 1914 - Gilbert, spoke with the captain this morning, as he made his rounds inspecting his barge. The captain mentioned to Gilbert, informing him they were making particularly good time. Due to their early departure time as well as the high-water levels of the spring flow. He informed Gilbert they should arrive at the port harbor of Le Havre, later this evening.

The captain mentioned to Gilbert, "Within an hour, we will be approaching Poses. There will be many interesting historical sights to see. There will be great landmarks, such as the hilltop ruins of the great fortress Chateau Gaillard. Later Saint-Quen Abbey Church, the Donjon De Rouen Tower, and many sights of interest. You and your family may spend as much time on the deck as you like. Please heed the warning, stay away from the outer rail." He holds up two fingers and said, "Two meters please monsieur, for you and your family's safety.

I myself instructed the crew to keep a close eye on your brood. I want no delays," emphasized the captain. The captain also told him, "I have arranged for someone to be waiting for you, to guide your family to the freighter. Once our barge is secured to our docking station, I will contact the harbormaster to inform Capt. Trudeau, we are here. It is my understanding he will send someone

Seeking to be Loved

to meet you, and to escort your family to the freighter. By the time we are ready to start unloading, they should be waiting on the dock at our starboard. Enjoy your day monsieur Guyon."

Gilbert thanked the captain.

Approaching the ocean was another exhilarating experience for the Guyon family. The Siene River became wide as they neared the ocean. One can barely make out the buildings on its banks. There were so many boats and ships of all sorts. Many tall ships, with high mast towering above them seemed to reach the sky. Huge cruise liners and ocean freighters moored to the docks, as far as you could see. Many of them within the bay made their barge which was huge yesterday, appears small to them today.

Nearing the end of the river journey the town of Honfleur was on the south bay, it is a port town. There are many buildings side by side as far as you can see. Boats and ships moored on every inch of its harbor.

Alas, Le Havre, the town was not as grand as that of the South side of the rivers Port of call. Large buildings, shops and businesses, homes above them. Docks stretch for miles, and the magnificent rock cliffs that border the edge of the sea.

It was an ordeal to get the barge to the dock. It took the coordinated effort of three steam powered boats, to maneuver it into its mooring station at the dock.

Ernest watched with much interest, he heard one of the crewmen call them remorqueurs(Tugboats). The barge was moored securely to the dock with ropes thicker than his arm.

An army of workers sprang into action. It was fascinating to observe all the activity that was taking place. It was like a coordinated attack of longshoreman. Setting up booms and platforms being laid, ramps being placed, and men pushing wheelbarrows full of things, all shapes, and sizes. Many men carrying items and bundles on their shoulders and heads. Once platforms were set into place, others were being assembled by crewman working in unison. Large sacks carried on men's shoulders being placed on them. It almost made him dizzy watching the mass of humanity. It was reminiscent to watching an army of bees, or ants, performing herculean task before his eyes.

The first mate had to order the swarm of men to stop. He had his crewman from the barge remove the Guyon's wagon from the deck. Ten men were waiting at the edge of the barge to assist rolling the wagon onto a ramp and down to the dock, with all its contents.

The captain met with Gilbert, he informed him that he already wired the message to Capt. Trudeau. "Bon voyage," the captain said, shaking his hand.

"Merci captain," replied Gil, as he prepared to lead his team off the vessel. Ernest and Henry had already finished harnessing the horses. They begin leading them off the deck, onto the ramp, down to the dock below. They were hitching the team to their wagon when a man approached Gilbert.

Seeking to be Loved

Chapter 9 <u>The Crossing</u>

"I am Jean from the SS Loreto, Capt. Trudeau, has sent me to meet you."

Gilbert introduced himself, "We are glad you are here, we will be ready as soon as we load into the wagon." Then he assisted Marilda, onto the buckboard. Next, he handed her Phillip, then helped Blanche and Joseph to their seat. He turned to Jean and said, "We are ready now."

It was slow attempting to maneuver through the crowd of workmen and passengers. With many stops, they had to wait for crews moving supplies, baggage, and equipment onto and off the many ships. The children kept peering at each other and their parents with wide eyes. Never in their life have they heard such language, the profanity and cursing. It seemed to come from so many mouths as they passed by. There was constant yelling, and screaming, along the way until they made it to the freighter. It was a bit unnerving.

Jean observing the many wide-eyed stares of the children, turned to Gilbert. He exclaimed, "Ay, now you see, and understand the term, ah the phrase, 'Cussing, like a sailor monsieur,' non."

"Oui," Gil replied.

Along the dock there are many magnificent ships, the size of some of them unimaginable. Marilda, thinking aloud to anyone who may be listening, expressed her amazement at the gigantic passenger steam liners they are passing. Finally, they arrived at the freighter, SS Loreto,

Gilbert turned to Jean and said, "What a ship."

Marilda responds, "Oui, it is, it is hard to imagine that we will be crossing the ocean on such a vessel."

It appeared darkness is setting in despite it being early in the evening. The sun is blocked by these massive ships. They can only see the dock area and the cargo holds of the ships. These areas provide the necessary light for the longshoreman to continue their work throughout the night.

Moments before they arrived, Captain Trudeau was wondering why they were not here. He ordered another crewman to go look for them. He is aware the dock is always a busy area.

Jean had not expected the many delays, the stops and waiting required on the dock. It would have been quicker for them to have directly exited the dock where they disembarked and traveled on the ocean boulevard. They could have re-entered the dock where the SS Loreto is moored. It would have taken less than half the time if they exited the dock for the transfer.

The captain became impatient waiting, he has many duties to perform and oversee. He instructed the crew when they arrive, do not let them unhitched the horses from the wagon. We will use them to pull the wagon up the broad ramp to the area the crew had prepared for them. They will use the team, until the wagon is maneuvered to where it will be secured on board. Only then have them unhitched the team and taken to the area we had prepared. When the animals have been secured, Jean was directed to bring the family immediately onto the main deck. There they will meet with the captain, and be assigned duties as he sees fit.

One of the cooks assigned to the crew did not report for duty. The captain had held off contacting the dock master to procure additional personnel as a replacement. He decided not to, until he met the Guyon's. He was holding the telegram from Monsieur St. Claire, which identified Marilda and Mary as cooks.

When they arrived, Jean reported to the captain, "This is the Guyon Family, Sir."

The captain introduced himself, "I am Capt. Trudeau." His demeanor and tone was one of no nonsense. The air of confidence and control were present, and easily detected in his manner.

He addressed the two ladies first. He told them, "My only concern was the needs of his crew." In reference to preparing provisions to sustain them during the voyage. He looked directly at

Seeking to be Loved

Marilda, "I understand you and your daughter are skilled in meal preparation."

Marilda responds, "Oui, we are captain."

"Très bien(Very good)," said the Capt..

He looked to Gilbert, "I understand you and your sons are capable manual laborers."

Gils response to the captain, "I believe you will find my sons, and I, quite capable of doing a man's days' work."

"Excellente," said the captain, "I will have a list of your work duties placed under your cabin door before the end of the first watch."

Gilbert looked questioningly, at the captain.

The captain acknowledged, he does not understand the number order of watch time designation. He explained, "First watch is at midnight and ends at 0400 hours. You will have your orders slipped under your cabin door before the watch ends."

He looked at Marilda and said, "The cooks come on duty at 0300 hrs. When you are awakened by the watchmen, you will find your orders had been slipped under your door and will be on the floor."

Marilda is pleasant, direct, and confidently firm in her tone and her demeanor as she addressed the captain. "We will perform as expected." She was certain, Mary and her own performance in the kitchen/galley will be better than what they anticipate.

The captain introduced the ship's machinist to Gilbert. "He is the one you will report to for your daily work detail. You are to meet him at the end of the second watch each morning at 0800 hrs... All assigned duties are to be performed that day no matter how long they take. Understood, Monsieur Guyon?"

"Understood captain," Gilbert replied!

The captain excused himself, "I have duties I must attend to."

The machinist took the Guyon's on a tour of the ship. The tour ended at the galley where Marilda and Mary will need to report at 0300. The machinist informed them, the watchmen will knock on their door, and see to it you are awake on time to report. He introduced her and Mary to Monsieur Bastine Casteau, the chef.

The chef is a pleasant man, obviously very devoted to his work. He turned slightly to point out the galley and dining areas. He explained the main duties and responsibilities, of he and his staff. The chef's day without his assistant, had been enlivening and long. It is just past 9:30PM, and he was still covered with grease and grime from the kitchen.

Marilda asked Gilbert, what will be done with the little ones? She is thinking ahead at her early and apparently long days in the kitchen. Who is going to watch the children? Little Gilbert, Blanche, Joseph, what are they going to do?

Gilbert stated, "Plus Phillip, I will -."

Before he can finish the statement, Marilda interrupted. "The baby is staying with me. I do not give a damn, what the captain will say or do."

Gilbert finished his statement, "I will take the two boys (meaning Joseph and Phillip) with me. The boys and I will keep an eye on them."

The machinist giving them the tour, heard the conversation. He said, "The captain is austere, well-seasoned and familiar with all expected duties on board his vessel. There is no better captain on any of the company ships. He also is a father and a very devoted grandfather. I know he misses his family greatly when we are away at sea for months at a time. I am sure he has something planned for them."

Marilda and Gil looked at each other, she grit her teeth and stiffened her jaw.

The guide bid them "Bonne nuit", and started to walk away. He stopped, turned to face them, and mentioned, as a warning to them. "The captain has no tolerance for insubordination, nor disrespect. Oui," He added, "Of anyone young or old who is on board his ship." He intentionally peered at the five younger children, then Marilda.

Seeking to be Loved

Gilbert nodded, "Merci, Bonne nuit." They entered the cabin. It was three times as spacious than the one on the barge they arrived on. It had sleeping bunks approximately the same size as those on the barge. Two sets of three on both walls, with cabinets extending from floor to the ceiling at the ends of each set of bunks. In the hall outside the room, there were two bathrooms to be used by crewmembers. Upon examining each on opposite ends of the hall, they had fresh paint on them. One door was marked Hommes, the other <u>Femmes Only</u>. That pleased the Mademoiselles.

The Captain, had the chef move to a smaller cabin, his near the galley would be more suitable for the family.

Marilda was beginning to like the captain, and was feeling a bit less concerned about safety of the children. She and Gil had a discussion with all of them, in reference to the three youngest.

Little Gilbert said, "I can work with Papa and my brothers."

Marilda explained to him, "You are a big boy now, we need you to be responsible."

He liked that word, he liked the idea that he was responsible, or, at least considered that he could be.

She told him, "You must look out for and protect Blanche and Joseph. We are counting on you to do that, while Mama, Papa, and the rest of us perform our duties.

While we are on this ship, we must work to earn our passage. Our duties may require us to be negligent of keeping all of you in our sight. We are depending on and trust you will be responsible for their safety. Just as we all are and were of you when you were little. We must and will be responsible for you and each other's safety. Oui, your job Gilbert is to be our eyes, mouth and hands to protect them and see nothing bad happens to them."

Little Gil thought about that for a few seconds. Then he said, "I have to be responsible like you Ma mee and Papa, to take care of Blanche and Joseph." He liked the feeling he got when he realized the others were willing to trust him. "They must trust me enough, to protect my little sister and brothers." The thought of that boost his self-confidence. The thought occurred to him, to protect someone, you must be strong. They think I am strong enough to do it. I am strong, he thinks proudly to himself. "I will protect them, Ma mee." Then he looked at his younger sister and brother confidently and exclaimed, "I will protect you whether you like it or not."

They just yawned.

"Oui," said Marilda.

His father mentioned to his son, "Gilbert, as far as I am concerned, that is the most important job of all."

Little Gill inflated his chest with pride. Then he said, "I can be responsible for them."

They instructed all three of their children, not for a moment let anyone of them out of their sight. No matter what anyone may tell you. Even if the captain orders you, you scream as loud as you can, all three of you, until one of us comes to you. Promise us you will do that, no matter what.

"Oui Ma mee, Oui Papa."

Marilda, had the children ready themselves for bed as she assists Joseph and Phillip. She told them, "Soon my darlings, we are going to be on our way to a distant land and a new life for my dear ones."

Phillip, who is always filled with excitement at the sound of his mother's voice, flared his arms in the air. It made her laugh, as it did all in the cabin.

Gil had gone to check the horses and he gave them hay for the night. He rubbed their coats with the curry brush. It always seemed to relax the beast, at the end of the day. He reminded himself that he must make it a point to brush them twice a day. That will keep you calm for the next ten days or so, he told them. He was concerned that the beasts would have no fresh air, during the journey for as long as they are at sea. When he got back to the cabin, everyone was already in their assigned bunks, sound asleep.

Seeking to be Loved

May 24, 1914 - A loud knock on the door, it sounded like a cannon blast within the cabin. It was followed by a partial opening of the door. The voice of the watchmen said, "Cooks on duty."

Those that were awoke by the watchmen's message, as the door gently closed, responded, "Merci."

Marilda needed to wake Mary, hardly believing she could have slept through the interruption. She whispered to her, "It was time for them to go."

She then whispered to Gil, "Ask the captain about the children's supervision. Be sure to remind the children, place the fear of God in them as to our instructions, administered to them last night." It was then, she noticed the paper on the floor.

Marilda picked it up; they stepped outside their door into the dimly lit hallway to read it. It read:
Monsieur and Madame Guyon:
- 0800 Your four youngest children will have breakfast at the Captain's table in the galley dining area.
- 0840 They will accompany the first mate and I on ship inspection.
- 0930 They will be on the bridge (at which time we will be in deep water, underway to South Hampton, England).
- 1100 They will accompany me on the second ship inspection.
- 1200 Second meal, in galley, Captains table, with Monsieur Guyon and his charges.
- 1240 They will be escorted to their cabin. *
- 1345 They will return to the bridge.
- 1445 They will be on the foredeck learning to tie knots and there uses.
- 1515 They will be in the galley. *
- 1545 They will be escorted to their cabin.
- 1700 Your family will have dinner at the captain's table.

  * - Means escorted by Mme. Guyon or oldest daughter.
Please note all child/infant cleaning, and nursing duties, will be performed by Mme. Guyon. She will be directed to report to where and when needed.

Seeking to be Loved

They both took a deep breath of relief, upon reading the captain's memo. Gilbert looked at Nattie and confirmed, "It seems to me the captain runs a tight ship. He is cognizant of all the appropriate needs of the ship, crew and the passengers."

Marilda acknowledged, "It appears so. Let us see if Mary Alice, is ready and we will be off to the galley."

The galley is at the end of the hallway, where it opens into a seating area. The tables have a high edge surrounding the surface, and chairs slide underneath. The cooking, food preparation tables are beyond a serving counter to the left.

She advised Gil to rest, he and the boys will be on duty for the day soon enough. She reminded him, "Be sure to check Phillip. He will need to be changed, keep him with you while he sleeps. I do not want him to be left in the bed alone, he might try to climb out, Joseph won't wake-up to stop him."

Marilda and Mary, were greeted by the head cook. He explained their duties to them. "We will be preparing three meals, for the thirty two crewmen and nine passengers. They must be prepared on time and served. The first meal will be continental and ready to serve at 0330 hrs. It is for crew going to watch and those coming off their watch. Then again at 0715 for other crewmen, starting their duties. The second meal will be served from 1130 - 1300 hrs.. Third meal 1630 - 1800 hrs., coffee, tea, and water, with fresh baked goods will be available on the counter for the crew at all times.

Between meals, utensils, dishes, cookware are to be cleaned, while preparation for the next meal is underway. 'Do you have any questions?' "

Marilda asked, to be shown where all the things he mentioned are stored. The only things that are visible, are hanging pots and pans.

He showed them where everything was stowed away. He explained, "Everything has a place where it is most secured. If not, rough seas could make a shamble of the galley." He emphasized

Seeking to be Loved

everything must be returned to the exact place, so we can find them when needed.

Monsieur Le Chef Casteau, ordered the girls, "You do what I say, when I say, we should have no problem."

He gave the orders and directions, they followed. He was amazed that the first meal came together so quickly. It was only 0400 and everything was ready for the first meal. Even the final batch of croissants, baguettes, Kouign-Amann and tarte talin pastries were baking.

The ham was warming in the oven, oatmeal and barley were simmering, coffee was ground, and ready to put in the percolator. He explained to the girls, where and how items will be set up and served.

Marilda asked, "Where will they all sit? There are only 20 places to sit. Plus, we do not have enough service settings for 41 people, at best 20," she stated.

"Indeed," said Bastine. He explained, "The relief watch will be approximately 10 to 12 men. Twenty minutes later, the men they have relieved will be served, another 10 to 12 coming off duty. Then the rest of the crew will be in at their leisure between 0630 – 0800. The captain is always the last one to show for the first meal.

After each serving, services are to be cleaned and dried, ready for the next seating. It is this way for each meal, as you see there will be more than enough place settings for each sitting.

Marilda had a concerned look on her face.

Chef Bastine said, "Do not worry, as efficient as you both were to prepare everything for the first meal, you will have no problem having things ready for all."

He was right, although once the first meal began there was no downtime. Not until the last of the dishes were cleaned and stowed away. Coffee and tea had been placed on the galley counter. There was a drawer full of baked goods, that the crewmen could help themselves to whenever they please. Preparation began immediately for the next meal.

Seeking to be Loved

    Marilda had been given ample time to nurse, and care for Phillip. Although time away from him seemed like an eternity, despite the busyness in the galley. She did not like being separated from Phillip. She missed not having him close to her. It would always break the monotonous routine of each day. When she could look at him and watch him smile. To see his reaction of joy, at the sound of her voice.

    Each time she thought about him, something within kept saying to her, "This was good practice." Whenever she registered that thought in her mind, she would declare to herself, "Practice, for what?"

    "This will help prepare him, for what?" she would question herself.

    "Preparation for what, being alone? Being without his mother?"

    The thoughts always left her feeling a bit uneasy, until she focused her attention on the tasks at hand.

    Mary Alice was pleased to stay in the galley and keep busy. She did not like the whispers, crude comments, and laughter of the crewmen.

    It was unusual to have a woman or young girl on board. She felt secure in the galley. The chef was always mindful of this. He would have her wait until the tables and benches emptied, before instructing her to gather the service utensils, and clean the tables.

    Both Mary and Marilda, were glad the Femme bathroom was close by.

    The crewmen were not use to having a sign in place on the door, especially labeled Femme. They thought it would be good sport to startle the femme, at every opportunity. Many would knock, bang or whistle whenever they went pass the door, whether someone occupied it or not. In an attempt to disconcert anyone who may be in that room.

    The girls learned quickly not to respond when this occurred, when they were in the bathroom. Marilda instructed the girls, not to

Seeking to be Loved

respond when using the facilities. Nor open the door to anyone who's voice she did not recognize.

Marilda and Mary were exhausted at the end of the day. They just wanted to get off their feet. It was nearly 1900 hrs. when they dried the last of the service ware and all had been packed away.

Chef Bastine, was pleased with the girl's efforts, and efficiency, he told them so. He bid them, "Bonne nuit, I will see you at 0300."

The first day for Gilbert and the boys, working was much different than what they were used to. They were assigned to wire brush all the bulkhead doors, steel framing on the engine room deck and walls. There were four doors, two on each end of the engine room. All needed to be scrubbed, cleaned, wiped dry, then painted. The three of them completed both sides, plus the interior walls, and bulkheads before noon. That left two exterior walls and four doors to complete after the break.

The Capt. invited Gilbert and the boys to join him at his table for the noon meal, with the three young ones. Marilda kept Phillip with her in the galley.

The captain complimented Gilbert, "Monsieur, your children are delightful. I must admit, I was a bit apprehensive about the youngest, your little Phillip. Your children are quite disciplined, their big brother Gilbert, is a good guardian and leader for them."

Gil chuckled at the captains' comment, looking at Little Gil, who is smiling with a proud gleeful look on his face. Gil asked his son, "Why are you smiling so?"

Little Gilbert's reply was, "I have never been called a big brother before," as he puffed out his little chest.

Joseph in a barely audible little voice, said, "You are my big brother." His statement, caused the captain and Gilbert to laugh.

"I hoped this is not an inconvenience on you captain. Having children around while performing your duties," remarked Gil.

Seeking to be Loved

"Not at all," said Capt. Trudeau. "I had always envisioned taking my children to sea, as well as my grandchildren. It is against company procedures. Rightfully so, I must admit!

I know you must be quite concerned about having them out of your site. Let me reassure you and your wife, they will be properly supervised, at all times," he emphasized. "I myself have given the assigned crewmen strict orders of diligent supervision, when in their care."

The Capt. divulged to Gil, "I plan to have ten to eleven days to get my fill of having little children under my feet. Monsieur Guyon, to me this is a dream come true. Plus, I do not have to break company protocol to experience it.

You see, it is the only regret I have, of going to sea. The fact that I have missed so much of my children and grandchildren's lives; watching them grow." He paused, "Oui, watching them grow; watching them do what children do, that is what I have missed."

Gilbert told the captain, "It is for us also an answer to our prayers, to be making this passage."

The captain silent for a few moments, awkwardly silent. He acknowledged there may be a God. He believes man is responsible for his own fate.

In the gentlest voice, which is greatly out of character for him. He does not recognize the tone of it. Even though he is hearing himself annunciate the words it was such a simple statement. For it is not his nature or his intent, at any time to display a tender side of himself while on his ship. "Oui, mine as well."

He realized he never prayed for children to be on board, his or anyone else's. The thought occurred to him, "Hell, I have not prayed since I was a child."

Gilbert said to the captain, "God many times answers prayers that are in our hearts."

The captain is out of his role once again and lost for words. "How did this man know what I was thinking?"

Seeking to be Loved

The captain is always processing, planning, evaluating, while things are happening all around him. He is lord and master of all on board once the vessel is underway. He is the ultimate and absolute authority on his ship at sea, it is his universe.

Captain Trudeau, is ever in the process of instantly analyzing, making decisions, and giving orders. It is in his blood, it is his nature, he is never lost for words. While he is processing this experience; he felt something is trying to connect inside. He inspects his own mind, his body; all is in order. Yet there is a sense, he was not getting something, or understanding a dilemma. This frustrated him. He and his men expect immediate and effective answers from him, for whatever the problem.

He wondered what can be causing this uneasiness, he is innately aware something is not right, something is not complete, something needs to be done.

He questioned himself, "It is not the ship. It is not the crew. What is it?"

There is something abysmal inside, trying to connect with him. He finally, responded to Gilbert statement. "Oui, oui, I suppose he does."

The ship's captain took control of his consciousness. Still he wondered, is there something about the ship that needs his attention, he is forever trusting his intuition in such matters.

He looked around the table at the children. "Get a good rest now, I have plans for you later."

The children are all smiles. Gilbert asked them, "What do you say to the captain?" In sequence they say, "Merci Captain, Sir!"

The Captain with a stern stone tight lipped look on his face, yet with a twinkle in his eye, ordered. "I will have my little mates on the bridge at 1330 hrs."

The children see right through his demeanor. "Aye, Aye," all three of the little ones say together as they leave the table.

Seeking to be Loved

Back to business, Gil and the boys were nearly finished with the days assigned duties. There was a whistle and a page, "All available crewmen on deck." Gilbert asked one crewman, if they should report on deck?

The crewmen said, "Non, we are getting ready to enter the harbor and to dock at South Hampton, we will be transferring and receiving cargo.

Gilbert told Ernest, "Go watch the team, the horses may get anxious. I expect there will be many unfamiliar people, loud voices, noise and business going on about them." He also told him to check, and clean their stall area. Be sure to place fresh straw down for them.

"How long should I stay with them, Papa?"

"Until I come and relieve you."

Gilbert and Henry went to finish scraping the last wall and returned their tools. They gathered paint and supplies from the machinists and finished painting all the doors and walls. They finished and returned to the shop. They cleaned the brushes and stored the tools and supplies.

"What should we do now?" Gil asked.

The machinists told them, "Orders will be in their room in the morning. I suspect you will be doing the same thing on the deck above and in the stowing area. It will probably be just the bulkheads within the cargo holds. That is all you will be able to paint. Cargo will be stowed and secured against all the walls. They will be little exposed wall to paint.

The captain may have another needed job for you to do, one will see. Go, your day is done."

Gilbert and Henry went to the horses makeshift stable to get Ernest. The whole area is full of crew, who are already closing the hatches and packing them tightly to make them seaworthy.

Ernest greeted his father and his brother. "Papa, you should have seen the men. The precision of their work, loading and unloading. Everyone seemed to know, exactly what to do. Barely a word was said. One man was holding papers; he would point, another man would be untying cargo. Others removed it, while some were securing things elsewhere. Everyone carried things to and fro, some were repositioning, packing, and stacking. All seemed to be working as a team, in proper sequence. It was quite fascinating to watch such coordination and efficiency of their effort.

Ernest said, "Someday, I think I might want to go to sea."

His father replied, "Maybe one day you will." Gil agreed with his son, it is amazing what can be done and accomplished when people work together for the common good and a specific cause. He has Ernest and Henry join the others in the cabin. When I come back, we will go to the evening meal.

It was past 1800 hrs. and the captain had not come to the evening meal. Gil told Nattie, he would see the children to the cabin and bring Phillip back to her.

Phillip was pleased to see his mother and she him. When he saw her, he reached for his mother. Taking him from Gil, she glanced at the chef.

The chef knew what she was thinking. "The little one needs to eat too, Mama. We can take it from here," he said.

Nearly all the crew have eaten, and have returned to assist on deck. They were now readying the ship to head back out to sea.

Gilbert realized, this is why the captain had not come to the evening meal just yet. He is busy preparing to leave the port. He began to think of how many tasks the captain must coordinate. Whenever a ship is entering or leaving port, especially among so many other vessels. He must orchestrate the efforts of crew, longshoreman, getting goods on and off the ship. Including storing cargo what and where, to assure all is balanced, proper weight distribution. Everything must be secured and in a timely and efficient manner. So many men doing so many different jobs, to make such a transition possible. He must see to the ships docking, unloading, and loading, then get underway in a designated amount of time in this

Seeking to be Loved

port of call. It boggled his mind, to think of it. He gained a tremendous respect for the captain, at that very moment.

The chef just received a message from the captain. Asking him to extend his apology to the Guyon's. He will not be joining them for dinner. He will see them at first meal tomorrow morning.

After they had dinner, Gill asked Ernest to check the horses. All the children wanted to go see them as well. Their father sent them to the cabin and told them he would take them later. Gilbert asked the chef if he could take Marilda's place for the rest of her shift.

"Oui" he replied, "It was just a matter of cleaning up and washing dishes and stowing everything in its place. Then we will fill the drawer with baked goods for the night, make fresh pots of coffee and tea for the crew. That will keep them happy throughout the night.

The chef informed Gilbert, "Your daughter is an exceptionally good worker, for such a juene fille(young girl) her age. Your wife monsieur, she is a master of the kitchen, she moves with grace and efficiency. Here she comes now with the little Phillip. Oh my, how content he looks now, he is in mothers' arms, full and happy," the chef burbled.

Nattie starts to hand Phillip, to Gilbert.

"Non, non" said the chef, "You keep him, your husband offered his service to help your daughter and I finish up."

"Well then!" she exclaimed using a somewhat perturbed tone in her voice, glancing at the chef then Gilbert who was nodding his head. Although smiling in delight and gratitude, for she is near exhaustion.

Mme. Guyon, "I was just mentioning to your husband how efficient you and your daughter preform your duties in the galley."

"Merci, chef. There is something I thought I wanted to discuss with you if I may monsieur."

"Please Madame," the chef replied as he rolled his eyes, in a quite peculiar way. While he removed the remaining items from the

Seeking to be Loved

snack drawer, replacing them with fresh. He suspected that a landlubber, is going to suggest how to operate his galley. He will listen in one ear, and let it go out the other.

"Well, I thought of those crewmen coming and going onto the first watch. Maybe they would like to have a more substantial meal. I thought if they can let us know by the end of our evening shift. What it is they would prefer for the first meal in the morning, limiting it to a few choices of course. It would not be too much trouble to have a meal prepared for them. Especially, if we are only cooking for 10 to 12 people."

"I must think on this Madame. Please do not mention this to anyone, especially the captain. Until we have talked some more on this matter."

"Oui chef, Merci again, I will see you tomorrow at 3 o'clock, I mean 0300 hours."

"Oui Madame, Bonne nuit!"

Marilda told Gilbert, she is going on deck to catch a breath of fresh air. I have not been in the open air all day long.

Gilbert recommend she take Henry, to accompany her.

"I will be fine," she told Gilbert. "I will stay just a moment."

Gilbert asked her to be careful.

When she stepped onto the main deck, the ships whistle blew. It was followed by four other loud blasts, from other ships, remorqueurs. The whistles were signaling readiness to assist the large freighter away from the dock. The noise of the ship horns startled Phillip, he started to cry. He turned and pressed himself against his mother. She veered to go back to their cabin, whispering to him, "We are okay my dear. You are fine right here in Ma mee's arms." When she entered the cabin all the children were waiting.

Shortly thereafter Mary Alice appeared from the galley. While in the doorway she pleaded, she and Ernest be allowed to go onto the deck. They wanted to watch as the freighter was moved away from the dock, and positioned to go to sea. "I have been in that stuffy kitchen all day, I need some fresh air."

Seeking to be Loved

Her mother understood, "Oui, you may go, just you two. Everyone else must get into bed."

It certainly would have been a rare opportunity, nevertheless their mother refused to let the others go. Her concern was for their safety, and them getting in the way. She told them, "When your father returns, maybe we will go on the deck. Hopefully by that time we will be out of the harbor." The children were disappointed, for they wanted to watch and observe the whole process of a ship heading out to sea. Henry stood at the porthole, watching what he could see from the small circular window.

The sensation of movement was apparent, although subtle. Then suddenly a jolt from forward starboard of the vessel, a moment later another towards the aft. It made all within the room standing stumble, before reestablishing their stance.

Marilda asked Henry, "What was that?"

He can only partially see what was happening. He said, "There are two small boats pushing them away from the loading dock." The loud whistles, blew again. She looked into Phillip's eyes, they were wide as saucers. She smiled at him; he returned a smile and kicked his legs with excitement. He does not show the fear, he sensed security in his mother's arms and recognized the calmness in her eyes.

They have the sensation of moving sideways as the vessel was being pushed.

When Gil returned to the cabin, he informed his family they have been invited to the bridge, by the captain. They were heading back out to sea. All within the cabin shout for joy.

As they entered the main deck from the hallway, they were met by a crewman to guide them to the captain. The harbor ahead was dark. Looking aft, they can still see the lights of the city and dock. They made their way to the bridge and were greeted by a spry looking captain and his first mate. Despite his long day of intense focus, the captain looked as though he just come on duty. He did not in the slightest degree, appear fatigued.

Seeking to be Loved

    Gilbert made a quick assessment in his mind, recalling the captain's words, earlier. Despite the longing for his family, the sea is in his blood. Gilbert observed the captain, and contemplated. He wondered if it was the excitement, the challenge, or, maybe the freedom, one experiences being in such a wide-open space, such as the sea.   That must be it!   He thought to himself, as he realized he felt the same way, when he is looking over his fields from his veranda.

    The captain apologized for not joining them for the evening meal. He explained, "Everything went exactly as planned which is unusual. I did not expect to be underway before midnight at best. If all fairs well, we should reach Québec ten days from now."

    He enlightened them of what is ahead, "The North Atlantic Ocean can be very fickle and rough seas are never a surprise and must be expected. So can the English Channel, or, as we like to refer to it, the French Channel. It too can be treacherous and rough, though not like the North Atlantic."

    He is pleased to tell them the chef and the machinist, praised their efforts in the kitchen and in the holds. I am beginning to think the company made a good decision, which will be productive for all.

    The Captain walked them onto the deck that wraps around the bridge. There are three upper levels above the main deck on the freighter. They look toward the open sea, it looked black except the occasional spots of light on the surface. The captain pointed out, "They are other ships."

    The only other thing they see is the glimmering, sparkling reflections on the ocean's vast surface, it is the moon casting its dim light upon it.

    Gilbert noticed the smell at sea, it is a fresh clean smell. It was not the salty, muddy, marshy, fishy odor in the harbor. He found himself smiling, it is a pleasant aroma. Taking in a deep breath, it rouses his spirit. He is beginning to understand the captain's energy.

    The captain turned and pointed out the fading lights of land on the distant horizon behind them. They could see the line of lights at the edge of the sea. The captain pointed out the dark, jagged silhouette of the English landscape. The outline of the landscape is enhanced, made visible against the night sky.

Several of the children and Gil, expressed how extraordinary and strange it appeared. Marilda agreed with them, even at night the view and the scene is fascinating.

The captain bids them, "Bonne nuit." He reminded them they must stay off the main deck. Unless directed otherwise and are accompanied by a crewman. They all wondered why; the sea seemed so calm and peaceful. No one questioned his order.

Everyone slept well, the gentle rolling of the ship had rocked them into a sound sleep.

The watchmen came knocking all too soon, as it seemed they had just fallen asleep. The night had passed quickly.

Marilda woke immediately, she had to wake Mary Alice. She picked up the children's schedule, and the men's work order from the floor. She thought to herself it looks like another busy day for all. She and Mary Alice made their way quickly into the galley.

The chef was alert and bustling about. They quickly got into the same rhythm as he. His method of preparation was already being initiated as usual, they took their places, and blended into the action.

The pots of coffee and tea were brewing, they began the preparation for the fresh baked goods. They started mixing the ingredients for the breads and pastry. Breakfast meats were being prepared, sliced bacon frying, and corn beef was boiling. The smells coming from the galley were more than enough to stimulate the pickiest of appetites. Soon the second watch will relief the first. A few more hours and the rest of the crew will be wandering in.

The children's schedule was the same, except during inspection. The captain took them into the engine room. He explained how the ships engines work. The Fireman was the busiest of all the engineers, keeping fuel in the furnace.

Seeking to be Loved

The heat generated by the burners, produced the steam. This is necessary to turn the gears thus causing rotation of the propellers to power and move the ship.

Even Phillip, seemed to be fascinated by all the activity in the immediate area. He was quite comfortable in the captain's firm grip. He turned his head to see where every new sound came from, as they toured the engine room.

That evening during dinner at the captain's table. The children told their father and older brothers, what they had seen in the innards of the ship. They attempted to explain how the propeller worked and made the ship move, to their father.

Blanche told them, she had learned to tie the square knot and a half hitch.

Little Gilbert bragged at the table. "I was the only one to tie a bowline, and Carrick bend correctly! The captain is making regular sailors out of us."

"Aye, and they would make worthy seaman and women," expressed the captain.

When the evening meal was finished, the captain informed them the sun will be setting soon over the horizon. "The sea is calm, you may accompany me to the bridge, if you would like. Sunsets and sunrises are wonderful and colorful sights. They are one of the great pleasures to behold when one is at sea." His intent was to entice them.

The sunsets are especially beautiful when the sky is clear, with a few clouds on the horizon. The angle of the sun's rays touching the clouds, illuminates a vast spectrum of magnificently brilliant colors.

Gilbert thanked the captain for his invitation. "We would be delighted." He asked permission to bring his wife and daughter Mary.

The captain said of course, "The invitation was meant for your entire family."

The captain called Chef Bastine, to his table.

Seeking to be Loved

Bastine, immediately appeared before the captain and inquired, "How can I help you captain?"

The captain requests that Chef Bastine, relieve Marilda and her daughter Mary of their duties, for the rest of the evening.

Bastine, displayed an irritated look on his face. Although, he knew better than to question the captains request. He does not express his distress, just responds, "Of course captain."

Gilbert recognized the chef's displeasure immediately. He made an appeal to the captain. "If you please captain, my family and I will assist them with finishing their duties in the galley. Then may we join you shortly? That is if you do not mind sir."

Gil noticed the expression on Bastine's face change to a less irritated appearance. The captain was also pleased with Gilbert's quick decision. He admired the man's willingness to sacrifice even more of his own and his family's leisure. So, they can share the experience together, without neglecting duties. He thought that to be quite noble, and he agreed.

The captain glared at Bastine, with his usual demeanor, maybe with a bit more annoyance. He does not take kindly to even the slightest questioning of his orders or request. He asked him, "How long will it take to get the galley in order this evening?"

Bastine, replied approximately 45 to 50 minutes. The Capt. looked at his pocket watch.

"I estimate the sun would be, touching the horizon in approximately 35 to 40 minutes. I will send a crewman to direct you to the bridge in 30 minutes," he told Gilbert.

He shifted his stare to the chef, until Bastine made eye contact. Bastine then excused himself, before the captain.

Gilbert, looked at his children and said, "I think we can cut that time down and be ready in 30 minutes or less if everyone lends a hand."

Marilda and Mary in the background, clapped their hands and giggle.

The captain said, "Very well then, in 30 minutes."

Seeking to be Loved

As expected, they made short work of it, with eight people instead of three cleaning. Each was assigned to a specific task; the job was complete in 20 minutes.

Bastine, was quite pleased, he too would have extra time to do as he wished for the evening.

The captain's prediction was correct, the sunset was magnificent. The western sky seemed ablaze, with the mix of colors that glowed in the sky. Yellows, orange, crimson and purple, the gray clouds seem to turn more pastel shades of gray mixed with blue and violet, against a soft blue sky that surrounded the explosion of colors.

When one looked to either side, away from the disappearing sun, there was a weaning of the skies soft blue that surrounds the display. It became darker and darker shades of blue. Turning around to face the East, they see the twinkling of the first stars of the evening, as one by one they make their appearance.

Captain Trudeau, shared with them, "There will be a very small or no moon tonight, you will see more stars than you ever imagined possible."

Henry, was the first to ask, "Can we stay up and watch the stars. Please Papa?" They all chimed in, it sounded identical to an echo chamber. All took turns making the request, please Papa, please Papa, please Papa?

Capt. Trudeau looked at Gil and Marilda and laughed. Then he said, "It would be best to come out of your cabin near midnight to see the stars. I will have a crewman come and tap on your door."

Marilda said, "Anyone still awake will be allowed to go, but only for a short while, we all need our rest. We all must be at our best and work hard tomorrow."

At midnight, the watchman tapped on the cabin door, no one stirred.

The morning of May 25, 1914 the watchmen made his rounds, waking Marilda, at 0300 hrs. They slept well with the assistance of the ship rolling in the open sea. Mary and Marilda made their way to the galley. Even though the distance was short it seemed longer. For some strange reason, their steps were unsteady. It was as if one step would stay suspended in midair for an extra moment. Marilda stated, "This must be the way a drunk man walks." For each step felt unsteady, until her feet touched the deck. Once in the galley, Marilda mentioned to the chef, how unsteady she felt on her feet this morning.

Bastine guffawed at her comment. He said, "You are not use to being at sea, you are experiencing what the ship is doing."

He told her to standstill for just a moment. They stood there as their body seemed to sway right to left, forward and back. "It is the motion of the ship, the sea is a bit rougher today. The rolling waves are causing the ship to rock, and to roll, more than you are used to."

"Why?" she asked.

Bastine explained, as they go about their business. "The winds may be greater, causing waves to get larger. We may be heading into a storm. It can be many things."

"It feels like, I have had too much to drink."

Mary laughed at her mother's comment. "Mother have you ever had too much to drink?"

Bastine mentioned to Marilda, "The best thing to do, is go about your work, as you do, your body will adapt. As it does, your head will clear."

"How long will that take?" she inquired.

Bastine pondered a moment, shaking his head side to side. "Usually just a few minutes, sometimes several hours, occasionally a few days. Your body will adjust and once it does, even on the roughest seas, walking about will seem as natural as always. What is important, is that you focus on the task at hand and not think about it. Your body will quickly adjust, it is a remarkable thing that God, has given us to live within."

Seeking to be Loved

The hot beverages were ready, the counter was full of the fresh breads and pastries ready to place in the oven. They began preparation for the later morning breakfast.

Bastine revealed to Marilda, "I have thought much about your suggestion last night. I want to know, how you propose to have a full breakfast ready for the first watch crewmen going on and coming off duty?"

Marilda started reviewing her idea. "You see it does not take long to prepare the coffee and hot water for tea. It takes just a moment to mix and to roll out the baked goods. If we knew in advance what the crewmen wanted, one person can prepare it. Breakfast items such as eggs, Spiced toast or even gravy can be served in just minutes."

Bastine, supported an interesting look on his face. He was thinking. He asked Marilda, "How will the crewmen let us know what it is we should make?"

Marilda opened her mouth and is about to respond.

Bastine began to think out loud, and said, "If we keep it to three items, I believe that will work quite simply."

Marilda began to share her next idea. Before she could finish, while she is still speaking. Bastine comments, "We can have those items on a list posted on the counter with those three foods, which they may check off next to their name on the watch list. That will be easy enough to get from the captain."

Marilda closed her mouth.

Bastine declared, "I think this is a wonderful idea. I can have my assistant, prepare those items very quickly. We can post a short list of food items on the first watch schedule."

He thought to himself, "This may help with the crew's morale as well. Normally after a few days at sea, they get tired of the same routine. They always take it out on the chef, and complain about the food. I will suggest this to the captain when he comes down for his first meal."

Seeking to be Loved

Bastine is quite pleased with himself, it is obvious by his gaiety as he went about his duties. He whistled and hummed the rest of the morning.

The chef watched the captain, as he has his first meal with the Guyon's, surrounded by the children.

Marilda is nursing Phillip, in their cabin.

He waited until the captain is almost finished with his meal. He brings a pot of coffee, to the table. He asked the captain if he would like more coffee. While he poured, he made a request of the captain, if he may have a word with him.

The captain replied, "What is it Bastine?"

"There is an idea, I would like to discuss with you. It may in a small way play a part in the men's morale."

The captain looked at Bastine, then Gilbert. He said, "I am always interested in how one may improve morale of the crew. What is it Bastine?"

Bastine began, "You see, I was thinking, how the first watch does not have a hearty first meal. Not like the rest of the crew. I thought how the men going on and off watch can have a substantial first meal. Simply by checking off a short list of breakfast items next to their name on the first watch list. If it would please the captain, we can get a copy of your watch list for the following morning. We can overlay it with a short list of breakfast foods next to their name. They can check off their preference when they initial it. We can prepare the selected food items quickly and have them ready for the 0330 - 0430 hour."

The captain processed it for a moment, then a smile appeared on his face. He looked at Bastine, then at Gilbert and he conveyed, "I think that will be a wonderful idea."

Bastine's face lit up as he gets another idea, the tone in his voice is giddy. He said, "I think I will call the early morning cook, The Short Order Cook." Hence the term begins!

The captain repeated the phrase, "Short Order Cook. That is exactly what they would be. Cooking select food items, from a short

Seeking to be Loved

list of foods, as well as a short list of crewmen. Excellent idea, Bastine." The captain stated jovially.

Bastine excused himself, "I have duties to attend to." He walked away from the captain's table. He can hardly control the giddiness he has inside. Knowing the captain was pleased with his idea...

The captain turned his attention to Gilbert, "I enjoy when my crewmen come up with new ideas, that will make things more efficient and better for all."

The plan worked well, the early watchmen were pleased to have options.

Several days passed at sea, it has been nearly a week, that they have been onboard. They have not seen any sign of land anywhere for days, they never realized they could miss the smell of the earth. Joseph asked his mother, is the sea ever going to end?

Marilda described to him, "The sea never ends, it flows from one ocean into another. There are great masses of land, great continents around the world as big as the seas themselves. We should be near the Americas in another four to five days. Then you will see land as far as you can see, just like you had in our beloved France."

Joseph asked his mother, "Will we see Grandmama and Grandpapa ever again?"

"I certainly hope so Joseph, I certainly hope so."

Blanche, repeated her mother's sentiment, "I hope so too, Ma mee."

Days passed, one after the other, the routine is the same. The only thing that is different is the weather. Each weather condition offers its own unique appearance. It sets the mood of those who observe it. Sunny days are pleasant, being the end of May, there are days with blue skies and bright sun, sea and sky is all that can be observed.

Occasionally the smoke from other ships could be seen in the distance and at times schools of porpoises playing at the bow of the ship. The spouting of whales can be seen by the watchful eye, sometimes distant other times close by as they swim near the ship. Rolling clouds are the only thing that breaks the monotony of the view.

Days of overcast and storm limit visibility. On such days, you are enclosed, what you see is even more limited. You see the ocean, at least what you can of it. Amid of a storm you may only see the waves which roll up against the ship and about you. Or the ocean that breaks over the bow and rolls over the sides onto the deck.

The air and atmosphere seem to cling to you, the ocean, waves, rain, mist, and fog are all about you. It is on you, you breathe it, it is in you, you have no choice but to accept it. You can fear it or become one part within it. You and the sea are one, both are but a share, a fragment of the whole.

Gilbert rose in the morning with his wife and daughter. He would go to the deck to enjoy the serenity, as he observed the sea, and breathes in its freshness.

One morning, while standing alone on deck looking out to sea, he was absorbed in his thoughts. He imagined how easy it must have been for sailors to come up with fantastic stories. How this similarity of days and task at hand, can allow the mind to wander. The routine day in, day out, and the view so consistent, must lend itself to let the imagination run as it will.

Sea monsters, marvelous stories about exotic places, about natural God's of the sea, or the sky, the sun, moon, and stars or even creatures of the deep. Which are just gods of one's own imagination. He wondered, what if instead they focused on the only one, and true God. The God, that created all that they observe, of all they can see, as well as the unseen.

He then imagined how glorious it could be, without all the distractions a person experiences when on land, to do so.

Seeking to be Loved

The philosopher within Gilbert began to focus as he started to contemplate. He thinks how easy it would be in such a vast openness for one to seek in his own mind, heart and within the soul of man, the presence of the Almighty. For here we are alone and at his mercy. "Amen," he said to himself!

At that moment, he himself experienced the lore of the sea, and the draw it has on men.

- He wondered, if it is the desire for adventure, or the calling to be close and exposed to your creator?
- Or is what we seek, deeper in our own subconscious?
- Is it, we must search for the answers to our heart's desires, amongst the world around us?
- Is it that? Which drives and sends men on their journey's around the world, despite dangers of the unknown and puts one at the mercy of nature, or, other men?
- Can it be for knowledge, or riches which draws us, so we should place our fate in the ever-present hand of God?
- Or, can it be, the calling from within our own depths, the soul? Where all knowledge lies, and our creator awaits that we are running from?
- Are we willing to roam to ends of the earth, in search of!

His sentence just stopped. In search of what, he ask himself? Adventure, Riches, Treasure, Answers?

Gilbert wonders, he questions his own motives as he is caught in his train of thought. "I can think of nothing I would be willing to risk, life or limb, nothing on earth." Then he realized he would for is family, chuckling to himself, "That is why I am here now. Oh oui, also for my Lord and Savior.

Maybe this is what the captain comprend déjà(already comprehends), or maybe something he hopes to understand?

He is giving up opportunities, that can never be regained.

- Is this, his true love, the sea?

Seeking to be Loved

- Or is it a greater more profound love that he seeks? He must feel it! It is present, it can be felt! I can feel it!

- Why would he want to give up that which he values most? Missing his family; That he admitted. It was that, which he said was the only regret he has had about his job.

Maybe it is the feeling he has, when at sea?

The captain has absolute authority of his vessel and crew in which he commands. He is judge, jury and executioner if need be, with total authority. Is it that, which draws him to sea?

What about the crewmen, they have no authority. What lures them?

- Is it the openness of the sea, which is so obvious. This we can see clearly in a moment by just observing in any direction?

- Or maybe the depths of it, that which we cannot see, and do not understand. Just as the depth of our own being cannot be seen, nor grasped, by mind or intellect, and many times not understood. Is that why one chooses the sea?

- May it be, we rather seek, what we do not know or understand elsewhere?

- Maybe it is reminiscent of the vastness of God, and the depths of our creator. Of which man does not understand, and may not be capable to fathom.

I know I want to understand, I am sure we all do. This knowledge exists within each of us. It is in the depth of our own being. It must be if we are created in Gods image. If we accept as fact that the spirit of God dwells within us.

- Is it easier for man to seek externally, what he can see, hear, and hold? Than it is to search internally, for the truths of our being, and purpose of our own creation?

I can feel it myself, and I know it makes me want to become more aware, now that I exist. To know why I am here, as one of God's creatures. It is he and his love that we must seek to guide us to our destiny.

Seeking to be Loved

Here on the ocean we are exposed, there is nothing to hide us from the face of God.

- Does the captain feel close to God, when at sea?
- Is this why he leaves everything behind?

For our Lord has said, **'Sell that which you have, leave it behind and follow me.'**

- Or could it be the similarity the captain has with God?

On his vessel he is the supreme being, he is the commander and law. Surely the captain does not think in that manner. That he is like God, or relishes in being the authority?

I know for many, it is in the nature of man, to Lord over one's own life and for some over others. It is only human to think we have control and authority over things in our life.

To have control in life, one must have consistency. To have consistency in an ever-changing world and in the environments in which we live is impossible. For us to seek control and authority, is only going to lead to disappointment and lack of satisfaction, from one's existence.

How hopeless, frustrated, and angry such people must feel. For whatever they do or whatever they have, it will never truly satisfy them.

We seek control, the power of our own strength and intellect, to find our own way. We control nothing of the environment or the world around us. For what we truly seek, is that which only God possesses, the creator of all, is the one who has control of all."

A scripture from the Book of Matthew, Chapter 6, verse 33 comes to Gilbert, ("Seek first the kingdom of God, and all else will be rendered on to you").

Gilbert praised God, "Merci Dear God, for revealing your word to me."

God must have been pleased! For he revealed the 23rd Psalm in Gilbert's mind at that very instant. He found himself reciting it out loud. The sun is just beginning to appear on the horizon to the east, as a new day begins.

Seeking to be Loved

The Lord is my shepherd; I shall not want. In green pastures he gives me rest; beside deep waters he leads me; it refreshes my soul. He guides me in the right paths for his namesake. Even though I walk in the Valley of death I fear no evil; for you are at my side. With your rod and your staff, you guide me and give me courage. You spread the table before me in the site of my foes; you anoint my head with oil; my cup runneth over. Only goodness and kindness follow me all the days of my life; and I will dwell in the house of the Lord forever.

The captain had observed Gilbert from the bridge, he was not accompanied, so he thought he would go speak to him and join him on deck with such a glorious morning breaking. Approaching Gilbert, he can hear the words, they sound somewhat familiar to him.

Gil had just finished reciting the Psalm.

The Captain said, "It looks to be a fine morning Gilbert!"

Gilbert turned around, the captain can see tears on his cheeks, yet see a smile and a glimmering sparkle in his eyes as well. He asked him, "Are you alright Gilbert?"

Gilbert chuckled, returned the greeting, "Good morning captain." He agreed with the captain, "It is a beautiful morning. Oui, captain, I am fine, better than fine. If you only knew how God has prepared a path for us, to follow on this journey."

"Look around, everything you see, the world, sky and the ocean, all brought to be, by our Creator. We control none of it, our heavenly father controls all of it. Nothing in this world is consistent. We men are the most inconsistent of all its creatures.

The only thing we can count on that is absolute, in this world or our life, is God's love for us! We know this from our history, so many examples has God given us. The very best of which is described in the book of John chapter 3, verse 16, **"For he so loved us, he gave his only begotten son."**

Seeking to be Loved

"Captain, this is the constant, the consistency, we all seek in our life. To know and even more so to believe, that we are loved perfectly, and unconditionally.

You have many more years of experience in life than I. I have learned when we follow the path our Lord lays out for us; it will never lead to any regrets. For His plan is much greater than ours." Gilbert turned to walk away, wishing the captain a fine day.

"And you Monsieur Guyon," replied the captain, as he nods his head and turned his face to the sea. His whisper is barely audible, he speaks aloud not being aware that he is, as he thinks of Gilberts words, of God's Plan.

"Oui, I am sure it must be."

A few more days passed, Gilbert noticed a change in the crewmen, they seem energized. There is joking and laughter in their speech. He mentioned it to the captain at the evening meal.

"We will see land soon; I estimate we have approximately 1000km left before we reach our docking bay at Québec. The men are becoming quite restless, with excitement of the moment they can put their feet on solid ground once again. Not to mention see people other than their shipmates, and the other things I will not discuss at the table with young one's present.

Oui, anticipation is always high. Then after a few days and nights of it, they are eager to get back on board and leave what they have made amiss in their wake." the captain explained.

Gilbert smiled and said, "I understand, I now see how it is with the men of the sea."

The captain replied, "They are a bunch of fickle misfits, many of them are. The sea is not their home, it is just a comfortable buffer, from two separate and different worlds and lives, they choose to live."

Sometime tonight or early tomorrow we will be in the Gulf of St. Lawrence. We may see Anticosti Island tomorrow before the day is done, as we cruise through the Honguedo Sraits.

Seeking to be Loved

"Will we be in Québec in a few days?" asked Gilbert.

The children by now are hanging on every word that is being said. They too have become bored with the day in and day out routine and the same scenery. They do enjoy the sunsets, when they can see them, on the few days when the sky was not overcast. They never woke early enough to watch the sunrise. Just Gil and Phillip enjoyed that privilege.

The captain said, "Maybe three days, it could be more. This time of year, shipping traffic is extraordinarily heavy in the Canadian ports."

It is the snow, ice, and the unpredictable North Atlantic Ocean, that cause many in the shipping industry to wait until the spring thaw to bring their goods to the ports.

We have locks to pass through. The miles on the St. Lawrence River will be slow. The only saving grace of this section of travel is the scenery. It will change, giving us some different landscapes and points of interest to look at and observe along the way.

The captain asked Gilbert, "How are your prize Percheron Stallions, are they faring well?"

Ernest answered before his father, "They are fine sir," he told the captain.

Gil proceeded to explain; Ernest eagerly burst forth once again. Informing the captain, "The first few days they were fine, apparently adapting to their new environment. After that period of time they seemed a bit eager, anxious about something. They were probably wanting to go out to work, that is what they are used to doing."

Gil looked at the captain, turned his head slightly to one side and nods and said, "There you have it."

The captain replied to Ernest, "Those horses may be as eager as you, young man." He smiled, looked at Gilbert and nodded.

"They seem to have traveled well. I am concerned that they have not had any fresh air, for over a week now." Gil mentioned to the captain.

Seeking to be Loved

"If the gulf is calm and weather is clear, I will have the crew open a few of the small hatches for a few hours."

Gil said, "Merci Captain, you have been very considerate of all our needs. We cannot thank you enough. Is that not right children?"

"Oui," "Oui Papa," "Oui," as you hear echoing all around the table. "We have had a wonderful time with the captain, aboard this great ship of his, have we not." The oui's, echo around the table again.

Capt. Trudeau chuckled and shared with them, how they have made this crossing quite enjoyable!

He apprised them, "The next few days, and final stretch will be very interesting. We will see many islands on the river. It will not seem like they are cruising on the river. It will appear in many places, as if we are still on the ocean itself. Not until they reach the first lock and dam system will it start seeming more like a river.

We will pass by several fortresses and castles, some on the banks of the river. Others high on the ridges overlooking the St. Lawrence. You will see along the river's banks grand homes and estates. Some of which will be on islands all by them self. I believe you will find the next few days very enchanting."

Blanche, pulled on her father's shirt sleeve, looking at him she asked, "What is enchanting, Papa?"

Captain Trudeau replied, "Magical my dear Blanche!"

"The river is going to be magical?" She questioned, alternating her gaze to her father and the captain.

The captain replied, "It will seem to be, especially to the young wondering mind. There will also be much construction as we approach the City of Tadoussac and of course that along the banks of our first port of call, Québec. What may be interesting to you Monsieur Guyon, is the vast stretches of farmland. From what I have read, seen, and been told, the land is quite fertile. A hard-working man and his family like yourselves, should make out well farming here."

Seeking to be Loved

"I hope so," Gilbert verbalized to the captain. "We will have to find work and earn our keep. Then hopefully save enough over time to buy land of our own. Then we can work it and make a future for our family."

"I am sure you will," replied the Capt.... He excused himself, "I must return to my duties." There is much for him to prepare before they get to Québec.

May 29, 1914, The worst maritime disaster in Canada's history. The Empress of Ireland, the beautiful, luxurious, Cruise Liner had been struck by a coal barge and sunk.

It had matched the Titanic, in its luxury ship class. Over a thousand passengers had died early that morning.

The freighter was less than three days from Québec.

The captain knew. He was made aware of the incident less than an hour after it happened. News travels fast on the river. He knew what to expect, there will be search, rescue and recovery. Shipping lanes will be altered, or stopped completely, for several days. Traffic on the river will be at a near standstill, he wished they had made it through the lock system.

The locks would be slower than usual while bodies of the victims are being recovered. The business on the river will not be on schedule until all bodies are accounted for. Many will be retrieved from the river and others that may still be on board.

Shipping will not return to normal at least for several days. The authorities know many may never be found. Unloading and loading will take two to three times longer. For many of the workers will be involved in the rescue and recovery effort. Many will have their work diverted to removal of all salvageable items of cargo and baggage from the sunken vessel.

The captain informed the crewmen and the Guyon's. He recommended a time of silence. Gilbert and his family prayed for the victims, survivors, and families of both. They prayed for their good

Seeking to be Loved

captain, crew and extended their prayers to all travelers and people in their beloved France.

They had to drop anchor fore and aft to hold their position in the Great St. Lawrence River. The captain was finally notified on June 4, 1914, he could proceed through the locks and to his docking bay. He informed Gilbert, that he and his family should prepare to disembark. They are to unload first, before the other cargo is released and delivered to the dock.

He told them they will be no time to waste. They must make haste, for he had ordered that no other hatchway's, or cargo bays be opened until he and his possessions are securely on the dock.

Captain Trudeau had request that Gilbert come to his cabin. When Gilbert knocked on the door, he heard the captain's voice, "You may enter." He instructed Gil to close the door and please have a seat. He proceeded to praise Gilbert, he and his family proved themselves worthy seaman. He was able to get his ship; well, "In shipshape." Due to all the extra work he and his family were able to perform on his vessel.

He asked Gilbert about the arrangements the company had made to reimburse him and his family for the services rendered.

Gilbert had a blank stare on his face.

The captain said, "I thought so, I expected as much. Monsieur Guyon. I would like to pay you and your family for your services. I will pay each of you six francs per day, times five workers times 14 days equaling Fr.420. You will find that the equivalent to 70 Canadian dollars. That is what you will receive."

"But captain, six francs for a day's work is a lot of money."

"Nonsense, Gilbert your family, all of you worked hard and admirably."

"But sir, what about the four little ones?"

"What!" The captain shouted, "You want to get paid for them as well?" He knew that was not Gilbert's intent. He displayed his harsh indifference, for it was his intent to mask the kindness in his heart.

Seeking to be Loved

"Non, non, captain you misunderstand, we should pay you and your crewmen for watching them."

"Nonsense again, you and your little ones, helped me see things, and look at life a bit differently. Not to mention an experience of a lifetime, for me. It is you, who I feel obliged, for these last twelve days."

The captain handed him an envelope. Then he told him that the first mate, will direct your exiting the ship.

"Capt., we will always remember you, and will keep you and your family in our prayers," Gilbert told him as they shook hands.

The captain with an out of character compassionate voice and with a softness seen in his eyes said to Gilbert, "And I will, never forget you and your family."

As Gilbert was leaving the captain's quarters he could have sworn, he heard the captain add with a whispered last statement, "I will Pray for yours also, Monsieur Guyon."

Seeking to be Loved

Chapter 10 <u>Finding his brothers</u>

Gilbert and Ernest hitched the team to the wagon. The pair seemed full of energy, they could not wait to use their bulk for what it was intended, and bred to do. They were ready to pull the load, labor, and feel the strength at their disposal. The huge Percherons, were out of confinement from the ship holds. The smell of fresh air, the busyness of the dock; all added to the spirit of these magnificent animals. Gilbert had to hold them back. Their hooves were stumping in pace on the dock, as they waited their command.

Marilda handed Gil the address they had for his brothers. He would ask for information at the dock master's office upon exiting the gate. The dock master directed him to the Constable office. They in turn directed him to the Québec city affairs building. It was there he was required to register. He had to list all in his family by name and date of birth. He had to declare his intent for entering Canada.

He was shown a map of Québec and the surrounding area. The address he had requested was pointed out to him. It was 5km upriver from where they were. The clerk offered him a sheet of paper and pen, to write down the directions and draw his own map. He was also given verbal directions to get them started from the present location.

It was already late afternoon, on a fair June day. The Guyon's were anxious to be on their way, in a new land a new country. The anticipation of seeing family was high. They have not seen them in nearly three years. Gil and his family could not wait to meet and surprise them.

Québec was an interesting city, it appeared new compared to what they had seen and been used too, in France. Although every street seemed to be full of life, people going about their lives and their daily business. As if everything were all so normal, unlike what they have experienced in their own country when they left.

Seeking to be Loved

They had been part of caravans of anxious people, taking up their roots, and going somewhere, someplace new. For some just to distance themselves and family from an uncertain threat.

For the first two weeks of their journey, from the time they left home, it was as if everyone was on the move.

Here it was different, the people did not seem the same. The feel and the atmosphere was dissimilar. War or the imminence of war, was not knocking on their door. It felt good to be there, it appeared by the expressions on the faces of people, they were in a safe place.

The citizens were home, they were not leaving, they were living. It was as though this was where they were supposed to be.

The streets were marked with signs, the directions were easy to follow. Walking was easier, not having to guide other animals, or other carts along the way. Progress was slow in the city, it took them almost three hours to go the 5km.

They came to Jacobs Street. Marilda halted the team, she saw the sign first. She asked Mary who was riding beside her holding Blanche on her lap, to look for house number 120. Many of the houses had the numbers on the crossheads above the front doors. "There it is," shouted Mary!

Gilbert walked to the head of the wagon and mentioned to Marilda, "I hope they got the letter."

She told Gil, it would be very unlikely. "Go," she urged him, "Go see your brothers. It has been nearly three years since you have seen them. Go, go, we will secure the team and meet you at the door."

He started laughing, and ran to the door, he knocked on it with excessive enthusiasm. He heard a familiar voice inside shout, "Hold your horses."

Gilbert hollered back, "I have been holding them for 8000km."

George recognized the voice, however he could not believe his ears. He yanked opened the door in astonishment. He could not

Seeking to be Loved

believe his eyes, he wrapped his arms around his brother. Nearly shouting in his ear, Frère(brother), Le Frère. They embraced and cannot stop laughing.

Finally, George's wife, came to the door and recognized Gilbert, Marilda and the older children. They joined them in the laughter. She ushered them all into their appartement, she told their eldest son, go get Uncle Louis.

George informed them, Frank died in October 1912, he has been gone for almost two years now.

Gil looked at Nattie and then back at George, our father just this spring shared your letter with me.

I had not written father since November a few weeks after Franks death. Before that, I had written him in October that same year, just a few days before Franks accident. He must have not received the second letter. I have not heard from him or any of you for that matter since we arrived here three years ago. He must not have received the other letter, George repeated. I must send him another, he said, slowing his speech. Considering whether he should or not as he thought of the many other concerns his father and countrymen must be facing presently. He knew his father must have his wits about him and not dulled by grief.

The thought and topic quickly changed to the present and immediate news of the area. We have many shipwrecks on the St. Lawrence, as you have just witnessed the horrible tragedy of the Empress of Ireland.

"Who would have thought that to be possible," George's wife exclaimed, as she and Marilda served tea?

"Louis should be here soon, he just lives a few streets down," said George.

Gil asked his brother about his Percherons, as to where they can stay.

Louis should be able to help with that. He and his family reside with the man that owns the local livery.

Gilbert asked, "Can I water them now?"

Seeking to be Loved

George waved his hand for Gil to follow him and Ernest joined them.

Louis saw them watering the horses and shouted to Gilbert. "What are you doing here?" He asked while grasping his brother's hand. They embrace and pat each other's back. "How wonderful to see you, I cannot believe it is you, you are here!"

"Are you not the one that said, you would never leave the lovely department(region) of Lorraine. Or the banks of the Moselle." Louis laughed with joy over seeing his brother.

Gil was the one, whom he thought of all his siblings, he would never see again, least of all in Canada. He knew the love he had for their area of France. It was where their ancestors were born, lived, and worked for so many generations.

George intervened and said, "Louis, about his horses."

Louis held up his hand and said, "We will take care of these fine specimens of French bred animals. Any stable would be proud to say, such great beast are being boarded at their livery. I am sure Monsieur Jauc, would be thrilled. Let us take them there right now."

"Jauc," Gil asked questioningly.

"Oui, Jauc Poincare, the proprietor of the Livery," explained Louis.

"Did you say, Monsieur Jauc Poincare?" Gilbert, asked with a wondering expression.

"Oui, why such a strange look on your face Gil?" asked Louis.

"Ah, it is nothing, it is funny how God, puts things in place." Was all Gilbert could say while he turned his head slightly wondering. If there could be a connection, with Jauc and the stableman at the Égilse Eustache.

A smile crossed his face as he thought of him, and the Priest Dominique.

They joined the others inside and reminisced until wee hours of the morning. The children were laid to rest hours ago.

Gilbert asked his brothers about farms in the area. He would prefer land on the countryside, putting his animals to work.

Seeking to be Loved

Both his brothers explain, the factories are full of recent emigrants, work may be a bit harder to find in town. It is good you are interested in the farms; they too have enough laborers. "But, brother you will be different, you are skilled and have those magnificent animals. I am sure any farmer would welcome you."

The need for agriculture, to help feed the masses descending on eastern Canada is great. The need increasing daily.

George suggest to Gilbert, "I can take you to the town chamber tomorrow." He realized the new day had already begun. "I mean later this morning. "They will know of several farms near the city. We want you and your family close to us little brother."

They laughed and bid each other good night, or should we say good morning. Let us just say, dormez bien(sleep well).

Gil kissed Nattie and went with Louis, to care for his team at the stable. I will stay with Louis; I will see you later today.

Louis introduced Gilbert, to Monsieur Poincare, in the morning when he arrived at the stable.

Poincare told Louis, he has been admiring these fine animals. "You have done well recruiting them to our stable. I hope they are not just passing through."

Gilbert spoke, "These are my horses, we only wish to board them until we find a farm, on which to work."

Poincare, grasp hold of the lapels of his jacket. "Young man, I have a proposition for you! You can keep these animals here free for one week, maybe longer. However, it must be at least a week. You see, such fine bred Percheron horses like these a rare here in Canada. I have only seen them once myself, growing up in Paris. Many French, have come here to Québec. I would wager, many would be interested in seeing them. I am willing to bet they would even pay a small fee to see these Fine animals!"

Louis knew the look in his bosses' eyes. He is usually correct on such matters of turning any opportunity into a profit.

Gilbert said, "That is a generous offer. These animals are bred to work and do heavy labor. The Percheron breed, would fare much

Seeking to be Loved

better working on a farm, where they can be using their bulk for what it was intended. I will graciously except your offer for one week, or, until I can procure employment on a local farm."

Louis can almost see the gears turning in Poincare's brain. He intervened, "Maybe my brother would consider letting these fine beasts stay, if one would sweeten the deal a bit."

Gilbert is not sure what his brother is suggesting.

Poincare does, and proceeded to make an offer to him. "If you will agree to keep them here for one full week. That would give me time to advertise and spread the word. Oui, spread the word that these fine rare gigantic animals, from their beloved France, are stabled here, in My Livery!"

Gilbert thought for a moment, about the beast and their need to work and get fresh air. He wondered how long it may take to find work on a local farm. He recalled the discussion with his brothers last night. He realized, it would be a good idea to take the pair with him. When visiting the farms and landowners, they could see his horses. George had identified several large farms in the immediate outskirts of town. He thought anyone of these farm owners, would be interested in hiring him, especially with such a fine team of draft horses.

Gilbert mentioned to Poincare; "I must have two hours a day to exercise them outside, to let them breathe fresh clean air into their lungs."

Poincare was only half listening, for he was imagining ways he can profit from this opportunity. "I can charge an admission, a viewing fee and I will give you 10% of the proceeds," he mentions to Gil.

Louis, coughed and cleared his throat.

Poincare said, "Okay, 20%."

Another throat clearing, by Louis.

"All right 25%, you must remember, I am offering free boarding, these beasts will probably eat three times that of an average horse," declared Poincare.

Seeking to be Loved

Laughter burst forth from all three men at that statement, they shook hands to seal the deal.

Poincare asked Gilbert, "Are these animals strong, Oui?"

Louis chimed in with his knowledgeable opinion stating, "The Percheron, is bred for great strength and stamina. They can outwork the finest draft horses in the world. They are some as big and some breeds larger. Sacre-bleu, the Percheron will outwork any."

Poincare looked at Gil, for confirmation of Louis's statement.

Gilbert stated, "They are the finest of the draft breed. What my brother identified, is true."

Poincare made another suggestion to Gilbert. Would you be willing to take one horse at a time, I will loan you one of my single hitch carriages or wagons, whichever you would prefer?

I will agree to that, Gilbert replied.

"Fine! Fine!" Is Poincare's reply, he is pleased. Although, he is always thinking, always planning of ways to expand his purse. Finally, he suggest, "I believe I can arrange a pulling contest, a test of the breeds strength." He folded his arms and placed one hand under his chin, pondering many ways to show off these beautiful, yet powerful equine.

Gilbert refused, "Non, that will have to be for another time. I will not submit them to any such contest, that they are not fully prepared. They have been confined for over two weeks. "Oui, they are strong, although not ready for such events."

Poincare, explained to Gilbert you may stand to make hundreds of dollars, not to mention hundreds more on side wagers.

Louis whispered in Gil's ear, that would be over 400 French francs. Gilbert's replied, "These animals are worth more than argent, or what you say here, 'dollars,' to me. I would make sure that they are ready for such a test of their true strength. They must be prepared, to assure they would not be compromising themselves to the danger of injury."

"You are a wise man Monsieur Guyon," stated Poincare.

Seeking to be Loved

Louis thought, and you are a shrewd one, of his boss. Instead he stated, "It runs in the family sir."

That afternoon Gilbert took the boys for a ride to the country, using one of the stable wagons. He planned to introduce himself to a few of the landowners, George had recommended. Local farmers, he believed would welcome help, that is experienced. He knew most would be willing and pleased to have a magnificent pair of horses added to their work force. The land along the St. Lawrence, was indeed fertile, from what Gil and the boys could observe.

Poincare's plan worked well, it appeared everyone in Québec, was willing to pay 10 cents to view these purebred Percheron's.

Gilbert, informed Louis, and George that evening, there was a farmer he met, who seemed to be quite interested. Even after it was explained it would be him and his family, needing to stay and work for them. He offered room board, monthly wage as well as a share in the overall yearly profits. Gilbert seemed extremely excited about the proposal.

George and Louis looked at each other, then George asked Gilbert, "What was the name of this farmer?"

Gilbert seemed a little embarrassed, in his excitement he had not ask the man his name. "I did not ask him," he told his brothers. "The owners name is on the paper with the list of farms, I know where he lives, and can find the farm easy enough."

George ask Gilbert, "Did you promise him anything or sign any papers?"

"Non," Gilbert replied.

George and Louis simultaneously respond, "Good!"

His oldest brother proceeded to explain to Gilbert; "Many of the landowners will not tell you everything. It is not that they are lying, but they are misleading. They will either deduct your room and board from your wage, as I have heard in many cases.

There are others, that will deduct the anticipated cost of you and each of your family members, from their overall monthly and yearly income. In your case even your horses, they may add

Seeking to be Loved

deductions above and beyond all the other expenses. Thus, in fact it appears the farm may be losing money or gaining very little. Some farmers, and many of the hired help work specifically for their own keep, only. They have room and board, but, end up with no income at the end of the month, or the year.

George explained, "This Gilbert I know, with your knowledge and experience, farming is in your blood. There is not a farmer who will not profit greatly, from having you and your family work for them. All of you seem quite capable, to be employed except the three little ones."

May I also suggest, you ask for a contract. Make sure that it includes and addresses all your and our concerns before you agree and sign it.

I know many of the new arrivals agreed to such profit-sharing. It sounds very intriguing and promising. By the end of the years growing season when all expenses are deducted, they end up with nothing. Many others end up owing the landowner, either compensation or more labor, because they show no profit."

Gilbert was thankful for his brother's advice. He never would have considered those things in his eagerness to start work, and to have a place for his family to settle.

He had never been employed by anyone, his family always worked together. Until he was old enough to work his own land, his only experience was seeing how his father worked and dealt with people. He was naive of the ways of the world. His only observation to this point was of his father and his own ways of doing business. When dealing with all business, or people, his habit was do so fairly and justly.

He did not know of such things as contracts. His verbal agreement and a handshake was all that was necessary. Ones word was all that was needed to put one's honor at stake.

He thought how absurd it would be to compromise one's own honor, self-respect, and dignity. What kind of man would even consider placing such aspects of his integrity in jeopardy?

Seeking to be Loved

    He told his brothers he would return to the farm he favored the next day on his way to visit others. That evening he, Marilda and his brothers, made a list of what they would expect for trading their family, and team, for labor and services.

    George also suggested, before he would sign an agreement or contract, to have a witness. Preferably the witness would be someone that is not involved with either party. He suggested someone from the Notary club. It is an organization, that he had just became aware of a few years ago. He had read about it in a newspaper. They do such things, as acting as a reliable witness in business matters for both parties.

    George volunteered to find out where the local office or contact would be. He suggests to Gilbert, "If you find a place where you would like to work and reside, tell them you will be back the next day to verify the agreement. Or better yet, tell them you will be back in the next few days. That will give you time to make sure someone from the club would be able to accompany you." He also told his brother, that he would be sure that they would be a fee. It would be a reasonable one.

    Gilbert and the boys were off early the next morning. There were three farms they wanted to visit. If time allowed, he wanted to stop by the one he favored yesterday. Two of the three were interested and willing to hire him and his family and were eager to have the Percheron's on their workforce.

    One was especially interested and expressed desire to have his horses for stud purposes, with his and possibly other farmers in the area. There was only one of the three, that was willing to sign a contract agreement.

    Gilbert was eagerly anticipating the prospect of starting work, in a new environment. He wanted to revisit the farm he discussed last night with his brother's. He had Ernest take the reins as he looked at the map he had drawn. He was hoping to find a quicker way instead of going back and retracing the route they had taken. He noticed there were several intersecting roads. He had hoped one

Seeking to be Loved

would bring him to the road they followed yesterday. The road that was close to and followed the St. Lawrence river. He instructed Ernest to take the first road to the right. Gilbert estimated it to be a half kilometer maybe a little more, it would end at the road they followed the day before.

After a few hundred meters or so, they noticed some beautiful pastureland. There are a few cows grazing on it, in the distance you can see the farmhouse. There did not seem to be a lot of activity in the fields, only grazing animals. He observed only one field the one closest to the house had been plowed. It appeared that only a portion of it had been planted and crops were growing. He wondered why in such a developing area, and the need for food so great, every inch was not being productive. The fields looked magnificent and fertile, why are they not planted full of crops, he wondered?

Something beckoned him to visit this farm, even though it was getting late in the day. The two hours had passed long ago. He fought the urge to stop. When passing the property, he gazed toward the house and the barns. It seemed to be well kept and sturdy, Gilbert thought.

Even Henry made a comment, how rich the soil looked where no crops were growing. He commented, "This would be a fine farm to work." He pointed out three separate fruit tree orchards. He bet Ernest and his father, they were pears, apples, and plums. "What do you think Papa," he asked?

Just as they had passed the entryway, a wagon path leading to the farm off the dirt road they were traveling on. Gilbert thought, we need to visit the owner of this property.

He wrestled with the urge to stop and inquire. He knew he had two farms already, that seem to be much better off and had quite enterprising operations. Although in the back of his mind he wondered about this property. He noticed a wagon up ahead coming towards them, as they neared, he noticed it was an older gentleman,

Seeking to be Loved

the wagon had several full sacks of seed. Gilbert waved and shouted, "Bon jour."

The man nodded his head and waved his hand, he did not speak as they passed by each other.

Gilbert was struck with the sensation, he must speak to this man. He turned his head and shouts Monsieur; he had Ernest pull in the reins, to stop the wagon.

The man turned around and asked, "Are you speaking to me, young man?"

"Oui monsieur! Do you know who owns this farm?"

"Yes, it is I."

Gilbert climbed off his wagon and approached the man. He introduced himself and stated, "It is none of my business monsieur. My boys and I were wondering; why such fertile land, in this area has fields not fully utilized?"

"It is only me and my wife now, I have had no sons. My three daughters have been married for years and have gone. Their husbands were not farmers, they have pursued other enterprises. My wife and I grow what we can, enough for ourselves and to pay our bills and debtors."

Gilbert informed him, "My family and I have just arrived from France. We are looking for employment and residence. I was wondering if you can provide us with room and board for my family and I. I have two fine animals; this is one the other is at a Livery, in town."

"Ah Yes, I have heard of them, where I picked up my seed," said the old man.

"We would be willing to work your farm for room and board and a share of the profits from the production. If such an arrangement would please you monsieur." The thought occurred to Gilbert, "Why did I make that proposal?" He knew there was one if not two landowners, that may be willing to bid on his services. While speaking, he understood, he may be forfeiting a guaranteed salary. "For what, the possibility of just room and board and a share of what

Seeking to be Loved

may or may not be?" He asked himself again, "Why did I say that, or even suggest it? If he agrees, I am committed."

The man did not say anything for a long moment. He looked beyond Gilbert at the boys in the wagon. He looked again at Gilbert and asked him, "You are willing to do this, Yes? I have 250 acres," he said.

Gilbert smiled, "Oui, they are beautiful fertile acres they are, I see you have three orchards."

The man said, "Yes, they are plums, apples and pears. I can rarely get them to market in time before they spoil."

Henry laughed and said, "I told you."

The man queried, "I see the five of you, do you have a wife?"

Gilbert said, "Oui, I have a wife two daughters and another infant son."

The man said, "We have rooms for you, but not enough beds for all. I think we can make an arrangement." Then he asked Gilbert, "When can you start?"

Gilbert explained the agreement he has with Poincare. "I, the boys and his oldest daughter can be here tomorrow and start working immediately." He did not want to speak for Marilda just yet.

It is still early in the growing season. "It is not too late for those seeds you have in your wagon to be planted. My team can plow three acres a day. On the land that I can see probably more than that. Gilbert in his excitement explained, what the man already knew. That would be another 60 acres turned, before the end of the planting season.

Gilbert bids him farewell, and indicated he will bring his things and will see him sometime midmorning the next day. While making their way back to the livery, he realized in his excitement he failed to ask the man his name. It did not matter; he made the commitment and would see him tomorrow. He suddenly became aware, he did not agree upon a contract. He knew his brothers would be concerned as well as Marilda. It just felt right. He thought to

Seeking to be Loved

himself, "The boys seem to be as excited as he about the prospect of starting a new life. Oui, and in a new land on this particular spot."

The large doors were closed, Poincare was stationed at the side door of his Livery. Gilbert approached with the wagon; he noticed the broad smile on the face of the owner. He heard him shout, "Here is the other magnificent stallion, you have come to see."

Poincare peeked his head in the side door. The doors to the Livery opened, Gil's brother Louis waved him in.

Gil observed the excitement on the faces of people in line, waiting to enter the stable. At his approach, the huge double doors opened wide to allow entry to the stable. Gilbert expertly guided the horse and wagon into the livery, the doors closed immediately.

Louis welcomed his brother, and nephews back from their job hunt. He explained to him and the boys, that it has been like this all day. People started arriving just a few moments after you left this morning. There has been many waiting in line to get a close look at your celebrity beast. Louis said to his brother, "Your horses are causing quite a stir of excitement. This line outside, has been there since before 10AM.

Poincare had been busy, spreading the word. It has interfered with my regular duties, trying to keep an eye on the people once they enter the stable. I have got none of the shoeing done today, keeping the stable's clean and the animals fed is all I have been able to do. Keeping an eye on the viewers and seeing to the safety of them, and the other animals as well. I have been answering questions all day, it has been a busy one. I know Poincare is pleased, but brother, I must say, I hope you found a place to put these beasts to work. I am afraid this livery will be a sideshow, until these animals are gone.
So, did you find a farm where you are willing to work? One that will accept your terms?"

Seeking to be Loved

Gilbert smiled at his brother and said, "I found three. On one we will start tomorrow."

"That is wonderful brother, which one did you choose?" Louis, could see the excitement on his brothers face, change slightly to a look of concern.

Gil did not know the farm, or the man's name. He did not want to explain the circumstances that transpired. He was glad the stable was so busy. Thinking quickly, wanting to change the subject; Gilbert said, "I am afraid Louis, I must honor my agreement with your boss. My Percheron's will stay here one week. Mary the boys and I will begin taking our things and start work tomorrow."

"Fine brother," said Louis. "Now, which farm did you choose, and you must tell me the terms you agreed upon." He noticed the strange look of avoidance in Gilberts eyes. He asked, "What is it Gil?"

Gilbert told him, "It is a farm of 250 acres, owned and operated by an old man and his wife. They have some cattle and a small dairy."

Henry in his excitement nearly shouts, "There are three orchards, apples, pears and plums, Uncle Louis."

Louis inquired, "Is it far away?" It seems you have been gone for a long time."

Gilbert told Louis, "We visited three other farms today. We were looking for the one that we liked yesterday to revisit. It was then we were looking for a shortcut to get there when we saw this farm. We were struck by how very fertile the land had appeared. It just felt right that we should be there to work this land and help this couple."

"Help!" Louis exclaimed in a questioning manner. "Do you not mean, work for. You did discuss the terms of your employment, in reference to your compensation for you and your families service and the use of your horses, did you not?"

"Not exactly." Gilbert replied.

"What do you mean, not exactly?" asked Louis.

Seeking to be Loved

Gilbert hesitated for just a moment then said, "I told him what we were looking for, room, board and employment."

"So, you did not discuss any terms?" questioned Louis!

Gilbert looked down sliding dirt with his right foot then back with his left, "No, I did not."

Louis looked at his brother with a serious look on his face, you did say, "You are to start working for him tomorrow, is that correct brother?"

"Oui," Gilbert said.

Louis raised his head looked to the rafters and lifted his arms fully spread. Then looked into his brothers' eyes and said, "I hope you know what you are doing Gilbert."

Gilbert just replied, "I know what I am doing."

"We shall see," said Louis, as he wrapped his left hand around his brothers' shoulder and laughed at him. They walked to the front of the wagon to unhitch his pack horse stallion.

Poincare revealed to the visitors who were in the livery; "Please give me your attention; they must prepare the beast, for its stall. Due to the fierce nature and power of the breed, for your own protection and safety, you must leave the stable at once."

Louis looked at Gilbert and Ernest, rolling his eyes, at the drama and fear Poincare is trying to instill in his audience. Knowing the word would spread and the stable will be even busier tomorrow with people coming, going, and asking the same ole questions.

Poincare turned to Gilbert, Louis, and the boys. He told them this is working out better than I had imagined. I wish you would reconsider, letting me keep the animals here longer. We can both make a lot of money and my livery will be the envy of all the others in Québec.

Gilbert uttered in a matter of fact manner to Monsieur Poincare, his plan is to start working tomorrow. "I will honor our agreement. He will keep the horses here for a week." He informed him, he will need his team to transport their own wagon and belongings to the farm he will be working, tomorrow morning.

Seeking to be Loved

    Poincare gets a distressed look on his face. Then he offered his finest pair, to transport their wagon and I will keep your stallions here.

    Gilbert considered it for a moment. He knew his horses need to exercise. He explained this to Poincare then said, "I must take my team." Nothing is said between them for a few moments, although Gilbert can see Poincare is thinking of another proposal. Gil told him, "We can leave before 6AM, my family and I can have everything unloaded and I can have the wagon back here, no later than 9:00 tomorrow morning. I will have my son Ernest return with me and stay here with Louis, to groom the animals and to assist in the stable. I will need one of your steeds, so I may return to the farm to put in a day's work. If this is agreeable."

    The smile returned to Poincare's face. He extended his arm to shake Gilberts hand and said, "I think that will work fine, just fine."

    It is already afternoon, Gilbert asked Poincare how long he will keep the stables open?

    Louis addressed his question, "The stable is usually open until seven each evening. Although when people want their own horses, for private use they come to me at my residence just across the street. Sometimes they need to get their horse and buggy, carriages, or other equipment they may need for the evening. It is expected to be scheduled in advance. On the rare occasions it is not, they will send their coachman to me to setup their private rigs. It is a rare request for one to come up unexpectedly. Most would prefer to have their rigs and things prepared for them when they show up."

    Gilbert expressed his concern about the safety of his animals, as well as the other horses in the stable, under these side show conditions. He knows it will affect their ability to rest peacefully. Louis agreed with him and added, "Now that the word is out, many people may want to stop by in the evening to view these fine beasts. There may be some people that have had too much to drink. Upon hearing the gossip about these fine Percheron horses, such people may decide to come sneak about to get a glimpse of them after hours.

The Guyon's, observe the sparkle gleaming in Poincare's eyes.

"Louis, do we still have some paint left over from painting the stalls last month?" asked Poincare.

Louis replied, "I believe we do sir."

He ordered Louis to paint a sign. "On it write, 'The proprietor cannot be responsible for any bodily harm that may occur to anyone disturbing the beast inside.'
That should stop any reasonable man from entering or breaking in, I would say."

Understanding how his boss thinks, Louis stated, "It also may stimulate more interest and curiosity. I am not concerned about the reasonable people."

Gilbert asked Ernest and Henry to start curry brushing the horses and feed them. He sent the younger boys in to see their mother. I will be along shortly and explain today's events and help prepare things for tomorrow morning.

Poincare looked at his watch, he is thinking to himself how much time he had before the stable closes the doors. I will resume letting people in to view these great specimens of horse flesh. He told Louis, to paint underneath the warning.

Daily viewing 9AM to 7PM, until June 13.

Seeking to be Loved

Chapter 11 New Beginning

June 7, 1914 - Marilda was the first to wake. She had Phillip cradled under her arm. She gently kissed the top of his head and whispered, "Today we start our new life."

She reflected on the last few weeks of their travels and how grateful she was for a safe crossing. She thought how all details seemed to come together, with every complication along the way. Whenever their journey seemed it would be delayed or come to a stop, almost instantly the Lord provided a way. The obstacle was always removed unexpectedly, allowing them to proceed to the next connection of their trek.

She was thankful for being away from the danger zone. She was full of excitement, she wanted to get up immediately to start her day. She did not want to disturb any of the others by waking them so soon. She imagined the farm in her mind, from the descriptions given by the boys and Gilbert. There was a new energy. She could see it in how each of her boys, and Gil were reacting and responding to questions about the farm. Despite having little knowledge of it. She thought how each have their own perception of what their new life will be like on this plot of land, in this new country. She was eager to see it for herself.

She strained to see Gilbert's watch on the table without moving so much as to wake him or Phillip. Lifting her head to see over Gil, proved to no avail, she was not able to see the watch face. She reached her left arm just above his head to grasp his watch from the nightstand. Only able to reach the chain. She lifted it gently from the table, slowly retrieving the watch. The moment the chain lifted the watch off the table it swung, hitting Gil on the nose. She could not help but giggle, he brushed away at his nose and rolled towards her.

He did not wake, holding it close to her eyes she was able to see the face of the watch, it was 3:45AM. She decided to ignore the

Seeking to be Loved

urge to get out of bed and start her day. She chose instead to pray, and offer thanks to the Lord for guiding them here safely.

Phillip rolled slightly under her left arm snuggling closer to her bosom and let out a breathy sigh. She thought what a gentle, pleasing sound he makes; it was comforting to her.

She rolled gently toward him lying on her side cradling him in her arms. She concluded her prayers with, "Merci Lord, for this little one." She whispered to Phillip, "Je t'aime mon cher(I love you dear one) so much, sleep well my dear child, grow healthy and strong, always love and serve God and you will do great and wondrous things." She had fallen back to sleep.

Gilbert woke and reached for his watch and chain. He could not feel it on the nightstand, he reached down to the floor. Not feeling it there, he wondered where the watch could be. He was sure he took it from his pocket and left it on the nightstand. He rolled over to look at Marilda, he raised up just enough to see Phillip. He appeared comfortable as can be, snuggled in his mother's arms. He slipped out of bed and dressed in the dark and left the room.

George was already in the kitchen. He had prepared a pot of coffee, and offered Gil a cup, as he sat in a chair at the table. He felt no need to continue the discussion from last night. He shared his concerns and respects his brother's judgment.

Gilbert had assured him that even with the very worst scenario, his family would be sheltered and well fed.

George knew his young brother was quite capable, in his chosen profession, and making things grow. It was his gift, he knew his younger brothers stubborn and determined nature. He was sure, given the opportunity he would do everything that was necessary to be successful. He shared his pleasure, that he found a place that was so close. He told his brother how nice it is to have remnants of family close again. It is nice to have you near, to be part of their life once more.

Gilbert agreed. He then shared his great concern with his brother about their parents, other family, and friends they left

Seeking to be Loved

behind. He mentioned the fact, that war was inevitable and they are on the Eastern front. They will be in the middle of it.

He was not aware of the fact that the French Government and its military have already begun a forced evacuation from the areas bordering Germany and along the eastern boundaries of France.

We must pray for the safety of our family, and countrymen and ask for God's protection.

"That we must do my brother," agreed George.

Gil asked George, "What time is it?"

"Five fifteen," he told him then asked, "What time did you want to pack and leave?"

Gilbert said. "Soon, I promised Poincare, I would have my team back, for his showing by nine this morning."

"Then you must get going."

It was a foggy day, the air was damp and visibility poor. They could not see much of the countryside, at best maybe only 50 meters in either direction. Pulling off the road at the farm, all was silent, almost dismal, thought Nattie. It was not quite 7:00.

Gilbert and his sons walked the entire distance behind the wagon. He carried little Gil all the way from the stable to the farm, their new home. Mary sat with Marilda, and the three younger children on the buckboard. Just as they were pulling up to the house, they can see light from within. The side door opened, the owner and his wife, must have been waiting. They greeted them with smiles, and a joyful welcoming tone in their voice.

Marilda picked up on the friendly sincerity of the couple immediately. She thought, they seem like very pleasant people. Next she thought, "I believe we will enjoy staying here." Marilda draws in the team to a stop.

Gilbert proceeds to meet the man, still carrying little Gil in his left arm. He shook hands with the man and introduced his family.

Seeking to be Loved

The woman walked to Marilda, and asked her to hand down the baby. "What a handsome child," she whispered. "Such bright, light blue, happy eyes he has, so early in the morning."

Marilda climbed down from the buckboard, she told the woman, "His name is Phillip." She turned to Mary, who handed her Joseph. "This is his older brother, Joseph." Next she pointed and said, "That is Blanche, climbing off the wagon." Then introduced Mary, "This is my oldest daughter, Mary."

A grand smile appeared on the woman's face, and a sparkle in her eyes. She suspects the woman must have been a loving mother herself. She already felt connected with this lady and sensed the warmness in her heart.

She at that very moment believed, her husband had made a good choice for his family.

You all must come inside, I have a pot of tea and warm milk. It is on the table and I will prepare a breakfast to celebrate your coming to stay and work with us.

Marilda told her, "We have already eaten our breakfast, Merci Madame."

"That does not matter," she said, "We all have much work to do. Preparing your rooms, sending the men and the boys to the fields, all must have a full stomach. You have already come several miles. We must meet with you, and break bread before the days labor begins."

Gilbert intervened, "It has been less than 3km."

The man directed Gil, "Let me show you where to take these fine animals."

Gilbert reminded him of his commitment to Poincare.

"It is good that you keep the arrangement you made. Keep the horses hitched. I will show you where they will be stabled when they are here.

These young men can start unloading and carrying things into the house. I must tell you right now, do not argue with the Mrs... she has never been so excited, from the moment I told her last night, of

Seeking to be Loved

your coming. She has set her mind to prepare a wonderful breakfast, for all of you, before the start of your day. You do not want to upset her, do you?"

"Most certainly not," replied Gilbert. He and the man walked towards the barn, he can hear Marilda, insist that she help prepare breakfast. She and the woman come to an agreement.

Marilda, is determined to find out the name of the couple. She can think of no tactful manner to do so; she felt foolish. The fact is, here we are already moving in, taking up residents and about to start working for them and we do not even know their name. Upon entering their home, Marilda stated, "Madame you know our names, but we do not know yours."

"Oh, I am so sorry my dear. I am Francine Chabot and my husband is Sean Chabot."

Returning to the house Gilbert realized he must return the percherons to Poincare's livery by 9AM. He had almost forgotten completely, in his eagerness to start to work the farm and fields.

He excused himself to Monsieur Chabot, "I must hurry to unload the wagon as soon as possible. We have many tools, may we place them in your barn, and bring the home wares into your home, monsieur?"

"Yes, Yes I will assist you," Mr. Chabot declared!

Gilbert and the children unload the wagon, it is the first time in more than four weeks, the wagon is empty. For some strange reason, the emptiness of the wagon makes Gilbert feel quite pleased with himself. Yet he is not quite sure why. On his way back to the livery he experienced a new sense of freedom within him. He thought maybe the wagon, emptied of all their belongings, is symbolic. Representing they are now settled, that must be it he thought.

Just like this season, the time for planting, maybe it is us, who are being planted. Our roots are being planted or at least replanted, in this new fertile land.

Seeking to be Loved

He reminded himself, first things first. I must get these horses to the livery. Then I need to get myself back to this farm. He is anxiously looking forward to test his team in the fields. He anticipates how this fine-looking rich soil will turn. He can smell the soil in his nostrils, and feels the pull of the plow when he snaps the reins and his team in synchronized steps, plod forward. Pulling the blade deep into the ground, exposing the dark loom of the earth. Rich soil waiting to nourish the seed. He can hardly wait, even though it is June, it is like Spring all over again.

Approaching the livery, he can already see people lined up. Poincare, shouted to the crowd here come the magnificent beast now.

He waved Gilbert into the livery, he has Louis immediately close the doors behind. He does not want the gathering to observe these Percheron stallions before they pay their fee.

Gilbert and Louis quickly unhitch the team and led them to their designated stalls. Grain, hay, and water were given them. Gilbert groomed the manes and brushed the coats of his team. He and they sense a contentment mixed with excitement. It is as if they know what is coming soon. They will be back in fields working together side-by-side, as they were trained, since they were colts.

Louis asked, "Where is Ernest?"

Gilbert apologized, "I left him at the farm, I completely forgot, to bring him back with me. Everyone was so excited about being on the farm and eager to get settled in. I am guilty also, I too am eager to begin working the land. I will bring him early tomorrow, to make up for today."

"That is fine, it is not necessary little brother," said Louis.

"Well merci, however, I think working in a Livery with his uncle will be a good experience," said Gil.

"Louis, what steed shall I take? I have no need to take the wagon back to the farm. All our belongings have been unloaded; all I need is a mount to ride back on."

Seeking to be Loved

Louis, pointed to a mare, that belongs to the stable. It was not scheduled for use today. Gilbert saddled the mount and off he rode back to the farm. He inhaled deeply a few times and was pleased to breathe the fresh air of the new land. Gil was ready to ply himself to what he was sure, he was born to do.

The sun was burning through the clouds and lifting the fog. Sun beams were shining through everywhere on the moist dew laden pasture. He guided his steed off the road unto the path leading to their new residents.

Marilda came to meet Gilbert. She told him, "**The Chabot's**," emphasizing their name. She knew Gil did not know it, "She repeated Monsieur Sean Chabot and Madame Francine Chabot." Then told him, she was quite pleased with the arrangements they have made for their living quarters. "I think you made a fine decision; I believe our family will make out well, and be very happy living here."

Gil dismounted, smiling as he and Marilda embraced.

He looked up, his eyes widen in amazement at what he observed. Phillip is crawling, so freely and independently. Before the journey, Gilbert with his older boys had spent the majority of their days in the field. He was not aware, his youngest son was starting to crawl. During their journey, the young children were so confined they did not have an opportunity to move about freely and independently. Still embracing he turned his head to Marilda, keeping his hand on her shoulder, she looked at him and grinned.

She mentioned to Gil, "As soon as I put him down, he started crawling around like a little mouse, scurrying across the floor. It must have seemed like home, to this little lad. Observing him was really quite comical!"

"Your son is growing up! His little arms and legs have been confined for so long. It has been just over a month now, he needed to move about freely once more. I am surprised his little limbs are strong enough for him to get around so. He has even stood himself up, holding onto their stairs and chairs. Thank goodness he has yet to practice climbing.

Seeking to be Loved

We have been quite busy, rushing about moving things into the house. We were afraid it might rain, before we got everything inside and in order. I guess he watched us go up and down the stairs so many times, he must have thought it is a natural think to do. We will have to keep an extra eye on him now!"

Gilbert asked, "Where are the boys?" Thinking they may have already gone to the fields.

"They are in the barn with Mr. Chabot," Marilda told him.

He kissed her and said, "I will go join them. I am ready to get started." He said as he walked toward the barn.

"Oui, you always are." She whispered under her breath, as she walked back to the house.

Gilbert found them hitching up the old man's draft horses. Gilbert had noticed his team earlier this morning. He did not take the time to examine them and look them over properly. He can see these were fine animals, in their day. They are well past their prime, like the Chabot's.

Mr. Chabot welcomed Gilbert, "You returned much sooner than I expected. I was thinking it would be nearer noon."

"I did not want to tarry. I wanted to hurry back and get started with plowing, or whatever task you would like for me to do," said Gilbert.

Ernest declared to his father, "He was going to have me start with the plowing. He wanted to see how well I could handle his team."

With a concerned look displayed on his face, Gil conveyed his apprehension to Ernest. "I believe it would be best, if I start with the plowing."

Ernest had only a few times put his hand behind the plow. Gil had tested him with his own team of Percheron's, though they are in their prime.

His father explained, "These animals we are not familiar with, and they were not as young as our team. We cannot be sure how they will respond." Another concern that he shared with Ernest and

Seeking to be Loved

his younger brothers, "We are used to our horses, we may expect these to be as powerful. We need to assess them, just as we do our own with new equipment and load. We must get to know them and they us, or, we, both man and beast may work too hard."

Ernest responded, "Oh father, I believe I can handle them quite readily."

"Oui, I am sure you can; I must insist I guide them first. I want you to observe how they pull, their pace and how they maneuver. Watch how they turn about with the plow, watch closely how they move and pull. I want you to see how they handle, how they move and respond. I will let you take over when I feel they are ready." Placing the emphasis on the animals, not wanting to discourage his son, but, wanting to keep both boy and beast safe.

I want you, Henry, and Gilbert to follow as usual. He noticed the slight disappointment on Ernest's face. Gil knew it is for the best, and he will also, one day.

"Where is the bucket?" Little Gilbert, asked looking up at Mr. Chabot.

"What on earth do you need a bucket for?" Mr. Chabot asked little Gil?

"My job is the rock collector." he stated with an exceptional glee!

"Where do you propose to collect rocks?" the old man asked.

"In the field of course!" said little Gilbert.

"Well, I think you will do a lot of walking, probably not doing too much gathering of stones." Mr. Chabot told little Gil. "You will have an easy job today little fellow."

"I am a big brother." said little Gil, "I can do a man's work." He announced in such a youthful, proud, determined voice.

The old man and the Guyon's chuckled, at little Gil's statement.

"Let us get on with it then. It will not be long till noon. Let us see how much we can get done before then. We will show Mr.

Seeking to be Loved

Chabot what fine workers we can be." Gilbert lead his troops, to the field.

I have seen already this morning what good workers you are. I saw how quickly your wife and children unpacked, set up, and organized their things. Even the little ones appeared to have made themselves quite the home. Mr. Chabot declared.

Mr. Chabot's team handled very well, although their pace was slow. Gil tested them on a few occasions, knowing that a quicker pace would allow the blade to be pulled more smoothly and efficiently through the sod. Despite making it easier on the beast, the team had their own methodical plod. So, he settled into their rhythm. Mr. Chabot was right, the deep loom soil was nearly void of stones, he knew things would grow well here.

He suspected silt deposits from the flooding of the St. Lawrence over the millennium, has left great deposits of fertile soil in the river valley. Also, the many years Mr. Chabot or those who farmed the land before him, have been tilling the land. Much of the debris had already been removed.

Nearly two hours had passed, when he noticed Chabot waving his arms. He looked up at the sky and the sun was high. It was near mid-day, he thought it must be time to take a break as he was finishing the row. Approaching Mr. Chabot, he estimated it was nearly an acre he had plowed, in a little less than three hours. He knew his team could have easily completed much more.

Mr. Chabot was grinning broadly, he told Gilbert you handled the team with expert care and guidance. He looked over his animals they seem to be no worse for wear. He uttered to Gilbert, "I am surprised you have turned this much field in such a short spanned of time."

Gilbert responded, "You have a good team, they have a comfortable pace." He smiled as he thought how impressed Monsieur Chabot will be once his own team is put to the task. "He will truly be amazed."

Seeking to be Loved

The boy's follow behind. Last, little Gilbert with his bucket. He showed his bucket to his father, "Look only three stones Papa."

Gil patted him on the head and said to him, "This is fine clean soil, the crops will grow well here. The roots will be free to grow, expand and draw nutrients from the earth."

"You men must be hungry, you should have worked up a good appetite," said Mr. Chabot.

They walked the team to the barn to be watered and fed. He asked Monsieur Chabot, "If this afternoon he would like for them to plow more acreage. Or would he rather them till the soil to ready it for seed?"

There was no hesitation in Mr. Chabot's response. "No we must not have them pull the plow this afternoon. The tilling will be much easier on the team. Tomorrow, they will rest, we will plant the seed."

Gilbert commented, "You care for your animals well sir, you do not overwork them."

Chabot said, "They are my friends, they have served me well."

Gilbert assessed the afternoon's work. He realized it will probably take them a little over an hour or less to till the soil. The leveling prepares it for the planting. They could have it seeded before the evening meal. He does not want to suggest that, at least not yet. He knew the old man must have his set way of doing his work, he has his routine.

He will see soon enough, how much will get done with our team and with the extra hands working on his farm. He is looking forward to seeing how this all will turn out; his anticipation is high.

He thanked God, for placing him and his family here to live and labor, with the Chabot's. He asked the Lord to help him and his family be fruitful, in whatever lies ahead.

Seeking to be Loved

Chapter 12 Unexpected Loss

    A new year had begun, eight months have passed sense the Guyon's left their land in the Lorraine region, of France. They have been living and working with Sean and Francine Chabot, for seven months. The life they created, or should I say, the life they have been led to, here in Canada has been pleasant. Living and working in this new country, felt as natural as the land they had left.
    The land Gilbert loved, was being torn to pieces by a fierce enemy!
    There was never any mention of payment on behalf of Gilbert nor the Chabot's after their initial meeting on the roadway. Meanwhile they shared the use of their home and boarding. The Guyon's were content and comfortable, with a roof over their head, food in their stomachs and hardy work to do each day. They had a warm place to reside and share the peace, only family and loved ones can bring.
    A new year begun, on a cold January evening, Mr. Chabot asked Gilbert to join him in the front room. This room of the house was reserved for the old man to do his business and paperwork. He reviewed last year's expenses for the farm with Gilbert. He had him tally the totals. He reviewed all the receipts of income. Mr. Chabot even had him total all the daily earnings, from the roadside sales of produce from a stand the children set up.
    The children had fun selling vegetables and fruit, that was not taken to market once it began to ripen. It proved to be a good take, averaging two dollars a day, at a penny apiece or 10 cents a dozen. In the city they believed, the stand could have tripled that total.
    Gil reviewed the bills and property taxes, which the old man had outlined in his record book.
    He asked Gil to deduct all cost of his farm's expenses, from the income to determine the bottom line. He then said to Gilbert, "You never asked about payment for you and your family's labor. I often wondered, why you had not?" He shifted his hands in front of

his chest palms up, as to suggest for Gil to tell him why he never asked about payment.

Gilbert proceeds to tell him the events of the day they met. That day and the day before he had visited a total of six farms. At each I shared what my expectations would be for reimbursement. I had a contract prepared to show them, outlining what I would charge for my family and I, plus my teams' labor. All the farms we visited were magnificent operations. We could see many people busying about their labors on those farms. My boys and I were on our way to revisit a farm we liked the previous day. We looked at the map, hoping to find a shortcut back to the livery. We decided to turn on to the road that led us to your farm. Just before we saw you, we were admiring the land around us, wondering why it was not yet plowed and full of crops. There seemed to be something special about this property, yet something missing on this land. There was a curiosity that I could not brush away from my thoughts. I wanted to find out who owned this land. At that very moment, was when you appeared. Something inside told me, "This was the right place to be, for my family and I."

I was so excited after speaking with you. I failed to share the written contract I had prepared, to barter with you and other prospective employers. It just did not seem to matter at the time. At that point, what mattered was, that it felt right. It was a feeling, actually it was more of an awareness, that we had found a place where my family would be comfortable. A place where we can work, to earn our living and where my children would enjoy growing. I must say, it was Henry, he was probably the most excited, especially when he saw your orchards.

My brothers thought I was foolish, since no agreement had officially been signed and witnessed. Just the word of two men.

"Why did you not bring up the business of payment once you were here?" asked Chabot.

Gilbert looked straight into the eyes of Mr. Chabot and said, "You and your wife, welcomed a large family of strangers into your

Seeking to be Loved

home. You provided us with everything we need, food, shelter and we traded for our labor. We are thankful to God, for the way things have worked out for us. My family is happy, despite having to leave everything they knew and loved behind. Look how healthy my wife and children are, look at how happy they are. We are living, working, playing, and enjoying life, what else can a man ask?"

"Gilbert, I am a simple farmer," Chabot began. "The land has been good, it has always provided us our means, to live and pay our bills, not much else. We need nothing more than what we have. You see the profits from last year's harvest. We have never had such a productive season; it is thanks to you and your family.

"Having two pair of horses made the work more efficient and twice as fast. Plus the extra hands allowed much more to be accomplished." Gilbert mentioned.

"Ah that helped, it was your fine Percheron stallions which have made short work of it, yes?"

"Oui, Mr. Chabot," said Gilbert, "Did I not tell you, what you could expect of them, sir."

"I think we will divide this equally. Now half of $1725.23, is, let me see." said Chabot.

Gilbert came to a quick round figure, that is over $800, I cannot accept that amount. That is double what I would have bartered for. This is much more than Gilbert had ever anticipated or expected. What about our room and board? Plus, we only worked for a little over six months.

"No, that makes no difference, you and your family, provided more comfort and pleasure to our life, than we have had in years. At least sense our daughters married and moved away. You have provided us with more profit than I dreamed possible. Not to mention enhanced this farms reputation in the marketplace. We never have had such a profit. It has always been barely enough to pay our debtors, with little left to continue operations of the land. Your family being here has enriched ours, in many ways. We will go to the bank tomorrow, it is settled. God Bless You!"

Seeking to be Loved

"God Bless, you monsieur," replied Gil, shaking his head in disbelief.

Neither Gil, or his brothers, have heard from their parents in France. The only news of what was happening in their homeland, they knew from reading the newspapers. They were thankful, for having been led away just in time. The German invasion started just a few weeks after their arrival in Canada. They prayed for the safety of those left behind.

Nearly three years have passed. The Great War, became a world war. It seemed to have come to a standoff, France had put up a valiant defense and had stopped the onslaught of the German forces. With the help of allies Canada, United States, England, and other countries, they were able to defend, their beloved France, just as it had for centuries.

The tide seemed to be turning, they were driving back many of the enemy forces. At a great cost of human life. Much of the country they once have known, has been destroyed. Many of its great cities and monuments are gone forever.

They prayed every moment they thought of it, which was almost constantly for the safety of the loved ones, left behind. George, Louis, and Gilbert talked and agonized over returning, to help defend their beloved country. Especially, with the onslaught of a changing economy and job market sweeping the valley of the St. Lawrence.

The cannery industry was closing; eel harvest was dwindling on the St. Lawrence Seaway. The global market for them was a driving force for many years. George had lost his job three months ago.

Louis, was not much better off. More and more people were purchasing automobiles and using the city transport system. The cities and providences of Canada are in the process of developing other means of transportation. The trolley and trains can carry crowds of people from one location to another.

Seeking to be Loved

At the end of the month, Louis was being let go by Monsieur Poincare. There was little work for him in the livery. The demand in the horse trade was not enough to keep the livery open.

George already moved south of the border, to the United States of America. He found work in the southern New Hampshire area. There was a great need for laborers in northeast Massachusetts as well. The area was booming, with factories, textile and pulp paper mills opening and in operation. The town of Haverhill, was becoming well known as the shoe capital of the world. A new paper mill is currently being built in Pepperell, Massachusetts. There was work for anyone that was willing.

In three short years, the Chabot farm had become well-known in the city of Québec and along the St. Lawrence countryside.

They produced the finest crops. There was no difficulty finding immediate markets for their produce. Gilbert, Marilda and their family lived on and work the land, as though it were their own. Farming was in their genes. Sean and Francine Chabot, became more like friends, and family to them, and grandparents to the children, than business associates. They have been more than generous.

It was early spring of 1918, late April, Mr. Chabot, was eager to start the spring planting.

The Guyon boys, were growing into fine young men. They have proven their mettle, and grit, in the fields and on the farm, as well as whatever they applied their efforts.

Ernest James, now seventeen years old, Mary Alice fifteen, Henry is now thirteen, Gilbert twelve, Blanche will soon turn nine in a few days, April 21. Joseph is seven years of age and eager to show his brothers, he deserved to be with the boys. He saw any opportunity to get out of the house and away from his sisters and women folk, something to strive for. Phillip is now four years old, Marilda worried about him, as mothers often do. He wants to be out with his brothers, she must keep a constant vigilant eye on him. When the door is open, he always made a beeline for it.

Seeking to be Loved

He always woke up early, when his father and brothers are getting ready to go out to do their chores. He climbs out of his bed and pulls on his little boots. He cannot reach his hat and coat, so he just follows them out the door, with neither on his head or his back. Marilda must catch him, before he sneaks out and gets too far. Sometimes he made it out the door with his father and brothers, who are not paying attention. She has to run outside to catch him, and snatch him up from behind. Spinning him around as she lifts him, hugging him tight against her and whispers in his ear, "Not yet, little one. Je t'aime," she repeats in English, "I love you, you little rascal. You will be working with the big boys soon." She would tell him.

"Je t'aime Ma mee, Je t'aime, let me go," Phillip repeats to his mother, as he wiggled and squirmed, trying to get down.

She laughed, and kissed him again, saying, "Non". Although it nearly breaks her heart, when he pushes against her with tears welling in his eyes. She squeezed him back to her with a firm embrace, telling him she needs him to be with her for now. You must let Ma mee help you grow big and strong. So, you can work hard with the men. You must let me help you grow and become strong like your father and brothers. One day you will be able to do even more work than all of them. For now Phillip, you need to let me help you grow, by eating a good hearty breakfast. When you finish your chores in the house, you can go outside.

Smelling breakfast, already being prepared as Marilda carried him back into the house reminds Phillip, that he is hungry and ready to eat. It distracts him from wanting to be with the others.

Phillip pushed back to look at his mother without struggling to be let down. Looking into her eyes, he questioned, "Eating a big breakfast, makes me big and strong?"

Marilda exclaimed, "It most certainly will young man." Adding as much excitement as she can muster to her voice!

Phillip squeezed her neck and said, "Je t'aime Ma mee."

She sat him down at the table, and Mrs. Chabot greeted him with a plate of scrambled eggs and sausage. Then she cut a slice of bread, she made herself, and just pulled fresh and warm from the oven. She slathered a piece with butter, churned yesterday and set it before Phillip.

Marilda looked on, she has tears filling her eyes, and tries to understand why.

Mrs. Chabot observed; she noticed a look of sadness on Marilda's face. She asked, "Are you all right my dear?"

Marilda looked at her attempting to smile, as she does the tears run down her cheeks. She chuckled, attempting to mask the deep forlornness she felt. She explained, "The strangest sensation just came over me. It was a sadness I felt inside, I have no idea why. It just happened, coming on for no reason. She laughed it off, repeating it was just something I felt inside."

Mrs. Chabot suggest to her, "You are much too young for that my dear." She consoled her, "It is something we all go through, once our child rearing days are over, usually after the children are gone. Are you sure, it is not something else?"

Marilda said, "I am sure it is nothing." She managed a smile for Madame Chabot. She then stated in jest, "Maybe I am starting early."

What sadness she felt, was more of a sorrow, yet she could not imagine why. It was like losing something very precious, her heart ached, as though it was grieving on its own. It was more intense than what she felt when leaving France; when she realized she may never see her parents and homeland again.

Mrs. Chabot changed the subject and conveyed to Marilda, even though there is still a little bit of snow left on the ground, Sean said, the ground has thawed. He believes it is soft enough to start plowing. He hoped to start doing so, soon.

She expressed to Marilda, "The last three years as you know have been so productive here on the farm. It has brought a new life to him. He looks forward to work in the fields with Gilbert and your boys. I have not seen him so full of life." There is a pause in her speech, while she thought. "It has probably been twenty years, since he has been so enthusiastic about working the fields."

When the men and boys came in for breakfast, he was smiling broadly.

Mr. Chabot sat at the head of the table, he made the announcement in a bold declaration. "We will start to plow the fields today. Gilbert and I discussed it, we will turn the fields and fertilize them. Then in three weeks we will till them, and they will be ready for seed. We think we can get 120 or better acres plowed and planted this spring and early summer."

"You seem to be awfully sure of yourself Mr. Chabot," declared his wife!

"I suppose I am," Mr. Chabot said. "It is a pleasure working the fields again and the farm. It has brought a new purpose and new excitement to life."

"Or is it the fact you have five additional pairs of hands to help you to work the land," questioned Mrs. Chabot.

"Aye, you are probably right my dear," he said, reaching for her hand. "The work has become fun once again, as it was many years ago."

Mrs. Chabot reminds him, "Just remember you are not as robust as you were that many years ago."

"Oui, I mean, yes my dear, I have strong men and boys here to do the heavy work and run the teams, I will do the planning and supervise, maybe some of the light work."

The weather was pleasantly warm on a lovely May morning. All snow had melted away along ago except the deepest drifts, hidden in the shadowed areas. Even they harbored only the slightest remaining patches of snow on the north facing grounds. Although they knew they can get another spring storm at any time.

Mr. Chabot and Henry went to the south pasture to check on calving. Their herd was getting a little larger and they were expecting at least 10 calves to be born this spring. Eight of which have already

Seeking to be Loved

been born. Upon reaching the field, Henry spotted the ninth arrival with its mother off to themselves at the far end of the field. He then spotted the tenth, although it was in the process of being born.

Mr. Chabot said, "Let us go see, what is delaying this poor old girl." He recognized the problem; the calf is coming out breech. He voiced to Henry, "I am not sure how long she has been attempting to give birth. I would suspect a long time; she looked very distressed. We must help her."

He directed Henry to go get his father, and a pail of warm water and soap. I will stay here with her and keep her calm. He patted her on the neck and spoke softly to calm her. He can see in her eyes, she is stressed, and in pain. He decided to see if he can help remove one of the calf's hooves. To get it out of the birthing canal, only the knee is exposed. He thought if he can remove that one leg, maybe the calf will slide out. He proceeded by attempting to pull on the knee, that was exposed.

The cow kicked and its hoof hit him just below the sternum. The blow was not that great. She was not trying to hurt him, just attempting to get him away. He thought, "I have felt much worse blows from a disgruntled cow or heifer." No sooner had he finished the thought, he felt an excruciating pain in his chest. It took his breath away, he dropped to his knees, holding his hands over his heart.

When Gilbert and the boys entered the pasture, they could see Mr. Chabot was lying down behind the cow. Neither had moved from their position, they ran to them. The calf was still stuck with only one leg and part of the other knee protruding. He handed Ernest the bucket, and went to Mr. Chabot. He was not breathing.

Gilbert ordered Ernest to move the cow and do what he can for her. He looked to Henry, "Run to the house have your mother send for a doctor."

Ernest applied warm soapy water to the exposed parts of the calf and as much to the birthing area as he could. With his hands he kept gently pouring the warm soapy water over the parts of the calf

Seeking to be Loved

that were protruding from the cow. Young Gilbert and Joseph were at the head of the animal. They talked soothingly to her, occasionally glancing over at their father.

Joseph started to cry watching his father trying to revive Mr. Chabot.

"Here it comes," Ernest shouts, he assisted the calf as it was slipping to the ground. His two brothers patted the cow, congratulating her on given birth. The cow turned to inspect her calf, and proceeded to lick it clean.

The boys went to their father. Gilbert kept speaking to Mr. Chabot and rubbing his chest in attempt to arouse him. He prayed to God at the same time, to please help this man.

Seeking to be Loved

Chapter 13 Burial

    They buried Monsieur Chabot, May 14, 1918. The widow's daughters, Molyn, Lori and Shirley along with their spouses and her dear grandchildren arrived the day before the funeral and burial service.
    Two days before the funeral Marilda told Madame Chabot, her family would stay with Gilbert's brother, while her daughters stay at the farm with her.
    Mrs. Chabot said, "This is your home now. I have doubts whether or not my daughters will arrive for the funeral service. They are very busy with their own lives."
    Marilda consoled her, "Surely they would be here. I insist we go. Gilbert made arrangements with Louis, and we have packed everything we will need. The boys will keep their work clothes in the barn. We will come daily, to do all necessary task, farm and domestic. This is the least we can do for you, during such a tragic lost. We will stay with this arrangement for as long as your daughters wish to stay. The girls and I will come each day along with Gil and the boys. We will take care of all the chores inside the home, prepare meals and cater to you and your family's needs.
    "That will be fourteen people if all three bring the spouses and their children. Including all of us, that is twenty-four mouths to feed," said Mrs. Chabot. "That is too much to expect of you." She stopped to reflect on the last time, she saw her daughters and grandchildren.
"I would love to see my grandchildren, how they must have grown, in four years."
    Marilda said, "Serving twenty four will not be an issue. When we were making the crossing, we had prepared for a crew of 41, three meals a day plus an open buffet of bread, desserts, and beverages for the men. We have no more need to discuss it any further, you have other things to concern yourself with. We will stay here until they arrive. We have everything prepared, the rooms have

been cleaned and ready. We will clean the rooms each morning when we rise. So, they will be ready for them, the moment they are here."

The three daughters had not seen their parents in over four years. They knew the Guyon's resided at the farm with their parents, through correspondence.

They made arrangements to stay at the Chateau Frontenac, and would have stayed nowhere else. It did not matter whether or not anyone was staying at their old homestead. All three were not suited for the farm, let alone country living, despite experiencing a pleasant childhood.

After checking in and getting settled in their luxurious suites, they hired carriages to take them to their parent's farm. The hotel maître d', made arrangements with the livery, to have two of their best carriages and coachman ready in one hour.

That meant Poincare would have to hire a man, for one carriage. He kept one Coachman on call, and that was Louis. When the coaches arrived at the Château, they were given instructions. Louis knew this had to be the family members of the Chabot's when they instructed him to the farm address.

He overheard the conversation of the daughters and their spouses. They discussed suspicions that this so-called Guyon family, were taking over the farm, and may have already done so. Their imaginations ran a full spectrum of possibilities with many unfounded accusations. Even questioning whether the death of their father, was brought about by the planned actions of a scheme, they devised.

Louis had all he could do, to contain himself. With every new statement and speculation, they brought forth, his anger rose. His only thought was, "Arrogant bastards."

By the time they arrived at the farm, his blood was boiling. He had to grit his teeth, to give the appearance of smiling, as he helped them from the carriage.

Seeking to be Loved

Their mother met them at the side door. The initial greeting and exchange of pleasantries and condolences to each other over their father's death, was touching.

Immediately after, no time was wasted reviewing the plans they had made for their mother. They told her after the funeral once they have buried their father, they would leave at once. As well as their plans for the sale of all the property. Richard one of the son-in-laws stayed behind at the hotel making appointments to meet and discuss options with real estate agents.

Louis started searching the farm, he was looking for his brother. He wanted to inform him of what he can expect, from the Chabot daughters.

As the afternoon passed, the Chabot's three daughters tried to convinced their mother, Mrs. Chabot, to come live with one of them. They told her, she would need to be close to them and her grandchildren.

She was indifferent about living in the city. The oldest daughter Molyn, lived in Montréal, a beautiful city with wonderful cathedrals. The two younger daughters lived in the Province of Ontario and the city of Ottawa. Neither they, nor their husbands had interest in farming.

Mrs. Chabot had discussed with Gilbert and Marilda the possibility of their managing the farm for her, the evening of her spouse's death.

Gilbert discussed it with his family, they were thrilled at the prospect. Gilbert even suggested that sometime in the future if they could save enough of their earnings, that they would be interested in purchasing the farm. They saw that pleased Madame Chabot tremendously, for she had begun to see and accept them as her own children. They have become part of her family, a partner in the farm, as well as maintaining their way of life. She was sure they would care for and maintain the property as she and her husband would, if not better. She believed this is what her husband would have wanted, and told them so.

Seeking to be Loved

    Marilda, Mary, and Blanche, did their best to stay out of the way of Mme. Chabot and her family. They catered to their needs, they wanted to assist in comforting them, during this difficult time of mourning. She and the two girls stayed busying in the kitchen preparing tea and sweetcakes for the Chabot's family. They all had to keep an eye on Phillip, so he would stay close and not wander about the house. Especially into the living room, or other area's Mrs. Chabot's family may be, they did not want to disturb them during their time of grief.

    Mary and Blanche were interested in the new guest. They could not help overhearing the conversations they had with Madame Chabot. They were very dismayed. Mary had to drag Blanche away from the hallway door, where they could hear what was being said. She stood there with her fist on her hips, in a stance of defiance. Mary was afraid she might say something that would embarrass her and the rest of the family.

    Marilda, warned them to keep their thoughts to themselves, and treat them with the utmost respect. They obeyed their mother.

    Despite the fact the Chabot daughters had no intensions whatsoever of staying at the farmhouse overnight under any circumstances. They were quite convincing expressing to their mother, that they were displeased for having to stay at a hotel in the city. This is our home, said Molyn, and the others murmured in agreement. We wanted to be near you, they told their mother. They gave the appearance of being very indignant about the matter, having to stay away, and take up lodging in town.

    Much of their rhetoric was not comprehended by Mrs. Chabot. All her attention was focused on her grandchildren, and the fact that her husband, was not there to enjoy them. "He would have treasured the opportunity," she thought to herself, and many times expressed it out loud ("If only your father, or grandfather were here to see you").

Seeking to be Loved

Meanwhile Mary suggested to her mother, they step outside for a moment.

Marilda told Mary and Blanche, "First serve the tea she had brewed, and offer items from the tray to Mrs. Chabot's family. She noticed the look on their face, she knew they were mad about something. She told them both to be very pleasant, and go place these on the cupboard in the living room. She instructed them not to look at anyone. Enter the room, place the items on the hutch, then returned to the kitchen. We will step out for a moment, to get some fresh air.

Marilda picked up Phillip, she and the girls stepped outside. It was a pleasant warm overcast spring evening. The time of day when the air is thick with the fragrance of spring. The fresh scent of loom, that has been turned in the field by her husband and her sons. A rich sweet smell of flowers and blossoms from the orchards, she always enjoyed the promise it brought. Fruit of the land, a fair trade for their labor.

They walked away from the house. Marilda turned to the girls and asked, "What is it my dears? What is causing you to have such scowls on your face?"

"Mother, you would not believe what they are saying about us, and accusing our family of," stated Mary.

"Oui, you should hear what they are saying about us. They are just mean, and do not know anything," said Blanche.

Marilda looked at them unsympathetically. She told them, "They have just lost their father, and you know Monsieur Chabot was a wonderful, generous, kind man. They are in mourning, and are grieving. They may fear many uncertainties of the future. Pay no heed to what they say about you, or any of our family. You must at all times be on your best behavior, be considerate of everyone and everything. Most of all, she said with a very stern voice, "Do nothing nor say anything disrespectful. Just think, how you would feel if you had lost your father, or me, or even one of your brothers or sister."

Seeking to be Loved

Mary and Blanche looking down, "Oui mother," they both replied.

Phillip in her arms recognized those words. His lower lip curled inside out, he began to whimper as he turned to his mother and squeezed her around the neck as tight as he could. He managed say, "I do not want to lose you, Ma mee."
Mary and Blanche were ashamed of their thoughts. They too began to weep and hugged their mother.

Dinner was served in the dining room, to Mrs. Chabot's family. Molyn's husband shared with the family, the results of the meetings he had with three real estate agents. He had mentioned that the Chabot farm had quite a reputation for the finest fruits and vegetables. They all thought we should have no difficulty getting a fair price for the property, and that they would line up potential buyers immediately.

Mrs. Chabot, now understanding the conversation intervened. She told them, she wished for the Guyon's to manage the farm on their behalf. Stating the arrangement she and the Guyons agreed to. Including the profit-sharing after all the farming expenses were taken care of.

As prosperous as the farm has been the last three years, that would have been advantageous for them. Mrs. Chabot and her daughters, would have to do nothing. Annually, each would receive their share of fifty percent of the profits. The farm would still be under their ownership.

From around the table, were comments coming from her daughters and their spouses. Stating to their mother and confirming amongst themselves, the absurdity of such a contract, 50% going to the labor.

How on earth could he agree to such an arrangement? No one, in their right mind would make such an agreement. What could they have done or said to father, to get him to agree to that? Did they, somehow threatened him? They have robbed him and you mother.

Mrs. Chabot began to cry. She could only say, "You do not understand."

One of the son-in-law's, Molyn's husband Richard, boldly proclaimed, "Oh, we understand, we understand perfectly, you have been cheated." He received several confirmations from around the table.

Another stated, "For how many years now? That money is gone forever."

Marilda and her family ate in the kitchen. They overheard much of the conversation from the room down the hall.

Gilbert held out his hands, in gesture for all to interlock hands during the prayer. He whispered a prayer for Madame Chabot and her family. "Lord help this family through their grief. Help them one day, to see the light that only you can shed on the world and their lives. Can we assist them in some way to comfort them in their struggle, guide us Ole Lord?"

When the prayer was finished Marilda told the older children, when we finish our meal, I want you to gather dishes from the table in the dining room. We will clean them and leave as soon as possible. We will leave Madame Chabot's family, to have a restful evening in their home together.

Gilbert said, "Ernest and I will go harness the team and get the wagon ready."

As soon as things are cleaned and put away, Marilda stepped into the living room to inform Mme. Chabot, that she would be back between 6:30 and 7AM tomorrow.

Mrs. Chabot's siblings looked at each other, after Marilda had left the room. They were quiet for the first time since their arrival.

The daughters were frantically wondering how they may excuse themselves graciously, and get back to the hotel. Without looking like they are abandoning their mother. When they heard the

Seeking to be Loved

door close as the Guyon's left their home, they asked their mother, "Where is she going?"

Mrs. Chabot asked them, "Have you not seen your rooms?"

Once again, they all look at each other, then turned to their mother and asked, "What do you mean?"

"Your rooms have been cleaned and prepared for you, and the children. They never looked so nice," she said, so cheerfully.

The daughters looked at each other, then to their mother once again. They are trying to disguise the disgusting tone in their voice. As they murmur collectively whispering to one another, "We are not staying here."

Lori's husband quickly stated, "The carriages will be here shortly to take us back to Château Frontenac." Then told his mother-n-law, "We will meet you at the Funeral Parlor, tomorrow. The wake is scheduled to start at 11AM, is that right?"

"One of the daughter's stated; "The service at the church is at 1PM. We must hurry back to the hotel."

"We have much to get ready," another exclaimed.

They all want to exit quickly, to avoid more discomfort. They gave no thought to the fact their mother would be spending the night alone, at the family farm.

On the way back to town Gilbert shared with Marilda, what Louis had told him. Marilda, Mary and Blanche, in turn shared with Gil and the boys, what they overheard the family suggesting from the kitchen earlier.

Just then they noticed two carriages approaching its Louis and the other coachmen. Marilda quickly realized that Mme. Chabot's family is not going to spend the night with her. She expressed to Gilbert, "I am going back to the farm."

She said, "Madame Chabot should not be alone. She will be so disappointed, her family is not staying with her. She spent so much time decorating their rooms. I know she will dread being alone

Seeking to be Loved

at this time, and she certainly should not be left by herself." She turned around to look at the girls, "Would you like to join me?"

Mary's a bit indifferent, she wants to get as far away as possible. She is furious over the things she heard.

Blanche said, "I will Ma mee. If they are not going to be there."

Mary reconsidered, after she thought the bed at the farm would be much more comfortable than the couch in the cramped quarters of Uncle Louis's living room. "I will to Mother."

She told the girls let us ride back to the farm, with Uncle Louis. She kissed Gilbert, and asked him, "Do you think we are doing the right thing?"

Gilbert watched her as she kissed the other children. He said, "You are a kind, considerate woman. I am sure you will bring her great comfort. We will plan to be here a little earlier tomorrow, to get the necessary chores done before the service."

Marilda and the girls load into Louis's carriage. She told the girls, we will stay in the barn until they leave, then we will go into the house.

She instructed Louis to wave to them, if the family does decide to stay with their mother. "We will be watching to see what they do, if they leave, we will wait until you are out of sight, before we go in. If they stay, we will wait for your signal. Then we will load into the carriage and go back with you. I hope this is not too much trouble for you."

"None at all," said Louis. "I think you are doing a good service for the old woman. I had to come out anyway. I must say, I was befuddled, why they were not staying with their mother in the first place, considering the situation."

The daughters and their family left with Louis and the other coachmen. Marilda observing through a space between the boards on the barn door, came to tears. She thought how sad it was that they would leave their mother alone under such circumstances.

Seeking to be Loved

She knew how Mme. Chabot, despite the reason for the visit, was looking forward to spending time with her daughters and grandchildren.

She and the girls left the barn when the carriages were out of site. Quickly they made their way to the side door. Upon entering, they heard sobs coming from the living room.

Blanche frowned, before bursting into tears herself as the girls looked at each other. They quicken their pace to the living room and Mme. Chabot.

She was delighted to see them. She wiped her eyes and tried to smile. She reached her arms to them. She whimpered, and started to cry again.

They gathered around her. Marilda and Mary on either side embraced her.

Blanche sat on the floor at her feet. She did not know what to say, she just laid her head on Mrs. Chabot's knees, and cried with her.

Mme. Chabot, patted her on the head and managed to say, "There, there my dear girl."

When tears finally dried, Blanche looked up, meeting Mme. Chabot's eyes. She opened her mouth, and was about to speak.

Mary instinctively kicked her, and placed her finger over her own lips, to keep her quiet. She knew by the look on her little sister's face, she was about to say something that she should not. Although she knew it would be the truth, it would not be appropriate.

Marilda thanked Mary nonchalantly, for her quick action. She would not have wanted Blanche, to share something about Mme. Chabot's family.

She also recognized the questioning look Mrs. Chabot had in her eyes. She answered it before she could ask, she just left out some details. Marilda explained to Mme. Chabot, "We saw Louis's carriage, he passed us on their way to town, both carriages were full. We knew your family must be going back into town, so we decided to come back and spend the night. We did not feel this was a time for you to be alone."

Mme. Chabot expressed, "I was so looking forward to have my daughters, and my grandchildren spend a few days here on the farm. This time of year, things are starting to bloom and the flowers bursting forth, it is such a beautiful time. You prepared their rooms so nicely, they never looked so inviting.

I had hoped it would bring back fond memories for them and be nice for the grandchildren to experience." She wiped her eyes, then looked at each of the girls, the twinkle returned, and they smiled at each other.

Marilda agreed with her, "It is a beautiful time of the year." Then she asked madame, "Is there anything you would like, before we go to bed?"

Mrs. Chabot replied, "I am just so glad you girls are here, thank you for coming back. When they left, I never felt so all alone in my entire life. I have spent several days alone over the years. There were many times when Sean has gone to meetings, or, went to visit his family. I never felt lonely, it was just a strange feeling that came over me, the instant they left. It was almost as if, I wasn't just being alone, it was like a complete emptiness. Like everything of value, everything in my life that was dear, and meaningful, was suddenly not there anymore, everything was gone. Everything inside and out, was suddenly gone." She started to cry again.

"Then you all arrived." She leaned slightly forward to hug all three of them close to her, and whispered, "My dear ones."

Marilda can only think of how our Lord and Savior when he was hanging on the cross bearing our sins, had to feel.

For the salvation of mankind. Our Lord allowed himself to live an absolute human life. To experience the joys, the temptation, the tribulations, and the sorrows, that go with it. So each one of us, have an example of how we can endure this existence, for the glory of the next. She reflected on Mme. Chabot's very words, "I felt so alone."

Seeking to be Loved

It brought to mind the last sorrow of our Lord and Savior. Where he had allowed himself to experience it to the deepest degree. The total abandonment of those he trusted, confided in, and taught. In his greatest moment of need, they left him. **"My God, my God, why have you forsaken Me?"** Matthew 27, 46.

He himself being the Lord, verbalized the words for all to hear. He had to be forsaking, and giving up even on himself, to experience total abandonment.

Only his Blessed earthly mother and one of his disciples had not abandoned him, John 19, 26. For they loved him so, refused to leave him to face alone, this last suffering and greatest sorrow.

After his body had been tortured beyond belief, his mental and emotional anguish of being totally abandoned by those so dear and loved by him, his misery was absolute.

When his suffering was complete, finally giving up even on himself, his humanness. His faith was not shaken. Though he never lost faith in the Almighty Father. His last words of his human existence testify to that fact, **"Father, into your hands I commend my spirit,"** Luke 23, 46.

Marilda suggested, "We should go to bed, tomorrow will be a busy, trying day for everyone, we will need our rest."

Marilda was up early, along with Mary and Blanche. They prepared breakfast for their family and Mme. Chabot. The boys completed the chores with their father.

They prepared a variety of foods, to be served buffet style. She figured some would want to eat, others may choose not to, after coming home from the funeral service and burial. A formal sit-down meal may not be practical, during the time of mourning. She felt it would be more appropriate, to let people choose for themselves what they would rather eat and when. Mrs. Chabot agreed, once Marilda discussed her thoughts.

Mrs. Chabot thanked Marilda, for all that she and the girls are doing for her and her family.

Seeking to be Loved

Marilda responded by saying, "That it was the very least we could do, for all she and her husband have shared with us." She proceeded to review her idea for today's reception of visitors. She began by saying, "Madame your family may have guest today, friends and extended family will be expected to offer personal condolences. The girls and I will prepare, a variety of food and hors d'oeuvres. They will be set on the table and buffet. Any guest that stop by, may help themselves to refreshments."

She explained, "There may be some who will bring things. It is customary when neighbors and friends visit the home of a deceased to pay their respects, they bring food to the grieving family."

After the funeral and burial, the priest had announced that the family of Mr. Sean Chabot, would receive visitors at the Chabot farm this afternoon.

Many showed up, people Mrs. Chabot has not seen in years. Local farmers, people from the church, friends, and family she had never met. Some born of family, she could barely remember. Many people she did not recognize, she was touched by the respect shown for the passing of her beloved husband.

The three realtors, Molyn's husband spoke with were in the midst, offering condolences and handing Mrs. Chabot their business cards.

She cordially thanked them, wondering why she would want their business cards. She paid no attention when they discussed the selling of her property. It did not sink in, not until later on in the evening.

When all the mourners and well-wishers had departed, Mrs. Chabot, her daughters, and their spouses were together. The adults were sitting in the living room. The grandchildren occupied other areas elsewhere in the home. The boys were outside playing games. The older granddaughters gathered together in the upstairs parlor area.

Seeking to be Loved

The eldest daughter was the first to reiterate the discussion from yesterday. She informed her mother, three real estate agents, were here today and had brought several interested parties. They wanted to come and make visits to the property tomorrow.

Mrs. Chabot appeared slightly confused. She asked, "Why?"

All at once, the response by several in the room was nearly shouted, "We had discussed this yesterday mother."

They were adamant that she sell the farm, and all its contents. "You will come live with us; whichever one you choose." Each secretly hoping she would not pick them.

Shirley, quickly added, "Until we can find you a nice little place of your own. One close by so we and the grandchildren could visit you as often as we like." Each managing a sicky sweet tone in their voice, wanting to make the latter statement sound intriguing.

"The grandchildren will just adore having you close by mother," said Shirley. Another added, "And we could spend all the holidays together. Wouldn't that be nice mother?"

"Yes, that would be nice, I have always dreamed of that," said Mrs. Chabot. "I always imagined it would be hear on the farm, where you all have been raised."

"Well, it all will be settled soon," someone said.

The son-in-law, who made the arrangements with the realtors, spoke joyfully. "I had asked them to bring the prospective buyers throughout the day. In hope that each one would be here simultaneously, and see there is much interest in the property. Possibly leading to a higher bid for the farm, for fear they may lose out on such a prime piece of real estate." I thought by having them view the property while many people are here, would be a good ploy. Making them believe there are many others interested in the farm.

The others in the room laughed and mentioned, what a wonderful idea. You are always thinking when it comes to business.

Seeking to be Loved

Mrs. Chabot began to understand, why there were people she did not know, at her home. Now she knows why, people handed her business cards.

Mrs. Chabot addressed her family, "What about Gilbert, Marilda and their children? They have been so kind to us, and had worked so hard and diligently with your father and I. They have become more like family. Your father and I love them, as we love you, all of you."

Her daughters and their spouses looked at each other, in such a manner, acknowledging their own suspicions as fact. Believing not only, have the Guyon's taken advantage of their parents, they moved in. They took up residence, and befriended them. All so they could take advantage of their parent's kindness.

One of the son-in-law's stated, "I have a mind to call the authorities, to investigate the whole incident, and circumstances of your husband's death."

Mumbles of agreement, were heard around the room.

Mrs. Chabot is beginning to understand. She confronted them, questioning, using a sharp tone, one full of anger. "Investigate What?"

Are you saying, you think they are responsible for your father's death? She is furious at their unfounded thoughts, they have of the Guyon's. To the point where she wanted to ask them to leave her home, which was once theirs. She had wanted them to feel that it still was. Now she does not know what to think.

She is beside herself with rage. For a moment she is dumbfounded. She does not know what to say to them. How can she make them understand that the last proposal, she had discussed with Marilda and Gil, would be to her and her children's own best interest and future benefit?

They can see the anger, and the fury in their mothers' eyes.

"Well", was all she could say for the moment. She looked around the room, there is deafening silence. She intentionally made eye contact with each, one by one. She waited for someone to

Seeking to be Loved

respond, if they dared, before she turned her gaze to glare at the next.

They can see the disgust in their mother's eyes, they have to look away. Some looked down at their hands, resting on their laps, others just turn their head slightly.

Mrs. Chabot slowly got up without saying a word, turned and walked to the kitchen. Marilda, Mary, and Blanche were sitting at the table. She recognized a deep sadness in Marilda's eyes, anger in the two girls. Mrs. Chabot looked at the girls, and said to them, "I feel as you do. And you are right, to be so angry."

She asked Marilda, "Would you please go get your husband."

"Oui, Madame."

She knew Marilda would fill Gilbert in with what had just transpired. She sat at the kitchen table with the girls. She told them, "They do not know you, and your family, as I do. You know Mr. Chabot and I, have come to love you very much, do you not?"

"Oui, Madame." They acknowledged without looking up although wore a heartfelt expression on their face, and a whimper in their voice.

"I have failed to raise my daughters to be kind, considerate, diligent human beings."

Marilda found Gil in the barn with the boys, they were making repairs on equipment in the building. Gil knew there was no need to continue to plow the fields at this point. They had discussed what Marilda and the girls heard last evening. He had shared it with his brother, while Marilda and the girls stayed at the farm. They had agreed, if there were to be any animosity between Mme. Chabot and her daughters, they would move south to northeast Massachusetts. They knew they can find work there. Plus be close to George, and all three brothers will be reunited again.

Gilbert mentioned to Marilda, it is unfortunate they think the way they do. Although there is some truth to at least one thing. I have always thought the profit-sharing was very, very generous of the Chabot's. I tried to convince him otherwise, he would have none of it. They have been good to us and the land has been very productive. We must not stand in the way of their wishes. We cannot change what they think, nor should we interfere with what plans they have. I know we can make this land very profitable for them and us. Although, we may be setting ourselves up for a lot of disagreement, and mistrust on their part.

Living, and working here would not be the same, not like it has been. We have had three good years. The team is starting to show their age, maybe we can find a small patch of land, where they will not be as much demand on them. Or maybe, a small farm! George had mentioned in his letter, there are plenty of farms in the area. Where we can either work or sell the team if we must.

They entered the house through the kitchen door. Mrs. Chabot is still at the table with the girls. She preferred their company at this point.

When Gilbert and Marilda entered the kitchen, Mrs. Chabot said, "This is so unfortunate, and on such a grievous day." She teared up once again. The anger rekindling, dried them quickly.

Gilbert told the girls, to go join their brothers in the barn. He then turned to Mrs. Chabot and said, "Whatever agreement..."

She lifted her hand, to stop his speech.

"You and Marilda come with me." She said, leading them into the living room. "You have met my daughters, and their husbands. I think they have something to say to you."

Before they do, I want you to know the last three years, have been the best three years their father and I have had in many. You have brought new life to the farm, and to us, as well as great comfort." She turned to her daughters and spouses, and said to them, "What is it you would like to say, to these two?"

There is silence in the room.

Gilbert decided he would be first to speak, and maybe relief some of the tension, and put all at ease. He told them, "I know what had been discussed amongst you." He proceeded to say, "We have been blessed with three years of living, and working for your parents.

Seeking to be Loved

You have been blessed with them your whole lives. Your father has been more than generous to me and my entire family."

There are murmurs around the room and sarcastic comments, such as. "I would say so." "Very generous." "More than reasonably generous."

Gilbert resumed, "We have been fortunate. It has been a privilege to serve you and your parents for these three years." He explained, "Running and managing a farm is hard work and as you may know, it is a job that requires 365 days a year. It is work that one must love in order to dedicate themselves to do it properly. Five of us had worked very diligently, day in day out, and gleefully, I might add."

To make a farm produce successfully, labor is required. If labor is to cost one dollar per day, that would be three hundred and sixty-five dollars per year."

The murmurs around the room, begin again. "Yes, that is correct." "You received more than double that," "Thieves." "You should be ashamed." "Robbers."

Gil continued, "Times five is $1825.00 per year."

"We received less than half that. The generous salary, we received, averaged less than $160 per year each. If one would limit the hours worked each day on the farm to ten, that would be 3650 hours per year. That would be an hourly wage of less than 5 cents an hour, averaging 45cents per day per worker.

Mrs. Chabot intervened and said, "But Gilbert, there are nine of you. Plus, you and your family worked more than ten hours a day, most days, except for the three youngest.

"Oui, Madame."

Gilbert chuckled uttering, "Joseph and Phillip's job for the last few years, has been staying out from under your feet."

She laughed at the thought, "You are right there," she said. "Gilbert you know you have worked longer than that. I know Marilda and your daughters are usually up by 6:30 each morning and many

Seeking to be Loved

times worked well after dark even in the summer, as you have also," exclaimed Mrs. Chabot.

Gilbert resume his spiel, "If that being the case on the average day, we had earned less than four cents an hour. Much less if you count seven laborers.

I do not know if you would consider that cheating your parents, or, overcharging for our labor. I do know our lives have been enriched, with the opportunity to have lived with and worked for your parents."

He turned his attention to Mrs. Chabot, and expressed his family's gratitude to her and her husband, for having given them this opportunity. Holding her hand, he explained, "We will be leaving next month. Poincare, is letting my brother go in a few weeks. We will be joining my brother George, in Massachusetts, at that time."

Molyn's spouse Richard ("Dick" for short) coughed to clear his throat and said, "Let us not make any rash decisions, now. We have not decided what we are going to do about the farm, just yet."

The daughters as well as the other son-in-law's looked at him quite strangely.

Lori, questioningly stated, "We decided to sell to the highest bidder, at the soonest possible date?"

Dick, cleared his throat again; attempting to end the conversation, so they can discuss it further later, privately.

Gil is quite observant about these things. He knew it would be advantageous for them to let him stay on, to manage the farm. He knew Dick, now sees easy profit with no investment on their part. Gil said, "We will have no further discussion ourselves. We will be moving on, you now must excuse me, for I have chores to attend to.

Just one last thing. The world has lost a wonderful man, there were none better, nor none fairer, than your father. Our lives have been, and will be the better for knowing him."

He turned to Mrs. Chabot and extended his arms to give her a hug. While they embraced, he thought what he could say, in an attempt to reassure her. He conveyed to her, "What is about to

Seeking to be Loved

happen will be Fine. Living near your children, and grandchildren will enrich yours and their life's, as it has ours, living here with you."

She blinked in an attempt to prevent tears, she did not succeed.

Gil assured her everything will be all right. He excused himself and left the room, Marilda followed him out the door.

"You are very tactful and suave," she exclaimed, adding "As well as an excellent mathematician. "You cannot tell me, you just came up with those figures and numbers off the top your head? If you did, you are quick to think under the stress of the circumstances. I would never have thought of those at the moment."

Gilbert hugged her, and said, "No, I had those figured out long before now. I do that stuff in my head all the time when I am working. Although Mme. Chabot threw me for a loop when she included nine into my figures. That took a little quick thinking, off the top of my head."

Marilda asked, "Do we really work for less than four cents an hour? That hardly seems worth it."

Gilbert reminded her, "You have to remember, we had room and board also and no other bills. We have had a good life here and we have been able to save nearly 800 dollars."

"Your right, though you got to admit you and the boys have worked hard and long. The girls and I did our share of the domestic chores."

"Long maybe, it never seemed like hard work. It with just work that needed to be done to make our efforts successful. It was pleasant labor," Gilbert stated.

"I agree, I love you, William Gilbert Guyon."

"I love you, Marilda Natalie Guyon!"

Mrs. Chabot's family comforted her, when Marilda and Gilbert left the room. They apologized for their actions, in an attempt to convince her they were only concerned about her best interest.

Dick asked, if she thought the Guyons might reconsider staying on at the farm.

Seeking to be Loved

Mrs. Chabot looked at him with an expression that silenced him instantly. At first it read contempt and disgust, the next moment, it changed to one of pity.

Her initial thought that appeared in her mind, before she made her comment, slowly changed. Thus her appearance and demeanor to a more civil and understanding smile. For she knew Dick, knew nothing of laborious work, honor, nor respect for oneself, or others.

She felt sorry for him. However, there was hope in her heart. Hope, that one day, he would understand such things. That he and all her loved ones will come to know, there are many more important and precious ways to profit in life. That of which is to, **"Profit, from life."**

She hoped, one day, they all would find the true worth of men.

She responded to Dick. "You heard what he said. He will not negotiate, he is a man of his word, it is done. He and his family will leave next month, just as you heard."

She let her words sink in, if they could. After a few moments she informed them; "I will not be going anywhere, with anyone, until I see them off. You all may stay if you wish. As for me, I will not leave my home, even if you sell it out from under my feet. I will not step foot out of this house, until I see them off and wish them farewell. I am tired, I am going to my room."

Gilbert told the boys, "We will be leaving next month. "We are going to America. The land of opportunity they call it. Uncle George says, there is work for anybody willing to work in a variety of jobs." He also identified, "They have schools and all children were expected to attend them, until they reach a certain age."

Henry and Gilbert said, "I liked school, I like to work as well. Can we not do both, father?"

Joseph said, "I have never been to school, except what Mary and Ma mee, had taught me."

Seeking to be Loved

Phillip uttered, "I want to work, and go to school."

His oldest brother laughed, "You might not like either one, you have never done them before."

Phillip a bit confused, questioned. "Which one is either one?" That brought them all to laughter.

His father picked him up under the arms, and swings him around, until they are both dizzy.

Marilda informed the girls, "The next few weeks may be difficult. We will continue to stay with Uncle Louis. We will pack our things, so they will be ready to load in the wagon. We will keep out only what we need. We will help your aunt and uncle do whatever they need to do and assist Mrs. Chabot.

America is a wonderful place, she told them. According to your Uncle George, it is a thriving, growing country."

She was reminded of Angeline, and said softly, "She was right."

"Who was right?" asked Mary.

"Oh, I was just thinking about Angeline." She was looking at and touched her vase, on the window sill. "Now we are going to America." Marilda suddenly felt the same odd emptiness, and blankness she experience when Angeline mentioned America, three years ago.

Mary giggled, and confirmed, "She was right." Then asked, "Are you all right, Mother?"

"Oui, I mean yes. We must start speaking English even more so now."

"How long of a trip is it to America, Ma mee?" asked Blanche.

"I do not know. You will have to ask your father."

They asked their father, he told them, "The letter they got from Uncle George, said, it was a little over 400 miles. "It took them a little more than four weeks. They left during the mud season, in the middle of March. The going had to be exceedingly difficult. We will be leaving the last week of June. The ground and roads should be dry and well packed. We should make good progress. I suspect to cover that distance a bit more quickly. It will still be every bit of three weeks, possibly more.

Seeking to be Loved

Chapter 14 <u>To the land of Opportunity</u>

    Gil, Nattie and the Guyon family, prepared the farm for the new owner and helped Mrs. Chabot, and her daughter pack.

    It was a sad goodbye, Mrs. Chabot's youngest daughter stayed, to journey with her to Ontario. The farm had been sold and she got a fair price, actually they made a tidy profit. The farm had gained a wonderful reputation the last three years. Her daughter handed Gilbert an envelope and told him this is half year's wage. He was reluctant to accept it, explaining to her, "The only crop in the field was corn and wheat. The fields intended for produce and market sale, have not been planted, due to the circumstances. I cannot justify taking advanced pay in wage, based on profits that have not been gained."

    Mrs. Chabot shouted at him, "That is nonsense, you take that you have earned that and more. There will not be another word on it."

    Gilbert looked at Marilda, she said to him, "She told you and that sounded pretty final." They laughed, and thanked Mrs. Chabot and her daughter, and wished them the best in their new life.

    Lori said to them, "I can see why my mother, and of course my father, have been so fond of you and your family. I enjoyed the last few weeks getting to know you. I also wish you well on your journey, and for a successful future."

    Mrs. Chabot handed Marilda her daughters address on a piece of paper and asked her to please keep in touch. "I will look so forward to hearing from you and about the children."

    Marilda promised she would; it was a promise she would not be able to keep.

    Louis's family will be going by train and will be there in less than three days. They are scheduled to leave June 24th.

    Gil and Nattie, could have taken the train as well, they had saved enough to do so. They have worked so hard the last three years.

Seeking to be Loved

They decided to see the country, between here and Massachusetts. The plan was to camp along the way, if it suited them to stay in a hotel due to weather conditions, they would. Gilbert asked his brother to find suitable lodging for him and his family. Since they would be there well before them. He gave them money to secure a residence, until they got there. They have heard much about Niagara Falls, it was one of the places they were looking forward to visit and maybe spend a few days. Their plan changed, when they realized how much further west and out of the way it would be. It would require another week at least.

The train his brother and family are taking, will travel southwesterly to Niagara, before heading east toward Boston. He did not think they had planned to spend time touring the Falls area, due to the train schedule. He thought, "What a shame to miss such a rare and unique sight, to be so close and not see such a magnificent spectacle of the natural world is a tragedy.

Starting the trip south early on June 25, along the St. Lawrence River, they made excellent progress for the roads were well developed. Progress slowed once they moved away from the river. Heading south toward the United States border, into the state of Vermont, progress was slower. The few roads were not very well maintained. For the next several days they averaged 35 to 45km a day. Gil mentions to Nattie, "This seems much quicker, and more pleasant than our last journey. Do you recall trekking across the French countryside when we had all the animals? Do you remember?"

"Yes," Marilda said, "Phillip was still nursing then, there were times I would walk with him in the sling. It seems so long ago."

Phillip now riding beside her in the wagon asked, "What is nursing Ma mee?"

Marilda just looked at him smiled and said, "It is when you were suckling my dear."

"What?" he said inquisitively?

"It is when babies are eating." She left it at that.

Seeking to be Loved

The pace was comfortable for all. They were in no hurry, they stopped to see spots of interest on the way. They made it a point for this trek to be more like a holiday, instead of a mission. There was a sense this would be the last move, so they wanted to take it in, and, enjoy what the new land had to offer, for sites and scenes.

They spent three days in the White Mountain region, of New Hampshire. The mountains were magnificent, they never seen a sight, so grand. Their own French Alpine Mountains, they only heard stories from those who had visited them. There were sketches and a few photographs they viewed during geography studies in school attended in the old country.

This land was not the same, the cities were different, coming through Vermont and New Hampshire. The cities were very spread out, they looked different, not as old as the cities and towns in France. Why should they be, this was considered the New World.

It took them twenty days to get to Pepperell, Massachusetts. As they neared the southern New Hampshire area the cities, were much closer together. It did not take long to go from one to another. Yet there was countryside and farms everywhere, they noticed on the way, many just on the outskirts of towns.

They had the address George sent them. That was their destination.

It was a warm sunny July day, when they reached George's residence. When they approached the house, they were somewhat surprised. No one was home to greet them. They walked to the front door and knocked, no one answered. It was obvious no one was home. The door was unlocked, so they entered to wait for them. He knew George would expect them to make themselves comfortable, until they arrived.

He thought they may be working, or running errands. Their home was nice, although not as spacious as the Chabot's farmhouse. They hoped the residence his brother may have found for them to live, would be a bit more roomy. He trusted his brothers, not giving it another thought. They were aware that living in the city meant

Seeking to be Loved

concessions would need to be made. Gilbert and Ernest fed and watered the Percherons. Noticing a shady place behind the house, Gil kept them hitched, while waiting for his brother. He will determine what to do with them for the night, after speaking with George. They sat on the front steps, watching people pass by. He wanted to be the first to see his brother, or his family members when they arrive. The others were taking naps inside.

It was nearing four o'clock in the afternoon, both Gil an Ernest were almost asleep on the steps. Loud blasts startled them. The sound seemed to come in every direction. The sound was very similar to the ships whistles they heard at sea. Some sounded like trains blowing their whistles along the St. Lawrence river. Within moments the streets around the home swarmed with people going to and fro. He realized the loud horns and whistles, must have been the signal that the workday was done.

He became re-energized at the thought his brother and their family may be home soon. He was anxious to see George again. It had been three months since he spoke with him. He turned to Ernest and said, "I suspect they will be home soon." Ernest nodded his head in acknowledgment. He was enjoying just watching the young ladies, as they passed by.

A middle-aged man slowed his pace, looking strangely at Gilbert and Ernest. He turned off the sidewalk, following the path leading to them. "Who might you be, and what are you doing here?"

Gilbert stood to greet him. "I am waiting for my brother and his family. I am William Guyon, they called me Gilbert or Gil, that is my middle name. This is my son Ernest. We are waiting for my brother George Guyon, who lives here."

"You are mistaken Mr. Gagnon, this is my residence. My wife and I have lived here for the last two months."

"You live here?" Gil pulled the letter from his shirt pocket, to show the man.

The man took the letter from Gilbert, he noted the date it was stamped. "This was postmarked in April. That man, your brother, apparently had moved out at least, if not more than two months ago. We started renting it May first. I have never met the former residence."

Gil was embarrassed for himself, and his family. He apologized for the misunderstanding, then asked the man if he had any idea how he could find his brother.

The man just shook his head no and reiterated, "Like I said, I never met the previous residents. They were long gone before we moved in. The house was empty when we looked at it before we accepted it to rent."

"Who owns the home?" asked Gilbert.

"I do not know that either, all I know is we pay the rent at the bank down the street."

"Do you know who showed it to you?" Gil inquired.

The man said, "Ask the gentleman at the bank when you go there. You might want to go talk to them, they might know something about previous residents. I certainly do not. If you do not mind, I would appreciate you getting off my porch. My wife will be home soon. I am very tired and had a long day at work. I wish you well, and hope you find your brother."

Just as the man was asking Gilbert to leave, his front door opened. Out marched Nattie, followed by what seemed to the man, as a troupe of children, of all sizes, one after the other. The man was astonished, wondering how many people are in his house. He looked at Gilbert in amazement. He exclaimed, "What do you mean by invading my home like this?" His voice was full of rage. "I am going to get the police, if you do not evacuate the premises immediately."

"What is this? We have visitors!" exclaimed a cheery voice.

The man heard a familiar voice behind him. It was his wife, who just arrived home from her workplace. "More like invaders," the man said, in a not so pleasant tone.

"What do you mean?" asked the woman. "Do you not know these people?"

Seeking to be Loved

"I have never seen them before, they were just here when I got home a moment ago. His brother lived here before we started renting."

"Where you coming from?" She questioned, looking at Marilda.

"We are coming from Québec, Canada. We had left June 25, we just arrived a few hours ago." Marilda told them.

"You must be exhausted, from traveling such a long way. Where do you plan on staying?" she asked.

Gilbert said, "We do not know? Is there a hotel or boardinghouse close by, where we can spend the night, or maybe a few days, until we find my brother's."

Gil questioned the man. "Has anyone else stopped by looking for his brother George, within the last few weeks? That would have been my brother Louis and his family."

The woman revealed, "Now that you mention it, last month, it was a Saturday afternoon, I remember." She looked at her husband, whose name is Matthew. "Matthew, do you remember the man that came to the door, a few weeks ago?"

"I do remember now that you mention it, he also, asked about a man and family. I think the one he was asking for, was George Gagnon, yes. We told him the same thing, we are telling you. Now I remember, there was a note left on our door a few days after that. It had a name and an address on it, if I can remember correctly. Yes, there was an address on it, I believe. The message on the note, was to give this to somebody. If I remember it had several names. I bet that somebody is you."

Gilbert with a glimmer of hope exclaimed, "Wonderful, may I see the note?"

The woman frowned just a bit, as she started walking past them mumbling, "If we still have it, I know where it will be. I keep all my notes and my addresses in a drawer, in the kitchen. I will be right back."

Seeking to be Loved

Meanwhile Gilbert resumed his apology to Matthew, for the inconvenience. He looked at Marilda and whispered, "I hope you left their house in order."

She responded by apologizing as well to Matthew. Then said to Gilbert, "Of course, I told the children not to touch anything until their aunt, uncle and cousins arrived."

Gilbert questioned the man once again, if he knew of place where they can spend the night.

He told Gil, "There is a hotel, actually three of them downtown, just a few blocks from here."

Gilbert gave Marilda a questioning glance, then he turned to Matthew, repeating, "A few blocks, what is a few blocks?" He was not familiar with the term.

Matthew chuckled and said, a block as the distance between city streets.

Gil's next question was, if he knew of a livery or stable where he can keep his horses.

"That I do not know, I never had to be concerned with the keeping of animals, myself," said Matthew. "I am sure someone at one of the hotels will know. You have horses?"

"Yes, they and our wagon are behind the house."

"You came all the away from Québec, Canada, in the wagon, being drawn by horses? It must be a very large wagon to carry all of you." Then in an anxious state, he asked the question, "Where did you leave your horses and wagon? I do not see them." He turned looking up and down the street.

Gilbert mentioned, "Usually only three rode on the wagon, the rest of us walked."

"Where is your wagon, MAN?"

Gil, calmly said, "They are behind the house."

Mathew took a deep breath to calm himself, his irritation increasing with each moment. He came to the conclusion, they as well as he are tired and weary. Not to mention being disappointed, not being able to find his brothers.

Seeking to be Loved

"You and your family should be exhausted, you must be very tired," remarked Matthew. "Although you do not look any worse for ware, from all that traveling."

Gilbert explained, "It was a vacation for us, we traveled at a comfortable pace."

The woman returned from the house with a disappointed look on her face. "I have looked everywhere, it may have gotten thrown away. I do not remember even keeping it, the note made no sense to me initially. I did not make the connection, so it was not important that I keep it. I apologize, I wish I had kept it now for your sake.

Someone at the bank maybe able to help. If you let us know where you will be, if someone may happen to return, we can forward them on to you."

The children were silent throughout the whole ordeal, they were fatigued from traveling. Gil and Nat looked at one another and recognized the disappointment on each other's face.

Gil said, "We will find a hotel. Once we are there we will return with a note. If it is agreeable to you Mathew."

Mathew nodded.

"Please keep it, to give to anyone looking for us. It will have information as to where we are staying and the names of my family. We would appreciate that greatly monsieur. I will include the names of my brothers George and Louis Guyon on the note, our address, once we know where we will be, if that is acceptable with you."

They agreed and mentioned to Gil, "We will not be home until after 5PM, on most days."

The Guyon's, apologized a third time for the intrusion and thanked them for any assistance they can offer.

This time of day the hotels downtown would have already been filled and no rooms are likely to be available, Gil thought to himself. All three hotels they stopped to inquire were full and reluctant to mention the only place they suspected might still have rooms available. It was a less desirable establishment. None of the

Seeking to be Loved

hotel desk keepers had suggestions to where they could board the horses. Nor could they suggest places to camp for the night within the city. They made their way to the south section of town.

One look at the hotel was all it took. Marilda, turned to Gilbert and just shook her head no, and snapped the reins. Gilbert caught up with Marilda and the wagon. He told her, "I have no idea where to go." He paused a second, looked around, turned to Nattie, and said, "I was just thinking, if we can find a church, we can ask there." He looked around, the shops and stores were closed. There were only a few diners, and meeting houses open. Nattie, noticed a gentleman staggering on the sidewalk. "Gil, ask him if he knows of one close by."

Gilbert waved to the man and walked toward him. "Pardon me sir, is there a church close by?"

The man looked at him oddly, confused by the question. He leaned closer to Gil. Trying to focus his eyes to see him, then the others behind Gil. "It is not Sunday, is it?" His speech is slurred, "Are you alright, No one looks sick or dead."

Gilbert said, "We are fine, we wanted to ask a priest if he knew of anyplace, we could stay and keep our horses."

"I see," said the man, squinting at Gil. "Saint Joseph's is just a short distance from here. Just keep heading;" he stopped to look at his hand as if he is trying to figure out, which one is which. "Is it south or west," he shrugs his shoulders; "Go that way," pointing with his right hand, "Until you get to Lowell Street. Then go that way," (pausing to lift his left hand and mumbling his words) "trwo or tree streets, until you come to Tarbells Street, turn left,"(looking at his right hand) onto it and you will see St. Joseph's church," here lifting his right hand higher. "Remember just tree or trwo streets." The man staggered on his way.

Gil thanked him, and they proceeded, in the direction the man first pointed. He found Lowell street, it was a few streets away. They saw St. Joseph's Parish, it was a handsome stone church, where Tarbells Street intersected.

Seeking to be Loved

It was small compared to what they have been attending in Québec, or the great cathedrals on the journey through France three years ago. They all wanted to go in.

Gil asked Ernest and Henry if one of them would be willing to stay with the wagon. They both agreed to watch their things, while the others went in.

It appeared that service had just ended for the evening. There were still a few people praying, and he noticed the priest. He was standing to the left of the altar.

They bowed, made the sign of the cross on themselves and knelt to pray.

Gilbert kept an eye on the pastor wanting to speak to him before he left the parish. He started walking down the aisle, Gilbert caught his attention and asked if he could speak with him. Gilbert introduced himself and his family to the priest.

"I am Father Jim, welcome to St. Joseph's Parish. How can I help you? I have not seen you here before?"

Gilbert explained where they were from, and how he was to meet his brothers and their family here in Pepperell, Massachusetts. He told him the address he had was no longer valid for his brother George.

The names were not familiar to the priest. He suggested maybe they go to another parish. "If you are going to stay in the area, you can check in with me. I meet with the other priests in the area on a regular basis at least weekly, sometimes more often. I will ask them if they have any new parishioners by that name."

"That would be wonderful Father, we would appreciate that very much. We have another request. We have no place to stay, or shelter for our horses. The hotels have no vacancy's, except for one."

"Yes, and you do not want to stay there." Father Jim, did not have to ask which one he was referencing, he knew. He told Gilbert that he had several parishioners that have farms in the area. "I am sure they would have space in one of their barns and would want such fine specimens to keep. Your animals look to be in fine

Seeking to be Loved

condition. They may charge you to board them, I am sure you can work out some suitable arrangement."

"That would be acceptable and expected," confirmed Gilbert.

The priest mentioned that there is a large dairy farm owned by the O'Sullivan's. "They have a boarding house, for many of the hired help. They may have a room or two to spare for you and your family. Though his farm is a few miles out of town, north of here. It is getting late you obviously have had a trying day. We have a small field here where your horses can graze. Although, there is no shelter for them. We have room in the rectory for you and your children. The problem is there are only two spare beds we keep for guest, and visiting priest. You are welcome to them. The others would have to sleep on the floor or on the couch. We will have plenty of blankets, you may use."

That is kind of you father, he looked at Marilda and she nodded her head, accepting the offer.

"Fine then, let me show you where you may stay. Tomorrow after our morning service, I will go with you on a visit to the O'Sullivan's."

"That is very kind of you father, we thank you very much."

Father Jim told Gilbert, "There are a few parishioners that have been sick, I have been wanting to visit them. If you do not mind making a few stops along the way."

Little did they know that the influenza epidemic was already underway. People were uncertain what the fatal sickness could be. Early January 1918, a doctor in Haskins county, Kansas, had reported unusual influenza activity in that area to the U.S. Public health service. In March it had spread to Fort Riley, the first reporting, was of one soldier with flu like symptoms. By noon there were hundreds sick.

World War I, had claimed an estimated 16 million lives, it will be ending later this year.

Seeking to be Loved

The Spanish flu epidemic that swept the world in 1918 to 1920, estimated to have claimed 50 to 100 million people. One fifth of the world's population was attacked by the deadly epidemic. Within months it had killed more people than any other illness in recorded history. It emerged in two phases, the first phase in late spring of 1918, was known as the, "Three-day fever."

It appeared without warning! In this first phase, few deaths were reported, victims recovered in days. Then the disease surfaced again in the late summer and fall. This time with a devastating and deadly effect. Health officials could not identify the disease, which was striking so fast, and so viciously. They could do nothing to control it, or treat it.

Many of its victims, died within hours of the first symptoms. Others after only a few days. With one's lungs being filled with fluid; the victim would suffocate to death. The plague did not discriminate, the young and strong which are usually not harmfully affected, were among the hardest hit by the disease. It struck in urban and rural areas, all over the world. In the United States, the densely populated East Coast, was severely inflicted. As well as the remotest parts of the country, even the least populated regions of Alaska.

In September at Fort Devens in Massachusetts, one day a soldier was diagnosed. The next day one dozen, it quickly increased to 1500, with meningitis like symptoms.

If you ask me, this may have been one of the major reasons for World War I coming to an end. Weaponry used by the enemy included chemical warfare, various gases, anthraxes', were unseen, unheard, but deadly. Maybe it was the fear that this deadly disease was another weapon of war. This unknown killer, being intentionally spread by an overzealous and evil enemy.

Could it have been more? May it possibly, have been a deadly plague, as mentioned in Scripture. That was to be let loose onto the human race, when we fall away from the Commandments. Especially the commandment, of loving God and our brothers as ourselves. Could it be another warning to mankind.

Seeking to be Loved

    The Guyons were awake and ready early. Mass was at 7AM finishing up at 8AM; they left shortly after. They were to make two stops on the way to the O'Sullivan farm. The first was an elderly woman who had been ill for several weeks. Her ill health was not unusual, she was in her late 80's. She had often failed to attend mass due to her age, and illnesses over the last few years. It was her sons and daughters, who informed the priest and asked if he would visit her. Upon seeing the priest, her energy was stirred. A cordial exchange of pleasantry followed. He anointed her and administered the Eucharist, her spirits were lifted.

    The next stop happened to be a family, who's youngest child was born with a severe condition that prevented natural growth. They did not want to place him in an institution, the family decided to care for him. "He is our child and our responsibility." His parents told the doctors at his birth.

    Staff at the hospital, some family, as well as others suggested institutionalizing the infant.

    They told the priest at the infants baptism; "This is the child God gave us to raise."

    The priest explained to the Guyons, "The boy was not progressing, not developing as it should, even for one with its condition." The child has not been responsive for weeks now, other than just eating and bodily functions. The father told me Sunday, that is why his wife, and the baby have not attended mass the last two weeks.

    Marilda had asked the priest, "How old is the child?"

    He turned four this spring. The priest added, "He looks no more than nine or ten months old."

    "How sad," said Marilda.

    Phillip was sitting beside her, Joseph to his right next to the priest who was to the right of him on the buckboard. Phillip responded to his mother's statement, asking, "What is sad, Ma mee?"

Seeking to be Loved

She glanced down at him, quite surprised that he was even paying attention. The simple questioned surprised her, although it should not have. She became aware of a queer sensation within when he asked about her sadness.

For some reason it puzzled her, and even more so, the feeling that came over her. Why when he just asked a simple question, did I suddenly feel odd? She knew there was more behind it, call it, "Mothers' intuition."

She saw the sincere look on his face. She for a moment studied his eyes, as he stared expectantly. There was something in the way he looked at her. She knew he was waiting for a response. She was set back, as she tried to understand the odd feeling she had. She looked at him for a moment. She knew there was something more than curiosity. There was a depth to his question, and the way he observed her. She could only respond by mentioning, "It is sad, that this young boy, had not grown normally, like you have in four years."

When they arrived, the priest started to climb from the wagon. "I will be back in just a few minutes." He expected them to stay outside, with their belongings.

Marilda asked, "May I come in?"

The priest thought it odd; she did not know the family. He shrugged his shoulders and said, "You may."

She told Joseph and Phillip to stay there. She told Gilbert to keep an eye on the boys. Phillip immediately started climbing off the wagon behind his mother. She said, "No, little one, you stay here."

Phillip exclaimed, "I want to go with you Ma mee."

She observed a sincere innocence, yet an intensity in his eyes. She is aware there is something, as she often had experienced with Phillip. She just does not know what it is, about the resolute expectant look he has on his face. With that thought, she wrapped him in her arms and said, "You come with me then."

Seeking to be Loved

Before they reached the door, it opened. The Priest was greeted by one of the children. The eldest son, who is nine years of age said, "Good morning Father, come in."

When the mother saw the priest, she began to cry.

Marilda, entered the home with Phillip in her arms. She instantly realized Phillip is about the same age as the woman's ill son. She is embarrassed that she had brought him in, he is so healthy, robust, and vibrant; compared to the child they are about to see. She put him down and instructed him, "Go to your father." She turned to face the woman standing with the priest.
Phillip stayed right behind her.

The priest introduced Marilda Natalie Gagnon, to the woman.

The woman apologized for her tears. She welcomed them to her home, and offered them a seat. She sat next to the priest and said, "Father I am glad you came. I have many questions. My faith is being shaken. My husband and I have tried to do the right thing. Why has God let this happen to us? I pray that he will make my handicapped child, grow healthy, strong and will be whole like other children."

The priest, with a gentleness in his eyes and sincere tone in his voice, looked at the woman taking her hand. He said, "His spirit is whole. It is the body, that is only temporary."

"Father I pray, and I ask every day that God grant me the patience needed to care for and accept my child as he is, and not be anxious and angry."

In the same soft caring voice, he said, "Patience is a byproduct of tribulations: it is not granted my dear, it is learned."

"Father, I asked God each day to spare us the pain, and suffering of seeing my son not growing and developing normally."

The priest, patted her hand, and whispered softly, "Suffering draws you apart from worldly cares, and brings you closer to your heavenly father."

"Oh Father, I pray to God each day for happiness, to make my family happy. I want all my children to laugh, and play as others do. I

Seeking to be Loved

pray for my son, that he would experience joy. I do not even know if he is able to, or can even experience what it is to be happy." She wailed again.

His compassion is obvious, it can be seen in his expressions, heard in his voice, and felt within one's own heart. "I know it is hard to understand. I would like to understand how and why things in life exist. I do know this; God gives us blessings every day. Happiness is up to us."

"Father, I pray every day and many times during the day, for God, some way, somehow, to give us the things, my son needs to enjoy life."

He answered, "My dear, God gives us life; so that we may enjoy all things."

"Oh Father, I feel that my spirit and faith is fading, as my son's body has stopped growing, and is at a standstill. I asked God to help it, to help make my spirit grow again. Alas, I get no answers."

He leaned toward her and whispered again. "The spirit is given to you. You must make it grow on your own. God always offers us what we need for our spirit to flourish. It is how we receive and perceive it, and then how we use it, that determines whether or not we may allow our own spirit to grow and benefit from its fruits."

The woman is silent for a moment. She stood and walked out of the room. She returned with the infant cradled in her arms. She sat next to the priest, "Father look at him. He breathes and occasionally moves. His eyes are open. Look how there is no expression in them. It is as if he stays within his own body and mind. I do not know if he is aware of me." The tears begin again.

Marilda wanted to wrap her arms around the woman, to comfort her. She wished she could say, or do something to ease the woman's pain.

Phillip peeked from around the chair his mother is sitting in. She had not been aware that he was there. She assumed he went to Gilbert. He walked toward the child. Marilda reached to stop him, but something demanded, **"Let him be."**

Seeking to be Loved

She drew herself back into her seat. The others did not notice him. They were just staring at the child. The priest, not knowing what else to say, just observed the mother, who he knew felt dejected from her silence and lack of response.

Phillip touched the child's foot and gave it a little wiggle. The priest and the woman immediately noticed the sparkle in the child's eyes. It was the first time in a few years she noticed the look of awareness, in her baby's expression. It was a look of recognition, between a child and its mother.

Marilda saw the glow on the mother's face and she followed the tears from the woman's cheeks as they dropped onto the face of the child. It was then that she noticed the child was smiling at the one holding him.

Phillip looked at the priest, who had reached over to caress the face of the woman. He said to him, in his four-year-old voice, "It's a happy baby."

The woman said, as she looked at the Priest, then up to the ceiling, "Thank you God! Thank you, God!"

Marilda scooped Phillip, into her arms and walked out the door.

Phillip asked her, "Why are you crying Ma mee?"

She just said as her own tears flowed, "My dear sweet child, My dear sweet child."

Gilbert and the others asked her, "What is wrong?"

She just put up her hand and was silent. When she was able to speak, she looked at Gilbert and all the children and expressed, "We are so blessed." Then sternly told them, more explicitly warned them.

"Do not any one of you, ever dare forget it."

Seeking to be Loved

Chapter 15 <u>Short stay</u>

The O'Sullivan's welcomed them to their farm, and were happy to offer them room and board. The farm had two vacant rooms in the boarding house for their workers. They let the Guyons, choose how they would like to use them. It was suggested they split up and have the girls in one, boys in the other. Another suggestion was for Marilda and Gil to stay in one with all the children in the other. It was left up to them.

Marilda and Gil decided dividing the sexes, would be the most comfortable thing to do for all. They only expected to stay a few days, or until they could find their own place to live.

Mr. O'Sullivan told Gil he would be paid two dollars a week, and that was only for Gil. The others were expected to work for their board. They were glad to have a place to stay, at least until they met up with Gil's brothers.

Gil assured Mr. O'Sullivan that his family would willingly work. He hoped he would hear from at least one of his brothers soon, so that they could determine their next move to settle themselves.

"Well and good then. Let me show you where you can keep your wagon and introduce you to Bill. He will direct your work for the day," said Mr. O'Sullivan.

The Guyons were satisfied with their present arrangement for the time being. Gilbert was getting anxious about his brothers. Three weeks had passed and now they were well into the month of August. He still had not heard from either one of them. Every Sunday they talked with the priest, hoping for news of them. Each week Gilbert would say to Nattie on the way to the Sunday service, "Wouldn't it be wonderful if they and their families are waiting for us there."

The priest kept in touch with other pastors, and priests in the area. There was no news of his brothers. Each Sunday Gilbert was hopeful there would be word of them, or someone had met them. He was confident someone would have information about his brothers whereabouts.

Seeking to be Loved

George stopped by the old address, where he and his family had stayed before moving. On two occasions, both times no one was home, and they never got the message that Gilbert had left for them. The brothers had similar priorities on their mind. They wanted to get their families settled into their new homes and communities. They figured they would have an opportunity to find their brother soon enough. Once they themselves were settled and providing for the immediate needs of their family, they would start a more serious search for each other. In the meantime, they would continue to ask about Gilbert and his family, as to their whereabouts. They would keep their eyes and ears open for any news, or letter, from who knows where.

They were confident one day soon, they would find him. "He will just show up," they thought, "Just like he did in Canada."

August, is a busy time on a farm. The dairy is always busy requiring milking twice a day. This is the time of year when produce ripens and needed to be gathered and brought to market. The grass has grown well for hay. It is ready to cut, dried and stored in the barns to feed the livestock through the long New England winter.

Each season on the farm is exciting. There is always work to be done, it becomes more intense, as fall neared. There is not much time to think about other things, for each day is full of tasks needing attention.

Marilda was not pleased with the cramped quarters. The farm itself was expansive enough and throughout the day all were busy. She longed for her own home, where she could spread out her things, instead of being limited to such compact quarters. She did not like having little to no privacy. She had grown accustomed to having a place, and space, where she could retreat for some peace and quiet. She cherished the time with her family, as it was when in France and had been in Québec.

The O'Sullivans were good people; they provided for the needs of their workers. The workers, who were all men except for

Seeking to be Loved

Marilda and the girls. They were courteous and pleasant when in their presence, however often crude and belligerent when not.

The walls between the rooms and the hallways leading to each room offered little buffer to noise. One could readily take part in any conversation that was taking place, on the other side, without having to raise one's voice much beyond a comfortable level. Let us just say, sounds from those in the adjacent rooms, depending on the volume even from across the hall, were quite disturbing. Often the sounds were very unpleasant and just as often, disgusting. She worried about the children being exposed to such language and behaviors. It was difficult enough for her, as a parent to teach proper manners, and etiquette, without examples of the opposite, constantly on display day and night.

She and Gilbert spoke daily, about needing to find their own place to raise their family. They both knew the wage that he was earning on the farm would never allow them the opportunity to save enough to purchase their own property, nor to rent elsewhere, away from the farm. They had their savings minus two hundred dollars he had given to his brother to find a residence for them. Gilbert told Marilda that as soon as the harvest season was over, he would look for employment elsewhere, unless, of course, they got news from the others. Hopefully finding other work would not be difficult as industry was booming in the Northeast.

Marilda's days were long. She assumed kitchen duties, meal preparation, canning and preserving food for all the farm hands. It was a day in, day out routine, with assistance from Mary and Blanche.

Joseph and Phillip, had their own chores and duties assigned by Marilda. Joseph preferred to be out with the older boys and men. He took every opportunity he could to be with them, as did Phillip. Although Phillip was still too small, the men would not tolerate him being in the way or under foot.

Four weeks have passed, and it was mid-August. Marilda was showing signs of weariness from her long days. She looked forward

Seeking to be Loved

to the winter season. Her main duty then would be meal preparation, which she enjoyed.

It was a pleasant August morning; Marilda, normally would rise early, to prepare hot coffee. Usually the men were awakened by the smell of fresh coffee brewing, not this morning. The men were up at 4:00AM to start the morning milking.

The rooster's crow woke Gil. He looked in on his wife and the girls, their room was next to his and the boys. He noticed she was still sleeping beside Blanche. Her breath was heavy and a bit labored. He decided to let her sleep, he knew how tired she had been, from the many long days.

Not long after Gil left, Marilda was awakened by the sounds of grumbling from the men. They were angry not having coffee before they went to the milk room. She had spoiled them. She quickly threw on her kitchen dress, apron, and rushed to prepare coffee. Then started preparations for the rest of the breakfast meal. Mary joined her and was followed shortly, by Blanche. When the coffee was ready, Marilda had the girls bring the pot and as many cups as they could carry to the milk room. She instructed them to apologize, for her not having the coffee available before they left the house.

After breakfast duties when dishes had been washed and put away, Marilda told the girls, Joseph, and Phillip, to go to the garden. She wanted them to pick all the ripe vegetables. She would ask Mrs. O'Sullivan for more canning jars to clean and sterilize. "If you come back with an excess of vegetables for the noon and evening meal, we will start canning," she explained to them.

"Is it fall already Ma mee?" Phillip asked. Even at his young age he associated picking vegetables and canning as something done during Autumn. "I like the fall Ma mee, when the weather turns cool and the leaves get pretty."

"No, my dear, it is still summer, there are many vegetables already ripening. The first of the season; fruit of our labor. We must prepare and enjoy their goodness."

Seeking to be Loved

"This is my favorite time of the year," she told Phillip.
"Why Ma mee?"
"Oh, the same reasons you like this time. Fruit and vegetables ripen. There are lots of good things to eat. I enjoy the delicious smells when canning, baking, and preserving the goods. Plus, soon some of the trees will start to show their pretty colors. I also, love the cool weather of fall. It means Autumn and winter are coming soon when life becomes dormant. A time for many to rest and refresh themselves, so they can burst forth with new life in the spring.

To me, my dear Phillip, it is a lesson in life. Spring bursts forth with new life. You labor through the spring and summer. When the fall months come, it is time to gather and prepare for the cold winter. To reap the harvest you worked for. When you do those things, you can enjoy a nice warm cozy house, with lots of good food, to share with those you love.

Just like people, we are born, grow, if we are cared for, we produce good fruit. Then we grow old, whither and one day we die, and are born again to a new life with God and his angels. Like you, my little angel!" She scooped him up, wrapped her arms around him and squeezed him tight.

He squeezed her neck and said, "Je t'aime, I mean, I love you Ma mee."

She watched them leave the boarding house, grabbing a basket on the porch and walking to the garden. She felt a heaviness in her chest, and found it difficult to take a deep breath to relieve it. She prepared to go to the O'Sullivan's farmhouse across the barnyard. Upon opening the door, she suddenly became very dizzy and felt as though she was going to collapse. She made her way to a chair in the kitchen, struggling to catch her breath and could not understand why. She thought, "I've not done anything yet, and I slept late. I should be well rested."

After a few minutes she felt as though she was breathing normally again. She got up, turned, and walked to the door. She

Seeking to be Loved

made it across the porch to the steps before she had to sit down again. She thought she must be coming down with a cold. She halfway expected it. She had not rested well the last few weeks.

The children came back with full baskets, no more than a half hour from the time they left. They found their mother sound asleep on the porch. Mary immediately asked, "Are you all right Mother?" She could not recall a time when she saw her mother asleep during mid-morning, or any time of the day. She looked pale. Mary turned to Joseph, and told him to find Father.

The commotion woke Marilda. She had not realized she had been asleep. She felt confused when she opened her eyes, thinking to herself, "It is daylight. What am I doing here?"

"Where am I?" she asked Mary. She was not making sense, of why she was sitting on the porch.

"Was I sleeping?" she finally asked Mary.

"Yes, are you feeling okay Mother?"

"I think so. I just feel tired, and dizzy. I remember now I was getting ready to go to the farmhouse to get canning jars. I needed to sit down to catch my breath. It was so odd, I remember thinking that I must be coming down with something. I think I am okay now." When she stood, suddenly she felt weak and had to sit back down.

"I sent Joseph to find Father." Mary told her mother.

"I do not think there is need for that. You just help me back to the kitchen. We need to start dinner if it is to be ready at noon."

Mary said, "I do not think you should worry about dinner or supper, Mother. We will take care of that, and if we need help, I will get Mrs. O'Sullivan. Let us get you to bed for now, so you can rest. You always told us when we were sick, or, not feeling well, to stay in bed. The rest will do us good. That is what you need to do now."

"I think you are right Mary, right now it feels like that is all I can do. You and Blanche, help me to get upstairs. Thank you, my dears."

Mary was frightened by the paleness and the coolness of her mother's skin. She and Blanche helped their mother get in bed. Mary

Seeking to be Loved

told Blanche, "You stay with Mother, until Father gets here. I am going to get Mrs. O'Sullivan. I will tell her about Mother. She may need a doctor."

"Okay, Mary. Do you think she will be all right?" Blanche asked, while tears filled her eyes.

Phillip was standing silent in the doorway, observing, he was not sure what to think. He was as worried as a four-year-old could be. The person he loved most in the world, was needing help just to stand and change clothes. He only knew something was terribly wrong, she did not look like his Ma mee. He just wanted to help her, to make her feel better. He wanted her to look at him with her warm, loving eyes, that made his whole life and world light up. He did not sob, though he felt streams of tears running off his cheeks.

Mary led Mrs. O'Sullivan, to the room where they laid their mother. Upon seeing her and surveying her appearance, stated, "I will send for the doctor right away." Leaving the bunkhouse, she met Gilbert at the door. "Your wife is very sick, I am sending for a doctor right now, go to her."

Gilbert thanked her, then rushed past. Hurrying upstairs, he did not notice Phillip standing just inside the doorway. His eyes were riveted on his wife's face, he never seen it so pale, not even on the coldest day of winter. He bumped into Phillip knocking him to the floor. Mary picked him up and held him. He never made a sound, although tears never stopped rolling off his cheeks, he just stared at his mother. He heard his father ask her, "What happened?" Gil took his hand rubbed it across her forehead lightly brushing her hair from the side of her face.

Marilda opened her eyes at the sound of Gilbert's voice. Phillip noticed the slightest of smiles appear from her lips, her face still ashen. Phillip wondered why the smile did not radiate about her whole face, and brighten the room, like it usually did. Yet he acknowledged from the slightest smile on his mother's lips, the brightness that started to shine in his own little heart. He felt the warmth of that little smile from where Mary held him across the

399

Seeking to be Loved

room. Moments later he noticed the warmth of the tears had disappeared. He can feel the tautness on his cheek as they dried.

Gilbert whispered, "Nattie, Nattie what happened? I think you have been doing too much, for too long, your days are so long my dear." He knew it was more than just fatigue, he had a fearful suspicion inside, this was different. He was afraid to think about it. He leaned toward her, kissed her on the forehead so lightly, he whispered, "Rest now my sweet."

There was no response from Nattie, her eyes were closed again. She appeared to be sleeping, the small trace of the smile still on her lips.

Gil slowly drew himself away. It was odd seeing her ill. He turned to his children and suggest, "We will let her rest until the doctor gets here." He escorted them downstairs to the kitchen.

Nearly three hours had passed, before the doctor arrived. He was ushered into the room where Marilda laid. He promptly initiated an examination, upon listening to her heart and lungs he made a quick diagnosis. "Lobar pneumonia, I suspect," he said aloud. "How long has she had trouble breathing?"

Gilbert glanced at Mary, then the doctor and said, "She was fine this morning at breakfast. That was the last time I saw her. She slept a little late this morning, although she seemed fine then. He turned and glanced at Mary, she nodded her head in agreement. My son came to the field to get me. He told me she was sick, that was three hours ago."

The doctor appeared puzzled. Gilbert asked, "What is it?"

The doctor explained it usually takes days for the lungs to collect this much fluid, she would have been coughing and had struggled with breathing long before this morning. "I have seen others already the last few days, two before arriving here, with similar symptoms and the onset this quickly as well."

Gilbert asked whether she needed to be taken to the hospital?

Seeking to be Loved

The doctor was deep in thought. His hesitation was brief, before he answered Gilbert. His first response is yes, his immediate second, is she should not be moved. She should be isolated, in case her condition is contagious. Not wanting to cause undue fear to the patient or family he advised, "Not just yet." He offered the usual advice, rest, plenty of fluids, if she is able to swallow it thoroughly and completely. Otherwise just rest and keep her comfortable, watch for the signs of fever. If she gets feverish, keep her body cool.

"I will check back again tomorrow morning, in the meantime keep her comfortable and avoid contact, as much as possible, Especially concerning the younger children, I advise you to keep them away from her."

Gilbert recognized the concern in the doctor's expression. He is aware of the fact that he is not saying all that he is thinking. He walked the doctor to the door and assured him, that he will follow his orders and keep a close eye on her.

The doctor reminded him to avoid contact with her as much as you can. He recommended wearing a kerchief over his mouth and nose, when caring for her, as a precautionary measure. He reminded him, "Keep the children away from her, as much as possible. Have them stay out of the room, for now. I will see you tomorrow, good afternoon."

Gilbert watched the doctor ride off, then he returned inside. He gathered the children around him in the sitting room. He explained to them what the doctor said, about staying away from their mother. The younger children began whimpering, he put his finger to his mouth to shush them. Only he and Mary will check in on her, and that we must wear a kerchief around our nose and mouth.

Gilbert stayed beside his beloved wife, throughout the night. He had blankets laying on the floor close to the bed, so he can rest and sleep by her side. The girls stayed in the other room with their brothers. Gil wanted to be close and attend her needs whenever they may arise. He was woken many times throughout the night. She struggled to breathe. He repeatedly repositioned her, hoping it

Seeking to be Loved

would help her breathe more efficiently. The night dragged on endlessly, never appearing to end. Gilbert prayed fervently, asking God to comfort her and give her strength to help her breathe, and get well.

It seemed every moment he finally dozed off to sleep, he would be roused. The sound of his wife coughing had grown weaker, and more pathetic with each passing hour. The sound of her struggle to breathe, was so disheartening, he could hardly bare it. All he could say was, "Dear God, Dear God, please comfort this woman."

He was so glad to hear the rooster crow. Dawn had finally come. He hoped the doctor would arrive soon. He heard the other men preparing to leave to start the milking chores. He felt no need to tell them he would not be there.

The dawn was near and sun rising, he was glad to see Marilda's eyes open. He knew that this was a good sign. He quickly hovered over her and knelt down beside her holding her hand in his. He patted her forehead, and moved her hair gently with his left hand. She looked so terribly weak and pale. Although he noticed a gleam in her eyes. She whispered to him; he could not understand her. He kneeled beside her, leaned closer, and turned his ear to hear the sounds coming from her lips.

She told him, "Get the children." She had to catch her breath. "Have them come in one at a time."

"The doctor suggested that they stay away," said Gil.

She squeezed his hand, met his eyes, and said, with a barely audible voice. "Bring them to me." **"Now."**

Gilbert hesitated, she struggled to propped herself up in her bed. She used both of her hands to run her fingers through her hair. She wiped her eyes and face, pinched her cheeks. With each movement she seemed to grow stronger and more alert.

Gilbert observed the loving glow, that emanated from her face, his heart filled with excitement, he thanked God.

She looked at Gilbert and said, "Start with Mary, then Ernest, the others in order oldest to youngest."

Seeking to be Loved

He went to wake Mary. He had not realized that she was already up, in the kitchen and had prepared coffee for the workers. She, Mrs. O'Sullivan along with Blanche, were preparing breakfast. He went to her and told her, "Your mother is awake and would like to see you. She had a rough night, but looks a little better," he added.

A grin appeared on Mary's face, she clapped her hands and proclaimed, "How wonderful and ran upstairs." She entered the room, her mother smiled. She motioned for her to come forward, and told her, "Close the door." Mary approached her mother, Marilda raised her hand to stop her, she whispered and gestured for her to tie on her kerchief.

Mary took it from her pocket, and tied it behind her neck. She pulled it over her mouth and nose. Mary approached the bed and her mother reached for her hand. They both smiled at each other. Mary spoke first, expressing how pleased she was that her mother is feeling better. She said to her, "You must rest and be at ease, until you are well."

Marilda smiled and began, "Mary, you are quite a capable young lady, and I am very proud of you." She reached out her hand and caressed Mary's face, with her fingertips on her cheek and her palm caressing her jaw. She communicated to Mary, "There is so many things I want you to know about womanhood."

Mary placed her hand over her mother's, and pressed it tightly against her face. "Mother, you have taught me so much already."

Smiling, Marilda stated, "There is much you still do not know. I am afraid, (she hesitated a moment) I will not be able to guide you. You will have to experience the milestones, in your life, that all women must face. I want you to know, I am always with you, and always looking over you. Look after your brothers and sisters, do not be afraid to correct them. Obey your father's wishes, always do what is expected of you and more.

Stay healthy, grow strong, always love, and serve God.

Seeking to be Loved

Be joyful, for it makes life easier and more pleasant.
Be considerate of everyone and everything in all that you do.
Do not ever, never ever give up hope, no matter what you are faced with or up against. Hope breeds faith and nourishes it, with faith in God, everything is possible."

Marilda felt Mary's tears, fill the valleys between her fingers. Soaking her and Mary's hand, that is being pressed even tighter against her daughters' face.

"Mother, you are going to get better!"

Marilda smiled at her daughter. "My time has come, I love you so much, you have blessed my life in so many ways. You were the first blessing from my womb. You paved the way for your brothers and sister. You must continue to do so."

They embraced, Marilda told Mary, to have her father bring Ernest.

Gilbert already had him waiting outside the door when Mary exited. Gilbert patted him on the shoulder, he entered into the room. Then he turned to Mary who was weeping, she hurried downstairs. He wanted to go after her, he decided to let her go. Gil wanted to understand why she was weeping, he would find out later, now he must get Henry.

Marilda gestured for Ernest, to come forward and close the door. He turned and stepped toward his mother, tying the kerchief around the back of his head. She patted her bed, so he would come sit by her side. She managed such a pleasant, proud look in her eyes when he sat beside her. Her weakened state could not prevent her from smiling.

Ernest who was apprehensive when he saw Mary leaving the room, now was a bit more relieved.

He asked what he thought to be obvious, "Are you feeling better mother?"

"I am feeling fine, I cannot help but feel fine every time I see you. I remember the day I first saw your face, there was something

Seeking to be Loved

so magical about it. We were just drawn to each other. I believe God, always intended for me to be your mother, and I am so proud of you.

You have grown to be a fine young man. You work so hard and diligently at your father side. You can out work any two grown men. She gurgled, covering her mouth as she coughed. The smile was still there when she removed her hands.

Ernest smiled, he does not know what to say to his mother. He only vaguely remembers that first meeting. He knows he was always loved and never felt anything different. Nothing more, nothing less, than all the other Guyon children.

His mother told him, "You have set an example for your brothers. You must always do so, you are the oldest, you must guide them and keep them on the right path. You have always been your father's son, his right hand. Continue to help him and keep the others in line. Guide them by your examples, as you always have.

Always do what is expected of you and more.

Stay healthy, grow strong, always love, and serve God.

Be joyful, for it makes life easier and more pleasant.

Be considerate of everyone and everything in all that you do.

Do not ever, never ever give up hope, no matter what you are faced with or up against. Hope breeds faith and nourishes it, with faith in God, everything is possible.

She reached out both her arms, so she could draw Ernest to her, as they embrace, she wept. She struggled to say the words, for they are deeply heartfelt and expressed with great emotion. She said to him, "You were my first gift from God, I love you and will always love you dearly." She whispered, "Get your brother Henry, I love you son."

Ernest stood up and said, "I love you mother." He turned and opened the door. Then with a head nod, he motioned Henry to go in.

Marilda, finished wiping her eyes and smiled broadly. "Henry, Henry, Henry my dear boy, come in here and give your mother a big hug." When they embrace, she has muffled laughter; it could not hide the gurgling sounds deep within her chest.

Seeking to be Loved

She expressed to Henry, "You brought such joy to your father's and my life. You have always been so rambunctious, so eager in all things that you do. You are growing to be a fine young man. You seem to enjoy life and every aspect of it, like no other. Doing so you bring much joy to those around you. Trace your father's and your older brother's footsteps, until you find your own path my son."

Always do what is expected of you and more.

Stay healthy, grow strong, always love, and serve God.

Be joyful, for it makes life easier and more pleasant.

Be considerate of everyone and everything in all that you do.

Do not ever, never ever give up hope, no matter what you are faced with or up against. Hope breeds faith and nourishes it, with faith in God, everything is possible.

She reached her arms out to draw him in for another loving embrace. She felt her own weakness and musters everything she can to squeeze him tightly against her. She whispered to him, "Have Gilbert come in." Upon releasing her embrace, she nearly faints.

Henry asked, "Are you all right mother?"

She pleads silently, "Dear God not this moment, just a little longer." Opening her eyes, Henry recognized the lovingly gleam and brightness he always saw in his mothers' eyes.

He said, "You had me worried for a moment."

She nodded and said, "Get your brother, I love you Henry and I will always love you!"

Leaving the room with a semi-smile on his face he opened the door. He looked at Gilbert and points with his thumb and said, "It is your turn."

Gilbert entered and closed the door behind him.

Henry wrapped his arms around his father and began to cry, intentionally muffling the sound against his father's chest.

"Come here Gilbert," Marilda waves motioning him to come here beside her. "My big boy," she said, then rephrased the statement, "My young man." Smiling she took a breath, then began, "You always wanted to grow up before your time. Always wanting to

Seeking to be Loved

work side-by-side with your older brothers and your father, and proved you can. You are your father's namesake and are very much like him."

Gilbert my son, always do what is expected of you and more. Stay healthy, grow strong, always love, and serve God.
Be joyful, for it makes life easier and more pleasant.
Be considerate of everyone and everything in all that you do.
Do not ever, never ever give up hope, no matter what you are faced with in life, or up against. Hope breeds faith and nourishes it, with faith in God, everything is possible.

Promise me this Gilbert, that in your rush to grow up, you never lose the magic of your youth."

"I will mother, I mean, I won't, I think? You know what I mean."

"Yes, I do." Marilda nodded, then grasped his right hand bringing it to her face and holds it with both her hands and kisses the back of it. Teared stream from her eyes, she squeezed them shut tightly to stop the flow. She attempted to take a deep breath and coughed, struggling to make room in her lungs. She managed to say, "I love you Gilbert and I always will. Go now, get your sister."

Gilbert opened the door to see his father and Blanche standing there. He stepped sideways as his father gave Blanche a gentle push from behind, as she walked in past Gilbert. Little Gil stepped past her and looked at his father. They both can barely hear Marilda, instruct Blanche, to close the door. Little Gil looked up at his father who knelt down in front of him, they just look at each other. Then wrap their arms around each other. No words were spoken between them.

Marilda, managed a grin and presents a happy tone in her voice, despite the struggle to breathe which is taking every bit of her concentration. Please Lord, just a little longer; her mind pleads.

Looking at Blanche, she reached out her arms and said, "My Dear Sweet child. Mother's little helper, how much you have grown. My dear one, how helpful you have become. You have done a very

Seeking to be Loved

good job, keeping your little brothers in line and helping your sister and I. You will make some man very happy someday and raise fine children. Blanche promise me, you will always do what is expected of you and more.

Stay healthy of mind and body, grow strong, always love, and serve God.

Be joyful, for it makes life easier and more pleasant.

Be considerate of everyone and everything in all that you do.

Do not ever, never ever give up hope, no matter what you are faced with or up against. Hope breeds faith and nourishes it, with faith in God, everything is possible.

Mind your father and your older brothers and sister. Keep a watchful eye on Joseph and Phillip. I love you my Dear Blanche, and I always will."

They embrace cheek to cheek, Marilda cradles her head with her hand pressing the child against her.

Blanche squeezed her around her neck and cried, "I love you Ma mee, I hope you get well soon."

"I do not want to let go of you. Mais(But)I need you, to get your brother Joseph. I love you dear, I always will."

Blanche opened the door and took off her kerchief and sent Joseph to go see their mother. Gilbert picked her up, they are face to face, "I hope Ma mee gets better soon."

"Yes, we all do honey." "We all do," said her father.

"Come here Joseph my dear son." She coughed, and tried to gather air into her lungs. Motioning for him to pull up his kerchief. When he does, he looked like a little bandit, in his everyday work/play clothes. He has a rough and rowdy look about him, the sight of him is comical. She cannot help but smile and almost giggled at the sight of his appearance.

"Hop up here next to me," she urged patting the mattress. "You like all your brothers are following the footsteps of your father. Hard-working, full of mischief and always ready to lend a helping hand. You my dear son are the fun-loving one."

Seeking to be Loved

So many, comical memories flashed before her, of the little boy. Thoughts of incidences, snippets of time, Joseph's actions, and antics. She wanted to laugh, as she had many times before when reminiscing of them. Her giggle turned to a gasping for air, then to a quivering tearfulness. She realized those memories have passed and will be her last.

"What is the matter Ma mee, are you not feeling good?"

She pulled him close beside her with her arm draped over his shoulder. With her left hand she wiped her tears from her eyes, face, and mouth. She managed to compose herself, enough to speak. "You have brought much joy and laughter into our home; you have a wonderful gift. I must ask of you, a big favor and give you a great responsibility."

"What is it Ma mee?" he stated questioningly. "I do not think I can do a big responsibility. I think I can do a little responsibility," he expressed in a suggestive tone.

She cannot help but giggle again, as she acknowledged, Joseph is Joseph, and will always bring such joy, to those around him. It is his simple honesty and openness, that defuses and makes light of many troublesome situations.

"Are you ready?" she asked.

"Yes," he said with the excitement he always seemed to possess. "What is it?" He asked as he turned his head and body to face her.

"I want you to be like a guardian angel." She observed the smile growing across his face and a sparkle in Joseph's eyes. She had to pause to relish and absorb the cheerful child, puffing his little self up to hear her request.

"I do not know if I can do that, I do not know what a guardian angel does."

"Oh, you can do this." She expressed with an absolute assuredness in her tone. He perked up even more, he is eager and can hardly wait to hear his mother's request.

Seeking to be Loved

"I want you to keep a very close eye on your brother Phillip, I want you to teach him to be brave and bold like you. He has your name as his middle one, so that is why I want you to be responsible to keep him safe. Teach him to enjoy life and every aspect of it, just like you.

I want you to look out for him, until he is old enough to look out for himself. Will you do that, Joseph?"

"I think I can do that Ma mee, but you know he can be a stubborn little rascal." He made that clear to his mother.

She nods her head, then managed a little chuckle in agreement. It required all the self-control she can generate within herself, not to cough and choke. She supports him saying, "I know if anyone could teach him those things, it is you Joseph."

She observed the look of confidence on his face, that her praise instilled in him. She nodded her head and told him, "I know you will do a fine job."

"Turn now to look at me," she proceeds on to utter the words that she hopes will leave a lasting impression on her children. The words that will echo in their minds, that will guide them, on life's journey.

"Listen to me my son with your heart and your ears.

Always do what is expected of you and more.

Stay healthy of mind and body, grow strong, always love, and serve God.

Be joyful, for it makes life easier and more pleasant.

Be considerate of everyone and everything in all that you do.

Do not ever, never ever give up hope, no matter what you are faced with or up against. Hope breeds faith and nourishes it, with faith in God, everything is possible."

"Give your mother a hug Joseph." She asked him as she held him tight against her. Her arms are going limp, she is losing strength, she does not want to let go. She is doing all that she can to hold on. Life is leaving her body.

Seeking to be Loved

She thinks to herself, "I have one more, I must be strong for him." Marilda is silent as is Joseph, still propped against her with their arm draped over each other. He felt the slackening of his mother's embrace, she becomes ever so faint. He slowly draws himself back.

"I love you my dear son and I always will, go now and have Phillip to come see me." As Joseph is ready to open the door to leave the room, she managed in a barely audible voice, "Have your father wait two minutes before sending Phillip in."

"Okay mommy! Can I take this kerchief off now?"

She started to giggle, then gasp for breath, nodded. She thought to herself, "Joseph is so fun-loving, I am going to miss him. I am going to miss them all so much."

She wanted to sob, she knew she must not. She only has a few moments to muster the strength, she is going to need now. She knew it is going to take everything she has left to keep her composure.

Every fiber in her being wants to fight, she knows not what, or, how. She only understood her time is at hand. She must use every single moment she has left to instruct, prepare, and protect her children. "I must hold on," she reminds herself.

"My job is not yet finished!" she screams in her mind. She feels as though she is abandoning them, the very thought haunts her. Life is fading with each breath and she feels herself weakening with each second. She refused to forsake them before they have all the tools they need for life.

Due to the lack of oxygen her lungs absorb, she became confused. She wondered, "What is this I am experiencing. Why such emotion, why this feeling? It is strange," she searched within her depths for an answer, for this sense of urgency within her. "I was fine yesterday, maybe a little tired. Why is it, I must say these things to my children? Why is it I know I must say these things now, this instant?"

Seeking to be Loved

Her subconscious knows her time has come, she regained clarity.

The door began to open, she took a breath and noticed a little hand grasp the edge of the door. It does not open any further. In a moment she acknowledged, Phillip is holding the door as his father is attempting to open it.

He does not want to come in. He knows something is not right with the person most dear to him.

She understands, she sensed his fear, his sadness. She knew he is aware something terrible is about to happen. She wants to encourage him, with the most confident, loving voice, the voice that he is so familiar. The voice that always created the grandest smile on his face and the brightest sparkle to his eyes.

"Dear God, she cried in her mind, let me see it one last time."

She managed to say in her loving mothers' tone, "Phillip come sit beside your mother." The lump in her throat and welling of tears filling her eye lids, prevent her from saying another word.

She noticed Gilbert had to force the door open. The door dragged Phillip forward, because he would not let it go. She saw the kerchief covering his little face. The image was a godsend, it made her smile, although she still cannot speak. It is the tautness in her throat, all she could do was lean forward and extend her arms. That was all he needed, he let go of the door. He ran to his mother. He climbed up on the bed and wrapped his arms around her neck. She could not hold back any longer, she wailed from the depths of her being and the tears ran forth.

Phillip could only say, "Je t'aime, Ma mee, je t'aime Ma mee." He pulled off his kerchief and kissed his mother on her neck as they hugged each other.

Gilbert still in the room, stepped to the bedside leaned over to pull Phillip's mask backup on his face.

Phillip removed it immediately, and kissed his mother on the neck again, repeating "Je t'aime Ma mee."

Gilbert leaned over to pulled up the kerchief once again.

Seeking to be Loved

Marilda held up her hand to stop him, and managed to say, "God will protect this child."

Gil nodded his head and gingerly stepped back.

Marilda took breaths, opened her mouth several times to speak, no words can come. Language cannot express what she held in her heart. Their connection transcends that of any typical mother child relation.

She could only moan, which came from her inner most being and repeat his name, Phillip, Phillip. She held him for what she knew would be the last time on earth.

She prayed, "Dear God, you have been kind and gracious for all of our lives. You have blessed me several times over and I thank you. I ask for just a little more strength and a few more moments. Please give me the words that will guide my child through life."

She finally heard herself say, "Phillip look at me."

He slowly draws away, sitting on her lap facing her. He sees the familiar glow coming from her face. The light and sparkle, the love and warmth in her eyes. He smiled and his tears stop.

Looking at him, she said, "Phillip Joseph Gagnon, that name has such great character. You have been through much in your few years of life and still, you have your whole life ahead you.

Mind your father, brothers, and sisters.

Always do what is expected of you and more.

Grow healthy of mind, body, and spirit, grow strong, always love, and serve God and you will do great and wondrous things my son.

Be joyful, do you hear me? Be joyful, (she repeated with a quivering in her voice) for it makes life easier and more pleasant.

Be considerate of everyone, and everything, in all that you do.

Do not ever, never ever give up hope, no matter what you are faced with or up against in life. Hope breeds Faith and Faith breeds Hope, they nourish each other. With faith in God, everything is possible.

Life can be difficult at times, you would be wise to always strive to do your best.

Seeking to be Loved

Expect the worst and hope for the best in all situations, if you do so, you will never be disappointed.

I love you Phillip and I always will, Au Revoir my dearest, Au Revoir, adieu...... (Goodbye, Go with God.....)"

Phillip, leaned forward and kissed his mother and said, "Au Revoir, Adieu Ma mee." He climbed off the bed, went to the door, opened it to see his father standing there. He said, "Ma mee is sleeping."

Gilbert picked him up and took him downstairs. He brought them to the kitchen where the girls and Mrs. O'Sullivan were preparing the noon dinner for the workers. He told them he was going back upstairs to check on their mother.

Mrs. O'Sullivan said, "The doctor should be here any time now."

"I hope so." Gil said as he left the room. He returned and entered the room where his wife laid pale and lifeless. He had suspected that she had passed, when he picked Phillip up and looked past him, to see his wife. He could not see that she was breathing, she looked still and peaceful. He knelt beside her and lifted her hand to his cheek.

"My Dear Nattie, what happened?   Why are you leaving us now?"

He kissed her forehead, He can only think that God was ready for her. He knew she had worked, hard and long. She was a perfect woman, wife, and mother in his eyes. He thanked God for her and bringing them together. He prayed, "Dear Lord, you giveth and taketh away, when it is right. Your ways are greater than ours, your plans greater and beyond our expectations. Thank you, for this woman, thank you for bringing us together. I do not know how we will get on without her; but I know you do, guide us now, show us the way. Please take her into your vast Heavenly Kingdom and allow her to watch over us especially, her babies."

He kissed her again on her forehead, cheek, and gently on her lips. He said, "You can rest now, my sweet Marilda."

Seeking to be Loved

Exiting the room, he quietly closed the door behind him. Leaned against it, he grits his teeth, tightened his jaw to allow no sound to escape from the agonizing moans, that came forth from within, the deepest recesses of his being. He wanted to scream to release what is exploding within him. Only muffled sounds escape him, as he slid to his knees covered his face and wept silently.

The doctor arrived, Gilbert was not sure how much time had passed, he was still kneeling in front of the door. Although the tears dried long ago. He only wished that he had told her all the things that were in his head and heart. He wanted to tell her one last time, how much he loved her and how wonderful and rich his life had been because of her. He wanted to tell her, what a wonderful wife and mother, she was to their children.

He wanted to hold her, to feel her loving, warm embrace one last time. He wished he had been able to comfort her in her last moment of this life.

The doctor had suspected as much, he knew she had died the moment he saw Gilbert. He asked Gilbert if he may go in. Gil just nodded as he stood up and stepped aside, he followed the doctor into the room, where his wife lay. He watched as the doctor checked for vital signs. He opened her eyes, to see only a blank stare. There was no reaction to the waving of his hand in front of her eyes.

He offered Gilbert his condolence. His immediate concern and fear was that there may be an unknown epidemic. Two of his patients have died just since seeing them yesterday, Marilda being the third. He asked Gilbert, if he may remove the body and have it brought to the hospital's laboratory. He explained, "We would like to run some test. We must attempt, to find the cause for this unknown, and apparently deadly illness."

Gilbert nodded his head in confirmation.

The doctor told him, someone will pick up the body as soon as possible. We will let you know what we find. In the meantime, he instructed Gilbert and Mrs. O'Sullivan, who had joined them, to clean and disinfect everything in the room and everything she may have

Seeking to be Loved

touched the last few days. Things such as the bedding and clothing should be burned, anything that she has touched since the illness appeared, must be cleaned in boiling water. The doctor is anxious, they can tell by the sound of his voice and his actions, while he assembled his things explaining, I must be on my way.

Mrs. O'Sullivan suggest to Gilbert, "You must tell the children, before they come remove the body."

Gilbert said, "I will gather them together and explain their mother is gone."

As Gilbert was leaving the room Mrs. O'Sullivan suggest to him, "Have them come to our house. I will go prepare the front room for you. You will have privacy and a comfortable place to stay with each other for as long as you need."

Gilbert thanked her, "We will be there in a few minutes."

She recommended, "Before you come, collect everything that she has touched in the last two days that you are aware of and just leave it here. I will dispose of them properly, immediately after they take her body away."

"I will do that right now." Gilbert said, as she left the room.

He asked Mary Alice to gather everything she remembers her mother touching in the kitchen. Any cloth items bring to him. He also instructed all his children to wash thoroughly under Mary's supervision. Leave all your clothes you are wearing in a pile on the porch, and put on clean ones. I will meet you all there in twenty minutes."

He burned everything as the doctor instructed.

Mrs. O'Sullivan boiled water to sterilize kitchen items and that which was piled in both their rooms, that were not burned.

With his seven children surrounding him, they made their way to the O'Sullivan's front room, in the big house.

Once they were in the room and seated, Gil informed his children, "God has called your mother home." He prayed for the right words to convey to them. "Her days here are done, her toil on earth is complete. She will rest and play with the angels, until the Lord calls

Seeking to be Loved

us all to his heavenly kingdom. We will miss her here on earth, she without doubt will be watching over all of us every day. Your mother will continue to send her love to us, in many ways. Her love will be in the wind that blows, the sun that shines and warms us. I know we will all feel the soft caress of her hand on our cheek and forehead as a breeze touches our face. It will be in the smell of the flowers, and the food cooking in the kitchen."

Joseph sniffed, "Humm I can smell it now, I can smell croissants and opera cake."

"I can smell relegieuse and mille-feuille," adds Blanche.

Gilbert at that moment sensed and acknowledged his children would be fine. He knew their faith, their resilience and strength. It was the inheritance that their mother gave them as well as her love. It had been demonstrated time and time again through her actions. She prepared them well for the life before them, the joys, struggles, misfortune, and tragedy's such as this.

Phillip cannot understand what was going on around him, during that family meeting. He did know that something about his mother was uniquely different. That it was never going to be the same. He sensed she was going someplace without him. He did not know it would be forever. He did not know, nor, understand he would never see his mother again. He only knew that there was nothing that can possibly separate them from each other's love. He was too young to comprehend what love was, or how to explain it. All he knew, was his mother who created such a radiance that he experienced when in her immediate presence. He could not explain or, understand the uniqueness of this magnificent, glorious, supernatural bond. The love that connected him with this special person in his life. He had no idea, no concept that it was gone forever. To him it was just another day, there was a sadness about it. He knew that before he entered his mother's room earlier. He felt it within him when he left the room.

Seeking to be Loved

How could he know exactly, what it was? He had no way of understanding, the love growing and evolving in him was going to be gone. Gone forever???

The days that followed were solemn, duties, chores, work on the farm continued as always. Mrs. O'Sullivan resumed the meal preparation, as she had done before. She now with Mary and Blanche to assist. Each day they waited for word from the doctor, wanting to know what had become of their mother. Gilbert was concerned about her burial, he mentioned it to the priest when they attended service on Sundays. A week passed, two then three with no word, the priest told Gilbert he would look into it. He told him that he has been visiting the hospital nearly every day.

Many people were falling ill, many were dying, it had been determined that a flu epidemic was sweeping the nation and the world.

Gilbert prayed each day for his children, that God strengthen, protect, and keep them safe from this terrible disease.

The Fall harvest was nearly complete. The work on the farm was busier than ever. All the vegetables had been gathered and preserved in addition to getting them into the markets. The always present daily and immediate requirements of the dairy kept everyone occupied.

Gilbert had acquired a nagging cough. Despite how hard he worked during the day his body seemed to be chilled, requiring extra clothing. This was unusual for him, he always thrived in the chill of the fall, and the briskness of the winter. One morning in the milk room, he started to stand after filling his pale, to pour it into the milk storage cans. He nearly fainted, he needed the assistance of the other men to steady him, until he regained his stability. He emptied his pale and resumed his work, he finished the day. The next morning when he woke and sat on the edge of his bed. He was dizzy, when coming to his feet he dropped to the floor. It was 5AM. Ernest and his brothers helped him back into bed. He had Henry run to the

Seeking to be Loved

house to tell Mr. and Mrs. O'Sullivan. They had one of the farm hands get the wagon ready to take him to the hospital immediately.

All the citizens were instructed to bring anyone falling ill, to the special clinic set up at the hospital. No one was exempt, when they became ill, no matter what the reason, they were to get them there without delay.

Gilbert died that afternoon. Word was sent to the O'Sullivan's. His last request was to give his children his blessing, his weakened state left him with little strength. He knew he had to choose his words wisely, he was nearly too weak to speak. His words to his children were written by an attendant who promised to pass them to his children.

"To all my children, May God Bless you, save you and keep you away from all evil. Always seek first the kingdom of God. Pray that you may always see and hear things in spirit and truth. I love you all, I love you so, I always do and always will."

The messenger for the hospital clinic told the O'Sullivan's and the children, someone from the hospital would be coming to speak with them. That was the only details that they were able to give them. They told them not to worry, arrangements will be made for all remaining family members in some way. They could not give them any other information. They only shared, what they had been strictly instructed to say, to remaining family as what to expect.

All family of those who fell victim to the influenza would be quarantined without exception.

That afternoon they were visited by two women, one was from the hospital the other one introduced herself with a title from the State Department of Health. They wanted to know if anyone was sick or showing any signs and symptoms of the illness, or disease which is spreading so rapidly.

The O'Sullivan's and all those on the farm were examined. None showed any signs or symptoms of illness, nor complained of any. When the two women were convinced no one else was showing

Seeking to be Loved

any symptoms of the epidemic. They conferred with each other in private. It was determined only the two parents had been afflicted. The decision was made, the children will be removed from the farm and isolated, to be observed.

They informed the O'Sullivan's of their decision and asked that they gather them together. The children were told that they would be taken to a special home for observation. They were only to bring two changes of clothes for themselves, nothing else and that they must leave immediately.

The children were ordered to gather the clothes they were to bring, and muster at the carriage waiting for them.

Mary collected the vase and doily on the nightstand of their room. She gave it to Mrs. O'Sullivan, and asked her to keep it in a safe place where the sun will touch it. She had no time to explain, they were hurried on their way.

"I will keep it safe for you." Mrs. O'Sullivan promised.

They had been taken to a home just outside of town. It looked much like an old school. It was an orphanage. They were ushered into a large room. The girls were separated from the boys. Each was instructed to remove all their garments. All clothing was to be placed in the baskets provided, along with other items they brought with them. They were told everything would be washed and sanitized and then returned to them momentarily. They were instructed to bathe themselves thoroughly. Each was given a garment to wear, similar to a nightgown. The children were directed to wait in separate rooms, until the clothes were delivered to them. All items were cleaned, disinfected, and folded neatly in piles when handed to them.

Mary had to comfort Blanche, along with other young girls placed in the same room.

Ernest, Henry, and Gilbert did the same with Joseph and Phillip in another room filled with young boys.

Ernest seemed out of place, he was older than all the rest, more like a man and carried himself as such. He asked the staff about

Seeking to be Loved

his father and mother. They could give him no answers. The only response was, they would look into it.

They were ushered into separate wards for the boys, and for the girls. There were many beds in the room, each had a box underneath to place their clothing and belongings. They were shown where the washroom was located, pans were provided for each. They were instructed how to dispose of the waste and thoroughly clean after each use. They were informed the meals, would be delivered to each ward, and reviewed procedures, they were to follow.

Ernest asked staff how long they would need to stay here?

Their only response was, "For that we cannot be certain, at least until we find that there were no more outbreaks of the influenza." They always added that you were here for your own protection, as well as keeping others safe. Each day he asked about his parent's bodies, and what will become of them. The only response was, "We do not know, you will be informed."

Days turned into weeks, weeks to a month, Thanksgiving had come and gone, Christmas was approaching. Some of the children on the ward did succumb to symptoms and they were quickly removed. Everything they had was removed and incinerated, new mats and bedding were replaced. Soon someone would be added to take possession of it.

For those that showed no sign of illness, for a minimum of two weeks, were released to family or next of kin. Others such as the Guyon's had no place to go. The rumor going around the ward was those who were healthy would leave. Those children not having family, would be put up for adoption. They would be leaving soon, to make room for others on the wards.

Ernest, Mary, Henry, Gilbert, Blanche and even Joseph, were given up to adoption. They were in that order, because of the age and ability to work. It was a plus, they were experienced in farming and domestic work. Phillip and others that were just too young, would not be sort after. They were no benefit to the families

Seeking to be Loved

adopting them. They would not be able to earn their keep. The children knew nothing of where they would be going or the people taking them. Once introduced and interviewed by the people who were adopting. They had all their personal belongings collected and waiting in the hall, for them to take with them.

Despite Ernest and Mary's appeal, not be separated from their brothers and sisters, no heed was given to their request. When they refused to leave, they were escorted out, reassured word would be sent to them of their siblings whereabouts and contact information. This only comforted them somewhat, only enough that they left with the adopting family, vowing to their siblings, they would be together again.

Seeking to be Loved

Chapter 16 <u>New Life</u>

    Phillip had only just turned five, no one was looking for a little boy who could not do a good day's worth of work, or chores. The adopting families out of need wanted children, people who could help. Hands were needed to replace those lost to the illness. Every family lost loved ones, and needed assistance to manage property, farms, businesses, and factory's.

    A baby or young child would only add to the hardship many were already experiencing. Another mouth to feed, in this trying time. No one needed, nor wanted extra duties, or add unwarranted responsibility to their life.

    Phillip wondered every day, what would become of him. He prayed the only way he knew how, the way his mother taught him. He prayed that he would be united with his parents, his brothers, and sisters each day, as soon as he woke before getting out of bed. After he prayed, he remembered the words of his mother, and would repeat them to himself. "To be joyful, it will make life more pleasant for him and those around him."

    That is what he attempted to do each day. He would take time getting to know everyone on his ward. Months had passed, they were well into spring. There was no one on his ward, that was there more than a month ago. They already had been adopted or had gone home with their parents, or other relatives claimed them.

    Phillip became familiar with and knew all the staff, along with the other children as well, that is before they left. He would be the first to wake each morning to play a game, or sometimes even a trick, on those on the ward. He liked to tease and have fun with his ward mates. He kept the atmosphere light, the attending staff, would be on the lookout for what trickery he would be up to today. Not a visit went by without a sound of laughter on that ward.

    It was one day in April right after lunch, one of the attendants told Phillip to gather all his things together. Phillip hoped one of his brothers, or sisters had come to get him and that they would be

Seeking to be Loved

reunited. With excitement he gathered his things and followed the attendant downstairs to an office he had never seen. There were two people waiting inside, when he was ushered in.

He recognized the headmaster, from brief visits he made onto each ward, the other was a woman. When he entered, she turned in the chair that she was sitting, to look at him. A small grin appeared upon the woman's face. His initial impression was she must not smile much. It looked like it felt awkward for her to present it. Young as he was, he sensed that the smile was a forced one, he knew it was not a pleasant one.

The Headmaster introduced, Phillip, to Ms. Rupender. She would like to take you home with her to live. I think you will find it a much more pleasant place than here. You will be able to do all the things that someone your age would normally do and should be doing, might I add. Can you say hello to Ms. Rupender, Phillip?

"Hello Ms. Rudepender," Phillip said, looking down at the floor.

Phillip prayed every day that one of his brothers, sisters, even his mother and father would come get him and take him home.

In the nearly seven months he spent at the orphanage. He saw many come and go. All his brothers and all the other boys on his ward, he was the only constant.

He would greet all the newcomers and despite his young age, the little five-year-old was the concierge of the ward. He took it upon himself to greet, comfort, console and show the newly admitted around the ward. He wanted all who entered to be at ease, and he wanted to befriend them. He made friends quickly, and as quickly it seemed all had left.

He had hoped one day someone would come get him, each night he prayed. He asked God, that tomorrow someone would want him.

He remembered his prayer, at that very moment, when he said hello to the woman.

Seeking to be Loved

The joy and happiness he anticipated was not there, he did not know why. He thought something was missing, it made him wonder? "Finally, someone who wants him was sitting right there. "I should be happy, someone is going to take me home. He said to himself. I do not have to stay here anymore. I will be able to do the things I used to do."

All he was cognizant of at the moment, was it did not feel the way he expected it would.

As days, weeks, months, and years went by, he understood the apprehension he felt that day, when he went home with Ms. Rupender.

Even at the age of five at the orphanage, seeing so many come and go, he became aware that children were being selected by size and stoutness. They were chosen by the adopters, wanting those that would be most helpful to them, free labor.

It was mentioned to Phillip, time and again by the attendants, when he would be overlooked by potential adopters. They told him, if he were only a little older or least a little bigger for his age, he would have been the first to go. Even though Phillip was healthy and strong for someone his age, he was not very tall, he was short in stature. So, Phillip even at his young age was apprehensive about this woman.

Thinking why does she want me?

She did not meet him before hand to speak with him, as he observed others have done. He had seen and overheard many of the conversations the others had with the children before they agreed to adopt them. One question that was always posed to the children was, "Would you like for us to be your parents?" Or "Would you like to come live with us?"

Phillip never had that option. Nothing was mentioned to him before hand by staff, or this woman. No one asked, nor mentioned anything to him about it. She had not even seen him, that he was aware of. She had not talked with or ask him, whether he would like to come live with her. No interview, no questions, before the decision was made. While he waited for papers to be signed the attendant had brought his things from his room in a cardboard box, and set it at Phillip's feet.

Phillip thought the woman sounded pleasant. Although there was still something about her. In the tone of her voice, that did not sit right with him. It made him very uncomfortable. Everything seemed to happen so fast. The next thing he knew he was in a carriage being taken to who knows where, with a woman he has never met, until fifteen minutes ago.

He did not know what to think, he just wondered where this was all leading. He suspected that he was going to live someplace else, that much he learned from his brother's experiences and all the other children adopted before him.

The woman did not speak, except to give the driver directions. When they reached the apparent destination, she was assisted by the driver stepping off the carriage. Phillip was lifted by the man and the box handed to Ms. Rupender. She nodded to the driver to hand it to Phillip, "Those belong to him." Her voice, dour and indifferent. She handed the driver something and said, "Come along Phillip."

They were in a town, which one he did not know, not that it mattered anyway to him. At his age that thought never even occurred to him, without his family, especially his mother no place was home. Like the orphanage, and as he perceived it would be here with this woman, it was just a place to be.

In his mind, it was a place to stay, until his mother comes to get him. Just before he entered the hallway of the building she was leading him, he took in a deep breath. He glanced about, unknowingly he let out a sigh before he stepped into a dark corridor, following her lead, they walked up the stairs.

Ms. Rupender unlocked a door, opened it, and turned to Phillip, "This will be your new home."

The sound of that statement jolted him. He stood still in the hall.

Seeking to be Loved

She told him to go in and put your things behind the sofa.

He froze, the word home, numbed him momentarily. The thought rushed through him, "This is not home." He had an urge to run, he did not know where to run, or what from. Next, the realization of the situation struck him. "If this is home, my home is gone, it is gone, it's gone. No, no, no." He thought to himself.

After the strange sensation faded, the word home echoed again and now it only reminded him of "Ma mee." Phillip for the first time feared, his thoughts. Finally looking up at the woman, asked, "How will she find me?"

"How will, who find you?" She questioned, looking down at the little boy, who now seemed even smaller, than he did at the orphanage.

He stood there holding his box of belongings, looking up at the woman, his vision blurred as his eyes filled with tears, that were about to overflow. "My Ma mee, my Ma mee," he repeated.

She placed her hand on his shoulder to turn and usher him into the apartment. She showed him where things were kept, in which closets and cabinets. Her room, which he was not to enter under any circumstances. He was told he would sleep on the sofa and keep his box of things behind it. She then showed him the bathroom down the hall.

She reviewed the rules, nothing was to be moved from its place. He was to stay clean at all times and speak only when spoken to. Meals will be at 6:30AM, dinner at noon when you are here and supper at 4:30PM.

He was instructed to place his box where it belonged, he looked bewildered. He just stood there, until he remembered it was to go behind the sofa. The moment of hesitation brought a swift blow to the back of his head. He ran to place the box where it was to stay for the next thirteen years, before she could remind him again.

"Now, I will show you where the school you will be attending is located. We are to meet with the principal in twenty-five minutes."

Seeking to be Loved

The school was only five city blocks from the little apartment. When they passed the playground, the sight of it excited Phillip. The anticipation of playing with others his age, lifted his spirit. Seeing all the children running, jumping with ropes, swinging, climbing, and screaming with excitement. He could not wait to go to this place. The building they entered seemed so huge, it reminded him of a church, although once inside that thought disappeared.

He noticed large hallways and many doors spaced equal distances apart. The rooms were filled with little tables and chairs.

They met with the principal, who walked them to the first-grade classroom to meet his teacher. The principal introduced Ms. Rupender, to Ms. Cameron, then he said, and this is Phillip Joseph Gagnon.

This was the second time Phillip heard his full name pronounced as such. Hearing it sounded good to him. It made him feel something he never really felt before. He did not know what it was, he just experienced it.

Suddenly, he had a good feeling about himself. It was similar to when his father or mother praised him for something. He did not understand pride. He looked up at the person who would be his teacher and smiled at her. Her face also seemed stern, she smiled back at him and he noticed a familiar twinkle in her eyes. He started to think this will be okay.

Miss Cameron said, "The children will be coming in any minute now. If you would like, I will introduce you to the class before you leave." She then said, "Of course you are welcome to stay for the next two hours and finished the day with us." She looked at Phillip and asked, "That is if you would like that Phillip?" Then she turned her attention to Ms. Rupender.

Phillip does not know what to say, everything is happening all so quickly. He wanted to cry. They are waiting for his answer. He turned to look up at Ms. Rupender, she looked down at him and nodded her head indicating yes. He just does the same, nodding his head up and down.

Seeking to be Loved

The teacher said, "That will be fine then."

Ms. Rupender expressed to the teacher, "That will work out perfectly. I have a few errands to run. Two hours will be just the amount of time I need." She looked at the boy and said, "I will meet you here at 2:45PM."

It was 15 minutes after three when she returned to pick up Phillip. The class had been dismissed, Phillip and Miss Cameron, were the only ones left in the classroom. The time he had to wait, seemed like hours. The door opened, in came Ms. Rupender, she did not seem quite as rigid, nor, as mean now to Phillip. She actually seemed more pleasant and sounded different, more warm, and friendly.

She apologized to Ms. Cameron, for being a little late. Then she turned to Phillip and asked, "Are you ready to go home, dear." He felt a little better about staying with her at that moment. He was happy not to be left alone, like he was so many times at the orphanage.

She talked to him all the way to her apartment. She did not ask any questions of Phillip, he just listened. Once in her apartment, she told Phillip to have a seat and she would put things away and fix dinner. The last item to be placed in the cabinet was a little bottle. It was only three quarters full of an amber colored liquid. She poured a small amount into a glass, before putting it away. She sipped on the glass during the meal preparation. Not much was said during dinner.

After dinner he was told to sit back on the couch, while she cleaned up. She said to him, "Tomorrow you will start school, and we must leave early."

The rest of the evening Phillip just stared out the window of the apartment overlooking the street. He observed what he could, just watching things going on, when evening darkened the streets as the sun set. It seemed awfully dark in the city. The only light was from corner lampposts. He noticed the light outlining window framing, escaping from the sides of shades drawn down for the night.

Seeking to be Loved

Ms. Rupender just sat in the chair humming to herself. Finally, she told Phillip that it was time for him to go to bed. I will get you a blanket and place it on the couch. With the lights out and things quiet, Phillip can hear muffled voices through the apartment walls of the building. It reminded him of the workers house at the O'Sullivan's farm. He heard women voices, reminding him of his mother. Occasionally a man's voice which reminded him of his father, he finally drifted off to sleep.

He was glad to be starting school. He knew this is what his brothers and sisters had done, when they reached a certain age. They always seem to come home, excited with things that they have learned and were willing to share with one another. He knew being around all those children his own age and to have a chance to go to the playground, would be fun. He knew he would enjoy his day, and he would make friends.

Phillip did enjoy school. It was a good respite from the confines of Ms. Rupender's small apartment. He followed the rules, they were made clear to him. He found out quickly there were consequences for not following them. He did what he was told, many of the things they did in class he already knew.

His older brothers and sisters had taught him. He usually had his assignments finished long before everybody else, and had to wait patiently.

His energy abound, so he took full advantage of it at the recesses. He would run, and play with abandon with the other children. Despite being a few inches shorter, and a bit younger, he could outrun and jump most of the other children. He was a sturdy little fellow. Probably due to the chores he did on the farm, and within the home. Also, the play and rough housing with is his brothers, made him a little stronger than many of the other boys.

He learned another valuable lesson early on which only restricted him somewhat. When he came home from school that first day his clothes were dirty from the play, roughhousing and the wrestling he did with the other boys at school.

Seeking to be Loved

Ms. Rupender was furious, she made him take off his clothes immediately and hand her his belt. She proceeded to strap him with it across his hind side. Then she told him, "In the closet is a scrub board, Get It," she yelled at him. She told him, "Put it in the sink and get yourself a chair to stand on. Now, you will learn how to wash clothes."

It was a chore he ended up doing frequently. Many times before Ms. Rupender would get home. He also learned to take his shirt off when he was playing in the playground, when the teachers were not looking, so he could keep it clean.

He looked forward each day to the interactions with the other children, as well as his teacher.

He especially enjoyed watching and talking with the janitor. The man fascinated him, he seemed to know everything, about everything. Whenever there was a problem in the classroom, building or playground, Mr. Russo, knew exactly what to do to fix it, and get it working again. He was always happy to answer the questions, Phillip would ask about how things worked. Or what was wrong with a particular item, and how did he know how to fix it.

Whenever Phillip had the chance he would stop whatever he was doing, to watch Mr. Russo working on something. He was curious, and always asked multiple questions. Mr. Russo always took the time to answer them, as well as explain how things worked. He enjoyed inquisitive children, and did not mind answering questions about his job. He liked to explain what he anticipated was the cause of the break down, or malfunction of whatever it was he happened to be working on. He always seemed to be right. When something was wrong in the classroom, the teacher would ask for a volunteer to go get the janitor. Phillip would raise his hand with enthusiasm.

Phillip became familiar with the places he was likely to be throughout the building. Sometimes it seemed to be a game for him, to find Mr. Russo. If he was not in his office, or the furnace room, where could he be?

Seeking to be Loved

Always a quick search would find him busy. He was repairing or maintaining some equipment item in the usual places, unseen to most. He never seemed to be in a hurry when there is a problem. He would look at the item, study whatever the issue may have been, then quickly proceed to repair, or replace whatever was needed. Like magic everything was back in order, in a short time.

Speaking of magic, this man had a knack for pulling pennies out from behind one's ear, with the snap of a finger it would appear.

Phillip was not allowed to participate in any the afterschool activities. He wanted to play sports, Ms. Rupender would not allow it. Occasionally he would participate in sandlot games on the way home from school, or during the summer. Whenever his clothes got dirty, or torn, he had to pay the price. It was not long before he was doing all the laundry, his and Ms. Rupender's.

He did what he could to keep the apartment clean and neat. He also learned how to prepare his own meals. He recalled watching his mother and sisters cook. Plus, helping Ms. Rupender prepare food in their little kitchen when she was not drunk. Many times, that first year living with her, he went without eating supper.

Occasionally when he came home from school, she was already asleep early in the afternoon. There were times she was not there at all, others she was to inebriated. Phillip had to keep his wits about him at all times.

She took out her frustrations on him, whether or not he did anything unusual to provoke it. For the next five years he took the responsibility upon himself to make sure the apartment was neat and clean. When he was home first, he would be the one to start dinner, if the time started approaching four o'clock.

He did everything he could to make Rupender's life pleasant and as easy as possible.

Years went by, Phillip thought less, and less, of his family, and more and more of the circumstances, and situation he was in. He adapted to his existence, only occasionally would he dream of his

Seeking to be Loved

family. The visions would fill his senses with the feelings he experienced in the past. In the dreams he felt security, warmth, joy, and a peace that only true unconditional love generates throughout ones being.

Sometimes he would even begin to see his mother's face. The brightness and light that came from the thought and image of her in his dreams. It would absorb him and made him feel as he was being suspended, floating, and secured in his existence. He would always wake feeling refreshed. Leaving him yearning for the feeling he had long since missed.

As time passed he could no longer see his mother's face in his dreams. They still possessed the feelings of warmth, comfort, and security as well as the light and brightness. Those were the sensations he felt, they are what lingered in his memory. At some point, he no longer recalled dreams of his mother. The experience of being loved, was foreign and nonexistent in his youth, adolescents, and teens.

He liked school, although he was quite pleased when Ms. Rupender suggested he get a job at one of the mills. There were other young boys in his fifth and sixth grade class that stopped attending school. He heard them tell the teachers, they were going to get jobs, to help earn money for their families.

He had often heard Ms. Rupender, complaining about not having enough money, for the rent or food.

He never considered how much a bottle of bourbon had cost her, during the early prohibition period.

Phillip felt that the job would make him feel more grown-up, more independent. He felt trapped, almost enslaved the way he has been living for five years. The job would give him a greater sense of freedom, along with an ability to do things that he wanted. He would have his own money to do as he wished. He knew he was on his own, after the first few weeks of living with Rupender. He knew he could not expect anything other than food and shelter, from this woman who took him home from the orphanage.

Seeking to be Loved

School, church, and Sunday catechism class, were the only places he felt the same as the other children. He knew something was missing, he just did not know what. It was more than just not being allowed to play or do extra curricula activities with classmates. It was more than not being allowed to interact with the children in his neighborhood. His dreams hinted, allowing him to feel the sensations he once had. As years passed they became less and less frequent. Phillip was too young to understand, what it was he was missing.

He like all young children, and every human being, needed to feel wanted, loved, and have affection and guidance. All want to know that their little life, is warranted.

He longed to be embraced, the way his mother held him. To feel the way, he felt when she wrapped her arms around him. Being held close and firm made him feel comfortable, it made him feel cared for and secure. It gave him a sense that, "This is where I belong. He cannot make sense of it in his young mind. It was just something from the past he remembered. Only in his dreams, did he experience that sense of belonging, that special feeling which kept him going, renewed, and filled him with joy and hope.

Tomorrow he will start looking for a job any job as Ms. Rupender instructed him to say. He was to accept what they would offer. She made a list with addresses of all the local mills, and shops. He was to visit each and inquire if there was work that he could do.

He never went back to school, never told his teacher that he would no longer be there. He knew he would miss it, but, the thought of the new freedom work might provide will make up for it.

He knew where most of the large mills were located. He started out at 6:30AM. Even Ms. Rupender was up early to send him off. She told him the early bird catches the worm. She hoped by him being there so early would show initiative and diligence.

She was right, he did not have to go far. The first mill he inquired hired him on the spot. The foreman was always looking for cheap labor, young boys unskilled. Willing lads, that can clean, pickup material, remove debris, to help make the work environment neater, safer, and hopefully more efficient. Anything to make the laborers and operators time more productive. Instead of being bogged down with the clutter that builds up around them at each of the workstations. Phillip did not ask about the pay, nor did he come prepared to spend the day at work. He had no lunch. He did not care. The thought of working gave him the energy he needed to make it through the day.

    Rupender, stewed throughout the day, she was furious with him, when he did not come home by noon. She expected him to inform her whether or not he was employed.

-She thought maybe he had gone back to school.

-Maybe he was out playing with other children.

-Maybe that lazy, good for nothing, is just sitting on the riverbank someplace.

    I will teach him when he gets home, to keep me waiting. "I will tan his hide," she said to herself.

    By five o'clock she was pacing her apartment, full of rage. "He will know never to do this again. I will teach him a lesson he will never forget." She fell asleep in a chair, her bottle laid empty on the floor.

    It was close to six o'clock, when the door opened, the exhausted boy was nearly faint from hunger. He had a big smile on his face. He could not wait to get home, to tell her, he got a job at the first mill he went to.

    She leapt to her feet, from the chair at the end of the small table where they dined, facing the door. She grabbed him by his left arm with her right hand. She slung him around slamming his lower back against the table. Her left hand struck him on the right side of his face. The blow would have sent him crashing to the floor, if not for her right hand holding him up. She reached back and slap him again, as she drew back once more, she yelled where have you been. He could not respond before her hand struck him again. She yanked him and swung him around 360 degrees, slamming his lower back against the table again. Still within her grip, she reached back to strike him again.

"I was working," he managed to utter. The words were barely audible, his energy was spent from the labor and the lack of sustenance.

She slowly lowered her left hand, and released her grip on his arm, with her right. Her rage seemed to have melted away.

Phillip leaned forward raising his body away from the table. Her only response was, "Why did you not tell me?"

Phillip did not notice any hint of remorse in the tone of her voice, only a lessening of her rage.

"Can I have something to eat?" he asked.

Only then in her response, did he noticed she may have regretted her reactions.

She questioned him, "What have you eaten today, I packed you no lunch?"

"Nothing." he replied.

"You sit down, I will prepare you something." She poured him a glass of milk and set it in front of him at the table. Her anger caused the alcohol in her bloodstream to reach its full effect. She stumbled about the kitchen, dropping pans, utensils, and food items.

Phillip helped her to her chair, in the living area. She promptly fell asleep. He prepared his own dinner, cleaned the kitchen, then went to sleep on the sofa. When he got up the next morning, she was still asleep in the chair. He packed himself his lunch, ate cereal along with bread-and-butter for breakfast. He cleaned up and went to work.

His existence in life was pretty much the same routine from that point on six days a week, for the next eight years. The freedom which he hoped for, and anticipated by starting to work, never materialized the way he thought. The meager pay he received the first few years had to be handed over to Ms. Rupender to pay the bills. She occasionally gave him a dollar to spend on what he pleased.

Seeking to be Loved

Thus, he could never save enough to buy things he wanted for himself, other than a tonic at the drugstore, or piece of candy.

After a few years, Phillip a young teenager, had ideas of getting his own apartment. This became one of his goals. He realized by the time he reached his mid-teens it was out of the question. Nearly all the money he earned paid Rupender's bills, rent, grocery's and her indulgencies.

He took pleasure in his work and learning other skills at the mill. The other workers, and his foreman, were more than willing to show him, when he demonstrated interest. He was always willing to jump in and operate a machine. He would help with other skilled task when asked by another coworker, while one took breaks.

Yes, they took advantage of him, he knew it.

It was his eagerness to learn and a passion to understand how things worked, that kept him energized and focused. He wanted to learn how to use every machine in the mill. At least all those on his floor, which he did. He was always quick to learn new task and operations. Phillip, was well respected by his foreman. His boss saw what the other men were doing. Still it pleased him to see Phillip's initiative. Whenever there was another job requiring more than just a minimum laborers skill, he would offer it to Phillip first. He knew he would be able to perform it and do well.

Phillip would always accept, wanting to please his boss as well as receive the extra pennies that went along with the hourly wage. This made some of the other workers jealous of him. Phillip was oblivious to the animosity that developed between him and one of his co-workers.

The labor and the learning of new things kept Phillip's mind active. He found little time to let his thoughts wander as he did when he was not working, sitting in the classroom.

He often wondered about the things in life he truly missed or was missing, he had a yearning. A yearning for something, that which kept him so motivated at the mill. Yet work, although always exciting to him, never really satisfied the desire within. Occasional dreams, or, sometimes during services on Sunday would he be given a hint. Watching families entering and taking their seats, he noticed they seemed so happy.

On restful Sunday afternoons, Phillip's memory would remind him of the things that he was missing. It was like a seed waiting to be planted, so it can burst from its shell and grow.

"Yes, part of me wants to grow, expand, bloom and flourish." He thought to himself. "I have strength. I know how to operate all the machines and equipment on our floor at the mill. I can take care of myself and others around me." Work and service, he could do well.

Something was still missing. Something inside was calling him and wanted to let him know somewhere, there are much better things in life to experience. What it was he never could put a finger on. He just had a sensation, a longing deep within him, for something much more important.

There was something beckoning beyond him, something out there in the world. Something, just waiting for him to find.

He acknowledged interest in some of the girls in church. He was now confirmed, and no longer had contact with them through Sunday school.

He began to notice and experience unique feelings within him, that he never noticed before. Yet within his depths there was a familiarity. Though there was an attraction to the ladies, he felt awkward when around them. Thus avoided situations that caused these feelings. His long hours at the mill kept him sheltered, yet it was an environment where he felt most comfortable and self-assured.

Time went by quickly, Phillip was passionate, strapping, and capable at whatever task he took on. Over the last few years he has been able to save up some money. Hoping one day he would move into his own apartment.

His own living space would be another step to independence and freedom. A step closer to his real dream, to build himself a home and family. A home where he could live, and one day raise a family, like he once had.

He laughed to himself when he would think about it. Knowing how he felt around girls, he wondered how he would meet one. Even more crucially, he wondered how on earth would he be able to court one?

Seeking to be Loved

Chapter 17 CCC

Phillip was 18 years old and had been living with Ms. Rupender for nearly thirteen years. He had not seen nor thought about his family for years and can barely remember his brothers and sisters.

He was not content although he accepted his present lot. He grew to respect Ms. Rupender, and her ways. She was really the only family he knew. Although he never felt like she was family, he always felt like he was subservient.

His childhood was gone and all the experiences that go with it, had been missed. As rambunctious and full of energy as Phillip was, he was not allowed the natural experiences childhood offered. The joy of growing up around other children and interacting and playing freely with them. As friendly as he was and kind to everyone he met, he had no close friends.

Coworkers, storekeepers where he frequented and patronized were the extent of his social existence.

Of course, the other tenants in the building also, they were all just acquaintances, not friends, not people he could share and explore life with as he grew into a man. His yearn to be independent and to interconnect on a personal level with others was always there. Albeit he learned the harsh lesson of consequences early on, those first few years staying with the old woman. Even today he was always very careful about keeping his clothes neat and clean as possible. Although now Ms. Rupender, did the laundry most of the time when he brought home dirty clothes. He suspected; it was because he was paying the bills.

He learned to heed her wishes, and demands. He started looking for other apartments and rooms in boarding houses in areas where he thought he might enjoy living. The cost was always prohibitive. For never completing six grades of his education, meant menial labor jobs was all he qualified for. Although he was quick to

Seeking to be Loved

learn and operate machinery, and to fix all kinds of equipment in the workplace. He never qualified for skilled worker, or specialist pay.

He was not about to complain to the bosses, or supervisors. He like many others, was just very happy that he still had a job during this depression, despite the pay. He considered himself lucky, to have a job, when so many men with better educations than he did not.

He wondered how men with families, especially large families supported themselves. He felt sorry for them, he was fortunate to be working and was thankful. When so many whom he would walk by each day, men with no job to go to, just standing on sidewalks or on the side of streets.

One day coming home from work, he stopped by the drugstore. Ms. Rupender, had asked him to bring home some coffee when he got off work.

That is when he noticed a new poster pinned on the wall. In big bold letters it read.

**Attention all young men 18 years of age and older.
The Civil Conservation Corps, Needs You!
To Rebuild America!**

Below in small print it read, **Room and Board plus Wages.**

Phillip thought, "That's for me! I will sign up right now. I am ready for something different." He thought about not having to take care of room and board. "Wow. Now I might have something left over. Heck, it will all be left over."

He asked the druggist, "Where do you sign up for this?"

The druggist told him at the Post office. He mentioned to Phillip, "The gentleman who hung the posters, was very excited about the program, it's part of the New Deal." He said, "This is going to put many people back to work."

The post office was closed when Phillip got there. He stopped by after work the next day to sign up. He inquired of the postmaster

Seeking to be Loved

when he handed him the completed application; when will he know whether or not he gets the job.

The Postmaster laughed! He mentioned to Phillip, "They will have a bus here in three days, to pick up any able-bodied men, that had filled out an application."

He questioned the postmaster, "That's it, I got the job? What do I need to bring?"

The postmaster chuckled again, this is all you need to bring, extending his arms with palms up at Phillip. "Just the clothes on your back. They will provide everything you need."

Phillip was beside himself. He started laughing. He thanked the postmaster and shook his hand. The postmaster slowly moved his head side to side and said, "It is not me giving you the job."

Phillip's excitement was almost uncontainable. He approached the school playground that he passed each day going to and from work.

He started to run. He hurdled all the benches. He ran to the monkey bars, grabbed them, and completed twenty chin-ups. Without releasing the bar, he started swinging until his momentum positioned him upside down on top of them. He walked across using only his hands. He reached the opposite end and swung down and dropped to the ground. He walked away grinning, pleased with the feat he just performed.

He was very excited about this new opportunity, no matter where it brought him.

He began to think about Ms. Rupender. He was concerned about her welfare. "Ah, old Ms. Rudepender, she will be all right," he told himself. "I am free at last." He jumped into the air swinging his fist. "I hope she does not get angry, when I tell her."

Upon entering the apartment, Ms. Rupender saw he had no package. She asked him, "Where is the coffee?" She slapped him on his forehead with her palm.

Seeking to be Loved

"It is in the cupboard. I brought it home yesterday like you asked."

She had been drinking again. He could smell it on her breath. He noticed yesterday, she had been a bit giddy. He did not understand alcoholism and blackout phases, when people seem to function well but have no memory of what they have done, or where they were. He just thought she was forgetful.

Dinner had not been started. Her only response was a mumbled, "Why are you late today then?"

Phillip paid no attention to the blow. It had not phased him in the least, nor did it surprise him. "I was at the post office." He decided despite her condition, this was a good time to tell her.

"When I went to the drugstore to pick up the coffee yesterday, I noticed the sign promoting the Civil Conservation Corps. I had to go to the post office today to sign up, after work. I will be leaving in three days."

He recognized the look that was so familiar to him. He had seen it so many times before. The look of rage in her eyes, the gritting of her teeth, the firmness of her lips. He braced himself as he did when he was younger, just before she would beat him. When he would come home with dirty clothes, from playing with the other children. Or stopping to help someone on the way home from school.

She drew back her hand. Phillip knew what to expect. He stood still. He thought, "She has not slapped me much the last three or four years. She cannot hurt me now." He watched her expression change from rage, to a pitiful look.

Phillip said, "In three days you will not have to put up with, or, be bothered with me anymore. If you like, I can make you some coffee now. I think I should start dinner." He knew she was confused and did not know how to respond. She seemed to shrink in stature before his very eyes. She slowly turned and staggered to the chair and collapsed into it. She has a bewildered expression on her face.

Seeking to be Loved

Phillip did not say another word. He went to the bathroom to wash. He came back shortly and prepared dinner. The old woman sat there, not a sound came from her. It was as if she had gone into a trance.

In fact, she had. She saw herself when she was about Phillip's age when she picked him up from the orphanage.

She saw that little girl laying on the floor in a beautiful lace dress with bright yellow ribbons holding her ponytails together. She was playing so contentedly with her dolls.

She saw herself as a school girl who was quite popular. She was selective of who she chose to be her friends.

She saw herself as a teenage girl with no shortage of boys trying to impress her with their escapades.

She saw herself as a young woman with many well to do suitors. There she was at the altar, exchanging vows with a man of wealth and position.

She remembered how she thought, "Now, I can have all the things I want. I will be in need of nothing." She loved her beautiful house, her wardrobe, and enjoyed the privilege of having a maid. She delighted in having the freedom to go about, to meet a friend for tea, or to host one in her home.

She remembered, how lonely she felt, staying awake at night until the wee hours, when her husband would not come home. She remembered the contempt she felt for many, which turned to bitterness.

She remembered, how she was left with nothing, no inheritance of her parents. They wasted every penny they had keeping an image. Her husband left her with nothing, except the home they lived in and the mortgage. The bank foreclosed, when there was no more fine furniture, or jewelry left to sell. She was unable to pay the bills any longer.

She remembered, how she felt abandoned, which was overridden by her own disdain of others. She wanted to feel that

Seeking to be Loved

same supercilious at this very moment. She cannot and is bewildered.

She was an only child with false airs of privilege.

She recalled her attempt at jobs when she had no more means to cover her expenses. She just could not get along with other people for any length of time. They expected certain things of her. It was always she, who had learned to expect things from others. For some reason it seemed to be easier, to live off the security and charity of others. Although she never got beyond this little apartment, and being alone for the last thirty years. She recalled the day going to the orphanage to select the boy. Not because she wanted to care for and raise a child. She wanted one old enough not to be making messes, and could follow her commands. A child who could help clean the apartment and run errands. Yet young enough so she can control, one who she could train to do things for her.

She realized she has become quite fond of Phillip. She had never told him or showed him. Now he, just like her parents, just like her husband will leave, and be gone from her life.

Something within, deep inside wants to weep. A part of her wanted her to know, this is not the life that was intended for her. Something wanted to tell her, there is a life meant for her and is waiting, and it is not too late. A life where she can find the peace, all the human race wishes to live within.

A phrase she has heard many times mentioned during service when she was sitting in the pew at church. Is now ringing in her ear. **"Seek, and you will find, Knock, and the door will be opened, Ask, and you shall receive."**

Yes, I heard that many times she thought to herself. She never thought then, as she does not now, the message was meant for her. She does not realize the spirit within her is wanting her to follow this instruction.

For we all must, in the days that we count of our life, Seek what the creator has prepared for us. To do so we must Knock on

Seeking to be Loved

and open the doors, we find and are set before us. Ask not what we want for our self, but, what our creator wants for us.

She chose not to relate these words to what she (each of us) must do. As always, the messages she heard while attending the services, year in and year out, were wonderful. They were not meant for her. She had other things on her mind. As now, her only concern is paying her bills, and feeding herself.

The vision of privilege she has always known for the first 28 years of her life, now does not even enter her thoughts and dreams of her future existence.

She sat and stared straight ahead, at what she does not know, nothing really, her gaze is blank.

She has no tears. Those are reserved for those who can feel the essence of life.

Only her guiding Angel, and the one preparing dinner are weeping. Her Angel has arranged many opportunities throughout her life. Where she could have made the choices that would lead her to the life God had planned for her. It weeps knowing another opportunity is passing her by.

The one weeping in the other room, used a towel covering his face to muffle the sound. His tears flow from the acknowledgment that this woman who sheltered him for thirteen years, is going to be alone. He realized she will be alone unless she is willing to make some changes in her life. She, like he, needs to allow herself to connect with others.

His tears are created from the sorrow he feels in his heart for this woman. Despite how she treated him, it is the empathy he experiences of her loneliness. He himself knows it all too well. He understands what it feels like to be abandoned.

When he is composed, he approached her quietly and placed his hand softly on her right shoulder. He told her he has prepared dinner. She reached across her body with her left hand and placed it on his and looked up at him. Even though her eyes have a blank glare, she managed a gentle smile, no more was said.

Seeking to be Loved

The three days passed. Phillip had packed the few things he owned. His belongings consisted of no more than three pairs of pants, one set of good clothes for church, a few shirts, socks, underwear, and nightclothes. He wrapped it all in his coat. Everything he owns is in the little bundle. He used a pair of the shoestrings to tie it at both ends.

Ms. Rupender was up early and prepared breakfast for Phillip. She asked him if he knew where he would be going and what he will be doing?

"No, I guess they will tell us once we are on the bus. As for what we will be doing, from what I heard from people at work is anything and everything. I am looking forward to it."

She reached across the table placing her hand on Phillips. For the first time in the thirteen years that he has known the old woman, this was the first time he saw even the slightest inkling of affection. She conveyed to Phillip, that he is a fine young man, and she will miss him.

Phillip had not heard those words in almost fourteen years. He had forgot about them. He heard his mother say those exact words before she died. He can hear his father's voice and see him very clearly, kneeling by her bed.

There was a deep longing, groaning silently within Phillip's being. He could not respond with words at the moment, he placed his other hand on top of hers and stood up. He walked around the table and reached both his hands underneath her elbows. Raising her up from her chair. He wrapped his arms around her and hugged her. Neither have ever done that before. It seemed a natural thing to do. For the first time in her 59 years, she felt someone cared for her. In that brief moment they exchanged an innocent solemn expression of genuine love.

Phillip whispered a prayer for God to bless this woman. He stepped back.

She reached into her pocket for a handkerchief to wipe her eyes.

Seeking to be Loved

Phillip said, "Goodbye Ms. Rupender, it is time for me to go." He picked up his bundle of belongings and walked out the door when he closed it, he heard her sob.

Seeking to be Loved

Chapter 18 <u>1939</u>

One afternoon the foreman of the day shift on the third floor in the factory where Phillip worked, made an announcement. Before everyone clocked out, he shouted in his gruff voice. "I need three men after the shift, to replace some broken windows." He shouted again, "I need three men for about an hour."

Phillip and two other of the younger workers step forward. Thinking they would receive extra pay for whatever work they would need to do.

The foreman looked pleased, he told them when they clock out to come to his office. While in line to punch their timecards at the clock, an older gentleman told the three, volunteering is what you are doing.

One of the three young men asked, "What do you mean?"

The gentleman told them, "That is why the foreman told you to clock out. He does not intend to pay you extra, especially not over time."

The three look at each other and two decide to leave. They punched their timecards and make a quick exit.

Phillip kept his commitment to stay, when the other workers ask what he is going to do, he told them, "I am staying. I will ask if we are to be paid for the work."

Several of the other workers laughed, for they knew the foreman's intent. When they are leaving in chorus several workers repeat, what they heard the foreman say many times. Every time he gives the boss a tour on the floor, during his weekly inspection of the shop.

"*Everything is in order sir, clean work areas, good workers, production up and Cost down.*"

They all laughed and a few pat Phillip on the back. One went as far to say, "Good luck sucker." "You will see boy," another shouts, as they were leaving.

Seeking to be Loved

Phillip does not mind, he has no family to go to. No extra money, to do anything with. He would just go to his room at the boarding house and wait for dinner.

He reported to the office, the foreman asked, "Where are the other two?" Phillip just shrugs his shoulders. The foreman's name is Mr. Katter.

Phillip questioned him, "Sir, will I be receiving extra pay for this?"

"No, but if you do a good job, I will see to it that I will put a good word in for you."

Phillip smiled, knowing that means nothing.

Mr. Katter said, "Panes of glass, putty and the tools you need are there on the table." He asked Phillip, "Have you ever changed windowpanes, Gagnon?"

Phillip was quick to think, knowing they are on third floor he would need an extra set of hands. Mainly to avoid the probability of dropping the panes of glass or the broken pieces when removing them. He knew the boss did not like to get his hands dirty doing any type of work. There is no ledge to stand on, or ladder long enough to reach the windows from outside. He would need an extra set a hands. Especially when removing and replacing the glass, someone to hand them to, and hand him what is needed next. He knew working alone, would take much longer. The constant moving and twisting, that would be necessary to position his body, would put him at risk. The maneuvering inside and out, on the window's sill, would be time consuming.

He knew if he said yes, he would be expected to do the job alone. Heaven forbid if he broke one of the new panes of glass. Not wanting to be dishonest, or wanting to be stuck doing the job alone, he answered his foreman, "Nothing like this boss."

He noted the discontented expression on his boss's face. Phillip immediately adds, "Not having a ledge on the outside of the window to stand on, I would not be able to hold the glass when taken them out, or positioning the new ones."

Seeking to be Loved

Mr. Katter is thinking his boss may be in tomorrow to perform his weekly inspection. He wanted the floor to look tidy and safe. "Oh, I guess I will have to help you."

They work together, with Phillip leaning outside the window to remove the pieces of broken glass first. Using great care so that they would not fall to the street below. He started to draw a small crowd of people, as he climbed out to stand on the sill. He noticed the spectators below. He thought, "They probably do not want to miss the spectacle, when I fall."

Phillip's nearly black hair, muscular build, and flashy smile, caught the attention of the young female office workers in the building across the street, as well as those passing below. He noticed them, however acted like he did not, as he went about his business, replacing the windows.

His foreman glanced at him from inside the window as Phillip busied himself, removing the broken panes of glass from the outside and handing them to him. Phillip has a broad smile, showing all his pearly whites. Mr. Katter asked, "What the hell are you smiling at?"

He stepped toward Phillip, to reach a broken piece of glass being handed to him. When he is close enough, he can see the crowd forming below. As well as the faces of the office girls pressed against the windows on the other side of the street. He said, "Ahhh that is it, just keep your eyes and your mind on what you are doing. It will be embarrassing as hell if you fall. Or worse yet if you drop a piece of glass, and cut one of those cute little things."

Phillip chuckled, while handing him the last of the broken pieces. He twisted his body around, facing out he could see the crowd. He noticed several ladies crowding the windows across the street. He smiled and waved, as he ducts under the window to re-enter the shop. He used a putty knife to scrape the dry weathered putty off the sash bars and muntins, from the inside. Mr. Katter held a tray to catch any glass or debris before it fell below.

Phillip, meanwhile was glancing down more often than he should, trying to get a look at the attractive young ladies below. He

Seeking to be Loved

noticed a young woman exiting an office building across the street the next building down. It was a glimpse from the corner of his left eye that caught the movement. He had to turn his head, his focus was instantaneous, he was spellbound. Many people were getting off work, the streets crowded with traffic. The sidewalks filled with pedestrians and amongst all the commotion, he noticed her.

Even with the task he had at hand, he attempted to keep track of her movement. With all going on below, his focus fell completely on her. He only saw this young woman for an instant, that moment captivated him.

His attention focused completely on her, it seemed that time as well as all movement was on hold. Although, it was only the briefest of moments, it seemed longer. When he came to his senses, he felt as if he had been watching a movie, he could see her face clearly. The clothes she was wearing, even the hat on her head and the belt around her waist. It was as though she was right in front of him. He even noted the directness of her pace as she stepped through the crowd.

All the while he was unaware, however he never stopped what he was doing and never skipped a beat with the work he was performing. If he had, his foreman would have let him know the second his focus drifted, or if his actions strayed from the task they were performing. It was the boss's intent to stay not one extra minute longer than he had to.

Phillip quickly reached for the new pane of glass being handed to him. He ducked under the window to replace the pane from outside. All the while trying to keep an eye on this young lady. Holding the pane in position with one hand, he replaced the metal staves with a pair of pliers.

He asked for the putty, he worked it in his hand to make it smooth and applied it with the knife as fast as he could. He ducked back under the window, and glanced up and down the street, back and forth trying to find the young blond headed lady.

His foreman asked, "What the heck are you looking for now."

Seeking to be Loved

Phillip's smile was gone, he could care less how many young ladies were still watching him. He just went about his work until it was finished.

His boss said, "Good job Gagnon, clean this place up and get out of here."

Phillip cleaned up as quickly as he could. He ran down the stairs and outside. He looked right and left, he decided to walk in the direction he had last seen her heading. He searched three blocks in the direction she had been walking when he last saw her. Glancing in every store and alley along the way, hoping to get a glimpse of that girl. He had yet to even think why he was in such pursuit of this person that caught his attention so dramatically. He was intent on seeing her up close.

Alas, he gave up the search realizing its futility. He started towards his own place of residents. He resided in a boarding house. It was an old Victorian style home. He had his own bedroom, he shared the rest of the house with three other men, who had their own rooms. The owner was a middle-aged woman, a widow, whose children had moved away. His weekly rent provided for the room and one meal a day, dinner. He was glad to have a place to stay so close to his work. Unfortunately, rent, food and keeping clothes on his back was all he could afford. He was glad to have a job, but had little expectation of anything else. He knew even this was better than what he had experienced for thirteen years living with Ms. Rupender. He was glad to have his own room, although he wanted a family and home of his own one day.

He missed what he experienced at such a young age from his siblings, father, and his dearest mother. The thought saddened him, yet creates a warmth in his heart. He wondered if he will ever experience that again.

There was never much conversation that took place at the dinner table of the boarding house. They have access to a very nice front room with a grand fireplace, and nice furniture. It would be a wonderful place to unwind and relax from the day. He nor the other

Seeking to be Loved

boarders rarely, ever took advantage of it. They all just seemed to keep to themselves.

For the next few weeks at work, Phillip would glance out the window every chance he had. He would look down the street in the direction of the building, he had seen that young blonde-haired girl come out of. On his way to and from work, he would always look for her. One day he decided, as soon as he got off work, he would wait outside on the sidewalk for her to pass by. He seemed to be waiting forever. He watched intently from a distance any time the door opened, and people came out of that building. Phillip hoped he would see her again. Over an hour passed the streets and sidewalks were nearly empty. He began to wonder if it was all just his imagination that day fixing the window. Did he really see her? He will wait again tomorrow.

All day long he wondered why he could not get this image out of his mind. He kept debating if it was even real, or just his imagination. He began trying to convince himself it had to be in his own mind. He thought, "How could I have seen her face, hair, and clothing down to the finest detail? I was three floors up, hanging on with one hand and working with the other. My boss breathing down my neck, and she was a 50 or 60 yards away. Who am I kidding? What a fool I am. It had to be my imagination."

He decided today he would get a little bit closer. He was determined to be the first to punch out, so he would not have to wait more than a minute or so in line. When the whistle blew, he ran to clock out, he rushed down the steps. He walked quickly to the corner. There was a bench near, where he could sit. He would have a perfect view. Although he realized sitting down, with all the people passing by he could not see above them. Stepping to the curb he took his position leaning up against the lamppost. Nonchalantly gazing about, keeping an eye on the people exiting the building across the street. He would soon realize his wait was not in vain. Soon as the door opened a group of young ladies were coming out. The young woman with blond hair, stood out amongst all the rest.

Seeking to be Loved

His eyes focused only on her, although she was in the middle of a crowd of young attractive lady's. He immediately focused on her only as they were passing through the double doors of the building onto the sidewalk. They quickly turned to their left, and walked to the corner of the street to cross at the intersection.

She chatted with the other young ladies.

He is on the wrong side. He wanted to cross the street opposite them. He thought, "I must get closer." He wanted to hear the sound of her voice. He did not know why that seemed important. All he knew was there was something special about this woman.

At the age of twenty-five, many young ladies were attractive to him, this one was different. He quickened his pace. He realized there should be a proper introduction. He thought how could that be since he did not know her. She surely did not know him, or anyone who knew him, not that he was aware of. He slowed his pace thinking this was awkward. He began to feel guilty about pursuing her, it made him think of an animal stalking prey.

What if someone would have noticed him following. I will just gaze from a distance at her, following on the opposite side of the street. Until she and one other girl in their group turned off onto a side street. By the time he crossed the street and got to where they turned, they were gone. He looked down the street there was no sign of her. "Dang," he said to himself.

He must come up with another plan. One where she could see him and if she appears interested, then he would introduce himself.

The next day he decided he would stand on the bridge, that goes over the Nashua River, the path she and her coworkers seemed to follow the few days he saw her.

He positioned himself, in such a manner so he can see her and her coworkers when they come out the door. Anticipating they would turn to cross the street and walk over the bridge, just as they had the day before. He was leaning against the rail of the bridge, "She will have to see me." He observed a dozen or more women

Seeking to be Loved

exiting the building they worked in. He hoped that she was with them. His heart is beating excessively, he can almost hear it pounding in his chest. He recognized her and is trying as hard as he can, not the stare. He turned his head slightly, so it does not appear he is looking at her. Although his eye's stay focused on this young lady who attracted him so. He glanced down at his shoes and then immediately raised his head as the ladies' approached.

His eyes look straight at the young blonde headed girl about to pass by him. She is in the middle of several other young girls, he sees no other. Her complexion is smooth, beautiful, and radiant. Her head does not turn, although their eyes meet. For the instant, her soft blue eyes met his, time stopped, the world was still once more. Just as it had been when he was replacing the windows and saw her the first time. There was no one else except them two. The ladies walked by, he was unable to move, his eyes followed her until she was out of sight.

When Phillip could no longer see her, the spell she casted finely released him. Upon returning to the moment, the sensation he is experiencing seems familiar somehow. Although, he can make no connection as to why.

In the recesses of his mind, was the memory of something Phil had been missing. It was similar to the gut feeling one gets when you lose something. Something you knew you had, and you need it, but, cannot find it anywhere. The emptiness and blankness you feel after searching everywhere to no avail.

He does not dwell on it long, he recognized the feeling. It was not new to him. His next thought was more demanding, "I must meet this woman." He could hardly wait until tomorrow. He would bring a clean shirt to put on and make sure his hair was combed. He wondered how they could meet, or how he could speak with her.

The next day he waited, as he did the day before, he had already changed his shirt, his hair combed. I am in position, he thought to himself. He could not help but grin. He scanned his mind, trying to think what he would say. What could he say? He did not

Seeking to be Loved

know any of these ladies. He could not just introduce himself or start a conversation. How can I get to know her name he wondered? When they approached the bridge where he is standing, she turned her head to look at him as they are passing by, their eyes met again.

Phillip said, good afternoon ladies. A few of them look and giggled, only the blonde returned the greeting. She said, "Good afternoon," as they walked on.

Phillip's eyes followed her once again, his body could not move. He finally realized she spoke to him.

He looked to the sky, thinking to himself and asking God, "Was that a sign?" He could not wait until the next day, he did not want to wait for the answer.

The next day happened to be Friday. Phillip was so excited. All night he thought about the woman's eyes. He could not be sure, but, he thinks there was even a smile. It was not a big smile, just a slight one, that caused the slightest dimple on the left side of her face.

He tossed and turned all night. He was not aware whether he slept or not. When the morning light came through his window, he jumped out of bed, made it, got dressed and was out the door. He wanted to be at work early and the first to check in and clock out and still have an entire shift in. He wanted to be waiting on the bridge long before any of the workers had a chance to leave their buildings. He did not want to miss her.

The Boss having checked the timecards, stop by Phillips work area. He mentioned to Phillip, I noticed you were here early this morning and hard at it, before anyone else got in. I want to remind you, we cannot pay you over time. Make sure you check out glancing down at the card, 15 minutes before the end of the shift.

"YES SIR!"

Phillip kept one eye on the clock, the other on his machine. The clock approached fifteen minutes before the hour. Phillip shutdown his machine, did an immediate sweep of his area and punched his timecard. He nearly flew down the stairs, once outside he caught his breath and casually walked across the street. He

Seeking to be Loved

hopped up on the stone railing of the bridge. He tried to act as nonchalant as possible.

Being Friday, many workers will be attempting to leave as quickly as they can. That is why he was in such a rush to get there before the streets swarmed with people. He wanted to be there early, ready, and planted in position. He was taking no chances at missing this young beauty. He knew there was something special about her, he was curious to know what it was.

Just as he expected the moment the clock struck four, people poured onto the sidewalks and street. It all seemed to be one big rush, everyone's steps were brisk. The voices sounded louder than usual, everyone was aware of the excitement. It is Friday, the night to be out on the town. He kept his eye on the building down the street. When he recognized some of the young ladies that usually come out together, he turned his head quickly and looked straight ahead. With his heart pounding he tried to look as casual as possible. Out of the corner of his eyes he strained, trying to catch a glimpse of the blonde beauty. He did not notice her with the group. He turned his head to find her, she was not amongst the crowd.

The group of young ladies were passing, a few look and grinned at him. He just nodded his head and said, "Ladies," in his most masculine cordial voice. When they passed, he continued scanning the crowd. He hoped to find the one he was looking for.

She was not amongst them. He thought, "If I only knew her name, I could ask the girls she walked with the previous days, where she might be." For a moment, he thought of hopping off the stone rail to catch up to them, and ask where is the blonde-haired girl, who usually walked with them. He decided that would be awkward.

He waited for what seemed forever, wondering where she could be. "Surely I didn't miss her, I couldn't have." He started to walk back and forth across the bridge. He heard the clock at the City Hall strike five. The streets were still busy, though not nearly as crowded as they were the last hour.

Seeking to be Loved

Of course, all kinds of things were going through Phillips mind. "Was she sick? Maybe she had an accident? She may have went another way, stopped at a store to shop, or maybe needed to pick something up.

She could be working late. Check that off the list, it is Friday, and surely a girl as pretty as she, would have been long gone by now. To prepare for an evening out on the town with friends, or."

His heart dropped as the next thought appeared in his brain. "Maybe she already has a man, a boyfriend, someone special she loves and cares about."

His excitement turned to a forlornness, his heart sank in his chest. The streets in this industrial section of town are nearly empty now.

He hopped up on the stone rail of the bridge. He swung his feet over the rail, and watched the water flowing under the bridge. He glanced upriver, and observed the many factories on its banks. Hard brick structures, they appeared cold and deserted. The shadows cast by the setting sun, started to touch them. They appeared dark and empty. He concluded, "They appear as I feel, a void inside, lonely and abandon."

Phillip hunches over resting his elbows on his knees, not sure what he wanted to do now. He sat there. After a while he scooted himself to the edge of the bridge, where the lamppost projects from the rail. He leaned against the stone column, as he lifted his legs onto the bridge rail. He crossed his legs right over left in an extended position. The street is quiet, most have gone on their way, happy and anxious to start the weekend.

He thought to himself, "Maybe, I should give the priesthood another thought. Or, maybe they have another position which I would be qualified."

"You look awfully comfortable!" "Hey!"

Phillip was deep in thought, he thought that maybe an Angel just spoke. The sound was sweet, almost musical to his ears. He

Seeking to be Loved

listened intently, he heard soft footsteps. He turned quickly, and saw that beautiful woman, starting to walk away.

He instantly was aware, that was her voice. His mind raced. He thought, "Why am I so stupid. I did not respond to her, if that was her!" He shouted, "Oh hello, did you just speak, or say something?"

She turned so gracefully. He spun himself around hopping off the bridge rail, all in one motion. He is staring right into her beautiful blue eyes, as he stepped toward her.

She said, "I just mentioned you look awfully comfortable."

Phillip smiled broadly, showing his pearly whites.

Thinking to herself, she conceded, "What a handsome fellow he is. All the girls in the office have noticed also, and the fact that he is a strong well-built man."

Phillip once again recognized the heavenly quality of her voice as he focused on it. He said, "I have been waiting for you." When the words came out of his mouth, he grit his teeth and said to himself. "Why did I say that?" He noticed her eyes opened a bit wider and her head tilt ever so slightly. "I meant to say, I was, (he paused to think, what he should say) comfortable." He uttered quickly, never gazing away from her eyes. His smile broadened again. He noticed, she is returning the sweetest of smiles. His heart soaring, he just wanted to shout, "Hallelujah, Yes".

The thought of her smiling at him and speaking to him with such a heavenly sounding voice, it was intoxicating. He does not hear or see anything except her. He stepped closer. He introduced himself, and she to him. When he heard her name, it was as if a light shone brightly within. It was a sensation of recognition. Yet he could not grasp what, or where it could be from. There was just something familiar about the name.

Phillip extended his hand, she grasped it with a very light firmness. He is conscious of the softness of her hand, yet she had a gentle meaningful grip. Once again time was stilled by the ecstasy of the moment. He did not want to let go. He was aware of her fingers separating ever so slightly. He released it with a matched gentleness.

Seeking to be Loved

Natalie asked, "Why were you waiting for me? Didn't you say, 'I was waiting for you'?"

Phillip chuckled, all the while maintaining his grin. "I must not lie.' Yes.' I had hoped you didn't hear that."

He continued, "I saw you a few weeks ago, when I was working on the windows across the street. Out of all the people that were walking by, you were the only one I could see."

"I remember that day, you were making quite a spectacle of yourself. You had all the girls in the office, in a tizzy."

"I don't know about that," Phillip said, "All I know is something inside, told me I must meet this girl. I mean, you!"

"Well now you have." She slowly turned, as though she was going to continue her walk home. Although, she also felt that she did not want to leave.

Phillip asked, "May I walk you home?"

She continued her turn and extended her elbow.

Phillip quickly wrapped his arm around it. They walked across the bridge.

"Why were you so late leaving work this evening?"

"My manager asked the girls if anyone would be interested in staying late. He had several things that needed to be typed immediately, and offered to pay overtime. So, I jumped at that opportunity."

Phillip said, "I do not blame you, it is rare when we get overtime pay. Actually, it was not long ago we were expected to work long hours, without extra pay. Heck, it is still like that sometimes. It is not as bad as it used to be."

They were passing the drugstore, he asked Natalie, "Would you like a tonic from the soda fountain, an ice cream, or something?"

"I do not get paid until next week."

"I invited you, it will be my treat," Phillip offered.

She was a little apprehensive, although she accepted.

Phillip did not stop grinning the whole time.

She even asked him, "Do you always smile?"

Seeking to be Loved

Phillip laughed, "I don't think so. I am so glad to meet you. I have no control over -- " He stopped mid-sentence.

"Control over what?" she asked smiling.

He thought a moment, processing what he is feeling and grinning about. Finally, he finished his statement. "I think it is joy. I have not felt this joyful, in a long, long time. I hope it does not embarrass you."

"Not at all," Natalie replied. She was very comfortable with Phillip. She too felt, there was something special about this man. He was not as charming as some of the men in the office building. They attempted to use their charm to impress all the young ladies in the office pool. He seemed to have an innocence about him, he is confident. Although not overly self-assured. That is refreshing and surprising to see in a man as good-looking as him. He certainly is not arrogant, she thought to herself, "Another plus in his favor."

They talked about their work, and some of the goings-on in this little industrial town.

Phillip wanted to ask her all kinds of questions, where she was from, whether or not she had family. Questions just kept coming to his mind. He wanted to know everything he could about her, not that it mattered. Everything about her he found to be fascinating. She was so pleasing to look at, it was pleasant to be near her. He loved the sound of her voice. He thought to himself, "This is the most comfortable I ever felt with anyone." It was mixed with excitement, contentment, and a joyful feeling, he never experienced before.

Yet it seemed to be familiar, maybe this was something he once knew, many, many, many years ago. He could not ever recall ever having a feeling quite like this. There was something in the depth of Phillip's being that recognized this experience.

Natalie looked at Phillip and said, "I really must be going." She explained, "The woman whom she has been staying with would be worried; we have become good friends."

Phillip asked Natalie, "May I walk you the rest of the way home? Is it very far from here?"

Seeking to be Loved

"That is not necessary, though it is getting late. If you do not mind, I would like that."

Phillips spirit was lifted to an even higher level if that could be possible. When they got to the house of her friend Kay, Natalie stopped and said, "This is it." She turned to face him.

He gazed into her eyes, his smile broadened more than ever. He can think of nothing, not a word to say, or what he should do.

Natalie, finally spoke, "Well good night." Her voice was soft, yet possessed a quizzical nature to it. She waited for Phillip, to make the next move.

He said, "Good Night."

They are still staring into each other's eyes. Moments pass, Natalie is getting impatient, wondering why he is not attempting to kiss her goodnight.

He noticed a slightly different look in her eyes. He felt the moment getting awkward. He finally said, good night again. He does not want to leave, nor for this moment to end. He looked down at his shoes. He asked, "If he can walk her home again on Monday?"

Natalie is a bit amiss. "Why is he not attempting to kiss me, good night? Maybe he is just being old-fashioned?"

Thinking quickly, she said, "I do not have anything planned tomorrow." hinting she is available.

Phillip nearly jumped. He told her he had to work in the morning until noon. He asked her, "Would you like to do something in the afternoon?"

Natalie replied, "I would like that." Not wanting to sound too anxious, she told Phillip, "First let me check with Kay, she may have something planned."

Natalie turned and quickly ascended the stairs to her apartment. She expected Phillip to be following behind her. He stayed on the sidewalk.

She was hoping to introduce him to Kay, a quick search found she was not there. Natalie rolled her eyes to one side, thinking this is working out nicely. She thought for a moment before opening the

Seeking to be Loved

door. "I will tell him, she must have gone out for the evening." She opened the door and informed him she is not home.

It does not occur to him to ask her out for the evening, or if she would like for him to come in. Not quite sure what to say, or do, he asked if he could see her tomorrow after work.

She is furious and really does not know why. She smiled and said, "Yes, one o'clock would be fine."

Phillip looked down again, then up at her and said, "You better make it two. Sometimes we have to stay later to finish the order. That should give me time, enough to go home and clean up and change first."

"Two will be fine," she said with a smile.

Phillip lifted his hand slightly to wave, turned and walked away. He was thinking to himself, "I can't wait until 2PM tomorrow."

Natalie closed the door being careful not to slam it, although she wanted to. She leaned against the door, looking up at the ceiling and is incensed, though smiling. She wanted to be kissed by him, it did not happen. She said to herself, "He is so handsome and masculine. His parents must have raised him right, for him to be so polite and respectable." She reasoned, "That is why he did not try to kiss me, or anything else on the first date. I like that in a man." She walked away from the door smiling. Repeating to herself, "I did want him to kiss me." Then she questioned, "Was this considered a first date? Maybe, although tomorrow will be the official one."

Saturday was the happiest day Phillip ever experienced. He and Natalie spent the afternoon in the park walking, sitting on the grass, enjoying the warmth and freshness of a spring day in the company of each other. He asked all the questions he wanted to ask the evening before.

Natalie Pauline Emerson, was from a large established family living in Haverhill, Massachusetts. The farm she was raised on had been in her family since the 1600s. It had grown to become a respectable size dairy, on North Broadway St. a few miles west of Lafayette Square, in the city.

Seeking to be Loved

One of the ancestors of her family was Hannah (Emerson) Dustin, a stoic heroine of the town. She had been captured during an Indian raid in 1697. Her newborn child was killed before her eyes. In the following days, she made her famous escape and was able to save herself, as well as the other captives.

Natalie grew up and learned to work hard and to discipline herself. She had been well educated and exposed to many things during her developmental years. She was an accomplished cellist, and played in the high school orchestra. She had been to business college, and had been meticulous in domestic task. She learned the sewing trade and was a talented seamstress. Yes, like Phillip, was headstrong, stubborn, determined, and hard-working. They shared many of the same traits, the things that really counted. Respect for others, kindness, and strong faith. She was Protestant, Phillip Catholic. Although, she always seem to know she was going to raise her children Catholic. She did not know why, she just thought that way. It was something, she just knew!

During each phase of her life, she was presented with new experiences, new opportunities, new challenges and encouraged. She with the guidance and love from parents and those around her, grew and excelled, through each stage.

On the other hand, Phillip who started life similarly, at the tender age of four years old, it was all taken away. The security, the familiar, the comfort and support of a loving nurturing family, were removed from his life.

The very footer and foundation of which a life is built. The solid ground that supports and allows one a firm foot hold on which to stand during lives challenges, which are inevitable, did not exist for Phillip. He had no family during those crucial phases. No base to support, confirm, and help him stand firm when facing what life presented. No one to comfort, or assist him. He had no one to prepare, warn, and guide him through the stages and experiences all must travel as we mature. There was no one to mentor, nor console

Seeking to be Loved

him socially, or emotionally as he survived each phase of his growth, and development through life.

He had old Ms. Rupender, who was ill equipped in these developmental areas as well. She did see to it, that he received spiritual preparation. He was never allowed to miss church on Sunday, or, on the special feast days and holy days of obligation. He knew all of them by heart.

Phillip and Natalie, made a handsome pair. They both enjoyed the attention they gave each other, the encouragement as well as the complements. When they were seen together, it was commonly expressed, how good they looked together. Comments such as, "You two look so happy together." "What a lovely couple." And Phillip's favorite; "You two were made for each other."

They actually were!

God knew in advance what the natural world had in store for these two individuals. He created them as such, to attract them to one another and to grow together as one. They were kindred spirits; they were designed to complete each other.

Natalie was accomplished, intellectual, and she excelled in all the necessary creative arts, music, and for the things necessary in this life and she was driven. Which was to be proved later, when providing for her family.

Phillip, accomplished in wisdom and spirit, he seemed quite capable of doing many handy and necessary task. He possessed a unbreakable will, that could not compromise his integrity.

What a magnificent person, these two human characters, would create when bound together. What a perfect human this creature would become. If the sacred vow of matrimony, allowed the two to mix, and compliment, each other, and grow as one.

The attraction was there, the path determined, and followed by both. The vows exchanged and the relationship established.

God's plan was in place. All the signs were there for both, Phillip, and Natalie. The joy, excitement and pleasure of an intimate

Seeking to be Loved

relationship and building a life, family and fulfilling their dreams together, is now a reality.

Then came the living, facing everyday struggles to provide for the immediate needs of family, each other, and oneself.

The distractions of the world around us can, and often will interfere with the pursuit of happiness. True happiness, which can only be achieved through virtuous love, and devotion.

The concerns and pursuit of life's necessities, test one's commitment to the Promise, and Vow to one another, and their own destiny in this life.

It is easy to get caught up, and trapped, in the day to day requirements of life. We too often react to the world around us. We may exhaust our energy, limit, or neglect to devote time to pursue the most important thing. Thus, forfeiting the maturity of oneself, the wholeness of our being and possibly the purpose of our existence in this world.

Phillip and Natalie busied themselves, caring for the daily needs of family and self. Feeding, clothing, sheltering, and providing for the needs of each child and their own.

The spirit that rejoiced within, once these souls met, is no longer sort, and rarely nourished and enriched. It is not forgotten, for it will always be present, only neglected.

The blessings of matrimony came quickly and often.

As with all, it is only natural to notice, recognize and pay attention to what is visibly present, and observed. Which is that of what one sees.

Something may come along, that stirs the depth of our being. Unfortunately, many do not look deep enough, to seek what stirs the soul, which in turn notified our senses. When one is constantly encouraged only by what they can see, or hold on to, one loses interest. Desire may be enhanced by what we hear when they share with one another. Alas, even that can be very superficial. For it is

Seeking to be Loved

difficult to see inside others. Even harder to understand what might be missing within one's self.

Our eyes only see, what they see. Too often we are content letting our vision reassure what our senses may have already known.

How unfortunate, if one does not explore further the true essence of the attractiveness, that which our soul has encouraged us to explore and understand. For only then our love can and will grow and mature as it is intended.

Phillip knew that something else had to be at work. Although not initially, it was later when he realized it. He knew there was no possible way he could have spotted Natalie, in the crowd below. Not while holding on with one hand, and working with the other, from the third floor. He still did not understand, how he could have seen her in such detail. He just knew, and the message was clear. He had no choice. His soul had guided him to initiate contact.

We all must come to the understanding, things we see from the start, may be attractive and arouse interest. Whether it be a person, or something else. For many it ends there, how unfortunate. For it will only become the distraction, thus will hinder the real attraction, which is not always seen. The true worth, true beauty of ones being, is what lies within our character, what we do not see.

If it is one's external appearance we are attracted to, or words alone, there will never be any depth to the relationship. The oneness created by the commitment to the vow of matrimony, and the whole being we are destined, will never be achieved.

Thus, those that take the vow without the earnestness' necessary by committing heart, body, and soul, to the vow before God, are destined to never be complete. Not the whole complete being, as God had intended.

A Devine plan always at work, manipulates circumstances, arranges opportunities, guiding each soul to its destiny. We the participants are for the most part unaware, we may even think it is chance. It is fate; the spirit knows, recognizes, and understands, thus will guide us, when we allow.

Seeking to be Loved

    Just as it was with these two, Phillip spotting Natalie, in the crowd while working. Natalie noticing Phillip, on the bridge, in the midst of a crowded street. More was at work than their vision acuity, their spirits alerted them to the presence of their intended mate. The part of themselves that was missing, the one who would make their life more complete.

    Now, that the spirits of these two have alerted them the special someone, has been discovered. The Intellectual Being, or shall I say, Intellectual component of one's self is driven to make contact. Communication verbal and nonverbal's are initiated and picked up by one another.

    It was the nonverbal's Natalie picked up on. For she heard all the lines many times before, and appropriately so turned them off. She was able to see through them. She relished in the sensitivity he demonstrated and the attention, Phillip showered upon her.

    Phillip loved her conservative boldness, in addition to her beauty. She was worldly and complete, he sensed that. He knew from the way she carried herself, and what she had shared with him, about her family and her upbringing.

- He was willing to provide her with everything he possessed. He had no understanding of what it was that she really desired and needed. He was willing to work anyway he could, to give her what she expressed, she needed.
- She was willing to provide him fruits of motherhood, and make a home for him and their children. She did not understand what Phillips needs were. She had no awareness of what was missing in this man she loved.

    What they both were willing to give, was all and everything they possessed, and presented it the only way they knew how. Things that were needed, things that everyone wants, the necessities of life, love, and support.

- They both knew they loved God, each other and God loves them.
- They had faith in themselves, in God, and each other.

Seeking to be Loved

- Both loved the other with all diligence, the only way they knew how. They were committed to each other, and willing to satisfy each other's needs and desires, the best way they could.

Neither understood what was beyond their immediate yearnings, and aspirations. The very reasons they were created for each other, and why God brought them together; To be Complete, As One.

Earning a living and providing for daily needs was allowed to consume them. The luxury of time to grow intimately with one another, to learn and understand each entity of their partner was sparse. Thus, love and its comprehensiveness was placed on hold, and not allowed to evolve to fulfill them.

Natalie needed a partner in life, not only a lover and a provider. She needed someone to hold her, and let her learn to enjoy the simplest pleasures, life itself offers.

Someone to teach her, to accept and allow herself to be showered in love and affection.

She needed someone who would convince her, everything is going to be fine.

Someone to always remind her that God will always provide.

Someone to help her understand our Heavenly Father will guide us, and trust enough to follow.

Phillip needed to allow his love to grow. To be more accurate, his love needed to evolve. He knew only from experience, the love a mother and child share. Even that was for just a short period of time in his life, a very incomplete lesson. The love he knew and knew so well, so very well was the love of an infant. A child helpless and dependent, trusting its mother for all its needs.

His love was trapped within the four-year-old child. He had no way of knowing that or why. He never experienced love as it advanced, and evolved, as he grew. His learning sources were removed from his life, taken away so completely, and suddenly. Unfortunately, we know why, it was due to the circumstance's life presented him.

Seeking to be Loved

The learning to love any other way, other than that of a child in need of protection, security, and nurturing during the young helpless stages of life, was at a standstill.

Phillip was willing and quick to learn, unfortunate for him and many like him, there was no one to teach and guide him, as he lived through the developmental associations. He was prevented from the natural exposure of relationships and interactive experiences, during his developmental growing years.

Natalie and Phillip Loving each other as they did, the family grew. Phillip's life became a routine of labor. He worked two, often three jobs for the meager wage of a laborer. Even with his multiple jobs, and willingness to learn new things they barely eked out a living.

Their love and dreams never faded. They had each other and were alive and the family growing. If nothing else, there was an abundance of love within their home.

All Phillip needed was to see Natalie with his children. That was all it took for him to continue his struggle as time passed.

Seeking to be Loved

Chapter 19 Transport

It was Monday morning, an overwhelming fear had struck, and swept over Phillip. The slight pain he experienced ever sense the incident at work Saturday evening, in his lower lumbar region of his back had not subsided. In fact, it was worse, much worst. The pain he was experiencing, which had stricken him to bed Sunday, kept him in silent prayer. Now the slightest movement sent shockwaves of pain, throughout his whole body.

He thought by staying in bed Sunday, and being still the pain would subside. At least that is what he prayed for all day long. He was very thankful that he did not feel the desire to relieve himself. Even slight movements and readjustments of his position in bed caused tremendous discomfort. The brief periods of sleep throughout the day were his only respite and relief. Although, he felt tremendous guilt, staying in bed all day, not attending service, and not enjoying the Lord's day with his wife and family.

It was shortly after 3AM, Monday morning when he made his first attempt to get to his feet. The excruciating pain he felt from the slightest movement and positioning, radiated from his lower lumbar region throughout his entire body. It was even more enhanced now.

The thought that consumed him since Sunday morning, and worried him throughout the day, was recovering enough to go to work. Now he is trying to get himself out of bed. All he can think of is how can he get himself to the mill.

He knew what duties he will have to perform, he wondered how will he be able to make it through the day. It was beginning to overwhelm him. All day Sunday, he prayed neither eating, nor drinking. He prayed the Lord would give him strength this day to do the necessary task his job would require.

He was constantly thinking to himself; "How can I just get up?
How, can I work today?
How, can I get myself there?
Oh, Dear Lord, please help me!

Seeking to be Loved

How, Lord can I do what I need to do?
Please, please help me, give me the strength.
Lord help me endure the pain. Help me get to work.
Help me to provide for my family.

Oh, lord my first family was taken away, and everything I had. I have been faithful to you. I do not mind hardship. I do not mind the pain. I have been dealing with it for twenty years now. That does not matter to me. Please just help me to move. Help me do my job, please, my wife, and my family need me. I do not want them to suffer, as I have."

Each attempt to prepare his body to get out of bed required he muster all his mental and physical reserves. He spent two hours readying his body. He tested every fiber within his frame for another attempt.

Okay, I can start to move now, slow, and easy, he convinced himself. I will just ease to the side of the bed. He started to tense the muscles in his left leg, so he can lift ever so slightly. Just enough to raise it above the indentation it had made in the mattress. Beads of sweat formed on his face, as he once again prepared himself, to make the slightest move.

Phillip thought, "I just need to get out of bed." He kept thinking to himself, "Okay, I am ready." He flattened his palms on the bed beside him, tensing his arms pushing down slightly to assist in helping keep his body stable. He made the first attempt to move his legs out of bed. The sweat is dripping from his face, he is aware that his eye sockets are full. He felt it drain off the side of his face, filling his ear canals. He tightens his eyelids, the saline from the perspiration stung his eyes, even though they are closed.

He smiled, in his mind there is a muffled chuckle. Although completely hidden, the best observer would not have recognized it. When he acknowledged the sting in his eyes, was actually a momentary relief. It created a distraction of his excruciating pain. The all absorbing, and consuming pain, made by the slightest movement to the core of his body.

Seeking to be Loved

He was confident, this attempt would be successful. Here we go, he readies himself.

He engaged the muscles in his left leg to generate the necessary action to lift itself. Another blast, a wave of pain pours throughout his entire being. For someone watching, the movement would not even have been detected. It forced his body into a hyper rigidness, paralyzing him. Forcing him to focus only on attempting to stabilize himself into a position where he could let the tension of his body and muscles ease. In hopes to relieve some of the agony.

The muffled heavy breathing and the heat generated from the intensity of his body's effort, woke Natalie. She gently reached over to touch him. Before her hand reached him, she felt the heat radiating from his body. She gently placed it on his arm, feeling the moistness of the perspiration on his forearm. She turned to him and asked if he was okay. He did not respond. She propped herself up to face him. She noticed the pools of water that filled his eye sockets. His body was covered with perspiration. She saw new beads streaming from his forehead.

"Phillip what is wrong?" Through the dimness of the morning light, she noticed his eyes tighten. She watched the stream of perspiration draining down the side of his temples. Squeezing his eyes shut, forced the pools of water that had filled his eye sockets to empty. She quickly pushed the wall button to light the room. Turning back to him once again she queried, "What is wrong, Phil?" She pulled the sheet off him, revealing his body and the bed around him, were soaking wet.

Gritting his teeth, refusing to open his eyes, he can only say the words, "My back." All his energy and mental capacity was focused on how he can relieve, what it was he is experiencing.

"Can you get up?"

He can only shake his head ever so slightly side to side. Due to the fear of movement, plus the anxiety associated with the rush of multiple emotions he was feeling, made it impossible to enunciate words. He did not want his wife or anyone see him like this.

Seeking to be Loved

Natalie asked, "Can I get you something, let me get you some cold water." He nodded ever so slightly.

It was just after 6AM, all the children were still asleep. Natalie went for a glass of water and prayed, "Lord please help him, we need him." She returned to Phillip, with a large glass of water. She realized he will not be able to drink lying down. "Let me help you up."

Phillip's eyes opened wide; he raised his left hand gently to stop her. "I can't," he managed to say.

"Phil, we have to get you up. You have not been out of bed since you came home Saturday night. From all I can tell, you have not even moved or spoken a word. I just thought you were exhausted, coming down with something, and needed to rest. You have to eat and get fluids in you. Let me try to help you up."

Phillip nodded in agreement. Struggling to speak, looking at Natalie he said, "Very slowly."

She placed the cup of water on the floor. She positioned herself on his left side on the bed beside him. She slid her right arm across his back to his right scapula. She placed her left hand over the front of his right shoulder. She observed some of the tension leaving his face, this is comforting to her.

Her touch has always been a relief, and a joy to him. For a moment he only experienced the pleasure of her touch, and the relief it brings. He looked into her eyes with a gentle smile as he nods, his own hands pushing against the mattress and she gently lifts. For a brief moment he is confident that he will reach a sitting position. His upper torso being lifted off the mattress by Natalie. While he simultaneously attempted to slide his left leg off the edge of the bed. The movement sent another surge of torturous pain, throughout his body.

Natalie felt his whole-body constrict, and they both froze. The heat from his body radiated again. This frightened her, she suggested, "Let me ease you back."

A slight moan came with Phillip's next breath.

Seeking to be Loved

Natalie was unsure what to do, she is worried. "We cannot afford to call a doctor. If I can get him up the children will be able to help him feel better, I am sure of that," she thought to herself. "If he can see and be with them for a while, it will take his mind off his pain."

She searched her brain for ways to get him up and finally decided, I will get my brothers to come help him out of bed. She feared Phillip may lose his job if he cannot work.

She reasoned that is not what matters at the moment. We just have to get him up, she told herself. He will be able to eat and drink, the nourishment will have to help.

She feared for him and her family. She is hesitant not knowing what else to do, she elected to go to the neighbors and ask to use their telephone, to call her brothers. They did not have a phone themselves, it was a luxury they could not afford. I will also call the mill and speak to his supervisor while I am at it. She explained to Phillip, what she was going to do.

He nodded and whispered, "I am so sorry."

She crossed the street to the neighbor's home. Mr. and Mrs. Hatcher have a phone. They told her, she or Phil are always welcome to use it for business or pleasure.

She called the farm, to get help from her brothers. Her mother answered and said, "They would be there as soon as they can. They are in the barn doing the milking, I will let them know when they come in for breakfast."

Natalie asked Mrs. Hatcher if she knew how to call the mill?

"The telephone came with a book with all the local telephone numbers listed in it for businesses and residents. It is called a telephone book, let me get it for you." She handed it to Natalie so she can look up the number of the factory where Phil worked.

Mr. Hatcher told her she would have to call the floor foreman. He is the one who she needed to talk to and let him know Phillip is ill and will not make it the work today.

Seeking to be Loved

When she called the mill, they told her they could not transfer her. She asked, Mrs. Hatcher for a pencil and piece of paper. She wrote down the number they gave her. She asked if she could make another call.

They told her, "Of course you may, my dear."

Phillip's boss seemed to be understanding. He mentioned, "I noticed Saturday evening when he was leaving that he was limping slightly. As usual he was smiling and joking with the other workers, when leaving the plant. So, I thought nothing of it and did not bother to ask if he was okay, he seemed to be."

Natalie thanked, the Hatcher's for letting her use the phone.

Mr. and Mrs. Hatcher wanted to know if there was anything they could do.

Natalie was embarrassed to ask for anything. She responded, "You already have, by letting me use your telephone, thank you very much, we should be able to manage."

The Hatcher's stood in the doorway, watching Natalie as she crossed the street. Mr. Hatcher turned to his wife and said, "We must help."

Mrs. Hatcher said, "I will prepare some food for them. I will also make a list for you, to get some groceries. Six small children in that little apartment. Who knows how they managed, up to now?"

"Phillip always seems to be working," said Mr. Hatcher.

Mrs. Hatcher turned to him and exclaimed, "You know that plant does not pay much."

"I know," was all Mr. Hatcher said in reply. Then he told her, "You make a list and I go get the groceries."

She corrects his grammar, "Then, I will go get the groceries."

He looked at her and asked, "You going to go too?"

She shook her head and just said, "I will make the list."

It was nearly 10:30AM when Natalie heard a knock on the door. Geraldine five years old, their oldest daughter had opened the door and yelled, "It's our uncles."

Seeking to be Loved

Natalie rushed to the door, and explained to them what has transpired.

Her brothers look at each other, "We will get the bastard up," Fred stated, in his matter-of-fact mannerism of speech. It was not at all, spoken in a malicious nature nor tone, just his way. Natalie led them into their room.

Phil attempted to turn his head, only enough to watch them enter. He was glad to see them and smiled, confident they would help. Then a worried look came over his face. "I think if I can get my feet on the floor, I will be okay. I might need help to stand," Phil whispered.

The brothers all stout, strapping young men, looked at each other. One positioned himself at Phillip's feet, another at his head, the other standing in the ready, if needed. Without discussing with Phillip, the brothers nod to each other. One said, "I am ready." In one quick synchronized motion, his legs and shoulders were lifted, his feet brought to the floor. There was a gasp of Phillip's breath. Followed by the loudest screams of agony they ever heard. His body went rigid and fell back, causing even greater unbearable pain. An uncensored barrage of screams, and cursing, spewed forth, as uncontrollable pain pulsated throughout Phillips body.

He pounded his hands repeatedly against the bed as he fell back onto it. Leaving his legs dangling over the bed and feet on the floor. The twisted position of his body caused severe contractions in his lower lumbar region of his spine. The pain caused him to pass out, and his body to go limp.

Tears immediately came to Natalie's eyes. She has never seen anyone in such pain.

One of the brothers decided to pick his feet up and rotate them back in the bed. He hoped it would help make him more comfortable.

Another shock of pain, caused Phillip to jump from his unconscious state to his feet. Screaming like a wild man, and cursing at the top of his lungs. Thrashing like a man possessed, despite the

Seeking to be Loved

pain being pulsated throughout every fiber of his being. Pain shooting throughout his body flooded his mind. Adrenaline flowed in mass dosages throughout his system. He could feel nothing anymore. He raged about the room, oblivious to anything around him, cursing hysterically, he was out of his mind.

One brother said, "He is crazy, he's mad."

One grabbed his arm, to stop him from raging about the room. A violent swing from Phillip, flung him against the wall. The others backed away.

Natalie gasped, as she hurried out of the room to gather her children into her arms to comfort them.

The brothers stayed in the room attempting to calm Phil, to no avail. One came out and suggested to Natalie, "He needed to be taken to the state hospital; before he hurts himself, or one of you. Where is your phone? I will call them."

Natalie squeezed all the children close to her. She told him, "The Hatcher house, is across the street. It is the white House with green trim." She began to cry.

He went to call, upon returning he informed Natalie and his brothers, "They should be here within twenty minutes." He suggested to his sister, "Maybe you should take the children across the street, the lady suggested it. We will take care of Phil."

The screaming, cursing, and yelling from the other room had stopped three minutes ago. Phillip finally passed out from pain and exhaustion. He was lying back on the bed asleep.

Natalie heard a siren in the distance getting closer and closer. It took all her determination to hold back her tears. She did not want to frighten the children, any more than they were.

The siren stopped, one of the brothers stationed himself outside to wave them in. Three men dressed in white outfits, followed Natalie's brother into the apartment. One asked, "Where is he?" No other words was said. They are directed to the other room.

Seeking to be Loved

One brother was sitting on the floor leaning up against the wall, while the other occupied the chair. They both stood up when the men in white came into the room.

Looking at each other and assessing the room, one man nodded to the other. He asked the brothers what happened?

They only said, "We attempted to help get him up. Then he went crazy, screaming and cursing, we could not restrain him."

"What is his name?" One of the men asked.

"Phillip," all three replied.

One of the men kneeled down beside Phillip. He started by whispering his name, then a little louder and louder, until he opened his eyes.

Phillip blinked until his eyes cleared and things in the room came into focus. At first, he is confused seeing three of his brother-in-law's and three large fellows, strange to him dressed in white. He wondered and asked, "Where am I?"

His mind began to clear, then fear befell him as he reasoned why there are men in white. That could only mean one thing, a state hospital. Where they will lock you away with the insane. He can hear Ms. Rupender, screaming it at him as a young boy crouched in the corner. "They will come take you away boy, and lock you up forever."

Phillip asked, "What are you doing here?"

The man in white replied, "You will be coming with us."

Phillip calmly said, "No. Where is Nat?" He asked his brother-in-law's.

Elvin said, "Taking care of the children."

The man in white mentioned, "It is time to go."

"I am not going anywhere with you," Phillip replied.

The man beside his bed looked at the other, and shifts his head to suggest they position themselves. They understand each other well, one maneuvers to the other side of the bed. While one monitors the expressions on Phillip's face. He then left the room, returning moments later with a straitjacket.

Seeking to be Loved

Phillip looked at his brothers-in-law and asked, "Hey, what is this?" They were silent.

The men in white asked him to get up and come with them peacefully.

Phillip explained, "If I could get up, I would have gone to work hours ago. I cannot move, and I will not."

The man nods to the two others. One grabbed his legs and jerked them to the floor. The others swiftly and simultaneously lifted his upper torso to an upright sitting position in bed. The wave of pain made his body convulse. He is too weak to struggle. He can only holler and groan in agony.

Within moments pain turned to fear, then rage took over the possession of Phillips body. It took all six of them with great effort to subdue him. They struggled with all their strength to place his arms into the straitjacket. They forced his arms into the jacket, despite the screams of anguish. They rolled him face down on the bed. One kneeled on top of his spine, paralyzing him in pain. The other two on each arm, forced his arms behind him, as they tightened the straps of the jacket.

Natalie's three brothers had to assist, to keep Phil's body from thrashing, and twisting, while they strapped his legs together at the ankles. They placed him on a board, the straps on it were buckled as tight as possible, one below and one above the knees to stabilize his legs, and prevent him from kicking.

The pain alone would have prevented Phillip from moving under normal circumstances. Although this was not a normal circumstance if the pain and the agony was not enough. Phillip was fighting for his life, and his dignity. Reasoning everything he has as little as it is, may be gone forever. The love of his life, and his children, who he loved so dearly would be gone, if he is taken away.

The thought raced through his mind, he may never see them again, just like he never saw his mother and father again.

All six men were needed to pick him up to remove him from their apartment. The realization of the situation and loss of control flooded his mind. Pain was no longer prevalent, only the feeling he may never see his dear wife, or his most precious children ever again.

He screamed, cursed, wept, and struggled with all the strength he had left. They prepared to carry him out the bedroom door, the men in the white uniforms position them self. One man is at the head holding the board. The other two held him, locking their arms under his arm pits, one on each side. The jacket was so tight they had to force their arms with great difficulty under Phillips. Natalie's brothers carrying the lower half of the board, attempt to help keep him stabilized.

When the order was given, "Let's go,"
Phillip, shouted "NOOOOOOOO."
With a quick lift and heave of the board, Phillip thrashed and twisted himself so violently in an attempt to stop them. The board was literally pulled away from the hands of the six men. The board dropped to the floor. They hear a most distressing moan; the brothers just look at each other. They watched the three men as they dragged Phil strapped to the board across the floor. They quickly recover, and rush to catch up and lift the board.

The white panel truck awaited him, the man at the head of the board opened the door. His back facing the interior of the truck, he waved the other men forward. They stepped up into the vehicle. The brothers lift the lower half. Phillip was slid into position on the floor, in the center of the paneled vehicle. The driver who had opened the door, closed it. He turned to the three brothers, thanked them, and told them, "We will take it from here."

They can still hear Phillip screaming for help, and pleading not to let them take him.

As soon as the vehicle started to move, the attendants look at the other and said, "It is time to keep him quiet." One opened the little box under his seat, he pulled out a course rope with a ball of heavy fabric knotted in its middle. The other straddled Phillip, and grabbed him by the chest of the straitjacket and lifted him up.

Seeking to be Loved

Phillip delirious with pain can only groan in anguish. His body contracts severely. He screamed at the top of his lungs from the agony and torment that he felt physically and mentally.

The other man holding the rope stuffs the fabric into Phillips mouth, stepped behind him and tied a knot behind his head. "That will keep him quiet now." he said, as he moved back to his seat. His partner released Phillip, letting his upper torso drop back along with the board he is strapped to.

Struggling to free himself is futile, he arched his back, to bridge himself in an attempt to achieve a more comfortable position, anything that may lessen the pain.

Both attendants sitting on the bench's secured to the floor and sides of the vehicle, grasped the bottom of their seats firmly with both hands and stomped on Phillips stomach. Forcing his back flat onto the board, where it laid atop the metal floor of the van.

An incomprehensible pain shot through his system. His body violently convulsed. They placed and secured another board over his knees. To stop him from wiggling the straps around his legs loose, preventing even the slightest bending at the knees. In the process of them doing so, created another shockwave of pain. Phillips upper body attempted to lift itself forward and up. Loosening and nearly breaking the straps holding him against the board. Next, they forced, his head and body back, only a muffled groan came through the gag in his mouth. They tied another strap over his chin and another over his forehead. This forced his head tight against the board, then secured the buckle as firmly as possible.

Phillip lost consciousness, again.

"Ah, that will keep him quiet now," one attendants said. The other added, "And still," they both laughed.

Phillip in an unconscious state, can see himself as a child bewildered. He is being taken from his home, nearly twenty-five years ago. No one explaining to him why, or, where he was going. He sees himself being dragged by his arm from one room to another room, and place to place. Being separated, from his home, from his

Seeking to be Loved

brothers and sisters. Remembering only the blankness on people's faces and tears dripping down his cheeks. How he cried for his mother; not understanding where she was and why she was not with him. Why is she not coming to get me, and take me home?

The only feeling and sensation he had was an ache deep within him. A loneliness, a sorrowful numbness, in his heart, an emptiness in his very being, body, mind and soul.

When Phillip woke, he did not know where he was. He was not sure if he was alive or dead. He was surrounded by whitewashed ceilings, walls, and the brightness of the sunlight shining in from the windows. There was a bright glow, produced by light coming through the white curtains surrounding his bed. He did know the bed of which he was laying, was not his.

"Maybe I am in Heaven." He thought only for a moment. His next thought was, "It does not feel like heaven," at least not the heaven he expected.

Where is the happiness, where is the joy my heart should feel? All he felt was the emptiness, sadness and uncertainty and a feeling of abandonment. Everything he felt from his now conscious state, was not pleasant.

He thought surely this cannot be the alternative. That acknowledgement caused him to weep, a great sadness filled his heart. He tried to lift his hand to wipe the tears and cover his face in his shame, he could not. Glancing down, he saw there were straps securing his arms and legs. He noticed them being across his chest and thighs, as well. At that point he noticed pressure against his forehead. He tried to look around to assess his surroundings. He could only move his eyes. He realized the straps were securing all his extremities, stabilizing his body.

He chuckled to himself, from the thought that came to him, "Wherever I am, I must have put up quite a fight."

Next he thought, "I do not feel pain, in my back or body." As his mind continued to clear, he realized he must be in a hospital. He

Seeking to be Loved

now noticed sounds about him, voices, sounds of pans clanging, moans, groans, and other sounds.

Another chuckle, as he felt joy inside, when he realized he must still be alive. He is not dead, and he will again, see his dear beloved wife and children. He whispered, "Thank you God!" He attempted to speak, his mouth is dry. He made a few swallowing attempts, then finally said, "Hello," and repeated "Hello."

Momentarily, the curtain is drawn, a nurse approached him smiling and bids him a pleasant greeting, "Good morning Mr. Gagnon. It is nice to hear your voice and see that you are awake. We were very worried about you. You have been asleep for three days. You must be very hungry and thirsty."

"Where am I?" he asked.

Her reply, "You are in the hospital."

"Which hospital?"

She did not answer his question. She asked, "Do you feel that you are able to eat, if I bring you a tray?"

He is hesitant, the thought of food was the furthest thing from his mind. At that moment he noticed the smell of breakfast foods coming from the trays being distributed. He responds, "I think I can."

"What would you like?" she asked.

Noticing how hungry he really was, he said, "Everything you got," then smiled.

She responded by telling him, "You must start slow Mr. Gagnon, your system may not be able to handle solid foods yet." She noticed a slight frown on his face. She excused herself, "I will be right back." When she returned with a tray, Phillip is pretty anxious about getting the straps off, and was looking forward to moving his arms and his legs.

The tray was placed before him, it was not quite what he imagined. He had envisioned bacon, eggs, sausage, toast with butter and jam, coffee, and juice. "Boy, a jelly donut and cup of coffee, would really hit the spot," he thought to himself.

Seeking to be Loved

What he saw, appeared to be cream of wheat. Accompanied with what looked to be smashed bananas and peaches, toast, orange juice and water. Even that as unappetizing as it looked, stirred the hunger pains in his stomach. He had not eaten in five days.

He was amazed and embarrassed when the nurse pulled up a stool beside his bed. Then placed a large cloth napkin under his chin, and took a spoon in her hand.

Phillip said, "I can feed myself. I would like to get the straps taken off."

She looked at him with kindness and an empathetic look in her eyes. "They must remain until you see the doctor."

A feeling of humility came over him.

The nurse noticed, for she has seen it many times. She told Phillip the doctor will be in this morning, hopefully you will be ready to have them removed. Now, you must eat to build up your strength, so you can get better.

He swallowed hard, as if swallowing his pride.

She reassured him, she is very glad that he is awake and alert. She expressed to him, "It is my pleasure to give you the nourishment you need to get better."

Phillip recognized the earnestness in her voice. He allowed her to feed him; despite the embarrassment, shame, and humility he felt. To him it was an attack on his dignity. The sensation was all too familiar to him, he had experienced it many times. In his childhood, ever sense his parents died, and occasionally as an adult.

With each bite a new energy flowed within him. A new hope, for he felt no pain in his body. The only thing he can remember was the experience of pain, nothing else of the incident, that led up to him being committed. After breakfast was finished, he thanked the nurse, and jokingly asked, "When is lunch?"

The doctor began to make his rounds, on the ward. Phillip can hardly wait to the doctor gets to him. He wanted to learn why he is here. When the doctor was standing beside his bed. Phillip greeted him with a smile and said, "Good morning Doc."

Seeking to be Loved

    The nurse handed the doctor his clip board, that hung at the end of the bed. He read the notes. He did not return Phillips greeting. After a few moments he looked up from the chart. He asked, "How do you feel today?" Glancing down at the clip board again briefly. Lifting his head to look at Phillip, "Mr. Guyon, or do you pronounce it, Gagnon?"

    Phillip smiling said, "I feel pretty good Doc, however you wish, I hear it both ways." Then immediately asked, "Why am I here?"

Seeking to be Loved

Chapter 20 <u>Examination</u>

The Doctor placed his hand on Phillip's forehead. He asked the nurse to take his temperature. Then he felt his pulse, as he counts the beats, while looking at his pocket watch. The doctor then turned to the nurse, and asked about his skin.

She reported the bruises, and abrasions are healing quite well, some are even starting to fade.

The doctor noticed Phillip's look of bewilderment. He said to him, "You put up quite a fight." Then asked, "Do you remember anything that happened?"

Phillip can only tell him, "The only thing I remember is being in pain, and not being able to get out of bed. That is all I remember. What day is this?"

The Doctor said, "Friday March 7, 1946, you have been unconscious for nearly four days now."

"Four days, the nurse earlier said three." He mentioned in a questioning manner? "What hospital is this? Why am I here?" He asked, glancing back and forth between the doctor and nurse.

Neither respond, the doctor set his clipboard on the bed.

Phillip, looked at the doctor's lab jacket, immediately noticed his name tag. The title, State Hospital, below his name. A hot flash came over him, and a moment of panic accompanied with fear, then a calmness returned. He knew he was not crazy, and surely these people would acknowledge that soon.

The Doctor opened Phillip's gown, to examined bruises on his chest and abdomen.

The doctor responded to Phillip's first statement. When you were brought in you were in a semi-conscious state of delirium. You have been asleep, ever since.

He asked the nurse, to remove the straps on his legs and thighs. "In fact, take them all off. I want to examine the wounds on his back and buttock as well." He examined Phillip's knees, and the heels of his feet. The bruises were starting to fade. The abrasions on

Seeking to be Loved

them, and the back of his head, appeared to have stopped oozing. He asked Phillip, "Do you think you can sit up?"

Phillip laughed and said, "Not with these on." Referring to the straps on his wrist, chest, forehead, and legs.

The doctor looked at the nurse and just said, "Nurse."

She proceeded to remove the straps.

The Doctor examined the wounds, and asked Phillip, to describe the pain he experienced.

Phillip explained, "It started in my lower back. I remember the last day at work which would have been Saturday. A coworker and I were asked to move a box. We started to lift the heavy crate, and the other guy slipped. I struggled to prevent the crate from falling on top of him. I made and awkward twist to shift the load before I could set it down. After we moved the box, I noticed an ache in my back. It was right about here." He attempted to show the doctor.

"Did you report that incident?" the doctor asked.

Phillip said, "No."

"Why not?"

Phillip looking sheepish replied, "It was Saturday evening I wanted to finish my shift and go home. Plus, I was afraid if I said anything, I may be replaced, and lose my job."

The doctor asked, "Were you experiencing any pain at that time?"

Phillip responded, "Yes, but...."

The doctor finished his sentence for him, "But, you wanted to finish your shift.

Phillip nodded in confirmation.

"Then what happened?" the Dr. questioned.

"I went home and went to bed, that is all I can remember. I was just happy, looking forward to Sunday, to spend time with my wife and kids. Except when I woke up, trying to move, caused the worst pain I ever felt in my life."

"Do you remember anything else? the doctor asked.

Seeking to be Loved

"No."

The nurse had the straps removed.

Phillip rolled his head gently side to side. The freedom of movement was refreshing. He lifted his muscular arms and stretched them forward. He brought his hands to his face and rubbed firmly. It felt marvelous to him. He opened his fingers and ran them through his black hair, rubbing his scalp as firmly as he could.

"Can you sit up?" the doctor asked.

Before Phillip reacted to the doctor's request, another flash of heat came over his body.

Both doctor and nurse noticed the beading of perspiration on Phillips forehead, the instant he was asked the question. They also noticed the hesitation in Phillips body.

His subconscious was telling him not to move.

They asked Phillip if he was okay, he nodded gently confirming that he is. He was not sure why he did not attempt to respond immediately.

It was because, he trusted his instincts, he always did. He had to. He remembered the pain when he tried to get out of bed, this past Monday morning.

Phillip pressed his hands against the bed. Thankfully, that did not generate pain in his lower back. It was not until he started to lift himself, when the pain returned. He told the doctor, "If I do, I am afraid the pain will start up again."

"Does it hurt now? questioned the doctor.

"Only when I attempted to lift myself."

"Did it hurt when you eased yourself back and released the muscle tension you just initiated? Does it hurt now?"

Phillip told the doctor, "It did eased up when I lowered myself back down into the bed."

The doctor asked, "Can you roll to the side either right or left?"

Phillip looked at the Doctor and asked if he should try?

The doctor nodded and said, "Let us see."

Seeking to be Loved

Phillip tested both shoulders; he suspects rolling to the left might be easier. His attempt was met with pain, he eased himself back.

The Doctor suggested to Phillip, "If the nurse and I helped, will you be able to roll to your side?"

"I know that I could, I just do not know how much pain that would put me in."

The doctor said, "Try, I want to examine your backside."

The nurse told the doctor, "We had checked his wounds each day while he was unconscious."

They had to assist Phillip to roll over. The Dr. explained to him, "We want you to relax as best you can. Try not to tense the muscles in your body as we roll it. Let us know if it causes any additional discomfort."

Phillip said, "Okay."

The pain is severe, Phillip tolerated it.

The doctor asked, "Are you in pain and did it increased?"

Phillip confirms, "Yes, and it did."

The Doctor apologized for the discomfort he experienced. He took off the bandages, to examine the abrasions on his scapulars, and on his lower lumbar and sacral area of his back. He also checked the back of his head and heels. The doctor asked Phillip, "If during the incident he had fallen, or slid?"

Phillip said, "No."

"Did you fall on the way home?"

"No."

"Did something hit you?"

"No."

"Could you have passed out and fallen unknowingly, before you returned home from work?" The doctor questioned him with a puzzled look on his face?

Again, Phillip responded, "No."

Seeking to be Loved

The Doctor checked the reports and notes on the clip board. After the examination he asked the nurse to clean and dress the wounds while he was in this position.

He asked Phillip, "If he can stay in that position until the nurse is finished?"

Phillip replied, "As long as I am still, I can tolerate being like this."

The nurse then asked the doctor, "Should I put the straps (restraints) back on when I am finished?"

The Doctor looked at Phillip, he recognized a sober calmness in his demeanor, even in his face down awkward position he was in. He conveyed to the nurse, "I do not think that will be necessary."

Phillip returned a confirming glance at the doctor and nodded his head slightly, then smiled.

Dr. Miller said, "Good." Then went to his next patient.

Before he left, Phillip asked, "How long will I need to be here?"

The doctor mentioned, "That will be up to Dr. Walker, he will see you later this morning or early this afternoon."

Phillip asked the nurse, "Who is Dr. Walker?"

"He is our psychiatrist."

Phillip told the nurse, "I am not crazy." There is a moment of silence, then he asked, "Am I?"

The nurse thought to herself, "How often have I heard that statement and question."

If Phillip learned one thing from all the years living with Ms. Rupender, it was not to ask questions. Just be silent and be still. He decided that will be a good tactic now. I will patiently wait to see Dr. Walker.

Dr. Miller had several questions about Phillips wounds. The chart had not explained how they occurred, nor were they included on the pickup report. He has seen similar wounds before upon examining new admissions. With no explanation as to what

Seeking to be Loved

happened to the patient once picked up. He was curious and wanted to know how the bodily trauma occurred. He speculated whether the wounds can be associated with the psychosis. He doubts that they can be self-inflicted. The doctor, has his suspicions.

He searched, however found no telephone number in the report. He wanted to call and talk to Mr. Guyon's wife. At the nurse's station he left orders with the charge nurse. The order stated, "If Mrs. Guyon comes in to visit or happens to call, contact his office immediately. If it was after hours, he instructed them to ask how the patient Phillip Guyon, in Bed-401, received the wounds/abrasions."

The nurse identified to Dr Miller, "Mrs. Guyon calls about the same time each day, around one o'clock in the afternoon."

He asked the nurse, "Please have someone notify me. Keep her on the phone, until I can get here. I will make sure that I will be in my office at that time."

"We will do that, Dr. Miller." She wrote a note and placed it on the desk at the nursing station, to remind all staff.

As he was exiting the ward, Dr. Walker approached. He stopped him and informed him that Mr. Guyon in bed 401, was awake and seemed to be alert and oriented.

Dr. Walker answered, "That is good, we were getting worried about him. It will be interesting to talk to him. He asked Dr. Miller if he is coherent."

"He seems to be very much so, I believe you will find him to be an interesting case."

Dr. Walker mentioned, "We do not have any background information. No family has been in, which is odd. I look forward to speaking with him."

"I think you will find him a pleasant fellow to talk to. I would like to know what you think." Dr. Miller said, as he continued walking down the hallway.

"I will keep you informed." replied Dr. Walker.

"Thank you, enjoy your rounds," said Dr. Miller. He presented an intriguing smile as he walked away.

Seeking to be Loved

Dr. Walker entered the section of the ward where Phillip's bed was located. The ward had sixteen beds, eight on each side, all of them were full. The only privacy was offered by white curtains around the bed, that is when they were drawn.

Privacy was a luxury that could not be afforded in state institutions. The drawn curtains separating the beds offered only limited visual privacy. Every whisper, every sound can be heard from almost everywhere in the room. Closing curtains was not allowed by patients, it was up to the discretion of the nurse on duty.

Noticing Phillip was awake and one of the few that appeared to be alert, Dr. Walker approached him first. He already reviewed the chart after speaking with Dr. Miller.

Phillip was the first to speak, "Good morning Doctor."

With his usual coolness Dr. Walker asked, "How are you feeling today? It is nice to see you awake," he added before Phillip can respond.

Phillip laughed and said, "It is nice to be awake. I am just concerned, why I am here in this type of hospital."

"What do you mean?" questioned Dr. Walker.

Phillip proceeds, "I have been called crazy, most of my life; but, never thought I was. So why am I here in this type of hospital?"

Dr. Walker noting from Dr. Miller's report, "All your vital signs seem to be good except that elevated blood pressure. You seem to be healing well. Although there seems to be some memory loss." He determined that from reading Dr. Miller's note from this morning.

Dr. Walker addressed Phillip, with a peculiar inquisitive tone to his voice. "When you were admitted, you were unconscious. The transport information, listed multiple diagnoses.

"What is that?" asked Phillip.

Dr. Walker began, "We have outlined here under diagnoses: reported by the transport crew upon admission. It means expected illness, or symptoms that led to your admission here.

Phillip is curious to hear Dr. Walker's list.

Seeking to be Loved

The doctor read the list:
- Laziness - "Staying in bed all day long the day before admitted."
- Cursing and swearing - "Uncontrollably."
- Combativeness - "Fighting the attendants and family."
- Out of his mind - "Stated by Family member."
- Possible possession - "It took six men to subdue him."
- (Possible Memory loss - Added this morning, by Dr. Miller)

What do you remember of these symptoms?"

Phillip proceeded to tell him, what he told Dr. Miller earlier this morning. He mentioned the work incident, the pain when waking up Sunday morning. How it was paralyzing him when attempting to get up. So, he stayed still in bed Sunday, hoping, and praying he would be better by tomorrow. Which would have been Monday, so he can go back to work.

"Do you remember coming here? Do you remember what proceeded you coming to the hospital?"

Phillip replied, "Only what I shared with the Doctor who was here earlier. When will I be able to go home?"

"Well, that depends!"

"On?" Phillip queried.

"First, we must get you healed up that includes, finding what is causing the pain. Have you tried walking yet? Second, you will have to be emotionally stable."

Phillip said, "No and added, attempts to move my body from my hips down or even to twist, causes pain in my lower back."

I will suggest to Dr. Miller, that he do a complete physical examination when he meets with you tomorrow. If you can get out of bed later this afternoon, I would like for you to come to my office. There we can discuss things in a more private manner. "Do you think you will feel up to it?

Phillip conveyed, "It might take me a while, I think with help I can get out of bed. I am not sure if I can walk. I feel that if I can get my feet on the floor, I will be able to."

Seeking to be Loved

The doctor informed him, "We can place you in a wheelchair if walking becomes an issue. If you can have yourself transferred from your bed to the chair. I will see you this afternoon, Mr. Guyon."

Phillip enthusiastically replied, "I will see you later." While the doctor walked away. Phillip rolled his eyes as he thought to himself. "He thinks I'm nuts."

Natalie called from the Hatcher's telephone the usual time. Nursing staff, had the note by the phone, and immediately sent the orderly to go get Dr. Miller. She mentioned to Natalie, "The doctor would like to speak with you." The nurse informed her, "Phillip was finally awake and is alert and oriented. He appears to be doing well." She told her, "Both doctors, had met with him this morning. He responded well and appropriately to all who spoke with him, including those caring for and working with him.

Here is Dr. Miller." She handed the phone to the Doctor.

Mrs. Guyon, your husband is finally awake and seems to be doing quite well. I have a few questions I would like to ask you.

"Okay," she replied.

"When he came home from work Saturday evening, did he appear to be in any distress? Did you notice if he had any wounds on his body specifically on his upper back, on the scapula's, on his lower back, on his heels, knees, and face?"

Natalie told the doctor, she was in bed when he came in from work. "It seemed to be the usual time. It was probably close to midnight. His shift does not get over until 11PM. Then he has to walk about a mile and a half to our apartment."

"Did you see any wounds Mrs. Guyon? What about the back of his head and around the mouth, or his abdominal area?"

"No, he did not turn the light on. I checked in on him several times throughout the day Sunday. I had not noticed any difference in him other than staying in bed, there were no visible wounds."

"Was there anything different about him, that you noticed?"

"No, other than staying in bed," she replied.

Seeking to be Loved

"Anything different in his routine when he got home?" the doctor questioned.

Natalie thought for a moment, "After changing his clothes, he usually goes to kiss the children good night. I do not think he did that. I do not remember him leaving the room to kiss them. Although I was still half asleep, it also seemed to take him a longer than usual time for him to get into his nightclothes. He just got into bed and stayed there until Monday morning. I knew there was something wrong. He mentioned his back was hurting, when I asked him, if he was ready to get up in the morning."

"Is it common for him to stay in bed all day Sunday, after working all week?" the doctor asked.

"No, Sunday is his only day off. He is up with the birds, earlier than anyone else. He always looked forward to Sunday, to go to church, and spend time with the kids and I."

Doctor Miller is puzzled. He asked Natalie, "Did you check the clothes he had worn that night at work?"

"Yes, and I have washed them since."

"Was there any bloodstains on the back of or on any part of his shirt or his sleeves? What about the heels of his socks, the front of his pants in the knee areas? Was there any on the bed, sheets, blankets, or towels?"

"No, there was no blood anywhere, just the usual dirt and grime on the front of his shirt and pants." The questions worried Natalie, wondering what happened to him.

Dr. Miller thanked Mrs. Guyon, and asked if she had been in to see her husband.

"No." She explained we have no transportation, nor extra money for bus fare. I have six children at home I can't just leave them." She caught herself, before she started to weep.

Dr. Miller sensed a tone of guilt in her voice, and did not question her any further. "I hope you can come in soon to visit him. I am sure he misses you and the children."

Seeking to be Loved

She asked the doctor, "When he would be released and could come home?"

His only response was, "We all hope soon." He thanked Natalie for calling.

She thanked him and asked, "If he (Phillip) would be able to talk to her?" She reiterated to the Doctor they had no means of transportation, nor do we have a phone. This phone belongs to a neighbor, "I hate to keep troubling them. Would it, could it, be possible when I call the hospital," she paused to control her emotions, until she can regain her composure. "Would it be possible to talk to him, could Phillip come to the phone?"

Dr. Miller told Natalie, he would talk to the ward nurse and make the request. "I will leave and order to allow your husband to come to the telephone the next time you call. If someone informs you to the contrary, you remind them, I said it was okay."

"Thank you Doctor, I know he will be worried about the children. I think to hear his voice will reassure them as well. I know it will make him feel better. I have to admit, I miss him and the sound of his laughter. We are all worried about him. If he knows we are okay, it will help put his mind at ease. I know it will," she expressed to the doctor.

He said, "I believe you are right, have a good day." He hung up the phone.

Natalie turned to Mrs. Hatcher; she had been looking on questioningly. "He is awake and alert."

Mrs. Hatcher noticed the encouraging tone to her voice and a hint of hopefulness in Natalie's eyes.

"The doctor said, we can speak with him next time I call." Natalie expressed her appreciation, for allowing her to use the phone and troubling her each day.

Mrs. Hatcher gave Natalie a hug, and replied, "You come and call every day. I am glad someone is getting use from that thing, that telephone. I seem to have little use for it. I do not know anyone else that has one." She looked at Natalie and said, "Who would I call? My

498

husband thought it would be a useful tool when needed. This is one of those times."

They disengaged their embrace, Natalie let her know what a wonderful neighbor she is. "Our family is blessed to have such a kind neighbor. I must get back home now the two older children will be home from school soon, thank you again."

That afternoon Phillip met with Dr. Walker, in his office. It was only with great difficulty, with the assistance of two attendance, that he was able to transfer from his bed into a wheelchair. Once he was on his feet, it actually felt good. Getting to that point was grueling. Sitting back down was very painful, a cushion provided help to ease the discomfort.

Dr. Walker was cordial, he questioned Phillip extensively. He examined him once again. Requesting that he reexplain the incident at work, and getting home that night. "Phillip, have you ever injured yourself in the past?"

"Yes, I have, actually twice Doc."

"Please tell me and describe the incidents and give me all the details you can recall for each."

Phillip began, "I never shared this with anyone."

"Not even when it happened?" the doctor asked.

"No."

"Why not?"

"Well, let me explain." Dr. Walker dipped his chin, Phillip proceeded. "It happened when I was nineteen, I had been working on a job with the Civil Conservation Corps. We were camped someplace southwest of Boston. I do not remember the name of the town close to the area we were working. We had been clearing forest for a new road. Actually expanding it, to make it two-Lanes. It was connecting Worcester to Boston. We may have been in the North Grafton area, at the time.

A few of the boys and myself were prying the downed trees in position to be hitched. We had to move them to a flat section of ground. Where the teamsters could get to them with their hitch of horses, to drag them to where they can be loaded and taken to the sawmill.

The ground was soft with lots of underbrush and debris. I remember we were working as a unit when we were ready to roll the log. When we started the push and roll. My partners timberjack snapped, he was thrown forward over the log. I was baring full weight of the log on my end. I was pushing as hard as I could. I was holding the log for all I was worth, it was not going anywhere.

My right foot sank deeper into the soft ground. I felt something, it was almost like I was ripping something in my lower back. I cannot swear to it, but, I believe I could even hear it. To me it sounded like cloth being torn in half as it happened. I did not feel anything at first, I thought it was my shirt, then a ping, ping, ping. It felt like fibers in my lower right part of my back were snapping. I know that must sound strange. Once others came to help roll the log into place, I remember thinking. "What was that sound and funny feeling in my back?"

I stayed still for a while, the other guys looked at me, and asked if I was okay. I told them, I think so, as I reached back to feel my lower back. I remember asking God, "Please, don't let me get hurt, not now."

"Were you?" the doctor asked.

"I did not feel hurt. However I knew something was wrong. I remember thanking God, and I was being very cautious the rest of the day. I made sure my footing and body were in good solid, sound, stable positions. Slight variations caused discomfort, when moving, especially straining."

"Then what happened?" the Doctor questioned.

"We finished the days labor, had dinner and I watched the camp's evening baseball game. I usually played, I always looked forward to playing, actually I loved to play. I was a pretty good pitcher and batter. Something inside warned me not to play tonight, so I just watched. I was glad I skipped it, despite the urging of my teammates.

The next morning, I was just so stiff and tight. The backs of my legs and in my back especially the lower portion was sore. It was not until after the morning exercise routine, my back felt loose. I was not so stiff, I felt I could move around without too much difficulty. I thought I would be able to work, which I did and was so glad for that. I could not afford to go back home. I had no home."

"What do you mean, you had no home?"

Phillip explained to the doctor, about his upbringing and treatment as a youth from the time he lost his parents. He did not want to go back to Ms. Rupenders.

"Did you not have any other place to go?"

"No, not really."

"Did you not have any money saved up, Phillip?"

"We were not allowed to keep any at the CCC camps. Just a few dollars each month, the rest we had to give them an address. Our pay would be sent to a home address. We were working for our family's support, that was how it was set up. All the other guys were sending theirs to their families."

"Well, you did not have any family." stated Dr. Walker. "SOOO?"

Phillip looked down at the floor, and there is a pause in his speech. He knew the doctor wanted an explanation. He sheepishly revealed, "I had mine sent to Ms. Rupender."

"You did say, you did not like living there? Plus, you were not treated well." The doctor has a peculiar look on his face, "So why did you send it to her?"

"I had no one else to send it to. I guess I felt sorry for her. The fact is, she is the only family I had for thirteen years. I figured I owed her something."

Dr. Walker asked Phillip, how he felt about the loss of his parents, and being removed from his other siblings. He observed a misplaced smile and a quick laugh, from Phillip. Something he referred to as the gallows laugh. When one laughs at something that is not funny. It was a means of brushing away the emotion, or, the hurt within.

"I did not have time to think about it really, I did not know what to think. I know I felt sad, indifferent, I guess. The first few years, I missed them a lot, and kept thinking why they, or, anyone was not coming to take" - he stopped - (a look of sadness mixed with disappointment, is read of his facial expressions by Dr. Walker), he continued; "take me home."

"What do you remember about that, Phillip?"

"Like I said, I do not remember much. I do remember seeing my mother lying in bed, the next thing I know she is gone. I remember my father holding me very tight, he was quivering. I remember him sobbing under his breath. No one would tell me where she was or why she was gone. I did not know why she left, or what happened. The next thing I know, my father was also gone. I just remembered being pulled everywhere and going to different places. I just could not figure out why. I just seem to be yanked here and pulled there. It seemed like we were always going someplace different, and never staying for more than a day." There was another delay, and an awkward silence. Then Phillip said, "Until the orphanage."

"What places?" question the doctor.

"Oh, I do not know all the places, or why we were taken to them. To me they were just buildings, what or where they were, made no sense to me. To me, it just seemed like another big house. Some places were kind of like this office, I remember. They seem to drag me in here, and out to there."

"Who are they, that you are referring to?"

"I had no idea, to me they were just people."

"What happened to your brothers and sisters? Did any of them succumb to the influenza."

"No, although then I was not aware of anything that was happening. I really wish, I knew where everyone had been placed. It

Seeking to be Loved

was not until I had signed up to join the CCC. I found several Guyons and Gagnons on the list our company commander had. One day waiting for him in his office, I saw a list of names hanging on his wall. It had the names of recruits in alphabetical order. I went to the G's and found Henry and Joe's names. I asked the commander where they were and what camp they worked. I told him they may be my brothers. He looked at the list and said, "They were sent to different areas to work on different projects."

"So, they were both in separate camps themselves?" asked the doctor.

"Yes, I asked to be transferred to where they were. Our commander said, that was not possible. He did say, I could write them, and he assured me the letters would be sent to those camps."

"And were they your brothers?" asked the doctor!

"Yes, they were in those CCC camps, I really did not know where they were located. The letters eventually got to them and they both wrote back. We eventually were able to hook up with each other at different times. When our camps were working close to one another our company commanders would set up inter-camp baseball games."

"Were you happy to see each other?"

"Oh doc, you better believe it, I was so happy. It was at those baseball games, when I finally realized what had happened to my parents, and my other brothers and sisters. They told me that our parents died during the flu epidemic of 1918. My mother died first in August, my father in late September or early October. I just turned five years old days before Dad died."

"Was there a funeral?"

"Not that I knew of, nor my brothers and sisters were ever aware of one. We have not even been able to find where they were buried. Neither Joe, nor Henry knew, no one knew. They would not tell us back then. I was too young to even know to ask," Phil made a sulking sound. "Is that not odd," Phillip asked the doctor?

Seeking to be Loved

Dr. Walker was fully aware of the mass number of deaths due to the influenza epidemic. Many of the bodies were incinerated, especially for those that could not afford caskets or burial plots. He explained that to Phillip, as he observed tears running down Phillips face.

There was another long moment while communication was suspended, as Phillip prayed silently, for God to forgive them.
"We did not have a proper burial service for our parents. Please accept them into your vast heavenly kingdom. I know they love you God. For it was they who taught me how to love you."

"Are you okay Phillip? Did you feel abandoned by them? Were you resentful of them, or of God, for taking them away?"

Phillip looked at the doctor, with a boyish grin. "No, how could I be. I know my parents loved me very, very much. I know they loved God, and I know God loves us. I also believe all things happen for a reason. I do not know how or why, maybe I never will, until my time comes."

He is amazed at Phillips words. He despite the necessity of his objectivity in this evaluation, he recognized a strong faith in this individual. Dr. Walker thought to himself, how can it be so simple, to believe in such a manner as he???

He asked, "Are you not bitter, angry or resentful with anyone, especially your parents for leaving you? What about your foster mother?"

Phillip looked at the doctor, then he said, "My parents did not leave me, they died. I have never forgotten them, and they are always in my heart. They will always love me, and I them. How could I be angry with them for that?"

Dr. Walker, intervened and ask Phillip. "How do you know they will always love you?"

"Because they told me many times, they loved me, and would never stop loving me. I remember hearing those words many times before they died. Those words, their words along with their love has been embedded in me."

Seeking to be Loved

The doctor nods, and wrote a few notes. He questioned Phillip further about Ms. Rupender. "Do you not have any ill feelings towards her, especially due to the way she treated you and beat you?"

"All I know Doc, is I was confused and sad. I missed my mother and my father, my brothers, and sisters very much. Although Ms. Rupender, did not treat me very well, she gave me food and a place to stay. All I felt was apprehension and fear the first five or six years living with her. Just pity, the next seven or so. When she got sick from drinking too much, I could sense she was not a pleasant person. She was not happy with her life. All I wanted, was to be able to do something that would make her feel better."

"Did you, or could you?" asked Dr. Walker.

"I do not know." Phillip stated with a questioning tone. "I like to think maybe somehow, sometimes I did. One never knows. I do know when I left her that day to start work with the CCC, I felt very sad for her. She had no one in her life, at least that I was aware of. I lived with her for thirteen years, we never had visitors, and we never went to visit anyone.

"You mentioned you injured your back a couple of times." Dr. Walker asked, inquisitively, changing the subject.

"Yes, the next time was several years later after Natalie and I were married. We were living in Pepperell, we had four young children all a year apart. Natalie was pregnant with our fifth. It was actually a few years, maybe a little over a year ago."

"What incident brought this about?" asked the doctor.

"Well you see, with our family growing, I was not making enough money at the Mill. I would work any extra shifts they would allow me, that still was hardly enough. I looked for a second job, they were hard to find. One of my coworkers asked me if I wanted to become a volunteer firemen. I told him no, but, he gave me his spiel. I listened to the duties and responsibilities.

When I went home that night, I discussed it with Nat. We thought the training, and experience I would receive could be helpful at home and work. If workers are injured, or if there is a fire, I would know what to do."

She said, "You never know, as a volunteer those skills, training and experience, may lead to a better job." We decided it would be a good idea.

"What type of job?" he asked.

"We thought that if there would be job openings in some Fire Departments, in other bigger cities surrounding us, I could get on the force. Especially, if I had experience and training."

"So, you are talking about a job as a Fireman?"

"Yes. The money I could make as a fireman, plus the fact that I could still work at the mill, would make things a lot easier for the family. Not to mention, I would be able to spend more time with them. I would not have to work so much extra time at the mill."

"So, what happened?"

"We, the volunteer fireman are always on call, whenever the alarm rings. We are required to get to the station as fast as we could. From where I live it was about a half-mile from the station. I found a short cut going through the woods, only a couple hundred yards from the station.

One night we heard the alarm go off, I quickly threw on my clothes, my shoes, zoom, out I go. I figured I could get there a little faster if I took the shortcut. I just started running through the woods, next thing I know, I am flying through the air. I tripped on something, maybe it was a root. I was going so fast. It was dark, and I caught my foot. I just went head over heels and landed right on my back hitting a rock. I remember thinking, What Happened.

I just got myself back up, and started running to the fire station as fast as I could. I guess due to the excitement, I did not feel anything at the time. I remember when I landed and felt that rock against my lower back, I thought to myself, 'Ooh dang, this is not going to be good.' I did not have time to think about it then. It was later when I was walking home, after we returned from the fire. That I noticed my back was hurting and I was walking funny."

Seeking to be Loved

"Did you hurt your leg?" asked Dr. Walker.

"No," Phil chuckled, he remembered his son asked the same question. "My leg was not injured or hurting. Actually, I had not even realized I was even limping. It was a couple of days later my son, who was six years old about the time, asked me, 'Why are you limping Dad?' I recall thinking, how did he notice. I just chuckled and said, I hurt myself running through the woods the other night going to the fire. He asked me, 'Does it hurt Daddy?' I looked at him and smiled and said, Only when I think about it. I did not say anything further to him, he may have thought I hurt my leg. But, it was my back."

"Did you miss any work from that incident?"

Phillip looked at Dr. Walker and made the sound, "Sheesh, I can't afford to miss work."

The doctor wrote a few notes, then addressed his patient. "Phillip, it has been delightful talking to you. I am sorry that it is here and under these circumstances. This will end today's evaluation. Do you have any questions for me?"

"Only one doc; when can I go home?"

"I must be honest with you Phillip. I want to observe you for another few days. I want to see Dr. Miller's report, then consult with him. In the meantime, rest, eat well, take plenty of fluids. Also, if you can without too much discomfort, exercise. Be cautious not to re-injure yourself. It is important that you, Do not overdo it, or push it too soon. The back is a difficult part of the body to heal and re-strengthen, especially the lower lumbar area."

Dr. Walker rang for the attendant, to escort and assist Phillip back to his ward, and bed.

Phillip felt more alert, he is noticing more detailed things about the hospital, as he went back to his room. Much of what he sees is not to his liking. He is looking forward to the day when he will be going home. There is a new energy in his being. He wished he can hear Natalie's voice, and to wrap his arms around her, and his children.

Seeking to be Loved

Natalie called the next day, Saturday afternoon. The ward nurse was pleasant, Phillip was in a wheelchair waiting for the call. "I will send someone for him," she told Natalie. Then she shared his progress, at Natalie's request. "Dr. Walker, has not completed his evaluation, she explained. Until he does, we will not know when he can go. It seems he is getting along quite well, Oh, here he is now!" The nurse handed the telephone and receiver to Phillip.

Phillip, as usual was supporting a broad grin, now larger and broader than ever, appearing on his face, ear to ear. He took the phone handset, "Nat, Nat," he shouts into the phone speaker holding the receiver against his ear. He paused to hear her voice; it is sweet music to his ears. He expressed how much he missed her and the kids. "How are those stinking brat kids?" He asked in the fondest voice and laughed.

She told him, "They are fine, they miss you." She asked if he is okay?

"I am fine, except for my back, it makes getting around tough. It is hard to sleep at night with all the screaming, yelling, and crying going on. Gee, I wish they could do something to help these people. I do not think I need to be here, in this type of hospital."

Natalie described to him, the way he had acted Monday morning. "My brothers and I, did not know what else to do. You acted crazy, the way you carried on so." Her voice changed, and she stated in a questioning manner; "I did not know what got into you. I told the kids to cover their ears, they were all scared and crying. I had to take them to Mrs. Hatcher's house, when they came to take you out of our apartment.

You acted so strange, not getting up, talking about pain, not moving, cursing, we were frightened. You really were acting crazy. I never saw you like that before. I was fearful, it took six big men to get you out of the house, you fought so."

Phillip explained, "I don't remember any of that. All I remember was being in so much pain when I tried to move. I am so sorry," he said to Natalie. "I am so sorry, that I scared you and the kids. Please tell them, I did not mean to and that I love them."

Natalie related to him, "When you did not get up Sunday, I knew something had to be terribly wrong. I just thought you were exhausted from working so much. That was why I let you stay in bed all day. I knew you had to get up Monday to work the early shift. You would not let me help you." Natalie started to whimper on the phone. She sniffed, and had to stop the conversation momentarily to collect herself.

"I called the farm from here, Mrs. Hatchers. I wanted to ask my brothers to come help. When they started to pull you out of bed, you just went berserk."

Phillip said sadly, "I know, it was like something just went blank in my mind. That was the last thing I remember."

Nat, started to cry.

Phillip's heart was breaking listening to her sobs over the telephone. He begged her to stop. "I never want to hurt you or the kids in any way. He promised that this will never happen again. I love you." He told her, "I am going to have to go back to bed now. I have to say goodbye, I love you and hope to see you soon." He was fighting back tears of sadness and sorrow, for the pain that he caused his family. He handed the phone to the nurse and whispered, "Thank you, I have to go now."

The nurse knew; she saw the emotion and she understood immediately. He did not want to distress his wife. She took the handset; "Hello, Mrs. Guyon, Phillip is required to lay down, Doctors orders. Yes, he is doing fine: he misses you and his children."

As he is being taken back to his bed, he pleaded to God.

"Never let me get like that again. No matter what pain or suffering I have to endure, I will. Please lord, I never want to hear or see Nat or any of the kids cry or suffer again, because of me. Please heavenly Father, I ask this in Jesus' name, Amen."

Seeking to be Loved

Monday morning Dr. Walker consulted with Dr. Miller, about the Phillip Gagnon case. He asked Dr. Miller, "What are your findings in reference, to Phillip's physical being."

Dr. Miller asked Dr. Walker if he has read the chart.

"I have."

"So you know how physically strong and well-built this man is. All his limbs are sound. There was swelling in the lower spinal area, the lumbar and sacral region. I was concerned about the bruises and abrasions. After speaking with his wife, I felt that he was, let us just say, not handled properly."

"Did the x-rays, show anything?"

"Yes, some slight misalignment of the vertebrae. There appeared to be some thickening of the bone structure. That could be from previous injury, and healing. Or perhaps some natural misalignment from birth, which is very common when there is some curvature of the spine, such as with scoliosis."

"Did you know that he was injured nearly nine years ago, or was it ten? I wrote it in my note," said Dr. Walker.

"No, I was not, he had not shared that with me."

"It occurred when he was working on a CCC project. He did not want to be sent home, he had nowhere to go, no home to go to. So, he apparently had continued to work, never receiving proper care," offered Dr. Walker.

"That would explain the x-ray image. He must have been experiencing some level of pain continuously since that injury." Dr. Miller stated to Dr. Walker.

"Yes, I have seen many patients that had back injuries, it affects their psyche tremendously. People with injury to the lower back, rarely seem to recover completely, which leads many to experience psychiatric issues," said Dr. Walker.

"It makes sense, with what we know about the central nervous system, and the spine. Everything is channeled from the spinal column to multiple networks of the body. All through the tiny interconnected vertebrae. When damage is done to the column itself, we can only imagine how that disrupts many bodily systems. If any of those tiny vertebrae become damaged and or the natural thickening of the bone when healing occurs, there can be many complications. With the slightest increase density of the boney vertebrae, or, a burr forms and develops, thus pushes against the column itself, the system is disrupted continuously," explained Dr. Miller. "What is your diagnoses Dr. Walker?"

"I have assessed from information given of him at admission and my first meeting, there is still *something missing*. I must wait until all test and results are completed, and confirmed, before I can make a proper diagnoses."

"That is the type of answer I expected from you," stated Dr. Miller as he chuckled.

Dr. Walker grinned, then proceeded by pointing out, "Despite those admitting diagnoses on the pick-up report, *Laziness, *Cursing and Swearing, *Combativeness, *Out of his mind, *crazy, *Loss of memory, etc. etc. (* = Common diagnoses in the early 1900's)

Plus, of course his blackout episode. Not to mention his history, and upbringing. I am not sure, nor, am I convinced at this time whether or not, this is the right place for him or that he needs to be here."

"What do you mean, Dr. Walker?"

"Well, the fact is, yes, he has an interesting history and a very unfortunate one."

Dr. Miller looked on questioningly, "Please continue."

"Examining his background, coming from a large family, that took flight out of France. Just before the outbreak of The Great War. He was only seven months old during that trek, it had to be very difficult and traumatic for one so young. Having to endure the hardship of travel during such a mass migration of people.

Of course, Phillip, he remembers none of that. He was told of the experience by his parents and older brothers and sisters. They were making their way along well as new immigrants, first in Canada and then to this area.

Seeking to be Loved

When he was only four years old both his parents died during the flu epidemic of 1918, within less than two months of each other. He was separated from the only love ones he ever knew. Too young to understand why, his parents died, and he was removed from his brothers and sisters." Dr. Walker, paused so Dr. Miller can construct the image he is presenting.

"On top of that, he had been placed in an orphanage. Then he was placed in a home with a woman. From our conversations, she was not a kind person, very controlling, very demanding, and quick to punish. From his description, he did not have an opportunity to interact or, play with other children. At best he could only observe. If he came home dirty from play, or any reason he was punished severely."

"From the sounds of it my good Doctor, we should have a monster on our hands," stated Dr. Miller.

"This is my dilemma," exclaimed Dr. Walker. "He does not demonstrate any of the typical behaviors, or dysfunctions, that I or staff have observed. His responses were normal to the typical questions. His wits seem to be about him. He does not seem to have lost his sense of humor. He presents himself well, despite the agony he must be in from the pain. Since he has been in the hospital, he demonstrated no agitation. Despite being on that floor. Staying there one night would make me crazy." Both chuckle in agreement.

"There is just something about him, there is a sparkle, a liveliness in his eyes and being. Despite the situation he is in, his physical injuries and history, he does not appear to be in despair. I am not ready to give a diagnoses just yet????

"I agree Dr. Walker, that is why I wanted to concur with you in person, on this case. I believe a mistake has been made bringing him to this hospital. Then there is the unexplained wounds."

"I have him scheduled this morning. I will finish my psychiatric evaluation, and run a few test. Then let us meet again and decide what we would like to do about this case," suggested Dr. Walker.

Seeking to be Loved

"Very well, I thing that is a good idea, I look forward to your findings. Good day," said Dr. Miller.

Seeking to be Loved

Chapter 21 Next Meeting

It is one week today that Phillip has been in the hospital. Upon receiving his breakfast tray, the nurse informed him, "You have a meeting with Dr. Walker at 9AM."

Phillip wanted to eat sitting up. One of the attendants watched him get his feet out of bed. He asked Phil if he may help him.

Phillip said, "Let me try on my own first. I think I can do it, just give me a minute."

His movements were slow and controlled, he made the transfer to the edge of his bed independently. He stretched out his arms, sat on the edge of his bed, and ate his breakfast.

When he finished his meal he freshened up, it was time for his meeting. He is taken to Dr. Walker's office. The good doctor inquired, "How are you feeling today Phillip?"

"Fine doc, I walked some yesterday, it felt good to be on my feet."

"That is good! Were you not experiencing pain?"

"Yeah, moving is difficult, especially the rolling and twisting, just to get to my feet. Something told me yesterday, it was time to stand up and start moving!"

"Something, told you?" the doctor questioned. "Are you hearing voices, telling you to do things?"

"Nah, nothing like that, it was something inside. I just thought, if I can get to my feet, I would be able to walk. Getting to my feet hurt some. Heck, sitting back down does also. Once I was on my feet, I could step without too much trouble."

"Do you feel better now?"

"Yes, actually I do, I feel quite stiff though. The pain is much less now, even when I am sitting in this thing, (He patted his wheelchair), it does not feel as bad."

"Tell me more about the voice inside. Can you explain it to me?"

Seeking to be Loved

Phillip chuckled, he knew that Dr. Walker is thinking he is crazy again.

"Please explain, if you can," the Dr. repeated?

Phillip can hear a phrase that echoes in the deep recesses of his mind. He accepted the challenge. "I will try Doc!"

"You see, it is not like it is a real voice. It is not sounds you can really hear with your ears. It is something inside, kind of like a thought. I remember my mother telling me more than once, when I was very young and growing up in those early years. Each of us have a guardian angel. It will guide us and protect us when needed. She would give examples we all experience. I am sure even you have Doc, (The doctor tittered.)

She would say, "You will always know right from wrong. Listen to your conscience." She would say, "If something inside, in your heart is telling whatever is in your head, not to do something, don't. Just walk away," she would say. "That voice inside you is your Guardian Angel. It is like the instincts in animals, it warns you of danger. We are given it by God, to be a constant guide. So, you always know what is right."

Phillip can see his mother telling him these things, while she is holding him. Looking deep into his eyes as she speaks to assure the message is sinking in. She has him promise her, you will always listen to your guiding Angel. That little voice inside of you right here. As she takes her finger and wiggles it into his chest. Making him laugh! Now promise me!

Phillip sees the ever-adoring love in her eyes, it touches his soul! He whispered aloud, "Je vais Ma mee" (I will Mommy).

Dr. Walker could not hear the whisper and asked, "What was that?"

"Oh, it was nothing," Phillip replied. Suddenly, he realized his pain is gone. It was as if a new life and energy surged through his body. Was it his inner being, or maybe just in his mind? Whatever it was, he wanted to get out of his wheelchair. He prepared to do so, he said to himself, "Oh (with a grimace) it is not gone yet."

Seeking to be Loved

Dr. Walker noticed the metamorphosis in Phillip, and the sudden change in his appearance. During those last few moments, he inquired, "Are you feeling okay?"

"You know Doc I am, for a moment even sitting in this thing, I almost felt comfortable," Phillip replied. "It has been a long time since I felt this good, even before I hurt myself, at work last Saturday. I was going to try to stand, just a second ago, that is when I realized pain was still there." Phillip answered, with a slight laugh.

"Your back is healing from the rest, and the treatment you have been receiving," the doctor suggest.

"Yes, thank you Doc!" Although Phillip, knows the rest and the food had to help. As for the treatment, the verdict is still out. He said, thank you to the Doc, thinking it might make him feel better believing his treatment is working.

Phil knew the thought of his mother, at that instant and the precious love that emanated from her, is what caused the refreshing surge. As well as the speaking of God, and his Angels. He knew he was given grace to endure, and a moment of relief.

Dr. Walker mentioned to Phillip, "I would like for you to take some test."

"Okay, I am ready!"

"Well, as soon as possible, do you think you will be up to it is afternoon?"

"I am up for it right now!"

Dr. Walker, explained to him, "I would like for you to be fresh and rested."

"I am never rested; my wife says that I am fresh all the time." Phillip looked out the corner of his eyes and chuckled. "Really no kidding, I feel up to it now."

"Well then, let us get started."

They spent the next three hours in Dr. Walker's office completing three test, one right after the other. It was grueling, though both enjoyed the experience, and laughed about the inkblots.

Seeking to be Loved

Chapter 22 Case Review

Dr. Walker and Dr. Miller met again during rounds the next morning, to discuss Mr. Guyon. "What is your verdict Doctor?" asked Dr. Miller.

"Well, the admitting diagnoses would be ample reason to be admitted to a psychiatric hospital. I believe the admission was justified. As we discussed yesterday and with his background." There is a temporary halt in his speech: "It would be legitimate, and I must say, expected for him to have a psychiatric condition."

Dr. Miller looked on with inquisitive eyes, as he listened for Dr. Walker's, next statement.

"My gut feeling, is there is something deeply embedded in his psyche that is affecting him. Although, after the testing, evaluation, as well as observations completed, I find nothing of the sort. I have questioned the nursing staff, and even the orderly's, he seems to be normal. If not more so than most of the people walking the streets outside this institution.

He is hard-working, seems to be a loving individual. He has kept his sense of humor, despite everything he has been through, even the pain he is experiencing now?? He does not seem to be a malingerer. But, there still seems to be something that I may have missed. Although the test indicate nothing so far. It is, well, let us just say, a good doctor's intuition, there is something gnawing at me, that I feel impelled to find. What about you Dr. Miller," asked Dr. Walker.

"I too have to admit, he is an interesting case. I am not a psychiatrist, although I suspected early on there was no psychiatric condition. At least one severe enough, to cause him to be in this hospital. It is very obvious he is in a lot of pain. From his back injury and I must say," he leaned toward his colleague to make his next statement, so no one else would hear. "This is off the record. The admission examination outlined multiple injuries, indicating trauma to many parts of is body in specific areas. His wife identified, he had no visible injury's, before he was picked up. He may have received them, or they were enhanced during the transfer from home to this institution. Yet he has never complained of those or harbored any ill will."

Dr. Walker replied, "That can very well be due to the blackout, he has no memory of it. He does not remember any of that due to the severity of the pain he suffered. Thank God."

Dr. Miller's serious expression quickly changed to one of astonishment; "Did I hear you say, Thank God?   You Walker??"

"It was a Freudian slip, I met thank goodness." said Dr. Walker.

"If word about the handling of this patient got out, it would look bad for this institution," stated Dr. Miller.

Dr. Walker stared at his colleague questioningly, "Do you think we need to discharge him? "Maybe we should have him transferred to the general hospital, for treatment of his physical conditions?"

Dr. Miller took a few seconds to process before he responds. "I believe things happen for a reason, Dr. Walker, maybe it was fate or maybe something else; Faith."

Now Dr. Walker, looked at him in a curious manner. The words Fate and Faith struck him in a peculiar way.   Dr. Walker questions, "What do you mean?"

"After talking with Mrs. Guyon, the family is doing fine. Although, they are just barely eking out a living, and I do not see how on Phillip's wages. Well, they can ill afford hospital fees. I would be willing to bet, if I were a betting man, the cost for a hospital admittance, test and treatment would be beyond their means. Phillip, if brought to another hospital would place a tremendous burden and hardship on his family. I am just saying, sometimes things are caused to happen in such a way, so that we can get the things we need to carry on, with our lives."

This statement caused Dr. Walker, to raise his eyebrows. He is trying to understand, what Dr. Miller is insinuating.

Seeking to be Loved

Dr. Miller recognized this; he knows his colleague well. He just reiterated, "Fate or Faith," to Dr. Walker. "If we wait until we know with absolute surety, it will be too late for any of us."

Dr. Walker asked, "What do you mean?"

Dr. Miller placed his arm on his fellow doctors shoulder and pats him on his back, as they walked down the hall. He chuckled and said, "Only those of faith will understand that statement."

"So, what do you think we should do with Mr. Guyon?" Inquired Dr. Walker, ignoring the comment. He knew Dr. Miller, is trying to provoke a religious debate. He did not want to give him the satisfaction of knowing that he struck a nerve.

"If you are with me on this, I have a suggestion, a proposal really," probed Dr. Miller.

"What is that?"

Dr. Miller made his appeal to Dr. Walker, "Let us keep him, at least to the end of the week. I would like for him to heal enough so he can walk. I want him to at least be able to get around his home, get in and out of bed, and be able to take care of his daily needs. I will show him some exercises, that he can do to help strengthen his lower back, without re-injury. Hopefully, that will help protect him from further injury in the future. I am not sure he will be able to go back to work. Although I suspect he would do everything within his power to do so.

Without a proper psychiatric diagnosis, you know we cannot let him stay here."

"Yes, I know, that is true," said Dr. Walker.

"Is there anything else you can do, any other test that you could or would like to run on him?" inquired Dr. Miller.

I do not feel that will be necessary, however I too would like to keep him a bit longer. You may recall from our earlier discussion of this case, I have a feeling there is something. I would like to get my finger on it. I just cannot say with any certainty at this time what it is, and that bothers me. My hunches have never been wrong. I will set up a few more appointments with him, and see if we can find or

Seeking to be Loved

uncover anything else. That should buy us some more time, hopefully that will give you the time you need to get him back on his feet."

"My good Dr. Walker, I feel we are doing the right thing with this case."

"I do as well, this will be interesting. I have met no one like this man. I believe it will be advantageous to learn more." replied Dr. Walker.

Dr. Miller stopped by the nursing station on the ward where Phillip had been recuperating. He asked the charge nurse once again, "When Mrs. Guyon calls, please forward the call to my office or have me paged."

That afternoon shortly after 1PM, Dr. Miller was interrupted while seeing a patient, when the call came. He excused himself, explaining he must answer this call.

He wanted to share with Mrs. Guyon their findings to put her mind at ease. In addition, he did not want her to have high expectations of him physically, at least not initially. He wanted to stress to her, Phillip will need extended time for proper healing to take place. He mentioned that he would most likely be discharged Friday afternoon, and would like for her to be here. I would like to go over instructions with you both.

Natalie thanked him for the information, and care they have given her husband. She is relieved knowing that his mind is sound and stable. She shared, how she worried all week about his mental state. She spoke of her concerns, if or how she may protect and shelter her children, if in fact he was unstable.

She assured him; she would make arrangements to be there Friday afternoon. She asked what time would he be discharged.

Dr. Miller assured her it would be sometime in the afternoon. The exact time had not been confirmed. He reiterated that he wanted to meet with her and Phillip together, before they left. His secretary would coordinate a time. "You can call my office Thursday.

Seeking to be Loved

The appointment will be scheduled by then. I must get back to my patient. Is there something else you would like to discuss, while we are on the phone."

Natalie said, "I cannot think of anything else at this time, thank you doctor."

"Call my office Thursday, goodbye."

Natalie, called Dr. Miller's secretary on Thursday. She was told the time for the meeting was set for 2PM Friday afternoon. She connected her to Dr. Walker's office.

Two days have passed since the last meeting, before Dr. Walker was able to schedule Phillip for another afternoon session.

Phillip was able to push his wheelchair to the doctor's office. He wanted to walk. The attendant recommended he take the wheelchair. It would be easier and safer since he was not going to be escorted. Phillip was given directions, even though he knew the way, from the previous two appointments.

Dr. Walker greeted Phillip. He is not surprised to see him show up independently, and unsupervised. As usual Phillip is supporting a smile, that familiar broad grin. "It appears you are feeling better and getting around more comfortably," stated the doctor.

Phillip's said, "Yes, I am feeling better and a little stronger each day."

"Mr. Guyon, I wanted to share the results of your evaluations and test, you completed last week and earlier this week."

Phillip chuckled, "You mean those ink spots and smears on those pieces of paper. I don't see how you can get anything from that."

"Yes," Dr. Walker returned the chuckle. "It is interesting how such things can give one a view, of one's subconscious."

"If you say so, Doc."

"Upon completing my review, all the test appeared to be negative."

Seeking to be Loved

"Is that good or bad?" asked Phillip.

"What that means, is there is no evident psychosis."

Phillip stared at the doctor in a questioning, bewildered manner. The doctor reading Phillip's expression, continued. "What that means is, mentally you are sound. Your brain is acting normally to stimuli and circumstances under normal situations."

"That's good, Right?" asked Phillip.

"Yes, that is good, it means for the most part you are quote, normal."

"Shooo, I thought I was, but who can be sure these days Doc. Does that mean, I can go home now?" Chuckled Phillip.

"If you are feeling well and your back continues to heal. We want you to be able to get around independently as well as perform your exercises. If that is the case, we hope to discharge you Friday afternoon.

I still have some questions and some exploring that I would like to do with you. Of course, if that is all right with you." The doctor mentioned to Phillip, "There are still a few concerns I have."

"Whatever you say, you are the doctor."

"Before we begin today Phillip, I want to ask you if you are comfortable. Would you rather sit in one of the other chairs, or, on the couch. I want you to be as relaxed as possible. Some of the questions I will ask you, will be very intimate. Things that you can remember about your past, especially before you lost your parents. We have found when people are in a calm and relaxed state, the mind recalls memories more efficiently. That is why I want you to be as comfortable as you can be. Is there a position you have found where you are most relaxed? Especially the last week and a half since you have been here?

Phillip looked around the room and spots a well-padded armchair. "That chair looks awful inviting. If I can prop my feet up, I think that will take even more pressure off my lower back."

The doctor slid an ottoman toward the chair, for Phillip to place his feet upon. "How is that?"

Seeking to be Loved

Phillip initiated the transfer from his wheelchair. He said, "I will tell you in a second. Oh, this is nice, you might have a hard time keeping me awake."

"That is good." said the doctor. "Phillip what is the first memory you have, going back as far as you can into your childhood?"

"Well, I am not sure how old I was. It had to be before I could walk. I remember we seemed to be always on the move. It was like we were always going someplace. I remember seeing the sky and my mother's face. I remember her looking at me. It always seems like; I can remember the feeling more than anything else."

"What was the feeling that you remember?" asked the Doctor.

"It was a peaceful warm feeling, every time I would see her smiling face and bright eyes."

"Did you love your mother?" the doctor asked Phillip.

"I thought I told you that the other day?"

"Yes, you did. Can you describe it for me."

"Well, if love is when you can feel happy, peaceful, and warm inside, or an indescribable joy, when you gaze at somebody. Or when you hear the voice of a person, your heart becomes light. I am not meaning light as in weightless. Well, I do mean that also. What I mean, is when it seems like there is a glow, or a beam, that radiates a brightness all around you. You know it just kind of wraps around you, its engulfing. Does that make any sense Doc? Is that what you mean by love?"

"I think you just described love perfectly, Phillip. Did you always feel that way about your mother?" the doctor asked.

"Yes, at least for the first four years of my life. I remember when she would either pick me up, or, hold me in her arms. There was not and could not, have been a care in the world. The only words I can think of to describe those moments are, peaceful, comforting and a secure feeling. Not just with my mother, my father also, even my older sister Mary. Although Dad was rougher and more fun. With him it was a different kind of security."

Seeking to be Loved

"Was it the same with him as it was with your mother?"

"It was a peaceful, contentedness, but no, not the same. Really it is just hard to describe, it was just a feeling, a sense I had inside. I guess, I would have to say with Dad, I may have felt more protected, maybe free? I don't know, the feelings were the same yet different. Does that make sense, do you know what I mean, Doc?"

"Your mother was very important to you, was she not Phillip?" The doctor is pleased with this question, he observed a reddening in Phillip's eyes and tears starting to well-up. He knows he struck a chord. "Did you, or do you, miss your mother?"

Phillip hesitated just for a moment, as he regained his composure. "I think that is a silly question," he said to the doctor. "Of course, I did."

"Phillip you said, Of course I did, instead of - 'Of course I do'."

"Yes," Phillip stated questionably?

"Do you feel that she is still around Phillip?" ask the doctor.

"In my mind and in my heart, she will always be around." Phillip stated.

"Do you ever see her? Hear her voice?"

"Only in my mind. I do not know, where you are going with these questions. All I can say, is what I remember of my first few years of life. It was a sense of being surrounded by people that cared about me, loved me, and each other. Then one day that feeling that sense of belonging, was no longer present in my life. Over the course of a two-month period of time, from what I can gather from my own memory, it all disappeared. It may have been longer, it may not have been that long, I am not really sure."

"I know you told me that your mother, and father both died within a short period of time of each other." mentioned Dr Walker. "Less than two months of each other, during the flu epidemic back in 1918. Where did you get that information?"

"Ms. Rupender, then later from my brothers and sisters," said Phillip.

Seeking to be Loved

"Did you tell me, you knew nothing of your brothers and sister's whereabouts?"

"Yes, that is correct, back then. I do now and we try to keep contact with each other as much as we can. Although, then I knew nothing once they left the orphanage. As to where they were, whether or not anything happened to them, or, they were still alive. I had no idea. I just did not know what to think. I had asked Ms. Rupender, about them occasionally. She would just say, I know nothing of them, or their whereabouts. That would be the end of it. Something about the orphanage policy she would mumble. I just never paid attention."

"I was not aware, you had contact with your brothers and sisters. You did not mention that, when we first met last week." Doctor Walker mentioned in a questioning manner. "I do recall you mentioned seeing two brothers at a CCC, inter-camp baseball game."

"You asked me to tell you about my childhood and my upbringing, that is what I shared with you last week. It was actually after Natalie and I got married. The wedding announcement was in the newspaper. My brother Henry, sister Mary, and Blanche contacted us, after they read about it. They found our address in Pepperell, from the article in the paper. They just showed up one day!"

"What about your other brothers and sisters?" asked Dr. Walker.

"We got all their addresses, Ernest, Mary, Henry, Gilbert, Blanche, and Joe's. I write them occasionally and send them Christmas cards, I have seen all of them at least once, since we were married. We keep saying were going to have a family reunion, but it has not happened yet."

"How do you feel about that Phillip?"

"Doc, it is so wonderful when we get together, a few of us had no contact with any of the others. Blanche, Mary, and Ernest, we have not seen for so long, not since we were kids. I guess because we were too young to ask questions, or did not know what to ask. We,

Seeking to be Loved

or at least I, had no idea how to go about finding them. We enjoyed the few times we have gotten together, we all get along great."

"Do you feel the same kind of love, you experienced as a child?"

"I can't say that I do doc, nevertheless, I can say, it is a joy being around my brothers and sisters. I can honestly say, we all still feel the love we have for one another. When we get together, we speak the old language, reminisce, and laugh. I have forgotten most of it, until I hear it again, it all comes back. The older ones remind us of where we were from and how we lived, in the old country. It makes me wish, I was old enough to have experienced it, see it, and live it as they did. We were a family in every sense of the word, we had parents who loved us. I must admit, I wish someday I can feel that love. That I once knew, or should I say, felt before my mother passed away."

"Can you explain it to me Phillip?" asked the doctor.

"Why do you keep asking me that?"

"Let us just say I am curious, sometimes when answering similar questions, something a bit different is expressed that may lead to a greater understanding. What is it you want to feel?" questioned, Dr. Walker.

"I am not sure I know how to explain it really, I guess I want to be able to trust somebody unconditionally. I guess I want to experience the same sense of security I once felt deep inside. When my mother's arms surrounded me, the sensation I would get when I looked in her eyes. It was such a loving, caring, re-assuring gaze. The feeling of being protected, and one of reassurance, that everything is going to be alright. I will never forget that look, it was always so radiant."

Phillip took in a breath and blows it out, he struggling to say the words. He through grit teeth, forced them out. "It was the look she had in her eyes, when she was lying in bed, the very last time I saw her."

Seeking to be Loved

Still struggling to say the words, that took him so long to admit. "It was just before she died."

He took another deep breath, it was the first time he admitted or at least said out loud, that he was aware his mother had died, while she was still embracing him. It was something he did not comprehend, nor want to acknowledge then.

"You know Doc, it is not that I can't take care of myself, or protect myself, or anything like that. Maybe the word I am looking for is a solid, unbreakable relationship, a security. A connection, an adhesion that can never be broken, is what I am looking for or would like to experience.

Kind of like the matrimonial sacrament, I guess. To have the faith in somebody, that no matter what, they are going to be there. To hold onto you and make everything all right, or at least seem so. I suppose I want to know, and feel that I am loved, respected, and cherished no matter what. To know that someone is always there to accept, protect and care. To have a person always by your side, whether they are present or not. I guess to know there is someone you can always depend on. To be, to see, to have that closeness around me once more. That is what I remember Doc, about my mother."

Phillip looked up, and watched Dr. Walker wiping his eyes. There is silence for a moment.

Dr. Walker cleared his throat, before he ask, "Phillip do you not feel that way about Natalie?"

"You know Doc, I do, but it is definitely different. It is kind of like a one-way street."

"What do you mean?"

"Well when I see her, I get tunnel vision and she is all I can see, no matter who is around. It is almost like that glow that radiance is wrapped around her, but does not return. I love her dearly, more than life itself. I knew that from the moment I saw her. I knew there was something very special about her. There is no question in my mind, she is the love of my life. She is the only one I want to be with,

Seeking to be Loved

I will do anything I can to make her happy. I will never look for, or be with another woman, as long as I live. Her life, happiness, and that of my children, are the only things that are important to me now.

"How would you describe your relationship with Natalie?"

"Loving, I would not have married her, and I am sure she would definitely, not have married me, if she did not love me."

"Do you feel secure in this relationship?" ask the doctor.

"That's a tough one to answer." replied Phillip.

"Explain it to me, you do feel secure do you not, in your marriage I mean?" queried the doctor.

"How can I explain it doc? Here I go, I will try! Where can I begin? There was something very special about Natalie. Not only is she the most beautiful woman I have ever known, and seen. She is also the best mother, I have ever known. Except for maybe my own, at least what little I remembered of her."

"Do you sometimes see her as your mother?" the Dr. questioned.

"Are you crazy," exclaimed Phillip! "She is my wife, I see her as a wife, I am attracted to her as a man is attracted to a woman. I see her as the mother of my children. I could never look at her as my mother. I am too attracted to her as a woman and my wife. If anything, I want to love, protect, and care for her. Also, to be able in every way to meet and gratify her wants, her needs and desires. I would like that in return but, I do not expect that from her."

"Why would you not, in a relationship such as husband and wife, expect a matching reciprocation?" the Dr. asked.

Phillip said, "It is okay to want, one should not expect or demand such things from others. I think, if you really love someone, you will want to do those things."

Dr. Walker paused again. Then he asked, "What do you expect from that relationship? Why not expect those things you just mentioned? Describing the experience, you had with your mother."

Phillip gets an angry look on his face, raising his hand as to gesture, he has something important to express. As well as to stop in

Seeking to be Loved

his tracks, the one questioning him. "Look Doc," he said in an aggressive tone, raising his hand up and down slightly. "I love my wife, as a husband loves his wife. I am attracted to her, as a man is attracted to a woman. That is, It! Let us just get that straight, right now."

"You seem to be getting very angry, Phillip."

"I am sorry, it is not that I am angry. I just want to make sure you get the right idea. I think of Natalie as my wife, not my mother. I love my mother dearly, I have from the moment I knew her. When I see my own children in Natalie's arms, I can see the same tenderness and caring."

"Do you get jealous or angry when you see Natalie tenderly caressing, and caring for your children?" Dr. Walker noticed Phillip's face getting red and skin tightening around his mouth and brow. Then he observed the facial, neck and shoulder muscles relax again. He checked his skin tone, as it changed back to its normal shade.

"No, to the contrary, it makes me feel happy, it brings on a very comforting feeling, if that makes sense. I want that for my children and Nat. It renews the memory I have and the sensation I once felt, so long ago; it refreshes me. It makes me feel everything I must do, is worth it."

"It does," asked the doctor in an inquisitorial manner. "Does that remind you of your mother?"

"Here we go again." Phillip stated, raising his voice slightly. There is silence, for a moment.

"How do you want to be loved Phillip?" ask the Dr.. "Can you describe what you want in your relationship with your wife?"

Phillip took his time, he described literally word for word what he mentioned earlier, when he explained, how we felt towards his mother and being loved. The doctor listened intently, as Phillip went on, occasionally jotting down a brief note on a pad he held in his hand.

Seeking to be Loved

The doctor asked, "Phillip how many years was it from the time you were separated from your parents, brothers and sisters?

"Well let me see, I was almost five years old when my mother died, and I just turned five a few days before my father's death. I was told my mother died in August, my father sometime in September, I believe, maybe October the same year. It seemed almost instantly, they removed us from the farm where we were living. Placing us in the orphanage, to me it seemed like the same day, but, that could be wrong, it all happened so quick."

"How long were you there Phillip?"

"It seemed to me like we were -- no, I mean, I was there a very long time. I was there for probably a couple months, I guess. Well, October to March or April, what is that six or seven months, I guess. It could have been longer, it seemed like a long time to me."

"Why did you change, what you were about to say?"

"Because, I was there the longest. All my brothers and sisters were adopted soon after we got there, at least from what I gathered. Everyone was leaving after just a few weeks, except me. Joseph and I were the only two of our family on our floor on the same ward. He was taken not long after we were there, maybe a month."

"Do you remember being there?" he ask. "Tell me about it."

"I do a little bit Doc, as I said, it seemed like I was there a long time. I was there longer than all the others."

"Why was that?"

"I did not know at the time, not until I was married, when I started to meet some of my brothers and sisters again. When we would get together and talk about it. From what I understand the oldest ones were selected first. Mary and Henry, told me that they believed it was because they could do a good day's work. The people that selected them had farms. That was the reason why they were taken so quickly. Blanche and Joseph, being a little older than I, could help with domestic work. I guess people thought, I could not do much of anything, Phillip looked down towards the floor as he spoke."

Seeking to be Loved

"You also got selected." The doctor said, in a somewhat cheery tone, for he sensed a bit of sadness and attempted to lift Phillip's spirits.

"Yes," Phillip chuckled. "Then mumbling, old Ms. Rupender." He laughed a little louder.

"Yes, you told me about her." Dr. Walker said, then he asked, "Did she love you? She must have cared about you, or she would not have adopted you." the doctor inquired.

"I do not know..." Phillip responds, with his mouth curling to one side of his face.

"You were much too young to do much work." said Dr. Walker. "Did you have chores to do? Did she live on a farm?"

"Yes, I mean no, well yes, I did have some chores to do. She lived in a one-bedroom apartment, in one of the tenement buildings in the town of Nashua. No, we were not on a farm."

"Where did you sleep, if there was only one bedroom?"

"I slept on a sofa, which was near the dining table. I had to make my bed each evening on the sofa. As soon as I got up in the morning, I had to fold up my blankets and put them along with my pillow behind the couch. I was too small to cook, or do dishes, for the first couple years. She had me sweeping the floor, polishing furniture on a weekly basis, dump trash stuff like that. Once I knew my way around the community, I would run errands to the store, you know typical stuff. If I got my clothes soiled, I had to wash them in the sink. She would get very angry, when I got my clothes dirty. If they got torn, I would really get it."

"What do you mean, you would get it? Punished," inquired the Doc! "How did she punish you Phillip?"

"She had an old leather strap, it was an old belt that at one time had a buckle. From the look of it, it had long since fallen off. She found it on the street one day, when we were walking back from the grocery store. It was near a trash can. I remember the day she had me pick it up. It was not long after I started living with her. She told me, reach down, and get that. I handed it to her.

Seeking to be Loved

"This will serve nicely." she said, in a harsh voice, glaring at me. It did not take long for me to figure out what she was talking about." Phillip laughed, "She liked to use that thing. If she could not find it fast enough, she would make me take off my belt, and use it on me." He chuckled again, "I learned quick to get along without wearing one." He laughed louder.

"What would she use it for?" Dr Walker asked.

"Well, let's just say, she kept that thing hot!" Phillip snickered.

"Please explain?"

"She would strap me with it, when I did something wrong, or if she were mad and felt I was in the way. She strapped me when I was late from school. If I stopped to play with the other kids, and came home dirty, or when she was drunk. I got a taste of that leather, often enough." he jeered. "Heck, sometimes when I breathe, I can taste leather," he said jokingly and laughed.

"It does not sound like she treated you very well, Phillip?"

"Well, I guess, I deserved it. I hated to see her get mad. It made me feel bad." Then he added, "In more ways than one." He chuckled again!

"Were you mad or angry at her?" asked the Dr..

"Well, I think initially, I was more afraid of her. I actually remember not wanting to leave the orphanage when I first saw her. I must say, I remember feeling sad when I was being taken away from there. The people there were nice to me and I was allowed to play with the other children. I actually missed that part of it when I went to Ms. Rupender's.

The first five years with her were difficult. Even through all that I felt more sorry for the woman, more so than mad. Not so much angry, maybe there was a little fearfulness of her at first. Although that changed, I guess I probably should have been afraid, but I wasn't. She seemed to be a sad, lonely person. She never talked about her background, nor did I ask, and I did not even know that she was ever married."

Seeking to be Loved

"We went to church, the store, and greeted neighbors when coming to or leaving the apartment. I was not sure she ever talked to other people. I do not know if she ever had any contact with others accept when necessary. I never seen her family, and no one ever had come to visit. I really did not have any idea, what she did during the day, when I was in school for all those hours. During the summer it seemed like she hardly ever left the apartment."

"Getting back to the original question Doc, I can't say that I ever felt any affection or love, from the woman. If I did, I was not aware of it. Hey, I had food and a place to stay! The first five years, I just tried to stay out of her way and do what I was told. That was not easy in a small apartment. The next five years were not quite as bad."

"What was different?" the doctor asked inquisitively.

"Those first few years I was very young and in school. I had just started my sixth-grade year. I remember returning to the apartment after school, she handed me a list of address's. The first had a name on it and told me tomorrow at 6:30AM, I was to report to this man. I had no idea who or where this was going. She just said, he had a job for me. It happened to be a textile mill. I did not know what I was going to be doing. I just thought maybe, he had a job for me to do, either before or after school." Phillip chuckled, "I did not realize it was a full-time job."

When I showed up, the man told me this is what you will be doing. I expect you here before 7AM every morning and that I cannot leave until the floor was clean. I was assigned to clean and sweep and empty every scrap bin as they got full. I had to wait until all the workers left.

"How long a day did you have to work?"

"Well everyone started at 7AM, it usually took me a little over an hour or more to pick up and clean benches and sweep the floor, after everybody else had left. Most days, people left at 4PM, unless they happened to be working overtime to get out a big order. So, I

Seeking to be Loved

would usually be there at least until 5:30 or 6 o'clock sometimes much later."

"You were putting in a long day, was that hard on you?"

"Not really Doc, it kept me busy and I did not have much time to think about things, except the work right there in front of me. Most of the men treated me right, they all liked to joke and tease with me. Actually, I liked working, it made me feel like I was doing my part. You know Doc, making your way!"

"What do you mean, making your way?"

"I guess you can say, I was earning my keep, and helping Ms. Rupender."

"How did that help Ms. Rupender?"

"Well every week when I brought home my pay, she told me I had to give it to her. She said, it was to help pay the rent, buy food, clothes, and things that she and we needed. So, I would have a place to live and be respectable."

"So, she took all of your pay?"

"Yes, she would give me a dollar, so I had some spending money. I felt like a big deal, carrying a dollar in my pocket."

"I bet you did," uttered Dr. Walker. "A young boy like you, that was a lot of money to be carrying around. What did you spend it on?"

Phillip grinned, "Oh I didn't need anything, sometimes I would buy candy, or a tonic at the drugstore on the way home. It felt good to be able to buy my own things. Most of the time I would just hold on to it. If I had anything left over, which I usually did, I would keep it in a sock, with all my clothes."

"After a year or so, they started teaching me how to operate some of the machinery, at the Mill. Occasionally if someone did not show up for their shift, I would be assigned to take their place that day. I still had to clean up after everybody left. I actually enjoyed doing that. The boss was a fair man, he was a hard man, but fair. The days I worked on the machines, I made a little more money. That is when I started taking out a little extra, before giving it to Ms.

Seeking to be Loved

Rupender. I always gave her the same amount but, I kept the extra for myself. By the time I was a teenager, the lunch that Ms. Rupender would pack me, just was not enough. I needed to buy extra food."

"Did you miss not being in school, Phillip?"

"No not really, the only thing I missed was playing sports. It just looked like so much fun, especially football. I would stop and watch the High School players, sometimes when they would still be practicing late, when I got off work. I see a guy give another guy the ball and he would run into the other boys. Butta-booooomm and plow his way through. It had to be fun!"

"Did you ever play Phillip when you were in school? You have a strong muscular built, I would think you would have been very good at athletics."

"No, Ms. Rupender was strictly against playing of any kind. Even in gym class if I got my clothes dirty, I got it good, when I got home." Phillip with a broad grin looked up at the doc then said, "But, it was worth it," and laughed.

One day, after work I stopped to watch, they were practicing late. One of the coaches asked if I wanted to play. I said, "Yes sir," and I jumped over the fence. I don't even know if I put my hand on the rail, I was so excited. The Coach asked me what position I played. I had no idea what he was talking about. I just shrug my shoulders. When they saw me jump over the fence and run, plus not being very tall, or as big as the others, they asked if I could run with the ball. I told the guy, "I will try."

Phillip started laughing, "I knew I had to run at the people in the line in front of me. I did not know they would be trying to grab the ball and take it away from me. Not to mention, they all wanted to pile on top of me."

"I remember the coaches laughing, then asked me if I want to try again? I said, you are damn right I do! We huddle up and the guy who was handing me the ball, this time told me where I should go and he said stay low, run fast, keep your head up and whatever you

Seeking to be Loved

do, do not stop, or drop the ball. That is what I did, I start running up the line, butta-boooommm. Everyone was grabbing at me. I ran as fast as I could. Someone got in front of me, I just lowered my shoulder, kept my head up and sent him flying. I did not stop until I ran out of field. I heard whistles blowing and the coaches yelling. I walked back to them with the ball.

One of the coaches asked me why he has not seen me in school. Or, have they just not noticed me. I guess at the time I was fifteen years old. I told the coach, "I have not been in school since I was ten years old."

He asked where have you been? I told him working at the Mill. He asked me if I was interested in coming back to school. I had to tell him no." There was silence, for a few moments.

Dr. Walker mentioned, "I sensed a tone of sadness and disappointment, or was it regret?"

"It was probably all three, Doc."

"You mentioned the first five years were difficult with Ms. Rupender, what about the next five?"

Well, like I mentioned Doc, once I was working, I felt pretty good and the fact that I was bringing home some money. It seemed to make things easier living with old lady Rupender. She was not taking the strap to me and she even started doing my laundry. We seemed to get along a little better, although as soon as I had an opportunity, I was going to move out."

"When did you move out?" asked Dr. Walker.

"Well by the time I was fifteen, I was looking for a place of my own. I started looking at apartments and boarding houses. I just was not making enough money, where I could stay on my own. I remember, a few years later, going to work one morning, or, it might have been coming home. Yeah, that had to be it I was coming home. I never stopped any place on the way to work. On the bulletin board at the drugstore was a flyer that caught my eye. It was an old poster of Uncle Sam, recruiting for the first world war. I thought maybe I

Seeking to be Loved

can sign up for the military service. Maybe join the Navy, and see the world.

I talked to my boss about it the next day during our break. He talked me out of it, he told me, I was one of his best employees. I knew how to run most of the machines on our floor, by that time. I also liked watching the machinist when he would be fixing equipment. I learned a lot about fixing things too. I noticed I got a raise a few weeks after that, chuckled Phillip. I kind of felt obliged to stay after that.

I thought maybe if I can start a Bank Saving Account and gain a little interest, it would be better and safer than letting all that money set there in my sock, doing nothing. My sock was starting to get pretty full. In a little over the five years, I was able to save $55. So, I thought I would just put it in the bank for a while.

That following spring the Mill put up a poster and sign-up sheet, for a company baseball club."

"Did you sign up?"

"Yes, I signed up for pitcher, I could hit that ball pretty well also. We had a lot of fun, there would actually be a crowd of people watching our games. Mostly family members and people from the local community. We played other companies, all us young guys were trying to show off for the ladies. I was a pretty good hitter, like I said. One game I was trying to show off for one of the girls. I saw her sitting on the ground with a bunch of the ladies, just outside the third-base line. I struck out, every time I got to bat that game, chuckled Phillip."

"Did you have a girlfriend, at the time Phil?"

"No, but, I was always looking," he laughed. "After that game, the guy coaching us, told me, I had better start looking at the ball, instead of the ladies," Phil snickered.

"So, you were not in love with anyone at this time? Did you have anybody caring about you? Anyone special in your life, you cared about?"

Seeking to be Loved

"No, not really doc, there was a few young ladies at church I would say hello to them on Sunday, and I thought I would like to ask on a date. I remember thinking during mass one Sunday, when we were leaving, I would approach this one girl, and ask her out."

"Did you?"

"Nah, I had no idea what to say to her. I was beginning to think, I was going to be a confirmed bachelor. I was probably seventeen when I first started thinking that. After several years, I was beginning to think, I would never meet or find, (there is a long pause in the sentence: then with a slight quiver in his voice, he finished the statement) someone I could love and would love me." He took a deep breath.

It was obvious to Dr. Walker, this man placed great value on this emotion called love. He saw the effects it stirred within him, deep within his mind and memory. He thought to himself, contemplating, processing, wondering in his own mind. I know there is something about him, what can it be? I feel it, I sense it, my professional experience, my intuition is convinced, I just do not know what it is. I cannot put my finger on it, is it something in his subconscious maybe. What is it? I must find out. I must know! *Something is missing*.

There is something buried, it is deep within his Heart. The good Doctor quickly erases that thought, the heart is an organ, a muscle within the body. Its only function is to keep us alive, circulate our blood to supply the body.

He questions himself for a moment, thinking even further within his own consciousness. Is it as deep as his soul?

Which he quickly eliminates as well. Reminding himself that the thing they call a soul, is just a figment of one's own imagination. He confirms to himself his belief, that it is our own human nature, desires, and the spirit of man that drives us.

Despite his intellect and his training, something within Dr. Walker is luring him. He realized there is something within this man

Seeking to be Loved

before him, he does not quite understand. "I have already concluded that there is no psychiatric diagnosis," he reminded himself. "So, why do I keep questioning Mr. Guyon. There has to be something here, appealing to my subconscious. I want to know what it is, it has to be important. I know if I find out, it will be beneficial to him and maybe many others. But What?

This case is perplexing, it is interesting, I must explore it and him further, to satisfy my own curiosity."

Dr. Walker picked up Phillips chart, he immediately focused on Natalie's name. He thought, "This might be a key, to help unlock this mystery." The he asked, "When did you meet Natalie, Phillip?"

"I met her in the summer of 1939, I had been working at the Mill for probably about seven months. It was two buildings down on the opposite side of the street from where she worked.

"How did you meet her?"

"I will never forget it; she was the most beautiful woman I ever saw. I just knew I had to meet this lady. I had seen her walking down the street when I was leaving work a few times."

Phillip did not want to go into the window replacement incident. He said to himself, "The good Doctor, would know I'm certifiably nuts then."

He told him, "I came up with a plan, of how I can meet her."

"Go on Phillip, I am intrigued!"

"Well it was Friday after work, now I was sitting on the bridge waiting for her and her friends to come walking out of the building. Her friends and co-workers all had come and gone, and I was still waiting for her, she never did show.

It just so happened, she was asked to work late that evening. Doc, it was almost as though God, had set it up. I just had to be patient and wait. I was kind of feeling disappointed thinking I might have missed her, or maybe she had not gone to work that day. Then all of a sudden, there she was, it is like the whole world got bright.

I have to say, it was the most exciting yet most comfortable, evening I ever had. I really do not know how to explain it, everything

Seeking to be Loved

just seemed to be more alive inside, and out. She seemed to glow, her voice to me sounded angelic, it was so soothing listening to her speak. There was just something very special about her doc. I could not wait to see her again, and I knew this was a person I wanted to be with. You know what is funny, I never met her before. Yet there was still something familiar about her, something I could not put a finger on."

"You must have made a good first impression," mentioned Dr. Walker.

"Maybe I did, I don't know about that, although I know that two weeks later I made a fool of myself."

"How did you do that?"

Phillip started laughing and began, "I met Natalie after work and was walking her home. She told me that a couple of the girls and their boyfriends were planning on going to the movies tonight and asked if I would like to go with her. I jumped at that opportunity! I asked her if she wanted me to come get her, or shall we meet at the theater. It was a few blocks away from where she lived. She told me that she was going to walk with her friend and meet the guys there. After I walked her home, I ran to my place, had just a quick bite to eat, hurried to get cleaned up and left to go wait at the theater.

I wanted to impress Natalie, around her friends. I decided I was going to pay for everyone's ticket to the movie. It was a double feature, so it cost more than I expected, I barely had enough to pay for all the tickets. After the movies they all decided, they wanted to go to the pastry shop to have coffee and donuts. I knew I spent all my money. I did not want to say good night to Natalie. I wanted to spend the rest of the evening with her walking around town. Or, go to the park and sit on one of the benches. Everyone else still had a pocket full of cash, I was broke."

Phillip laughed, "I tried to talk them out of it but, I was voted down. When we get to the Donut shop, they all go in except me. I was penniless and too embarrassed, I would not be able to pay for Natalie's refreshments. I just told them I was not hungry. I would wait outside, despite the urging to come join them, I refused. I patiently waited until they finished, so I could walk Natalie home. I sat on the bench outside, I can see them laughing, talking, and enjoying themselves. I had wished I could have joined them, I was too proud or stupid one or the other."

"Did Natalie ever find out, why you did not go in?"

"Not until after we dated awhile, it was that following spring."

"What did she think, or say about that?"

"When I told her, she said, she just thought I was being thickheaded and foolish," Phillip said, laughing heartily.

"She obviously seen something in you, since she married you," said Dr. Walker.

Phillip chuckled again, (the doctor could not help but notice the joyful, fun-loving, warm hearted man before him, so quick to smile, so quick to laughter. ???)

Phillip then mentioned to the doctor, "She told me, she knew that night there was something special about this man. Despite his foolishness and stubbornness, she said, I saw something else. She said,(the doctor observed Phillip, starting to choke up again with emotion, he knew Phillip, was about to say something that was heartfelt, something in his subconscious. There is a long pause, as Phillip prepared to present the words.) She said, I knew this was the man I needed to marry. She continued, anyone who would spend their last penny, when it is so hard to come by. To impress me, without considering their own needs, is rare. She said, something inside told her, 'If this guy was willing to sacrifice everything, he had for me and others, in such a small matter, how much would this man sacrifice for the important things, we may face.'

I think it was shortly after that Doc, that I asked her to marry me," Phillip said, grinning with eyes sparkling and full of moisture.

"You had not known each other very long," said Dr Walker.

Seeking to be Loved

"No, it was about six months, I think we both knew, we were made for each other. It was almost as though I have known her all my life. It was not until after we were married, when my other brothers, and sisters, looked me up. We finally, were all able to get together. I believe it was Mary, my oldest sister who mentioned to Natalie, that our mothers middle name was Natalie. The others also chimed in, saying that was what our father used to call her, "Nattie," short for Natalie. I did not realize that, until Mary mentioned it."

"What did you think about that Phillip?"

"I just thought it was interesting, maybe a coincidence. I often wondered after that if it may have been the name, that gave me that sense of familiarity about her. Or, maybe it was just that we both had known, we were made for each other."

The doctor jotted down a few more notes, then looked up at Phillip. "Once again I enjoyed our conversation, I think I would like to meet with you one more time." He checked his appointment schedule there are no openings the next day, he knows that he is leaving Friday. "I will have my secretary change one of my appointments tomorrow afternoon."

Phillip request, "Do not change anything for me Doc, these people need you."

Dr. Walker told him, "I will adjust the schedule. I am not sure when I will see you. The attendant will come get you when it is time. I may want to meet with both, you and your wife, before you are discharged."

"I will be here," said Phillip.

Seeking to be Loved

Chapter 23 The Dream

When Dr. Walker went to bed that evening Phillip's case was on his mind.

Earlier over dinner, he and his wife talked highlights of their day. These table discussions you might say, had become a way of winding down from the good doctors' day. He mentioned to his spouse, "We presently have an interesting gentleman in the hospital. His admitting diagnoses does not match his demeanor, his test results, nor his behaviors. The odd thing is they do, or shall I say, should match his history. There is just something I cannot figure out about this man. There just has to be *something missing*?"

His wife humorously remarks, "You the diagnostic wizard who usually has the most complicated cases dead on, as soon as you set eyes on them. I certainly must hear this!"
Then on a more serious side she asked, "Why is he there?"

"Oh, the same old stuff, laziness, combative, excessive cursing, screaming, amnesia etc. etc. Yet for nearly two weeks he has displayed none of these behaviors. Being at that hospital, on an open ward, it is hard to believe. Just being around so many others that are demonstrating such bizarre behaviors, twenty-four hours a day, has to work on one's nerves."

"Anything else?" she asked.

"He has a reoccurring lower back injury."

"Is he malingering?" She inquired, knowing that is the case with so many who were trying to get out of responsibilities, work, or other stressors in life.

"No, he is very committed to want to provide for his family. Despite his injuries, he allowed himself very little, if any time to recover thoroughly."

"Can the pain itself cause a psychosis?" she questioned her husband. "**Do** you remember last year, when you strained a muscle in your back? **Do you, Recall That Episode**?? When you were reaching for that box on the top shelf. Do you recall how much,

Seeking to be Loved

PAINNNNN you were in?" There is a smile on her face, as she reminded him, how he carried on for days. "I thought you lost your mind, the way you carried on, moaning, and groaning at the slightest movement. And What Was Your Diagnoses, that Dr. Miller told you, after he examined you?"

"Yes, but, it had to be more than just a slight strain." He uttered trying to defend himself.

"I had thought for sure when you came out of his office, you would be in a complete body cast. What I had hoped he would have done, was order a gag, no a muzzle, to be placed and worn over your mouth. No, no a tourniquet would have been much better, something to cut off all that moaning and belly aching. You were driving me crazy, listening to all that groaning," gest Mrs. Walker. She laughed, he grumbled at the thought of that experience.

Getting back to her original question, he stated, "I guess over time, I suppose it could. The pain does not seem to affect his emotional state. At least from what we have observed, from the time he became conscious."

"Conscious?" she inquired.

"Yes, he was unconscious from the time he arrived, for nearly four days, may be longer."

"Is that unusual?" she asked.

"Very much so, although it does happen occasionally. Usually upon awakening they are even more disoriented, confused, and become very agitated. That is when you see their craziness. You know why they are here, and belong in this hospital. There is no question, they are in the right place. That is not the case with Phillip." "Oops!"

He recognized his error mentioning the name of a patient and explained to his wife, "Please do not ever mention, I said his name to anyone."

"Yes, Doctor," she replied. "Phillip," she said questioningly, "You must have become pretty familiar with this man."

Seeking to be Loved

"To the contrary my dear, it is not that I have become familiar, he is puzzling. He is just very interesting. There is just something about him, that I want to understand. There is something, I feel if I can put the pieces together, the findings I think will benefit many in the future."

"Whoa, whoa: I heard you correctly, did I not, you said, I FEEL? You the analytical master mind problem solver, is now resorting to FEELINGS? This guy has you hogswaggled."

"I know, I know, may I go on please?"

"Most definitely, I am intrigued!" she said smiling.

"I may be onto something, a breakthrough that may help many to overcome their mental illnesses. Where they may be able to get on with their lives. Who knows, it may even help unlock the mysteries they/we all have within ourselves..."

"You said, he keeps re-injuring his back, is that verifiable? Do you think it is intentional?" questioned his wife.

"Each incident was totally different, although now that you mention it, there is a common denominator, that I can see. Each time he was in the process of helping, or attempting to protect someone. Which makes me think that it could not have been an intentional act."

"You mentioned you have not observed any bizarre behavior. What about the staff, have they witnessed, anything unusual, in reference to his behavior?"

"Other than being in pain, he is quite jovial. He is actually, happy-go-lucky. He smiles and laughs a lot, he likes to joke, interacts with staff and with what other patients that can communicate with him. He seems to be a kind, caring, loving person. He should be resentful, bitter, and angry, with what life had dealt him. Instead I see just the opposite? Plus, on top of all that, he has a strong faith??? You know me, and what I think about God."

The good doctor mentioned to his spouse, "On top of his back issues, you do not even want to know half of the other injuries he had upon admission."

Seeking to be Loved

"Yes, I do," she said, with an inquisitive look in her eye. She leaned toward him, and stated, "Faith cannot be denied." Then proceeded to clear the table; she had intentionally attempted to provoke him. She was waiting for him to comment on her last statement. He did not.

"Well, he had fresh wounds, abrasions, bruises, literally all over his body. Almost every major surface of his body."

"Was he beat up, or in an accident?"

"That is the funny thing, No." He explained, "If he had been, the face and hands are always damaged. That is due to the fight they put up and being struck. In his case they were the only things that had limited damage. Both corners of his mouth and the back of his head. There were no other facial injury's other than his mouth, just rope burns and bruised lips from the gag. They commonly apply it if someone is biting, spitting or, using excessive abusive language, when being picked up."

The doctor retired for the evening, and as usual he started reading his Psychiatric Medical Journal. Upon falling asleep, he began to dream of his own childhood.

He is visiting his grandmother, who had passed on years ago, when he was a young lad of eleven. He is sitting beside her and she is reading the Bible, as she often did. She is reading Corinthians Chapter 13. He heard her voice read the words Faith, Hope and Love. Even in his sleep, his consciousness is aware of his own snicker.

In his dream his grandmother looks down at him beside her, as she repeats those words. She adds and the greatest of these is love, as I love you. The little boy looks up to see his grandmother's loving smile. He remembers it vividly in his mind, even in his own heart he feels the warmth, the peace, the joy.

He can see the essence of a radiant glow that is surrounding him with comfort and security, in the loving arms of his grandmother. He enjoys the comfort that his dream is offering him, he settled into a deep sleep.

Seeking to be Loved

The subconscious mind of the good Doctor began the exploration. He envisioned himself searching into the deepest recesses, the inner most chambers of his own mind. This dream excites him, he himself is full of wonder, this could be interesting, he thought in his dream.

He is met there by an elderly woman. She seemed very familiar to him, although he does not recognize her.

She told him, "I have something to show you." She turned and he followed, a door opened before them.

He ask, "Where are we going?"

She only replied, "Inside."

"Inside where?" he asked the old woman.

"Inside you, my dear."

The voice is familiar, still he makes no connection. They pass through the door. He feels a coolness as he entered into another area. There is no light in the initial passage, it seemed to be complete darkness, nothing was visible. He kept straining to focus and waited for his eyes to adjust. There was nothing to adjust to, the area was void of any light, as though he was totally blind, living in complete darkness.

He can only follow the sounds of the footsteps of the one leading him. Once inside, it became illuminated. He noticed in front of them was a fog, thick like a cloud, they walked into it. It surrounds them as they continue their steps. Then everything lightened, he could see clearly. He was looking at the back of the woman standing in front of him, guiding him. As they come through the cloud, he sees five little shapes. He knows they are boys, although the shapes are nearly indistinguishable. He cannot make out their faces although everything about them was quite intriguingly familiar.

He has an urgent need and desire to meet them. The yearning to know, and understand each one of these little boys, is almost overwhelming. He thinks how odd, why such a passionate longing, to know and understand, these strange unknown lads. He asked the old woman, "Who are they?"

Seeking to be Loved

"You!"

"Why are there five? he asked."

"Each one is part of you. There are five unique entities, that The Great One, creates before each one of us can be born into the world. Once they are formed, then we are allowed to be born."

"Who are they, or, should I say, what part of me are they?"

"Let me introduce you, to yourselves. This one is your Physical Self. It allows you to have a place to live. To have a place to grow, to move and to carry you wherever you need to go."

As he observed it and understands, he began to see the image, then the face, which is his.

They step to the next. "This one is your Intellectual Self. It allows you to learn, to understand, to make decisions. It allows you to choose paths you will take in life. It allows you to solve problems, and to bring things to light, in a way that only you can."

Looking on as the old woman describes this entity, he begins to see the image more clearly, never completely.

She moved to another, and introduced the next part of him. "This one is your Social Self. It allows you to connect and grow with others. It permits you to fulfill that for which you were created. It enables you to be a part of them, and them of you. It allows you to meet your needs, and to meet the needs of others. This is a bond that can only be created in its pureness. It grows and evolves as our body and mind progress in life. The respect and dignity of one, is the respect and dignity of all."

"I do not understand." he declared.

"Only when the decisions that you make in your life, match that for which you were created, will you understand."

Something struck him as he is dreaming, as the good Doctor struggled to understand and desperately wanted to make the connection. "Does this mean, if the body and the mind do not progress, the social self will not evolve?"

There Is no answer from the old woman.

Seeking to be Loved

They move on to the next. "Here is the Emotional You. This Self takes you to the higher plane of life. This is where you can touch beyond one's physical being. This is the center of your life energies force. It is here where you determine whether you accomplish your objectives, goals, and destiny. It is here where one defeats himself, thus overcoming one's greatest enemy. It is here where, the essence of your Humanness and your Spiritualness collide. It is here where you can rise to your greatest heights. It is here where you can devastate yourself to the lowest possible depths of life. By choices you make."

"Why is this self, this image so unclear? It does not seem to have a solid form, it is as if there is no skeletal structure, holding it in place? Are you sure it is me or mine? It is unclear, it also seems to constantly change."

The old woman explains, *"Not until one completely understands himself, does this part of him, his emotional image of self, become solid and clear."*

"This Self needs nurturing, which is the food for its growth. The milk this One needs, begins with The Great One, who loved it enough to bring it to existence. Next, his mother feeds it the love it needs to grow. Followed by the love of others at each planned stage, as this one grows, and moves through the tests of time in this worldly life. Without the nurturing, without the connections The Great One had planned, they can be no growth of this part of you."

"So, the social self and the emotional self can cease to grow? How can that be if one grows physically and intellectually?"

"The answer to your first question, is yes. The answer to your second question is, when the nurturing and love are not fed to the soul, growth of these Self's is not likely. Care, love, and protection can be removed, or traumatized, by of which there are many forms. When this happens, the nourishment that feeds this precious Self no longer exist. Then growth of these Self's ceases. If one is not allowed to experience life, as planned naturally, by The Great One, at the

Seeking to be Loved

proper stage, the evolution of one's growth to these Self's, is not possible."

"Are you saying, trauma whether physical or mental, or lack of natural exposure and protection can stop these Self's from growing, or as you put it evolve? If they shut down at specific stages, are they stuck there forever? Or, is just the progression of development slowed?"

"You ask good questions." Was all the woman said... Then whispered, "When Love is missing."

"What was that?" he asked.

They move on to the next self. "This is your Spiritual Self. It allows you to find your way in the world. It allows you to continue to live in peace and joy, no matter how devastating the circumstances you must face in the world. It allows you to continue to love and to seek love always. It is the homing device that will guide you to your destiny, and guide you home. It can supersede all the other Self's when necessary. It allows you to see the possible, despite the impossibilities," said the Old Woman.

This one has no eye's, no nose, no mouth, no ears, nothing hinting that really makes it appear human. Even its shape is vague, its form shapeless.

"Why is it like that? If this one is so great and wonderful, why does it look, loook so???"

"It is you that must give it shape, it is you who must put a face on it," said the old woman.

"How can I do that?"

"You must accept it, acknowledge it and where and whom it came from. When you do, it will grow within you and continue to guide you."

When the old woman finished saying these things, she turned around knelt down, hugged the young boy, and kissed him on his forehead. Just as she did many years ago, when he was sitting by her side, as she read Scripture to him.

Seeking to be Loved

She then disappeared from his dream. He realized at the moment she kissed him on his forehead, it was his grandmother. He stood in the cloud all alone, he shouted come back grandma, come back, I love you Grandma, I Love you, I Love you, come back, I love you, Please come back!!! As he said the words, shouting them repeatedly he noticed the entity before him changing. The image was beginning to become a more solid form. The eye's started to appear on the blank face. He could feel something growing within him. While light seemed to radiate from within first, then around him. He felt something deep within, an ecstasy he never felt before. He whispered to himself, to his own amazement, "I love you God."

He saw the image of himself standing whole and complete before him. His very image, now is as though looking into a mirror. Yet it was real, they embraced each other and laughed. He felt a wholeness, he had never experienced before. He felt tears of a profound joy running down his cheeks.

He was instantly awake, and so full of this new part of himself. He cannot hold back his tears, nor does he want to. He wants to shout his joy to all the world.

He hugged his wife sleeping beside him, whispering in her ear, I love you. As he laid back, he cannot help but notice, how light, comfortable, warm, secure, and content he felt. It occurred to him, this is what Phillip described and experienced with his mother, and Natalie. There must be a connection, was the last thought he had before falling into a most pleasing slumber.

The next morning on the way to the hospital, he analyzed his dream which he remembers vividly. Each scene, each word penetrated deep into the recesses of his mind.

"When Love is missing!"

"Excuse me," said The Good Doctor, as he turned to see who spoke to him. No one was near him. How strange, he was sure someone spoke to him. He continued on. He recalled his own questions and his own thoughts, in reference to his questions. He

Seeking to be Loved

knows his grandmother, was trying to show him something about the complexity of the human creation. He understands the physical and the mental Self's. He has studied them in the greatest detail from the time he was in college, medical school, and practicing his profession the last two decades. He always believed there was something else missing.

Something else in the human development, especially that of the mind. Why some people break down, and others do not, when faced with the same, or very similar circumstances. Where is the breakdown, is there a flaw in one's own make up, or chemistry from birth? He questions himself further. What was it the old woman, his grandmother described to him? I know she said something about lack of love, lack of nurturing, lack of protection.

"When Love was missing"

Who, saaaaid that, he queries looking around him as he walked along, seeing no one? Thinking it odd, he is certain he heard someone.

Yes, I remember, it was something about mental and physical trauma during particular stages of development in our lives. "What was it?" Aaaahh, One can cease to develop, or stop development of that particular self, the Social and Emotional Self. They get stuck socially and emotionally in a particular stage, of life.

"When Love is Missing"

"Who said that?" He turned completely around looking for the one who keeps repeating the phrase; "Humm no one."

Yes, this is all making sense now. If one may be stuck, let us say in a pre-adolescent stage due to accident, injury, abuse, illness, or neglect. That is where his social skills may stay, even as their body and mind grow. If one is not properly exposed at proper times, during proper stages as one develops.

It must be the same, or similar, with one's own individual emotional capacities. If one is a fully-grown adult of reasonable intelligence, one would think, they can solve adult problems, and adult emotional conflicts. Yes, Yes, that must be so!

Seeking to be Loved

If that part of them did not grow, and did not successfully evolve through all the necessary prerequisite experiences, and interactions of the growing years. They must be stuck in that state of being. What was it the old woman implied?

Where or how could they learn to solve issues that occur during certain, and proper stages in their life? If for whatever reason such experiences are removed or withheld, as with Phillip? How can they be expected to as an adult, or at an adult level, when one's emotions are involved?

I have seen this many times, in my treatment sessions, my groups, and work with families. Where one looks adult, sounds adult and acts like an adult. The other one looks the part but seems to say things, and describe things, in such a childish manner and acts as such.

Their social and or emotional reasoning, may still be stuck in the preadolescent stage, or whatever stage they may have evolved to, when trauma, or abuse had taken place. It certainly appears that way when treating them. I can only imagine it has to be even worse, when they are on their own, without someone supervising their interactions, like parents, and as we do when they are in treatment. It is no wonder so many people are committed to institutions.

Phillip, on the contrary???

"Love was Missing"

What, excuse me, who, where does that keep coming from? How odd, the good doctor said aloud. I am sure I keep hearing someone speaking. He looked around, hoping no one is observing him. "They will think, I have gone off the deep end," he said to himself.

"Phillip still does not seem to fit into this mode of reasoning. Or does he?   What were the words that were so familiar to me in that dream? I remember how I felt last night, upon awakening from my dream. Love, that is it, Love."

"When Love is Missing"

"That's right, When Love is Missing, it was also the key to the fifth, the fifth self, the Spiritual Self."

Even as he is saying it again, he feels a lightness about him, the warmness of a brightness inside of him. He pauses for a moment to observe and relish, this change, this metamorphosis'. As it is happening within him, he is observing and processing it. He is questioning himself, is this a biological, physiological, or psychological change? "Is it an adjustment of my perception or just a whimsical play of my imagination? Is it, I think what I am experiencing and feeling, is real? I believe that it does not matter.

What does matter is, if we can find the point or period of development when, where, and how a particular component of self-shuts down. Then we will know at what social, and emotional stage, or, level of skill the patient is working from. Then we can reasonably suspect the skill, and experience level we are dealing with. Then we can educate them, teach them, or at the very least understand how best to associate with the individual. Thus provide them the most appropriate treatment." He started to rethink: "The question will be, whether one will be able to mentally grasp the social skills, or emotional reactions once that stage of life passes and time elapses?

Can this be accomplished, without the associated experiences, we all have during our growing and developmental years?

This will lead to some interesting experiments. I will share this concept with my colleagues, during our next meeting."

"What about Phillip? He seems to have all the Self's and they too have developed quite well. How else could he survive his childhood and his growing years without love, without the basic unstructured interaction with his peers. Those natural experiences we all have playing, fighting, growing up, that just occur naturally during our development and interactions during the stages at the proper times in our life.

Seeking to be Loved

- How did he get through, the emotional trauma, the physical pain, the isolation???

- How could he get through the sheltered, harsh environment of the woman who adopted him? During those crucial stages of his development, yet be as he is???

There was something in my dream, my grandmother had said, what was it? He can hear her voice, as though she was standing there beside him, *"It is this one, that can supersede all the others, when necessary."*

That is it! He said to himself, Phillips Faith in God, is what helped guide and bring the other self's / parts of him along.

Dr Walker, can hardly contain himself. He cannot wait to share his revelation with the Guyon's, as well as his colleagues. His meeting with them is set for 1PM. He wondered if an hour will be enough time. He reminded himself to speak with Dr. Miller, maybe coordinate extra time if needed. His meeting follows mine.

Seeking to be Loved

Chapter 24 Family Meeting

Natalie met Phillip on the ward, he had been waiting in the hall. The instant he set eyes on her, he was struck by the glowing splendor of this woman. He stood, and walked to meet her. It is reminiscent of that first time he saw her leave the building across the street, nine years ago. They embraced, both are pleased to see each other.

The nurse reminded them, they only have two minutes to get to Dr. Walkers office. Reaching his office, the secretary greeted them.

"Good afternoon, Mr. and Mrs. Guyon, Dr. Walker is waiting for you." She ushered them into his office. They exchange greeting formalities; the Doctor offered them seats.

Dr. Walker about to proceed, finds himself hesitating momentarily and noticed his mouth is still opened. What he was about to say initially, eluded him, which is in itself extraordinary. As is his nature and training dictate, he finds himself processing why. He closed his mouth and smiled at the couple. There is another delay before he begins, "Let me say Mrs. Guyon, your husband is a very, (another halt in his speech) unique individual. He has puzzled me!"

Natalie, snickered softly and said, "That makes two of us." The mood is lightened.

"Yes," said Dr. Walker. He quickly reviewed the test results and his findings and opinions.

Both Phillip and Natalie are pleased, with what the good Doctor shared.

Dr. Walker continued, "I believe some time ago, during Phillip's infancy an interesting phenomenon took place. I have come to believe the human character, person, individual what have you, develops in many ways, as we grow and mature in life. Each as I like to refer to them, Components of Self. These unique and separate entities can, and may, develop independent of each other.

Seeking to be Loved

Please let me give you an example. The physical body grows, when properly cared for and nourished. The brain's intellectual and mental capacities, will learn more as we are taught. The social, emotional and spiritual components continue to evolve with exposure during proper stages of our development."

Dr Walker, intentionally paused, to allow them to absorb the information and brief descriptions he just presented them.

He saw their interest, as they listened and understood. He resumed by saying, "When hardship is endured for long periods of time without relief, stress, tension, and anxiety continue to mount and build. To the bearer of such, there is always a price to pay. Something must give, that something is always the bearer himself. Physically, or, mentally, sometimes both, something must give, or break down, as we often refer to one's condition," explained Dr. Walker.

They are listening intently.

Dr. Walker continued, he looked at Natalie. "I am sure you know Phillip had an unusual upbringing. He endured an extended journey across country and ocean when he was an infant. He lost both parents. In addition, he was removed from all his many siblings, at a tender age. All very dramatic and tragic, for such a young infant.

There are many experiences, one has at crucial times in their growing years, Phillip just did not have. This has nothing to do with his physical, and mental status mind you."

The more the good Doctor continued his speech, the more blank, Phil and Nat's stare becomes. He said, "Let me get to the point."

"Please do Doctor," they both said simultaneously.

"I believe Phillip needs to learn and to experience the evolution of love as it matures."

She looked at him inquisitively and said, "What?"

He looked at Phillip and resumed his hypothesis. "What I suspect, and has become apparent, (He stopped for just a moment as he analyzed his own choice of words. [*apparent - A parent*]

Seeking to be Loved

Interesting he thought to himself.) that you started your life with an extremely loving and nurturing mother and family.

"Yes, I agree," acknowledged Phillip.

"Love is what brings us into this world." (The Good Doctor stopped again. Thinking, "What am I saying." His mind feels like it is racing to understand the words he is speaking? "I am a disciplined well-known Psychiatrist.") He hears the voice again.

"Love was Missing, Love was Missing, Love was Missing"

"Love was missing," he repeated out loud, not realizing it.

"What do you mean? You just said, I had a very loving family," Phillip questioned.

"What did I say?" inquired the doctor. "Oh yes! You see, love must evolve and grow once we are born. Growth is a natural thing and as we mature, we experience things as our mind and bodies develop. When we do so naturally at the correct time and in the appropriate stages, we develop the skills necessary to be successful in the next stage we evolve, and grow into."

Natalie and Phillip, are following him so far.

He looked at Phil and said, "You have only begun to see and experience love as an infant, a very young child."

He turned to Natalie as he continued, "He may not have learned how to love through conflict."

Nat and Phil glance at each other, then back at the doctor.

"Let me explain, and review my theory. I will give you a brief example. When a child is born, it has a special connectedness with the mother. It is part of her, it is part of both parents actually. Although for nine months it is solely given everything it needs to grow from its mother, during the gestation period. Initially, once born the infant is totally dependent on its mother."

"Yes, we understand that," Natalie said, and Phil agreed.

The good doctor continued. "Within the family, especially when there are siblings in the house there are rivalries and spats, as the children grow and interact with others in the household."

Seeking to be Loved

Phil and Nat laugh, both identify they are very familiar with that from our own.

"Yes." The doctor proceeds, "You, the child, or, both get mad at one another. You the parent correct them, and their behavior. As they get older you may argue. Children may fight with siblings, yet they still live with and love one another. Also, within the family unit the parent will discipline a child. Teaching them, right from wrong, good behaviors from bad, so all can learn to respect one another, and live peacefully.

We learn to live within the rules and expectations of that unit. If you break the rules, there are consequences; you get punished. Your parents and siblings still love you, and you them. When one matures, they make friends beyond the immediate family unit. Maybe cousins, neighbors, or, other acquaintances close by. They are people familiar to the family, and many times the same thing occurs.

As we mature socially we venture forth, making other connections and friends at church, school, playgrounds, and neighborhoods, etc., etc.. We naturally develop a more global base, there will be disagreements, and conflicts. We may get angry, say things, and do things we wish we had not, and may regret. When it is all over and done, we will still love one another. We will; let me rephrase that a bit, if we forgive one another and reestablish the relationship we had with the person, we pick up where we left off. That is if we love them. Let me reiterate that more simply. Once again conflict may lead to arguments or fights. During this process, you learn to make up, and maintain your friendship.

Later in life, as we grow through adolescent years, we start experiencing different feelings, developing within our being. There are specific things about certain people we find interesting and attractive. They may even spark emotions within us. We learn to make contact, despite the anxiety created by these new feelings and emotions. It is from the successful experiences, we have during those early interactions, that provide the skills necessary to connect at more mature levels.

We start to love in a new, unique interpersonal way. We begin learning about others and their needs. With each stage, there are unique associated social exposures. During those particular stages, if love is not missing in our life, in its various forms, our ability to love grows and develops.

I mentioned, each successful experience, better prepares us for the next level. It is within these unique and particular encounters that our love grows, blossoms, develops, matures, and evolves.

It is obvious to me Phillip's evolution of interpersonal love, has never evolved beyond the mother and child affiliation."

Phil and Nat, ease back into their chairs, to absorb the words and the meaning.

Then Dr. Walker resumed, "This is due to the circumstances he had to face, (the Doctor emphasizes) Alone.

Natalie understood what the doctor was saying on an intellectual level. Knowing she can and does get her physical and social needs met, within this relationship. She is tearing up and the good Doctor, hands her his handkerchief. She partially acknowledged, she may never get her own emotional needs met. This caused her to force out the words, the words that cut Phillip to his core. "I do not need another child to nurture, I need a man. One who understands ME!"

Phillip wanted to say something to reassure her, he is lost for words. He reached his arm around her in an attempt to comfort her the only way he knows how. It breaks his heart to see her cry. He said to her, "I love you Nat, more than anything."

She replied, wiping her tears, "I know you do," she blurted out in her matter-of-fact manner.

The sound of her remark, penetrated Phillip. His emotional senses are keen, he relied on his instincts to get him through life. As we all know our instincts never steer us wrong, they are designed only to protect us. What Phillip interprets into Natalie's statement

Seeking to be Loved

is, it is not going to be enough. Instantly he is hurt, and angry, at the same time. He remained silent and slowly withdrew his hand.

She regained her composure. She asked the doctor, "What can be done?"

"I am not sure." exclaimed Dr. Walker, "This itself is theory, at this point. Although I believe it to be true, whether or not it is fact, will take much study. All behavior is learned by life's experiences, success depends on how well one is guided through and reacts to them. I suspect it is the same with emotions, especially of love. For there are many levels, phases and stages of it."

"Do you have any suggestions?" Natalie asked.

Phillip looked on intently.

Thinking for a moment the good Doctor, began sharing his thoughts. "Phillip being strong well developed physically and intellectually, I suspect all his components are as well. Although one part maybe stuck." Dr. Walker chooses his words wisely. "He may possibly benefit from experiencing various social situations, that the average developing child goes through."

Phillip and Natalie both question, "How?"

Phillip stated, "I cannot go back in time. I will look foolish doing childish things at my age."

"Maybe," the doctor hesitated for a moment before finishing his statement. "You are raising five young children at home, is that right?"

They both answer, "Yes." Then Phillip corrects the good doctor; "Six but who's counting."

"Well, Phillip will need to observe them, and not intervene when certain conflicts arise, let things happen. Observe how they deal with different situations. I would specifically focus on acts, displays of kindness and love as to how, your young ones express them to each other."

Phillip and Natalie both look at each other. Phillip mentioned, "That sounds fine and good, however I am not home while they are

Seeking to be Loved

awake except on Sunday. I often work late, or, do extra jobs in the evening."

"That will be an issue, the doctor admits. Well, maybe Natalie can make notes of such moments, then share and discuss them with you, when you are home. Maybe at least this will give you a start in developing a greater understanding of how love grows."

The doctor, himself is not convinced this will be of much benefit. He knows this is a poor substitute for actual experience. The business of living, learning, developing and of course, Loving is crucial at all the appropriate ages, and times in one's life.

Suddenly, the good Doctor is reminded of his fifth self... He told them, "You both have great faith, and what is impossible for us humans, is only child's play for God." The words he is expressing at this very moment, he can hardly believe they are his. In his mind, he saw himself in his dream, looking on with amazement. He recognized a body, a face very clearly, a smile appearing on the face of his own fifth entity - Spiritual Self. He also instantly acknowledged the warmth, the luminosity within his own being.

Phillip turned to Natalie, and he declared with all sincerity, "I promise to do anything and everything necessary to understand. I love you and the kids. I want to love you how you need and want to be loved." Tears trickle down his cheeks, he does not feel them, he is totally focused on his commitment.

Natalie, smiled confirming his commitment, "I know you will Phil," she said wiping her eyes. His spirit is lifted a few more notches. She looked at the doctor and asked, "Is there anything else?"

He said, "No, I know Dr. Miller wants to meet with you both before you are discharge. Actually, I may want to see Phillip again sometime in the near future. I would be interested in exploring my theory for further study on this diagnosis and prognosis. May I contact you in the future?" the doctor inquired.

Phillip stood up and said, "Why sure Doc." They shook hands and left his office. Before they have a chance to get back to his ward,

Seeking to be Loved

an attendant intercepts Phillip and Natalie and informed them, "Dr. Miller is waiting for you. Oh, here he is!"

Dr. Miller introduced himself, Natalie confirmed, "Yes, we spoke on the telephone."

Dr. Miller suggest they find a place to sit.

Phillip is in his wheelchair, Natalie hinted to him, "I have been sitting long enough."

Dr. Miller guided them to the side of the hall. "Very well then, let us step over here, out of the way."

The good doctor proceeds, "Phillip's lower back has suffered severe and repeated damage." He explained how the vertebrae which protects the spinal column and how the disc cushion the vertebrae. He reviewed how the spinal column works. He explained its role sending signals and messages to and fro throughout the body. Many nerves are interwoven throughout the column and vertebrae. He identified how even limited damage or disruption can provoke acute pain and possible paralysis.

Phillip has had repeated injury and severe damage done to his spinal column. "I must say, in all truthfulness, it amazes me he is not paralyzed. Yet as of today, he is walking short distances and performing all functional activity."

Phillip interjects by adding, "And it feels good to walk!!"

Dr. Miller explained, "The healing of the surrounding tissue may take weeks if not months. He is strong, young and a hard worker. I must tell you, and I cannot emphasize it enough, to take all the time necessary to rebuild. It will be important to re-strengthen the supporting tissue surrounding the spinal column and especially in his lower thoracic area. It will take patience and diligence to recover effectively. Too much stretching, twisting, and bending can damage what took weeks to regain. He has been given exercises to do.

Yes, he has been cautioned, many times about overdoing. The rebuilding is a slow process, and re-injury can and does frequently occur. You must be very, very careful and allow the time necessary for healing and strengthening. The support tissue takes a longtime to become pliable, flexible and resilient once again."

"When can I be expected to go back to work?" Phillip inquired. He chuckled and said, "Soon I hope!"

"Only, time will tell." stated Dr. Miller.

"Should he come back to see you?" Natalie asked.

"I do not believe that will be possible."

"Why is that doctor?" she asked.

Dr. Miller attempts to explain, "You see, to be admitted here one must have a psychiatric diagnosis. We do not believe Phillip has one."

"Well, that is good," Natalie affirmed.

Dr. Miller knowing the family's predicament, wrote down his phone number and handed it to them. He mentioned, "If you have any problems, questions or setbacks, call me. I cannot make any promises, but you never know."

"Thank you, Doctor..."

Seeking to be Loved

Chapter 25 <u>Home</u>

They say home is where you hang your hat. I would rather believe, it is where your heart is! I found this to be so, "*When Love is not missing.*"

Alas, there was one aspect of the Emotional Self within Phillip, that had never fully caught up.

Although it allowed him to survive and sheltered him, in times of difficulty. It made it so easy for him to naturally connect and share with the youngest of his children, grandchildren, and his great-grandchildren.

The misfortune was that his love was stuck in the glorious pure radiance of the mother-child pledge. The mother's unsaid oath to nurture, protect and guide one of her own flesh. On part of the infant, there is an absolute dependence, unmeasurable trust, and certainty it possesses of its mother. It is that which causes joy and a sense of completeness, to its little being. Through those many years, until he met his true love, his only reference point to love, and how to love, was as a four-year-old.

He loved Natalie with all his heart, all his soul and with every fiber of his being. It could not break through or grow beyond the stage barriers. His love was stuck in the stage of life he was in when the love he had known was taken away. It was not replaced nor, could it resume development in the environment and circumstances he was consigned.

As it was, he had grown up in an atmosphere where he was not allowed enough natural experiences, to permit his love to evolve and mature. It should and most assuredly would have during each developmental stage of his young life. He had the strongest of foundations established to grow from. If it had been replaced and if *Love was not Missing, during* and through those crucial early developmental years, it would have blossomed.

He had such a strong base, the love of family and of God.

Seeking to be Loved

Growth with family and with friends, in anything other than rigid structured settings were not part of his existence as he developed into a man.

How does a handsome, masculine, diligent, hardworking, honorable, decent man, love the woman he was destined? When he never had opportunity to experience the phases and qualities of love, beyond that of an infant.

He met the physical requirements, he met the intellectual requirements, he met the spiritual requirements.

I credit them both, Phillip, and Natalie, they passed all the test, endured all the struggles.

They had to battle something they did not comprehend. Something unseen, only felt deep within their hearts. How can one come to grips, with what they do not understand?

I recall the last few times I met with my father. He shared that his only regret, was that he could not give us more. He would state it in a material sense.

I knew what he truly meant. His words were to be understood at a much more profound level. He meant it in such a way, as to connect with us as we grew and matured.

He told me, he did not know what it was, or how to say it.

I knew it then, although, I myself did not know how to put the empathetic understanding into words. Now in my older years I know without doubt. For I am, my father's son.

I knew, only after my own struggles to learn to love more perfectly. That he wanted to grow in love with us. How unfortunate, he did not know how, no one ever told or showed him, he was never allowed.

He was wise enough to realize he could not go back and retrace steps and stages in his life. To experience life and love in each stage as it develops naturally, until it matures. Time passed, experience gone by, opportunities are lost.

Although Phillip's love did mature. It was the very last thing he taught us. He experienced it, on his dying bed. He would not let

Seeking to be Loved

go of his life. Despite the severity and fatal nature of his injury, he refused to die. No, not until he knew each one of his ten children and his dearest wife were going to be okay.

When he knew that our hearts would once again experience joy. Only then when he heard the sound of laughter. The cheer of those he loved so dearly, the laughter of his grandchildren and adult children, happy and joyful.

Only then did he lay down his life......

My Father and Mother gave us and left us a great inheritance; the greatest gift, the greatest treasure of all!

Love was not Missing in our home. It was the only thing in abundance. With it, we had everything we needed, and more than any human being should ask for!!!

We observed both our Father and Mother, with complete dedication, providing for their family and loving each other as they knew how.

Our Father with labor, joy, and laughter.

Our Mother with unwavering will, and determination.

Brothers and sisters, turning over all their earnings, from after school jobs to our parents, to help make ends meet. Without question or regret. There was a willingness, to sacrifice personal needs, and interest. Even delaying one's own future, as my oldest brother was willing to do. If necessary to secure the immediate needs of our family.

I suspected my father's dilemma, for many years. The life and lives of those around him grew and changed, he saw the experiences of his children and grandchildren. There is no doubt he realized they were living and going through the very things he had missed in his youth. Though it was by observation only he could take it in. He could even probably imagine the emotion and relish in the excitement, and joy, on his adult level.

Could he Love in any other way?

Seeking to be Loved

Did he learn to meet the needs of his wife in the way only a mature love can?

After his children were grown, moved away, and he retired; leaving the only social environment, outside of family where he was truly comfortable, it was now gone also. He once again was left alone for most of his day. Where he can readily experience the fear, the loneliness, the uncertainty, the difficulty to connect.

He always rose to the occasion, at family gatherings and when we would visit.

I knew then, and even more so now, my father was a remarkable man. I have witnessed many times his guidance, protection, and kindness. I never understood what he experienced.

I would ask him about his childhood, and he would explain, never with bitterness, never with anger nor sadness. He always gave truthful, lighthearted explanations, with a smile and chuckle.

It was not until my wife and I started raising our children, that I began to acknowledge my Fathers wisdom. As well as his ability to bring joy and cheer to any situation.

Not until recent years, twenty after his death, did I have any idea of what he suffered, endured, and overcome.

I am so glad and grateful my three children had a chance to meet him. Before our first child arrived, I envisioned each of my dear ones, one day walking into my father's loving embrace.

During yearly visits when each was barely able to stand on their own two feet. I can vividly recall, as I knelt behind them, steadying each one of my children in turn. I whispered into their ear. "Walk to him. Before you, is the Greatest man you will ever know."

Their Grandfather, would reach out his arms for them to walk into. I could see the purest unconditional love in his eyes, as they stepped into his embrace!

I did not have the words to express what is in this book, until I had matured enough in my own understanding of love.

It has been my desire and mission for the last twenty plus years of my life, to learn to love more perfectly. In my morning

Seeking to be Loved

prayer, in closing I ask this;   "Jesus, teach me to love as you love, Blessed Mary and Saint Joseph, teach me to love as you love, brother Andre teach me to love as you love, so honestly and humbly. Dad and Mom teach me to love as you loved."

I do not know if my parents ever did achieve the complete oneness, their matrimonial vows promise, during their fifty-seven years of marriage.

To achieve it, one must accept the sacredness of it. Then commit absolutely and devoutly to it and to each other. As well as the Commandments of our Lord. When we do so, the treasures of this life will follow.

Alas, Phillip and Natalie did find each other. They did experience many of the treasures that this life offers. Although, there was the tests and the struggles of this life. They had them in abundance, which we all must face.

Each day they had to contend with that which required, and received much, if not all of their attention. Raising, caring for and teaching their children, Phillip Joseph, Geraldine Anne, Maralla Ralphine, Cynthia May, Twila Alice, Rachel Genieve, Eleanor Louise, Izora Ellen, William Ernest James, Jeremiah Lee. The duties and responsibility of providing a home, food, finances, and other worldly needs, had consumed them.

They had each other, and absolute trust in God. They endured, survived, weathered the storms, passed the trials and tribulations, life will and did present.

Only at the closing moments of their lives, it seemed they had experienced the truest and purest love. The ultimate test with the ultimate reward.

You read about Phillip on his deathbed, not letting go until he knew his children and wife would be okay.

It was my sister Rachel, who shared with me years after our dear mother, Natalie passed away. She had mentioned to me during

Seeking to be Loved

a conversation in preparation of this book. There was one day, not long before our mother died, she was having great difficulty.

It started in the morning, she needed help getting out of bed and moving around. Our mother told Rachel, her back was hurting excessively. Apparently for no other reason, other than of course her age, she was well into her 90s. It was nothing that she had done the previous day, that could have brought this on. Nor, anything she ever experienced before. She made the comment, "I now have some idea what your father suffered all those years."

She had the privilege of experiencing what he had to suffer most of his life. Empathy, that which moves the spirit within, to a much higher plain of one's awareness in life. A plain that sings to the soul and to souls, so one can and does understand truly what another is experiencing.

I know Phillip, was the first to greet Natalie at her passing. With open arms and a smile as broad as heaven itself. Along with a hardy joyful chuckle.

While I was writing this the vision within my mind is the two embracing. The light of each forming the purest light, of one. I hear a heavenly host, the sound not of voices. As I concentrate and listen, it is more like the soft harmonious sound, created by a celestial choir and orchestra. Yet, I cannot detect a voice, nor single out a certain instrument, that I can attached to the sounds. It is just a glorious resonance, that is the only way I can describe it.

I only at this very moment acknowledge they did not or could not, maybe none of us can, ever be able to experience the greatest gift on earth. <u>Love</u> in its most purest form. It may only be once we pass all the obstacles on earth, the trials, temptations, and test of time. Only when we have in earnest reached the finish line, and have kept the sacred vow in our hearts, may we achieve the oneness. When all the parts, each other's parts, will form a whole. Thus, the creature God, intended all along, Finally becomes complete!

Seeking to be Loved

Closing:

Our Priest's homily, the Sunday following Christmas 2018, spoke of "Family," "The Holy Family." The perfect example, of Love and devotion to each of its members and the peace that emanates from true love and devotion. He discussed the three rings that go along with developing a family.

My first thought of my family, when he mentioned three rings, was that of a circus.

He proceeded to explain the rings:

First> Suffe<u>ring</u> - This brings us together to comfort, secure, heal, and it draws us closer to God.

Second> Ca<u>ring</u> - This brings about nurturing, guiding, and teaching.

Third> Sha<u>ring</u> - The giving of our self and what we have to offer, so each is nourished and can grow.

May we not waste time seeking to be Loved, for we already are in the purest possible way!

Let us make the journey, *Seeking to Love,* purely as we ourselves are Loved. Let us do so with joy, consideration of all and with faith; then the peace of God that surpasses all understanding, will guard our hearts and minds in our Lord. Phil. Ch. 4 verses 4-9.

May Love conquer all!

Seeking to be Loved

Author's Note:

Worldly circumstances took Phillip away from the sources and prevented the learning, and experiencing, what we all need in each of our lives. Despite his struggles, throughout his life, he taught others how to love more perfectly. Still teaching on his deathbed, not by words, by example.

I know the suffering he endured. I have been privileged to feel and empathize with what he had experienced. To be able to acknowledge and understand the physical pain, and anguish suffered. As well as the loss of love, and protectiveness, that can only come from the care of the most nurturing parents, where unconditional loved exist.

Although, I must admit, it was in no way near the degree of which our father endured.

Both parents had learned to accept, and to live with the humiliation, pain, and illness. This man experienced and lived through the mental anguish, his entire life, at least from age four, until he died at age 82,

His wife, our mother, had dreams and visions of what she wanted for her family. And by God, there was nothing in this world, that was going to get in her way, or stop her. She would not allow cost, illness, fatigue, or insults, prevent her from reaching what she saw as important for her family.

Due to the poverty, illness, and sacrifices, they put aside any thought of their own comfort, and or security. Their life was devoted, to make sure they endowed their children with dignity, self-respect and that of others, a willingness to work, to do what was necessary no matter what the cost.

Most importantly, instilled within each of us a deep abiding faith in God.   Plus, the desire to preciously LOVE.

As I am writing this manuscript, approaching the final phases of the story, I have come to the realization that the story is about our journey in life.

Seeking to be Loved

Oh, the time, scenes, situations, and struggles, have changed and are unique to each one of us.

I would like to think I have inherited some traits, from my parents. We cannot help but to be influenced by ones so close to us. Through heredity, I hope I acquired some of their best traits and quality's, probably to a greater degree their worst.

I can see even though they have passed on years ago, they are still teaching us, as they always have, without judgment. Yet they are still guiding and showing us a better way. It is through our memory of their actions, and words of their teachings, and guidance. Never neglecting at every opportunity to correct, discipline and show a better way. Never letting us forget, **Love was not missing.**

I only hope this book may inspire others, to seek the greatest treasure. Understanding the pursuit of it is a wonderful adventure and one that does not end until the final test, and last battle won. May we not waist time seeking to be Loved. For we already are, in the purest possible way!

Let us make the journey, **Seeking to Love,** purely and preciously.

Other works by the author:

Lifestyle Management an Ever Changing and Evolving Process
The Dove Story
Christmas Memories From Haverhill Massachusetts

Made in the USA
Monee, IL
30 May 2021